MASTER'S HANDBOOK ON SHIP'S BUSINESS

MASTER'S HANDBOOK ON SHIP'S BUSINESS

THIRD EDITION

TUULI ANNA MESSER

Based on earlier editions of
Shipmaster's Handbook on Ship's Business
by Ben Martin and
James R. Aragon

CORNELL MARITIME PRESS

A Division of Schiffer Publishing, Ltd.
4880 Lower Valley Road • Atglen, PA 19310

Published by Schiffer Publishing, Ltd. 2011
Master's Handbook on Ship's Business was originally published by Cornell Maritime Press, Inc. in 1969

Copyright © 1969 by Cornell Maritime Press, Inc.
Copyright © 2011 by Tuuli Messer-Bookman

Library of Congress Cataloging-in-Publication Data:

Messer, Tuuli Anna.
    Master's handbook on ship's business / Tuuli Anna Messer.—3rd ed.
    p. cm.
    "Based on earlier editions of Shipmaster's handbook on ship's business by Ben Martin
and James R. Aragon."
    Includes index.
    ISBN 978-0-87033-531-0
    1. Ship captains—Handbooks, manuals, etc. 2. Ship's papers. I. Aragon, James R.,
1951– Shipmaster's handbook on ship's business. II. Title.

    VK211 .M47 2001
    387.5'068—dc21

                                                                    2001047413

ISBN: 978-0-87033-531-0
Printed in China
First edition, 1969. Third edition, 2001; second printing, 2011

Schiffer Books are available at special discounts for bulk purchases for sales promotions or premiums. Special editions, including personalized covers, corporate imprints, and excerpts can be created in large quantities for special needs. For more information contact the publisher:

Published by Schiffer Publishing Ltd.
4880 Lower Valley Road
Atglen, PA 19310
Phone: (610) 593-1777; Fax: (610) 593-2002
E-mail: Info@schifferbooks.com

For the largest selection of fine reference books on this and related subjects, please visit our
website at **www.schifferbooks.com**
We are always looking for people to write books on new and related subjects. If you have an
idea for a book, please contact us at
proposals@schifferbooks.com

This book may be purchased from the publisher.
Include $5.00 for shipping.
Please try your bookstore first.
You may write for a free catalog.

In Europe, Schiffer books are distributed by
Bushwood Books
6 Marksbury Ave.
Kew Gardens
Surrey TW9 4JF England
Phone: 44 (0) 20 8392 8585; Fax: 44 (0) 20 8392 9876
E-mail: info@bushwoodbooks.co.uk
Website: www.bushwoodbooks.co.uk

To deck cadets and those who aspire to command at sea

Contents

Preface to the Third Edition

Since the publication of the second edition of *Shipmaster's Handbook on Ship's Business* twelve years ago, many substantive changes have been made in the operating environment affecting seagoing vessels and their crews. Pervasive legislation affects many facets of vessel operation. Rapid advances in communications, including Internet access and satellite e-mail, have changed the way the modern master communicates with the home office and have probably taken away some—many say most—of the master's autonomy. The book has been revised and expanded to reflect these changes, and the title has been altered to emphasize that the information applies to masters of all seagoing vessels. The third edition is titled the *Master's Handbook on Ship's Business*. To incorporate all the new information, several chapters have been added to the book, and all the original chapters have been updated. New chapters include the following:

> United States Laws
> International Codes and Conventions
> Vessel Security
> Communications
> Flag Etiquette
> Appendix D – Agencies and Contacts
> Appendix E – Foreign Medical Evacuation and Travelers' Insurance
>   Companies
> Appendix F–Acronyms

I hope you find the book useful, and I encourage you to send recommendations for the next edition to the publisher.

I would like to thank all the people, agencies, and companies who offered their time and information, especially Lela Perkins of the San Francisco Customs Office, Al Kirschner of the Coast Guard's National Maritime Center, and Alan Maciano of General Steamship Corporation.

My gratitude also extends to my colleagues at the California Maritime Academy, especially Captain James Buckley for his input and advice on publishing, Scott Saarheim for his contributions to the communications chapter, and the faculty of the Marine Transportation Department for their support and guidance. I also wish to thank Captains John Keever and Paul Leyda of the Maritime Operations Department for their support and assistance.

I couldn't have done any of this without my parents, Sidney and Laila Messer, who placed my getting an excellent education above all else.

Finally, I nod in gratitude to the many masters I've sailed with, who taught me, by their fine examples, how honorable and satisfying the position could be.

Thank you all!

Preface to the First Edition

There has, for some time, been a real need for an up-to-date, practical guide book to assist the new shipmaster in the preparation and completion of the large amount of complicated paperwork which is required in the operation of the present-day merchant vessel. The primary object of *Shipmaster's Handbook on Ship's Business* is to provide a useful source of information and ready reference regarding the many phases of ship's business and paperwork with which the master must be concerned.

The paperwork necessary for the efficient operation of the modern cargo vessel may appear onerous at first, but it will be noted, after a voyage or two, that the work will be less troublesome and difficult if it is started as early as possible on the voyage and as much is done towards completion as available information and details permit. This is especially true of making up the payrolls and other accounting items. There will be occasions, however, when some paperwork, involving reports and official documents, must be done on short notice. The details of such reports and documents may not be known in advance so to attempt their preparation early could lead to serious errors.

This book is principally for the newly appointed master of a merchant vessel but it may also be of assistance to more experienced masters as a check in completing the paperwork required; and much of the information herein will be found useful by masters of foreign flag vessels calling at U.S. ports.

Of necessity there is some duplication due to various subjects coming under several headings. However, all subjects are covered by the index, which has been made as comprehensive as possible.

Much of the paperwork throughout the voyage is for the home office or charterer and many special forms are issued by both. These differ in various companies but the information required is essentially the same.

An attempt has been made to cover all phases of paperwork connected with the duties of the master. Many of the forms used are shown in facsimile. It must be kept in mind that forms issued by federal agencies are occasionally changed in size or text, or the form number may be changed, usually with the idea that the new form will save work. The master should endeavor to learn of these changes from the customhouse broker or from his home office. Too often the altered form comes as a total and not particularly welcome surprise, especially if the old form has already been completed with no small effort. However, the completed old form is usually accepted up to a definite date. Obsolete forms should be disposed of as soon as new ones are received.

Most companies issue "Instructions to Masters," which are written by men who have a thorough knowledge of the shipmaster's business and problems. Generally, such instructions allow much latitude to the master's prudence, discretion, and common sense, taking it for granted that he will at all times endeavor to protect his company's interests.

In some foreign ports it is necessary to use metric figures in making out certain reports. Included in the appendix are U.S. and metric conversion tables as well as other tables and information of interest to shipmasters.

Ben Martin
1969

MASTER'S HANDBOOK ON SHIP'S BUSINESS

CHAPTER 1

The Master

The office of master is one of great personal and professional responsibility. The master is in ultimate command of the vessel and has various levels of authority over all on board, but that authority should be exercised without arrogance or harshness. Regardless of fault, the master may be directly, even personally, responsible for all actions, procedures, and incidents connected with the vessel.

GENERAL RESPONSIBILITIES

A primary responsibility of the master is to ensure compliance with various laws at all levels: state and federal laws that apply to the vessel and crew in United States waters, the laws of foreign countries when the vessel is in their waters, and international law. It is also the master's responsibility to ensure that company policies and procedures are followed.

Modern legislative trends are increasing the responsibilities placed on individual shipboard personnel, particularly officers, as well as shoreside administrators and managers. Many modern environmental laws carry with them not only civil penalties, but the potential for personal criminal liability as well. The legislative atmosphere surrounding maritime transportation has been affected primarily by a few major events: the *Exxon Valdez* spill in 1989, which prompted the passage of the Oil Pollution Act of 1990 (OPA '90); the phase-in of international Standards of Training, Certification, and Watchkeeping for Seafarers 1995 (STCW '95); the National Invasive Species Act of 1996 (NISA); and International Organization for Standardization (ISO) 9000. The laws affecting maritime activities are enacted largely as a response to catastrophes of one sort or another, or as a reaction to international pressures and trends.

The modern master faces many of the same concerns that shipmasters confronted in past decades regarding vessel operations. However, unlike in earlier times, masters now must contend with issues such as the following:

1. Reduced manning
2. Increased automation
3. The elimination of radio operators due to the implementation of the Global Maritime Distress and Safety System (GMDSS)
4. New documents required of personnel signing aboard
5. International, national, and union work-hour rules
6. Additional required logs and recording documents
7. Twenty-four-hour communications accessibility to the vessel

A master should become familiar with all the legal responsibilities of the position and with all the laws affecting the vessel and crew in the various waters the ship plies.

On accepting command of a vessel, the master tacitly agrees to act honestly and to the best of his or her ability to protect the interests of the company; to look after the safety of the vessel, cargo, passengers, and crew at all times; and to do whatever is required to keep the vessel in seaworthy condition. Additionally, the master has a legal and moral duty to protect the environment.

As the direct representative of the company and, on some chartered vessels, the representative of the charterer as well, the master is responsible for all damage, accidents, and incidents that happen on board or are otherwise connected with the vessel. These include incidents caused through personal fault or neglect, and also in many cases those caused by the actions of the crew or others on board. The master is responsible for all authorized persons on board and, in some cases, even those on board without authorization.

The master also has a duty to render assistance to any individual found at sea who is in danger of being lost, as long as such assistance can be provided without serious danger to the master's vessel or to persons on board.[1] When engaging in any rescue attempt, the master and crew must exercise the level of skill reasonably expected of mariners. Heroics are not expected, but negligence on the part of the rescuers may lead to civil penalties.

It is taken for granted that the master will exercise care, prudence, discretion, and his or her best ability in all business transactions with various government officials and other shoreside individuals in the many ports the vessel visits.

THE VESSEL

The master alone is responsible for the safe navigation of the vessel. Even when acting on advice from the home office, an agent, or others, including surveyors or the Coast Guard, the responsibility for any occurrence resulting from such action is still entirely the master's. Safety should at all times be the paramount consideration.

Cleanliness and Safety of Crew's Quarters

The master is responsible for the cleanliness, sanitation, and good condition of the living quarters on the vessel. Inspections should be made frequently of the messrooms, washrooms and toilets, galley, storerooms, refrigeration spaces, hospital, and other such areas.

Additionally, the master must ensure that no unauthorized personnel are permitted aboard while the vessel is in port or at anchor.

Public Areas of the Vessel

Public areas such as lounges, gyms, workshops, and eating areas should be kept clean and orderly. Most vessels now have designated smoking areas and smoking should be confined to these areas only. The bridge, considered a workplace, should be a nonsmoking area.

The master should ensure there are no displays of material that may be considered offensive in public areas of the vessel. Posted artwork, jokes, and calendars should be appropriate for a professional environment.

Seaworthiness

The master has the responsibility to ensure that the vessel is seaworthy. To this end, regulators have enacted several "whistle-blower" protection statutes that protect mariners who inform the Coast Guard or other authorities about unsafe or unseaworthy conditions aboard vessels.

If a vessel is ready to begin a voyage, and if the chief and second mates—or a majority of the crew—determine that the vessel is unfit to proceed on the intended voyage, they may request official intervention into the matter. Unseaworthy conditions may involve crew, hull, equipment, tackle, machinery, apparel, furniture, provisions of food and water, or stores. The master should immediately apply to the appropriate district court of the United States for the appointment of surveyors. At least two complaining crewmembers must accompany the master to the judge or justice of the peace. The court will appoint at least three experienced surveyors to examine the vessel. If the complaint involves food and water, at least one of the surveyors will be a medical officer of the Public Health Service or appropriate agency. The surveyors will issue a written report stating that the vessel is fit for sea or, if not, in what respect the vessel is unfit. The court will review the report and determine if the vessel can proceed to sea or to another port for repairs, or whether it should be confined to port. The master or company is required to pay all costs of the survey, report, and judgment.

If the complaint appears to have been without merit, the master or owner may deduct from the wages of the complaining crewmembers reasonable costs and damages for the detention of the vessel.

Any three mariners may complain that the provisions of food and water are at any time of bad quality, unfit for use, or deficient in quantity. This complaint may be made to the commander of a U.S. naval vessel, a consular officer, or chief official of the Customs Service. The officer receiving such a complaint should examine the provisions (or have them examined) and certify to the master if the provisions are unfit. The officer should also make an entry in the vessel's official log on the results of the examination and submit a report to the district court of the United States at which the vessel is to arrive.[2]

THE CARGO

The primary purpose of the merchant marine industry is the transportation of goods and passengers. The phrase "cargo is king" is as true today as it was decades ago. In addition to keeping the vessel and crew safe, the master bears the responsibility of delivering the cargo intact and on time, which is the ultimate reason for the maritime endeavor.

Loading and Stowage

Like almost everything else aboard, the proper loading and stowage of the cargo is ultimately the master's responsibility, even though in most trades the loading, stowage, and discharging of cargo is the duty of the chief officer and/or shoreside personnel. In many ports the cargo is loaded under the directions of cargo supervisors employed for this purpose by the company or charterer.

Generally these supervisors, many of them former seagoing officers, are highly competent and experienced. If the cargo operations do not meet with the master's approval, the supervisors will usually abide by the master's orders, though perhaps not without some heated discussion or persuasive argument. A new master, and even a seasoned one, is well-advised to cooperate as much as possible with all concerned and to refrain from making changes or issuing orders just to exercise authority. The chief mate should be similarly counseled.

However, if the vessel is ultimately overloaded, or if loading has been done in such a way as to make the vessel unseaworthy, it is the master who will be held responsible.

Load Line Regulations

In the 1800s, Samuel Plimsoll promoted the idea of putting marks on the sides of ships to indicate safe freeboard and discourage overloading. He saw his idea put into action with the British Merchant Shipping Act of 1876, which required ships to be marked with load line markings, or "Plimsoll marks." These marks are now required by every seafaring nation.[3]

Under no circumstances should the vessel be loaded beyond the allowable stress limits or beyond the maximum approved draft for the season and area. (See illustration of zones and seasonal areas following appendix B.) The master should not be influenced by coaxing, threats, or blandishments of the agent, company, charterer, or others. If the vessel's draft is excessive, cargo, fuel oil, or freshwater should be discharged to bring her back to the proper draft. If the loading or stability conditions of a vessel change, the master shall record the following in the official logbook before moving the vessel: (1) the position of the assigned load line relative to the water surface, and (2) the draft of the vessel, measured both fore and aft.

If a vessel is overloaded, it may be detained by the Coast Guard or other enforcing agency and fined per day of violation. Customs has been specifically designated as an agency that can enforce load line regulations.[4] Violations of the load line regulations may result in a fine against the master, owner, managing operator, charterer, and/or agent.[5]

If the master is fined for load line offenses, it is doubtful the company will provide reimbursement. Well-managed companies issue instructions from time to time that their vessels are not to be loaded beyond the applicable draft. If it is necessary to take remedial action in order to remedy overloading, the master should enter such action in the logbook.

PERSONNEL

The master should work in close harmony and cooperation with the deck and engine officers and foster an environment where people want to work harmoniously. A prudent shipmaster will listen to suggestions made by the chief mate, chief engineer, and even junior officers and mariners but will always bear in mind that he or she alone is responsible for whatever action is taken.

Bridge Resource Management

Modern concepts of bridge resource management encourage a less dictatorial and more collaborative bridge and watch environment than was the norm on ships in past decades. Evidence of the effectiveness of collaborative management techniques has been so well documented that the military and most industries now subscribe to some similar management concept. The most important crewmember aboard may indeed be the able-bodied seaman (A.B.) on the wheel or the lookout on the bow.

A vessel can be made safer by the use of good communication techniques. How something is said can be as important as what is said. Even body language communicates a great deal.

The master should encourage watch officers to acknowledge lookouts for reporting lights, even if they have been tracked on radar. Acknowledgment and praise for good behaviors promote more good behaviors. As a general rule, it is better to chastise in private and to praise in public.

Most masters probably consider themselves good managers. But even the most seasoned master should consider periodically thumbing through a personnel management book to get new ideas on how to better manage people.

In the multicultural work environment that exists on most modern vessels, good management is key to a safe and efficient operation.

Language Issues

On a vessel with crewmembers of differing nationalities, language may be a barrier. STCW requires basic proficiency in English, but this standard varies from assessor to assessor. A mariner who cannot communicate effectively in English cannot fully participate in the vessel's mission and should be let go.

Confidentiality

The master is the keeper of shipboard personnel files, which include personal information on the current as well as former officers and crew. These records are to be kept under the strictest confidence. A crew list should never be left in a place where unauthorized persons could view it. Crew lists show birth dates, next of kin, home addresses, and social security numbers, and they are to be kept confidential. Identity theft and other crimes related to the illicit gathering of personal information can be avoided with proper records management. Some vessels keep a crew list taped inside the back cover of the deck logbook. This is not a good practice. Crew lists and other documents containing personal information should be kept under lock and key to ensure their confidentiality.

Conduct

The master is responsible, through the heads of the various departments, for the maintenance of good order aboard the vessel. It is the master who may be held to account for disorder, irregularity, or a violation of the law committed by a member of the crew. Problems include smuggling, oil spills, throwing refuse or garbage overboard in port, harassment, or any other illegitimate acts that may have been prevented by proper supervision and instruction. Existing case law holds that the presence of a crewmember who is known to be dangerous can render a vessel legally "unseaworthy." It is the master's responsibility to make the vessel safe in all respects, and this may include handling internal threats from unruly crew or passengers.

Aboard ship, the master has the backing of federal maritime law in maintaining order aboard the vessel and may restrain dangerous crewmembers until they can be discharged to shoreside authorities.

If a situation escalates to the point of imminent physical harm to the vessel, cargo, environment, or crew, it may indicate a lack of awareness and supervision on the part of the master and/or company. Despite the restraints on firing mariners imposed by many union contracts, the master's first duty is to protect his vessel. Union grievances can be settled later and may be cheaper and less troublesome than retaining an unruly or unpredictable crewmember aboard.

Harassment and Offensive Behavior

In addition to assault, battery, and other personal attacks, sexual harassment and sexual offenses are considered serious offenses. The master is responsible not only for the professional conduct of the mariners under his charge while they are on duty, but for their conduct off duty as well. The old image of gruff, nail-spitting sailors is no longer accurate. The modern legal environment permeating most workplaces responds to the most sensitive and most easily offended employee. A crude joke or a sexually explicit description that is merely overheard or seen by a passerby can spark claims of harassment against the master and the company. Increasingly, the law is becoming less tolerant of sexual harassment and sexual offenses. One fairly recent statute requires, for example, that a master must report a complaint of a sexual offense to the Secretary of the Navy (via the Coast Guard) or face a civil penalty.[6]

Even when there has been no wrongdoing, once a suit is filed the cost of defending the innocent is so expensive that most companies choose to settle out of court. Most large firms now require sensitivity and sexual-harassment awareness training for all their employees. On board, it is the duty of the master to see that the policies of the company are followed in spirit as well as in action. Free speech is not free in the workplace, even if one is off duty. Masters should protect themselves and their employers by removing potential liabilities from the ship.

The master can and should set the tone for the whole ship. Talk at mealtimes should remain enjoyable and professional. Crude or offensive language should be squelched. People aboard ship have no choice as to where they have meals or with whom. They have little choice but to spend time in public areas for recreation. Every effort should be made by the master and the officers to ensure an appropriately courteous atmosphere during meal and coffee times and at other communal activities. Ideally, the master will manage the ship so well that all crewmembers will be courteous to one another as a matter of professional pride. Crude language, sloppy or tattered clothing, poor personal hygiene, or rude behavior does not belong on a well-managed ship. It is ultimately the master's responsibility to provide a safe and hospitable work environment for all aboard.

Drug and Alcohol Abuse and Testing

Most companies require a preemployment drug and alcohol test. The drug screening programs used by most companies have gone far toward eliminating sailors with serious drug addictions. Alcohol addiction is harder to detect with simple blood alcohol tests. When at sea, the vessel does not have access to the third-party drug and alcohol testers that are normally used by the company, and if a drug or alcohol test is required, the testing, collection, and breathalyzing requirements must be performed by the master. U.S. law requires that no one aboard who has a safety duty (i.e., has a duty on a station bill) can have a blood alcohol content (BAC) over 0.04 percent and that no alcohol can be consumed within four hours of standing a watch.[7]

Chapter 4, "Vessel Accidents and Incidents," provides further guidance.

Work Rules, Rest Periods, and Safety Gear

It is the master's responsibility to ensure that regulations regarding work hours, rest periods, working conditions, and the donning of safety gear are strictly observed. Federal and state laws dictate rest periods for various personnel aboard, and international recommendations are made by labor organizations.[8] Where regulations overlap, such as STCW and OPA '90 rules, the most stringent rule should be applied.

Most well-managed shipping lines have incorporated these laws and recommendations into their operations and procedures manuals. Masters should understand that even if a manual does not explicitly so state, many of the company manual's provisions and practices are required by law.

Gratuities

The master should see that no gratuities, presents, rebates, commissions, or kickbacks are offered to any of the crew by persons doing business with the vessel and that none are accepted by any of the vessel's personnel. No member of the crew should be permitted to inappropriately influence the purchase of supplies, stores, equipment, or repair services.

Training

STCW requires various types of training for personnel aboard ship. It is the master's responsibility to see that each crewmember is properly trained for the duties he or she is expected to perform and that each person who is expected to use a piece of machinery or equipment has been familiarized with that equipment and is competent to use it.

Ethics and Fairness

The master's personal value system will be tested daily. A strong code of personal ethics and a sense of fairness will ensure that the crew knows where the master stands on various issues and will help them serve the ship more effectively. There should be no doubt in the minds of officers as to what behaviors are expected of them. The crew should be treated fairly and with dignity at all times.

As noted earlier, federal regulations now exist to protect whistle-blowers. A master may not discharge or in any manner discriminate against a mariner because the person in good faith has reported, or is about to report, to the Coast Guard that a violation of 46 USC *(U.S. Code)* or a regulation issued under 46 CFR *(Code of Federal Regulations)* has occurred.[9]

ON TAKING COMMAND: THE TURNOVER

Arguably no amount of planning can fully prepare a person for his or her first experience as master. No matter how many questions are asked or how many checklists are completed, there will always be additional questions or issues that arise once the ship has sailed. Modern technology allows instantaneous communication with the home office and other shoreside resources, so the new master often has shoreside advice and support, even after the ship has sailed. Despite personal and cultural pressures to the contrary, the new master should not hesitate to seek advice and input.

Inventory

The outgoing master will probably have prepared an inventory of items for which a receipt will be required. At a minimum, the inventory will list the cash on hand; it may also include the controlled drugs, any firearms and ammunition on board, the more important ship's documents (including a slop chest inventory), and various items of valuable equipment such as sextants, binoculars, laptop computers, and so forth. It is usually sufficient for the new master to sign a duplicate copy of the list. If a new master is taking command of a new or laid-up vessel where there is no former master, or if the master is not on board, the documents and certificates may often be found in the vessel's safe or files, or else in the company's office.

The new master should learn the combination of the safe as early as possible. If not available from the former master, it can be obtained from the home office. If circumstances warrant, the master may consider having the combination changed.

A new master should check the following items when taking command:

1. Combination to safe
2. D-1 aliens in the crew. (D-1 is a visa permit for crews of ships and aircraft.)
3. Crew changes to be made before sailing
4. Outstanding deficiencies or unfulfilled requirements of the Coast Guard, customs, or other federal agency. Clearance may be denied if certain deficiencies are not corrected.
5. Status of shipping articles
6. Amount and type of ballast and where stowed; ballast reports made and records kept
7. Bonded stores on board
8. Cargo on board and cargo orders for the current voyage and, if known, for the next voyage
9. Cash on hand and whether any cash has been ordered
10. Charts and publications for the voyage
11. Freshwater on board, water ordered
12. Fuel on board, where stowed, fuel ordered
13. Logbooks, both deck log and official log
14. Light lists, tide tables, almanacs, etc., ordered for the next year if the voyage is to extend into the next year
15. Narcotics on board. All narcotics should be kept in the safe; the amount on board when a new master takes over should agree with that shown on the stores list.
16. Slop chest sufficiently stocked
17. All forms for the countries the vessel is scheduled to visit
18. Drug testing collection kits and forms
19. Repairs needed or ordered

Vessel Operations

As soon as possible after taking command, the new master should ascertain the operating details of the vessel by conferring with the chief engineer and chief mate on fuel consumption, speed, ballasting, and cargo operations. Much information can be obtained from the logbooks. When time permits, a complete inspection of the vessel should be made.

Master's Notebook

This is an important item, which, if properly kept, will prevent many headaches. Regardless of how good an individual's memory may be, it is wise to make notes of what is required or what should be checked. A list should be kept showing requirements for entering and clearing harbors as well as information for the office, such as draft, fuel, and water on arrival; crew replacements; stores required; and so on. However, the master should be aware that in the event of an incident, personal notebooks will most likely be considered "discoverable" in any subsequent legal actions, which means that the notebook, in its entirety, may be reviewed by the parties involved in the litigation and possibly entered into evidence in a court of law.

Communications with Home Office

Given the advent of modern instant communications, shoreside personnel, perhaps unaware of specific conditions, may advise the master to do something that could be considered imprudent when viewed from the onboard perspective. Often there is no hard copy of this request or advice. Even when responding to a home office directive, responsibility for any action lies with the master. A master may occasionally be placed in the unfortunate position of having a company directive conflict with his or her better judgment, sometimes indirectly suggesting the master bend a rule or statute; if the order came over the satellite phone, there will be no hard record of the verbal exchange. In an ideal world, it wouldn't be necessary to balance personal and professional integrity with a desire to remain employed. Many recent laws now hold management liable along with shipboard personnel for policies and procedures that encourage and allow mariners to violate the law. Yet, sadly, some less-than-scrupulous shipping companies will attempt to push masters beyond the practices of good seamanship in order to make a timed arrival or to save a few dollars. Each master must determine how to handle such conflicts to maintain a personal comfort zone.

Standing Orders

Standing orders should be made up for the guidance of watch officers, and the master must ensure that these standing orders are strictly complied with. Many officers read and sign the standing orders but later become careless about following them. These orders should be supplemented with night orders whenever circumstances require. Both standing orders and night orders should be signed by the watch officers to indicate they have read and understood them. If the standing orders say to "call when in doubt," the master must ensure that he or she will be available when called to respond to the watch officer's request. Such standing orders will not be effective if calls to the master are met with brusque replies. Standing orders should not be so detailed as to be confusing or readily forgotten. All officers should receive a copy of the orders to take with them to their cabins.

Paperwork

A master taking a first command may be dismayed with what appears to be a vast amount of paperwork and greatly concerned about having the necessary papers properly made out and in order when required. Starting the paperwork early in the voyage, rather than allowing it to accumulate, will ensure that it can all be done in ample time.

It is important that the master read carefully all instructions or information on forms required at different ports. If such forms are in a foreign language, the local agent can usually translate them. Many foreign countries print the text in English as well as in their own language. Naturally, the master should not sign any papers without understanding exactly what is being signed, particularly anything that will needlessly obligate the company or cause it unnecessary expense. The master should try to obtain a copy of any form or paper signed, especially bills.

A file should be kept of all papers made up on the voyage, including manifests, stores lists, bills of lading, crew lists, passenger lists, crew's effects lists, and so forth, as well as copies of all letters and radio messages sent out. Many modern computer programs keep such copies on disk, and this may be sufficient. For documentation surrounding any incident, keeping a hard copy is prudent for later reference. The date, name of the vessel, voyage number, and port should appear on every letter and every form.

Ship's Documents

Many of the permanent documents and certificates on the vessel will be checked by government officials from time to time, so these should be kept where they are accessible at a moment's notice. It can be very embarrassing and irritating to be unable to find the papers and documents asked for by the boarding officers. Most vessels have a binder or a specific drawer for such documents.

One of the first things a new master should do after taking command is to check that all the required documents are on board. If any will expire soon, a notation can be made to see that they are renewed promptly. Chapter 9, "Documents and Certificates," has a description of the more important documents.

Reports issued by the American Bureau of Shipping (ABS) and other classification societies when repairs are made to the vessel should be kept in a separate file, as they may be called for when the vessel goes through inspection or survey. They should be filed as soon as they are received.

Other Papers on Board

Special forms are issued by shipping companies and these will vary in accordance with each company's requirements. The following will cover many of these, although some may be known by different titles. The ship's company will have complete lists.

1. Blank customs and immigration forms
2. Spare logbooks
3. Master's cash statement or other form of settlement
4. Cash receipt book or similar record
5. Company operations and policies manuals
6. Company safety manual (safety management system)

7. Telex addresses, telephone and fax numbers of agents, domestic and foreign; e-mail addresses where appropriate
8. Telephone numbers (office and home) of company officials to be contacted in case of emergency; access to corporate legal and insurance guidance
9. Slop chest account forms
10. Bill of lading forms
11. Wage and overtime scales
12. Overtime support sheets
13. Payroll sheets
14. Stevedore damage report forms
15. W-4 forms
16. U.S. Coast Guard (USCG) forms required for the shipment and discharge of mariners, for marine casualties, and so on.
17. Wage vouchers
18. Stores list forms
19. Union agreements with supplements and clarifications issued by the company
20. Illness and injury report forms
21. Medical attention forms
22. Drug and alcohol screening and collection kits and forms
23. Crew information forms

Checklist of Items to Complete During the Voyage

Forms that are to be completed during the voyage should be filed in a safe place, ready on arrival at the first U.S. port. They are explained in detail in the appropriate chapters.

1. Customs Form CF-5129, Crew Member's Declaration (fig. 10), should be distributed a day after sailing from the last foreign port. Crewmembers should fill out, sign, and return the forms within a definite time, usually twenty-four to forty-eight hours. A crewmember with nothing to declare should write "none" across the form and sign it.
2. Form CF-1304, Crew's Effects Declaration (fig. 7). This is filled out using information from Crew Member's Declaration. A crewmember with nothing to declare is not listed on the declaration, but all curios to remain on board (termed ROB) must be listed.
3. The inward foreign manifest
4. I-418, Crew/Passenger List (fig. 23). If the vessel has passengers, an alphabetized passenger list must be made (if this was not supplied by the agent). If passengers were taken at several ports and a passenger list supplied at each port, the names should all be put on one list in alphabetical order.
5. Form I-94, Arrival/Departure Record (fig. 20), for each alien passenger on board

6. Form I-95AB, Crewman's Landing Permit (fig. 21), for each nonresident alien crewmember (not for registered aliens)
7. Crew discharges
8. Wage vouchers
9. Payroll
10. All entries in the official log properly signed
11. Overtime sheets checked and tallied weekly
12. Stores requisitions checked and signed
13. The voyage letter, if the company requires one. Notes should be kept throughout the voyage of things to include in the letter.
14. List of miscellaneous vouchers, totaled and balanced
15. Slop chest account forms and inventory
16. Master's expense account

No list of this nature can be all-inclusive as each company and country has different requirements. Before taking over a ship, the new master must have a clear idea of what forms are necessary. One benefit of modern communications is that most questions that arise for the new master can be readily answered by someone ashore.

CHAPTER 2

United States Laws

The United States regulatory system has been criticized for the impractical procedures that are followed to enact laws. Because most elected lawmakers cannot know how to regulate specific activities such as flying planes or operating ships, the legislators write acts and statutes that use fairly broad language. The appropriate regulatory agencies, most of which fall under the executive branch of government, are then tasked with writing the detailed regulations that will guide the specific behaviors of the affected industry, supposedly in accordance with the intentions of the legislators. The regulatory agencies are considered the "experts," and they do consult with the public and industry leaders in the drafting of regulations.

Regulations change so quickly, and there are so many regulatory agencies—government and nongovernment—publishing "recommended practices," it seems almost impossible to keep abreast of the law. Nonetheless, those who want to work in the shipping industry must be willing to work within an increasingly stringent set of regulations and industry practices.

CRIMINAL AND CIVIL LIABILITY OF THE MASTER

Criminal and civil liability extends to the master personally and also to shoreside management and possibly even charterers for various environmental crimes, even crimes that have no criminal intent requirement. These are called "strict liability crimes," and the master can be liable no matter who is at fault.

Under the concept of "willful blindness" and the criminal doctrines of "aiding and abetting" and "obstruction of justice," persons can be found criminally liable even if they were not present at the incident. The master must never approve, encourage, endorse, or command anyone to violate the law, and violations—or even the potential for violations—must never be ignored. Additionally, criminal penalties can be assessed for hindering investigations, intimidating or tampering with witnesses or documents, and falsifying statements or logs.[1]

Generally after an incident, the Coast Guard is the first agency on the scene to begin the investigation. Usually during Coast Guard investigations persons are questioned without being read their rights or "Mirandized." The Coast Guard has the authority to Mirandize and subpoena, demanding that the master provide documents on-scene, but it rarely exercises this authority. Interestingly, even though the Coast Guard does not Mirandize before questioning (as required before questioning in a criminal case), Coast Guard policy dictates that the collection of evidence should preserve both civil and criminal options. This means that when the Coast Guard collects evidence, they must follow strict guidelines. Though this policy clearly applies to the collection of physical evidence, it does not require the investigators to read people their rights before questioning them.

With serious incidents, several federal and state agencies may be involved from the start. It is not unusual to see Coast Guard investigators, the Environmental Protection Agency (EPA), the Federal Bureau of Investigation (FBI), the U.S. Fish and Wildlife Service, and multiple state agencies all represented at a major marine incident.

Coast Guard investigators may board out of uniform, as they have found people are more relaxed and more willing to answer questions if the guardsmen are in civilian clothes. Additionally, the FBI may work closely with the Coast Guard and other agencies in pursuing their own investigations. For instance, a Coast Guard officer, though not conducting a criminal investigation for the Coast Guard, may ask questions and collect documents on behalf of another agency, such as the FBI.

Once its investigation has been completed, the Coast Guard may decide a criminal investigation is warranted, in which case it will contact the U.S. attorney's office. All information collected during the initial investigation now becomes available to agencies conducting the criminal investigation; thus, statements that may be used against a person in a criminal hearing were probably collected without the person's having been read his or her rights. This creates a dangerous gray area for the mariner being questioned with respect to a maritime incident.

Mariners must never impede an investigation; however, they should be entitled to seek legal counsel, especially if the potential for criminal liability exists, before answering questions or making statements about the events leading up to the incident. Crewmembers should avoid hindering any mitigation or cleanup efforts, but they may tactfully request legal counsel before discussing the circumstances leading up to the incident. Chapter 4, "Vessel Accidents and Incidents," provides more information on handling similar difficult situations.

Persons found guilty of environmental violations can be punished at multiple levels of government and in many different ways. The possibilities include any combination of the following:

1. Administrative civil penalties (fines) assessed by a regulatory agency like the USCG and/or EPA and/or Fish and Wildlife Service
2. Administrative proceedings against a license or document
3. Civil fines imposed by a court
4. Criminal sanctions imposed by state and/or federal courts

All the above penalties may be applied for the same incident.

With a flood of tangled regulations pouring forth, operating companies are scrambling to hire legal experts to draft company procedures and policy manuals to bring their operations in line with the rapidly changing state, federal, and international requirements. Mariners are often left to educate themselves, usually by sifting through multivolume manuals that are filled with corrections and updates to keep them current. Frequently, when modern mariners sign on a ship, they are handed a ten-pound manual and are then asked to sign that they have read and understood its contents before being allowed to assume a watch. Masters and companies should do all they can to provide their employees with concise guidance and enough lead time to absorb the material they are expected to assimilate.

Many mariners now carry license insurance, which, depending on the coverage, generally provides for legal defense in administrative hearings (and possibly civil and criminal trials). Most plans offer some sort of income replacement while a license is suspended awaiting a hearing or trial. Given the high cost of legal representation and the legislative trends focusing on individual responsibility, license insurance increasingly makes good sense. When comparing license insurance policies, one should ask about coverage of legal defense costs in criminal proceedings as well. Given the criminal component that may be present in newly enacted strict liability "environmental crimes," mariners on tankers face more exposure to criminal proceedings than mariners on container vessels. Premiums will vary widely depending on the scope and type of coverage and the mariner's license level, experience, training, and work pattern. Most major providers advertise in industry publications and many have Web sites. Before settling on a provider, coverage and premiums should be thoroughly researched and compared.

The modern master is under more stress and has fewer personnel resources than ever before. Many feel the master has more responsibility and less actual operational authority today than in previous years. Following is an example of an ethical and legal dilemma involving a major oil company.

A female third mate signed on to a large tanker. About four weeks into the trip, the master learned the third mate was pregnant. She had not been asked during her preemployment physical if she was pregnant, nor had there been such a question on any form she filled out. She knew that if her pregnancy was discovered, she might not have gotten the job on a high-paying tanker. The tanker was carrying a product known to cause cancer and birth defects. The master was aware that women of childbearing years would not be allowed to work within a certain radius of shoreside tanks holding this product. The master also knew that he could not discriminate on the basis of sex or pregnancy, unless the condition affected the mate's ability to do her job, which, at the time, it did not. The master and company potentially faced a lawsuit if her baby was born with defects, but they also faced a discrimination suit if she was let go.

These types of problems are becoming increasingly common with the plethora of overlapping and competing regulations and the bulging body of case law being decided each week. Masters must constantly weigh operational efficiency against legal requirements, and personal and professional ethics against cost reduction.

In the past, sailors were rightly characterized as a rugged lot. Some were poorly educated; some were criminals who'd been given the option of going to jail or going to sea. Today, the opposite is true. A criminal conviction, a drunk driving offense, even failure to pay child support can adversely affect a mariner's ability to maintain a license or document.[2] Most feel that the tougher regulations on mariners' personal requirements are a boon to the industry. The ships are safer, the environment is better protected, and (some) crews are happier with the new batch of purged and sanitized sailors. However, there are some mariners who miss the character and adventure of the old days.

The following list is by no means exhaustive, but it does address some of the major legislation affecting mariners of the twenty-first century. Should a major environmental incident occur, all applicable environmental statutes and regulations would be brought to bear, including statutes like the Migratory Bird Treaty Act and other wildlife and environmental laws.

FEDERAL WATER POLLUTION CONTROL ACT (FWPCA) AND CLEAN WATER ACT (CWA)

A long history, starting with the 1899 Rivers and Harbors Act, has led to present-day water pollution regulations. The Federal Water Pollution Control Act (FWPCA) was passed in 1972 and was improved by subsequent amendments, such as the Clean Water Act (CWA) in 1977, that strengthened enforcement and broadened the scope of the original legislation.[3] These acts prohibit the discharge of oil, hazardous substances, or pollutants upon the navigable waters of the United States, adjoining shorelines, contiguous zone waters, or waters seaward of the contiguous zone that may affect U.S. natural resources. Such discharge is also prohibited in connection with activities under the Outer Continental Shelf Lands Act or the Deepwater Ports Act. Pollutants include dredged materials, solid waste, incinerator residue, sewage (not from vessels, which is covered under MARPOL), garbage, sewage sludge, and biological and radioactive materials. Under CWA, pollutants also include such things as heat, stormwater runoff, rock, and sand. Toxic pollutants include sixty-three substances listed in 33 USC §1317. This act covers all inland waters as well as waters out to the 200-mile exclusive economic zone (EEZ).

In 1990, FWPCA was amended to allow the president to ensure effective and immediate removal of a discharge and to mitigate or prevent a substantial threat of discharge of oil or other hazardous substances by taking various actions, including removing and destroying a vessel posing such a threat. As of 1990, the required coverage of the National Contingency Plan extends out to 200 miles.

In January 1998, the Environmental Protection Agency proposed additional amendments to CWA, which will regulate discharges of pollutants under the National Pollutant Discharge Elimination System (NPDES). Section 301 of CWA prohibits nonpermitted point source discharges of pollutants into United States waters. Section 402 of CWA establishes the NPDES, an EPA permitting program that requires permits for certain point discharges of pollutants. Under CWA, point discharge sources now include vessels. EPA regulations found in 40 CFR §122.3(a) list certain discharges which are exempt from NPDES requirements.

Under CWA, criminal sanctions are warranted for negligent acts or omissions that lead to a harmful discharge, tampering with a monitoring device, failure to report a harmful discharge, or providing a false statement regarding the incident. Negligence means a person did not use reasonable care.[4]

OIL POLLUTION ACT OF 1990 (OPA '90)

The Oil Pollution Act of 1990 (OPA '90) was written partly as a legislative response to the *Exxon Valdez* spill in 1989. The act was probably the most pervasive legislation of the decade but only the major effects of it will be discussed here. OPA '90 amends various sections of the Clean Water Act and is codified in 33 USC and 46 USC.[5]

CWA/OPA '90 established a three-tiered system of civil penalties that may be assessed against an owner, operator, or person-in-charge of a vessel discharging covered substances. These penalties are based on strict liability, which means if there is a prohibited discharge, regardless of fault, a civil penalty will almost invariably be assessed. A summary of the provisions and effects of CWA/OPA '90 follows:

1. OPA '90 permitted the Coast Guard to review National Driver Register information about an individual applying for a license or document. As part of this heightened scrutiny, time windows were developed to limit an applicant's eligibility for certain documents depending on the recency, severity, and frequency of various driving offenses.[6]

2. OPA '90 encouraged the enactment of increasingly rigorous state legislation of tankers and bulk liquid trades. States are free to enact standards that are more rigorous than OPA '90, and many have done so. Most major ports now require their own Certificates of Financial Responsibility.

3. Tanker escort regulations required that all laden, single-hull tankers over 5,000 gross tons must be escorted by at least two suitable escort vessels while transiting Prince William Sound and Puget Sound. Most coastal states have imposed their own additional escort regulations.[7]

4. Work hours and rest rules were imposed aboard all U.S. tankers.

5. Blood alcohol content of crewmembers must be below 0.04 percent while aboard a U.S. flag vessel.

6. As a result of new regulations on alcohol and dangerous drugs (not all due to OPA '90), employers must now conduct a multitude of drug and alcohol screens.[8]

7. Strict criminal and civil liabilities, including fines and jail time, can be assigned under OPA '90 regardless of actual fault.[9]

8. Criminal penalties were added and/or increased for not notifying the Coast Guard after a spill or pollution incident.

9. Limits on liability due to oil pollution and a fund for cleanup were established.[10]

Since enacting OPA '90, according to Rear Admiral Robert C. North, USCG, in his 2000 newsletter *Perspective,* the following trends have been noted:

• The average number of spills over 10,000 gallons has dropped by 50 percent from pre-1991 levels.
• The gallons spilled per million gallons of oil shipped has decreased by 50 percent.
• There have been no spills over 1,000,000 gallons since 1991.
• The total volume of tank ship oil spills in the U.S. peaked in 1989 and has remained below 200,000 gallons since 1991.

INTERVENTION ON THE HIGH SEAS ACT, 1974 (IHSA)

On March 8, 1967, the *Torrey Canyon,* then the thirteenth largest ship afloat, grounded in international waters off the coast of England. Her cargo threatened disaster to the coasts of both England and France. The English authorities were unclear about their right to intervene while a distressed vessel was on the high seas, and as a result, Britain waited ten days before acting. The vessel eventually spilled 60,000 tons of crude oil onto the shores of England and France.

Two years later, in response to this incident, the International Convention Relating to Intervention on the High Seas was drafted. The United States, modeling this convention, drafted the IHSA to protect her shores.[11]

Prior to IHSA, the United States had no clear authority to intervene on waters beyond the 3-mile limit. Pollution incidents within the 3-mile limit were covered by CWA and FWPCA. As a result of IHSA and the 1973 protocol that broadened the scope of covered pollutants, the United States can intervene on the high seas should her coasts be threatened by an actual or potential discharge of oil or other hazardous substances.

ACT TO PREVENT POLLUTION FROM SHIPS (APPS)

The Act to Prevent Pollution from Ships (APPS) is the implementing act incorporating into U.S. law the provisions of the International Convention for the Prevention of Pollution from Ships, as modified by the Protocol of 1978 (MARPOL 73/78). It prohibits the discharge of oil or harmful substances from U.S. flag ships anywhere and from foreign flag ships in U.S. waters; it requires the immediate and complete reporting of discharges, probable discharges, or even allowed discharges in emergency situations. This act also covers garbage discharges from ships. An intentional violation of MARPOL in the United States is a class D felony, and any violation of MARPOL subjects the violator to both civil and criminal liability. Up to one-half of fines collected may be awarded to persons providing information leading to a conviction under this act.[12]

APPS was amended by the Marine Plastic Pollution Research and Control Act of 1987 (MPPRCA), which implements annex V of MARPOL (garbage and plastics). Under these regulations the discharge into water of all plastics, synthetic ropes, fishing nets, and even biodegradable plastics is prohibited.

RESOURCE CONSERVATION AND RECOVERY ACT (RCRA)

The Resource Conservation and Recovery Act (RCRA) applies to generators or transporters of hazardous waste. This would primarily apply to cruise ships that generate dry cleaning, photo lab, cleaning, and beauty parlor wastes. Regulations can be found in 42 CFR §6900 et seq.

REFUSE ACT

The Refuse Act prohibits the discharge of any refuse matter of any kind into the navigable waters of the United States, their tributaries, or their banks.[13] Both civil and criminal penalties may be imposed and, as in APPS, up to one-half of fines collected may be awarded to persons providing information leading to a conviction under this act.[14]

NON-INDIGENOUS AQUATIC NUISANCE PREVENTION AND CONTROL ACT OF 1990 (NANPCA)

As amended by the National Invasive Species Act of 1996 (NISA), the Non-Indigenous Aquatic Nuisance Prevention and Control Act of 1990 (NANPCA) applies to all U.S. and foreign vessels that operate in the waters of the United States.[15] It imposes mandatory ballast water handling methods for vessels voyaging to the Great Lakes or the Hudson River and for vessels engaged in the foreign export of Alaskan North Slope crude, and it recommends voluntary procedures elsewhere.[16] It also imposes mandatory record keeping and reporting requirements (found in 33 CFR §151.2045) for all vessels within U.S. waters. Ballast water reporting forms (fig. 17) are found in appendix B, "Figures: Sample Forms." The Coast Guard stated in its *Navigation and Vessel Inspection Circular* (NVIC 8-99) that the current recommended voluntary ballast handling procedures might become mandatory for all vessels, with civil and criminal penalties, if operators do not voluntarily comply during this initial period.

The act applies to all ballast water and sediments taken less than 200 nautical miles from any shore or with water that is less than 2,000 meters (6,560 feet) deep.

Four types of vessels are exempt:

1. A crude-oil tanker engaged in the coastwise trade
2. A passenger vessel equipped with a functioning treatment system designed to kill aquatic organisms in the ballast water
3. A Department of Defense, Coast Guard, or armed forces vessel subject to the Uniform National Discharge Standards for Vessels of the Armed Forces[17]
4. A vessel that will discharge ballast water or sediments only at the same location where the ballast water or sediments originated

Masters of vessels are requested to take the following voluntary precautions:

1. Avoid the discharge or uptake of ballast water in areas within or near marine sanctuaries, marine preserves, marine parks, or coral reefs.
2. Minimize or avoid ballast water uptake in the following areas or circumstances:
   A. Areas known to have infestations or populations of harmful organisms or pathogens (e.g., toxic algal blooms)
   B. Areas near sewage outfalls
   C. Areas near dredging operations
   D. Areas where tidal flushing is known to be poor or at times when a tidal stream is known to be more turbid
   E. In darkness, when bottom-dwelling organisms may rise up the water column
   F. Areas where propellers may stir up sediment
3. Clean the ballast tanks regularly in midocean to remove sediments. Cleaning can also be done at drydock or under controlled arrangements in port. Dispose of sediments in accordance with local, state, and federal regulations.
4. Discharge only the minimal amount of ballast water essential for operations while in U.S. waters.
5. Rinse anchors and anchor chains to remove sediments and organisms at their place of origin.
6. Remove fouling organisms from hull, piping, and tanks on a regular basis.
7. Maintain a ballast water management plan designed specifically for the vessel.
8. Train the crew on the application of ballast water and sediment management and treatment procedures.

Masters of vessels that carry ballast into U.S. waters after operating beyond the EEZ are requested to employ at least one of the following ballast water practices:

1. Exchange ballast water beyond the EEZ in an area at least 200 nautical miles from any shore and in water that is at least 2,000 meters (6,560 feet) deep before entering the waters of the United States.
2. Retain the ballast water aboard the vessel.
3. Use an alternative, environmentally sound method of ballast water management before the vessel begins the voyage.[18]
4. Discharge the ballast at an approved reception facility.
5. Under extraordinary conditions, conduct a ballast water exchange within an area agreed to by the U.S. Coast Guard Captain of the Port (COTP) at the time of the request.

Vessel compliance with mandatory reporting and record-keeping requirements (see chapter 8, "Logbooks") will be monitored by the U.S. Coast

Guard as well as by state officials (such as California State Lands Commission) via random boarding inspections.

COMPREHENSIVE ENVIRONMENTAL RESPONSE, COMPENSATION, AND LIABILITY ACT (CERCLA)

Combined with other acts, the Comprehensive Environmental Response, Compensation, and Liability Act (CERCLA) requires the posting of certificates of financial responsibility (COFRs) or the posting of a bond ensuring that the maritime operator has the financial resources to pay for the cleanup of an environmental incident. CERCLA also sets forth reporting requirements and provides for criminal sanctions for the nonreporting of hazardous substance releases.[19]

SHORE PROTECTION ACT OF 1988

The Shore Protection Act of 1988 concerns the transportation of municipal and commercial waste. The act was enacted on November 18, 1988, to minimize the amount of trash, medical debris, and other harmful materials being discharged into U.S. waters by vessels handling such wastes. The EPA develops the regulations and the Department of Transportation issues required permits for vessels engaged in waste-handling operations. Permits are obtained from the U.S. Coast Guard Headquarters.[20]

FEDERAL ALCOHOL STANDARDS

A Coast Guard official, other law enforcement officers, or a marine employer or master may direct an individual operating a vessel to undergo a chemical test when reasonable cause exists. Reasonable cause exists when the individual was involved with a marine casualty or when the individual is suspected of being in violation of the intoxication standards defined in 33 CFR §99.020 or §95.025.[21]

Federal alcohol standards apply to persons operating a vessel. Per 33 CFR §95.015, "operating a vessel" means simply being a "crewmember (including a licensed individual), pilot or watchstander not a regular member of the crew" aboard a vessel that is not a recreational vessel. While aboard a nonrecreational vessel, the following regulations apply: A person operating a vessel

1. shall not perform or attempt to perform any scheduled duties within four hours of consuming any alcohol;

2. shall not be intoxicated at any time (having 0.04 percent BAC or 0.01 percent BAC for any person under twenty-one years of age or showing the effects of intoxicants on manner, behavior, disposition, speech, muscular movement, or general appearance;
3. shall not consume an intoxicant while on watch; and
4. may consume a legal nonprescription drug or prescription drug provided it does not cause the individual to become intoxicated.

A refusal to test will result in the presumption that the person was intoxicated.

PORTS AND WATERWAYS SAFETY ACT

The Ports and Waterways Safety Act set up a national system of vessel traffic services (VTS) for certain ports. Although the regulations state that under certain conditions the VTS may "issue directions to control the movement of vessels," the regulations also state that nothing in the regulations is intended to relieve the master, owner, operator, charterer, or person directing the movement of a vessel from the consequences of any neglect to comply with any laws or regulations. Each user of a VTS must carry aboard a current copy of the applicable VTS manual for the system being used. Vessels within a VTS are tracked using a vessel movement reporting system (VMRS). Copies of the manuals occasionally are printed in the *Local Notice to Mariners* for the involved port.[22] To date, VTS is in use at the following ports:

Port	Name	VHF Channels
New York	New York Traffic	Ch. 11, 12, 14
Houston	Houston Traffic	Ch. 11, 12
Berwick Bay	Berwick Traffic	Ch. 11
St. Mary's River	Soo Control	Ch. 12
San Francisco	San Francisco Offshore	
	Vessel Movement	Ch. 12
	San Francisco Traffic	Ch. 14
Puget Sound	Seattle Traffic	Ch. 5A, 14
	Tofino Traffic	Ch. 74
	Vancouver Traffic	Ch. 11
Prince William Sound	Valdez Traffic	Ch. 13
Louisville	Louisville Traffic	Ch. 13

This same act, in response to the killing of an American citizen aboard the passenger ship *Achille Lauro* in 1985, was amended in 1986 to include provisions of the Omnibus Diplomatic Security and Anti-Terrorism Act, which imposed security measures and procedures requirements for passenger terminals and ports and also required the development of security contingency plans.

PROTECTION OF NORTHERN RIGHT WHALES

The United States has two newly imposed USCG mandatory ship reporting systems along the East Coast of the United States for the protection of endangered right whales.[23] All ships of 300 gross tons or greater must participate. Government ships that are exempt from the International Convention for the Safety of Life at Sea 1974 (SOLAS) need not participate but are encouraged to do so. Participating ships must report to the shore-based authority when entering a covered area. No reports are required for movements made within an area or when exiting the area.

The northeastern reporting area, called WHALESNORTH, operates year-round and includes the waters of Cape Cod Bay, Massachusetts Bay, and the Great South Channel east and southeast of Massachusetts. The southeastern area, called WHALESSOUTH, operates from November 15 through April 16 of each year and includes coastal waters within about 25 nautical miles along a 90-mile stretch of the Atlantic seaboard in Florida and Georgia.

Ships equipped with INMARSAT C must report in International Maritime Organization (IMO) standard format (fig. 39) as follows:

WHALESNORTH OR WHALESSOUTH

M   Vessel INMARSAT number

A   Vessel name and call sign

B   Date, time, and month of report (Six-digit group giving day of month and time, single letter indicating time zone, and three letters indicating month: for example, 1230 GMT on July 22 would be written 221230ZJUL)

E   True course in three digits

F   Speed in knots and tenths (9.3 knots would be written 093)

H   Date, time, and point of entry into system (date and time expressed as in B, latitude expressed as four digits with N designating north, followed by a slash, then longitude in five digits with W indicating west. For example 32°18'N, 124°33'W should be sent as 3218N/12433W)

I   Destination and ETA (name of destination port and arrival time expressed as in B)

L   Route information can be reported as a direct rhumb line to port or a series of waypoints. If reporting waypoints, coordinates should be expressed as in H, and intended speed between waypoints expressed as in F. For vessels transiting within a traffic separation scheme, only the entry and departure waypoints within the TSS need be given.

The remaining right whales (approximately three hundred) found along the East Coast of the United States are federally protected under the Endangered Species Act. Right whales are highly vulnerable to vessel collisions because they are slow moving and hard to spot. They don't move out of the way of approaching vessels, and they mate, rest, feed, and nurse their young at the surface. The National Marine Fisheries Service recommends that the following precautionary measures be taken when transiting right whale critical habitats:

- Prior to entering the reporting areas, check the Coast Guard Broadcast Notice to Mariners, NAVTEX, Coast Pilot, local pilots, and other sources for information on recent right whale sightings.
- Maintain a sharp lookout by people familiar with whale characteristics.
- Avoid nighttime transits of right whale habitats.
- Reduce speed when transiting right whale habitats, ideally to speeds below 14 knots.
- Do not assume right whales will move out of the ship's way. Right whales are slow moving and seldom travel faster than 5 or 6 knots. Maneuver around the whales or avoid recently reported sighting locations. Federal regulation prohibits approach within 500 yards of any right whale anywhere in the U.S. Atlantic EEZ. The same regulations have been implemented by the state of Massachusetts.
- Any whale accidentally struck, any dead whale, or any whale observed entangled in fishing gear should be reported immediately to the Coast Guard on VHF channel 16, noting the precise location, date, and time of the sighting. In the event of a sighting or strike, information such as the size and speed of the vessel, water depth, wind speed and direction, description of the impact, fate of the whale, species, and size should be reported.
- Right whales can be sighted anywhere along the East Coast. Mariners are urged to exercise prudent seamanship at all times with regard to right whales while transiting the U.S. East Coast.

Reports of sightings should be sent to NOAA:
  telex: 236737831
  CAMSLANT Phone 757-421-6226
  Fax 757-421-6226

Ships not equipped with INMARSAT C must report using narrow-band direct printing MF or VHF voice communications to the Coast Guard's Communications Area Master Station Atlantic (CAMSLANT) in Chesapeake, Virginia.

UNITED STATES SUBMARINE CABLE ACT

The United States Submarine Cable Act makes it a federal offense to damage a submarine cable and requires the master of a vessel to keep the ship's gear at least one nautical mile from a vessel engaged in the laying or servicing of a marine cable. Many submarine cables are filled with oil and would cause a pollution incident if torn. Also, most modern submarine telecommunications cables carry up to 8,000 volts and any attempts to cut or untangle the cable could be lethal. Vessel operators may contact AT&T by calling 1-800-235-CHARTS for free charts showing cable areas. The vessel's name and documentation number should be handy.[24]

FEDERAL BENZENE REGULATIONS

Benzene regulations published in 1987 parallel the Occupational Safety and Health Administration (OSHA) exposure regulations and set forth threshold limit values and other regulations pertaining to benzene exposure.[25]

CLEAN AIR ACT 1990

The Clean Air Act of 1990, augmented by more stringent state and local air quality acts, limits the amount of harmful emissions from vessels and provides for financial penalties for violations. Although it is a federal law, most of the related work, such as monitoring, permitting, and enforcement, is done by the states. As an example of how the act will impact commercial vessels, the EPA is issuing new emissions standards for commercial marine diesels built after 2004, superseding emission requirements outlined by IMO.[26]

CHAPTER 3

International Codes and Conventions

International conventions and treaties to which the United States subscribes are codified into federal law in the *U.S. Code* (USC) with detailed regulations available in the *Code of Federal Regulations* (CFR). However, during codification, the provisions of an international convention, treaty, or U.S. act may be broken up and inserted into different titles of the USC or CFR, as appropriate. For example, the provisions of OPA '90 can be found in EPA regulations as well as USCG regulations.

THE INTERNATIONAL CONVENTION FOR THE PREVENTION OF POLLUTION FROM SHIPS, 1973, MODIFIED BY THE PROTOCOL OF 1978 (MARPOL 73/78)

MARPOL covers all types of marine pollution violations, from misdemeanors to felonies.[1] Each day a violation continues is considered a separate violation, so it behooves masters to ensure their crews are fully versed on the requirements of MARPOL. Persons giving information that leads to convictions and fines against violators may be entitled to up to half of the fines collected. Some annexes have designated special areas of the world where either no discharges are allowed or the restrictions on discharge are stricter than the annexes' basic provisions. MARPOL is composed of five annexes. These provisions are codified throughout the CFRs and are not found as one coherent regulation.

Annex I—Regulations for the Prevention of Pollution by Oil
Special areas for Annex I listed in 33 CFR §151.13 include areas of the Mediterranean Sea, Baltic Sea, Black Sea, Red Sea, Gulf of Aden, and Antarctic area.

The particulars for compliance with Annex I can be found in 33 CFR §151.10. This section includes information on oily-water separators, maximum oil concentrations of overboard discharges, and the requirements of maintaining an Oil Record Book. Additionally, shipboard oil pollution emergency plans are outlined. Requirements for International Oil Pollution Prevention Certificates (IOPPs) can be found in 33 CFR §151.19 and information of Shipboard Oil Pollution Emergency Plans (SOPEPs) is found in 33 CFR §151.26.

Annex II—Regulations for the Control of
Noxious Liquid Substances in Bulk

Special areas for Annex II listed in 33 CFR §151.32 include areas of the Baltic Sea, the Black Sea, and Antarctic areas.

Annex II is codified in 33 CFR §151.30 et seq. This section lists applicability and certificates needed to carry various noxious liquid substances (NLS). It outlines the procedure for obtaining an attachment to an IOPP certificate for the carriage of NLS.

Annex III—Regulations for the Prevention of Pollution by
Harmful Substances Carried by Sea in Packaged Forms, or in
Freight Containers or Portable Tanks

MARPOL Annex III is codified primarily in 49 CFR §171 et seq.

Annex IV—Regulations for the Prevention of Pollution
by Sewage from Ships

These requirements are addressed by sections of the FWPCA (33 USC §1322) and are found in 33 CFR §159 and the EPA regulations of 40 CFR §140.3–4.

Annex V—Regulations for the Prevention of Pollution
by Garbage from Ships

Special areas for Annex V listed in 33 CFR §151.53 include areas of the Mediterranean Sea, Baltic Sea, Black Sea, Red Sea, Gulf areas, North Sea, Antarctic area, wider Caribbean region, and Gulf of Mexico.

This annex is codified in 33 CFR §151.51 et seq. and includes information on record keeping requirements, waste management plans, placards, and inspection and reporting requirements.

No person may discharge garbage into the navigable waters of the United States. Plastic or garbage mixed with plastic may never be discharged into the sea or navigable waters of the United States.

Discharge requirements and distances off the nearest land are as follows:

1.   Plastics can never be discharged; they may be held aboard or incinerated.

2. Dunnage, lining, and packing materials that float must be discharged at least 25 miles from the nearest land.

3. Victual wastes and all other wastes including paper products, rags, glass, metal, bottles, and crockery must be discharged at least 12 miles from the nearest land. If the material has passed through a grinder it may be discharged outside a 3-mile distance from land.

4. Mixtures of garbage having different requirements must be retained aboard or discharged in accordance with the strictest applicable requirements.

Vessels must post prominent placards stating the MARPOL Annex V requirements. The placard most mariners see aboard ship applies to vessels operating outside of special areas. When operating in a special area, no garbage is to be released except victual wastes, which may be discharged as far as practicable from land but in no case less than 12 nautical miles from land or, if in the wider Caribbean region, discharges of victual wastes which have been passed through a comminuter or grinder shall be made as far as practicable from land but in no case less than 3 nautical miles from land.

Vessels must maintain a waste management plan and a log. Masters should endeavor to keep all records of garbage discharged ashore.

INTERNATIONAL CONVENTION FOR THE SAFETY OF LIFE AT SEA (SOLAS) AND INTERNATIONAL SAFETY MANAGEMENT CODE (ISM)

In 1994 the ISM Code became chapter 9 of the SOLAS Convention and compliance is now mandatory for signatory nations. The ISM Code has thirteen parts:

1. Introduction and General Explanation
2. Safety and Environmental Protection Policy
3. Company Responsibilities and Authority
4. Designated Persons
5. Master's Responsibility and Authority
6. Resources and Personnel
7. Development of Plans for Shipboard Operations
8. Emergency Preparedness
9. Reports and Analysis of Non-Conformities, Accidents, and Hazardous Occurrences
10. Maintenance of the Ship and Equipment
11. Documentation
12. Company Verification, Review, and Evaluation
13. Certification, Review, and Control

By July 1998 all oil, chemical, and gas tankers as well as passenger ships, bulk carriers, and high-speed cargo ships of at least 500 gross registered tons were required to be in compliance. All other ships, including mobile offshore platforms, of at least 500 gross registered tons must be in compliance by July 2002.

Vessels are required to have a safety management systems (SMS) in place, usually comprised of a manual or document listing plans and procedures for various emergencies and operations both ashore and aboard ship. The primary goal of an SMS is to ensure the commitment and involvement of all concerned—the shipping company's top management and representatives of shore and ship personnel—to continuously improve safety management skills, including preparedness for both safety and environmental emergencies.

Compliance is evidenced by a vessel's Safety Management Certificate, which is valid for five years and is usually issued by a classification society after an audit. Presently, only the ABS is certified by the Coast Guard to audit and issue certificates to U.S. flag vessels. External audits are conducted every five years. Internal audits are to be conducted annually.[2]

While there are numerous other codes and conventions dealing with safety at sea, the ISM Code is the first mandatory code to focus on the human element from the managerial level down to the operational level. Other regulations, codes, and conventions address building standards, operational issues, safety, and pollution control, but the ISM Code is designed as a proactive tool—a type of safety quality control—that management can use to further enhance the safety of vessels, cargo, crew, passengers, and the environment. The airline industry has long been steeped in an atmosphere of safety consciousness. The maritime industry may well be the last frontier for international and national regulators to infuse with the modern safety culture. Professional mariners will need to grow with the times and adopt new attitudes and new management styles to remain effective and competitive.

Traditional statistics reflect that over 85 percent of marine casualties and incidents are due to human error (the numbers vary widely depending on the source). Modern thinking is that almost 100 percent of marine casualties are attributable to human error. For example, if a hose blows out on a tanker, that incident historically would have been called equipment failure. Today's thinking suggests that a human somewhere, not necessarily aboard the ship, probably made a mistake. Perhaps the hose was poorly designed or improperly tested, or there was a flaw in the manufacturing process, or the mate allowed the hose to overpressurize. Whatever the reason, the failure was most likely due to human error. The ISM Code seeks to address the whole picture of marine operations, not just a specific evolution.

It is the company's responsibility to generate a safety management system for its vessels and to create and facilitate the liaison between ship and shoreside personnel. It is the master's job to implement such policies and procedures.

INTERNATIONAL ORGANIZATION FOR STANDARDIZATION (ISO)

The International Organization for Standardization (ISO) in Switzerland offers over 13,000 internationally accepted standards for business and technology. ISO promulgates international standards and offers voluntary certification, much like the Good Housekeeping seal of approval, to member companies meeting certain standards. ISO standards are documented agreements offering technical specifications or other criteria to be used as guidelines by a certain industry. For example, the format of credit cards (their size, thickness, and digital data) is based on an ISO international standard so the cards can be used worldwide. Among the best known standards are ISO 9000, which deals with management practices, and ISO 14000, which concerns environmental practices.

ISO 9002 is a voluntary certification pursued by companies wishing to demonstrate their commitment to quality assurance to prospective customers and clients. ISO is comprised of representatives of over one hundred participating countries. It recommends documentation, record keeping, and written procedures similar in format to those required by the ISM Code. Like the ISM Code, ISO 9002 recommends written shoreside and shipboard contingency plans, policies, and operational guidelines. Most classification societies provide a service whereby a company can get all of its management programs and vessels certified under ISO, ISM, and STCW (if applicable) by means of one audit, thus avoiding duplication of effort. The master's role is one of ensuring compliance with company policies and procedures aboard the vessel and among the crew and providing valuable feedback and input to shoreside managers on any improvements, corrections, or upgrades that could be made.

The master has the responsibility of implementing and enforcing company policies and procedures and of preventing and correcting any nonconformities. The master's responsibilities under any company policy should be clearly written, distributed, and updated as necessary. The master must be given appropriate autonomy and authority as well as any required shoreside support. The master's ability to execute his or her responsibilities can quickly be rendered less effective by overly controlling shoreside micromanagement.

ISO 14000, once implemented, will offer a technique for standardized environmental management and will be a symbol of a business's commitment to sound environmental practices.

INTERNATIONAL CONVENTION ON STANDARDS OF TRAINING, CERTIFICATION, AND WATCHKEEPING FOR SEAFARERS (STCW)

The 1978 International Convention on Standards of Training, Certification, and Watchkeeping for Seafarers (STCW) entered into force on April 28, 1984. The United States signed the 1978 STCW treaty in 1991. Many member nations felt the 1978 convention was not ensuring the competency of ships' crews (as was its intention) because, among other reasons, the requirements were too vague. In 1993 IMO's Maritime Safety Committee decided to make the review of the STCW convention a priority. The revisions were completed in 1995 and were readily accepted. The United States has codified it into various sections of the CFR.

The convention consists of seventeen articles and a completely revised eight-chapter annex containing regulations. Supplementing the annex is the STCW code, which contains eight chapters of technical requirements and guidance, some of which is mandatory. The code is divided into parts A and B. Part A contains the mandatory requirements and part B offers guidance and recommendations.

Amendments to the STCW code entered into force on February 1, 1997, with allowances for deferrals of some provisions. By February 1, 2002, all candidates and sailing officers and crew must meet the provisions of STCW '95 and hold a valid STCW '95 certificate appropriate for the level of their position aboard. Until February 1, 2002, mariners can sail without having STCW '95 certificates if their maritime training started before August 1, 1998, or if the mariner entered active seafaring life prior to August 1, 1998.

While conformance to STCW '95 standards is primarily the burden of administrations and flag states, the master, chief mate, and senior crew, as parties responsible for shipboard training, competency assessment, and sea-time documentation, should have a basic knowledge of the STCW code. Per the code, the master is responsible for ensuring that any crewmember assigned to the vessel is thoroughly familiar with the vessel and any safety or pollution control equipment relevant to assigned duties.

Per STCW '95, the master must ensure that any person assigned as an officer or rating of a watch is provided with a minimum of ten hours rest in a twenty-four-hour period. The hours of rest may be divided into no more than two parts, one of which must be at least six hours in length. These requirements need not be maintained in case of drills, emergencies, or overriding operational concerns. Notwithstanding the previous exceptions, the minimum period of ten hours may be reduced to not less than six consecutive hours, provided that any such reduction does not extend beyond two days and that at least seventy hours rest are provided each seven-day period.

The STCW, as yet, does not apply to seafarers aboard warships, vessels owned or operated by a signatory nation, fishing vessels, or pleasure yachts.

Unlike the United States system of licensing (for officers) and certification (for unlicensed crew), the STCW code divides officers and crew into three levels:

1. Management level: master, chief mate, chief engineer, and first assistant engineer (called second engineer by Europeans)
2. Operational level: officers in charge of a navigational or engineering watch, designated duty engineers in unmanned engine rooms, and radio officers. This would be the equivalent of U.S. second and third mates and engineers.
3. Support level: crew performing tasks under the supervision of persons at the operational or management level, the equivalent of U.S. unlicensed crewmembers

Also, to bring certification standards in line with the International Tonnage Convention, standards in the deck department will be based on 500 and 3,000 gross tons, instead of 200 and 1,600 gross tons. Engineering licenses will be based on main propulsion machinery power thresholds of 750 kilowatt and 3,000 kilowatt.

Most of the operational requirements of the STCW code have been codified into the appropriate titles of the CFR. For example, the STCW code mandates certain rest requirements for officers standing watch. The U.S. *Code of Federal Regulations* already addresses these and other issues. Most states have enacted legislation incorporating or exceeding the minimum STCW requirements and it is the law of the flag state that governs.

As a result of the revised STCW, new obligations have been placed on the administrations of flag states, operating companies, and masters and crews. Companies must ensure that each crewmember is appropriately certified and familiar with the vessel and his or her duties, that personnel records are kept on crewmembers in their employ, and that vessels are properly manned with a well-coordinated and properly rested crew. Additional training and certification may be required on certain types of vessels, such as passenger carriers or tankers, and it is the company's responsibility to see that the crew is properly trained for these specialized duties.

The master is responsible for implementing any company policies based on the new STCW requirements. The master must identify all newly reporting mariners before assigning them any duties, provide them with an opportunity to visit their assigned working spaces, and familiarize them with any equipment they will be using, including giving them instruction on activating and using the equipment. The master should give new crewmembers the opportunity to ask questions of persons already familiar with specific tasks and equipment. The master is also responsible for supervising new crewmembers in order to confirm their competence in their anticipated duties. In addition, one of the more important regulations the master must enforce pertains to rest requirements. Many flag states have incorporated these and even more stringent requirements in their legislation.

Mariners have the responsibility to familiarize themselves with all spaces and equipment with which they will be working. If anyone is unfamiliar with any equipment, it is the crewmember's responsibility to ask for assistance.[3]

In addition to the regulations of the STCW, the 1995 appendix makes several recommendations to the body of signatory states including the following:

1. Development of international medical standards for mariners
2. Regulated training and certification for maritime pilots and vessel traffic service personnel
3. Promotion of women in the maritime industry
4. Development of requirements that operating companies train and assist mariners in maintaining or enhancing their competency after they are employed

GLOBAL MARITIME DISTRESS AND SAFETY SYSTEM (GMDSS)

With the implementation of the global maritime distress and safety system (GMDSS), many vessels have eliminated the radio officer's position. All ships were to be in full compliance with the system by February 1, 1999.[4]

INTERNATIONAL LABOR ORGANIZATION (ILO)

Founded in 1919, the International Labor Organization (ILO) is now a part of the United Nations. This organization issues recommendations that are often adopted and incorporated into law by port states.[5] U.S. flag ships and foreign ships operating in U.S. waters must comply with various ILO recommendations such as the following:

1. Safety standards, competency of officers and crew, work conditions, hours of work, and manning levels

2. Workers' rights
3. Benzene level thresholds
4. Repatriation of mariners
5. Conditions of employment and shipboard living conditions
6. Safety of women at sea
7. Other recommendations affecting the safety and welfare of mariners

CHAPTER 4

Vessel Accidents and Incidents

O f all the components of the maritime venture, accidents and incidents aboard vessels pose the greatest legal, physical, and financial threats to the master and company. While individuals don't know how they will act in time of crisis, preparation and contingency planning can enhance performance in emergency or postincident situations. The International Safety Management Code requires ships to have checklists to dictate the steps to be followed in most anticipated types of accidents and incidents. These checklists should be kept at the ready and should be reviewed by the master and crew at frequent intervals.

The best mariners may not be the ones who tell of their heroic deeds or the daring feats involved with saving their imperiled vessel. The best mariners may be the quiet ones, the people to whom nothing extraordinary ever happens. Why? Because through proper preparation and planning they have ensured that nothing extraordinary happens. Unfortunately, the company may view the master who puts out a blazing shipboard fire as more of a hero than the master who, through proper ship husbandry and personnel management, prevented the fire from happening in the first place. A good master will recognize the crewmembers who take such precautions and will heartily praise behaviors that prevent mishaps.

CASUALTY REPORTS TO THE U.S. COAST GUARD

By federal law, the Coast Guard must maintain reports on certain marine casualties and, if necessary, investigate them.[1] Failure to report a marine casualty as required by law or regulation carries a civil penalty. The reporting requirements apply to all accidents occurring in U.S. waters (including those involving foreign vessels) and to all accidents involving U.S. vessels, regardless of where they occur.

There are two classes of marine casualties that require both immediate verbal reporting and written reporting on form CG-2692 (fig. 15): a reportable marine casualty and a serious marine incident. Following are examples of reportable marine casualties:

1. An unintended grounding or unintended allision with a bridge
2. An intended grounding or allision with a bridge that creates a hazard to navigation, to the environment, or to the safety of a vessel
3. The loss of main propulsion, primary steering, or any associated component or control system that reduces the maneuverability of the vessel
4. An occurrence materially and adversely affecting the vessel's seaworthiness or fitness for service or route, including but not limited to fire, flooding, or the failure of or damage to fixed fire-extinguishing systems, lifesaving equipment, auxiliary power-generating equipment, or bilge-pumping systems
5. A loss of life
6. An injury that requires professional medical treatment beyond first aid and, if the person is employed aboard a vessel in commercial service, that renders the individual unfit to perform his or her duties
7. An occurrence causing property damage in excess of $25,000. Damage cost includes the cost of labor and material to restore the property to the service condition that existed prior to the casualty but does not include the cost of salvage, cleaning, gas-freeing, drydocking, or demurrage.

The following circumstances describe serious marine incidents:

1. One or more deaths
2. An injury to a crewmember, passenger, or other person that requires professional medical treatment beyond first aid and renders the person unfit to perform routine vessel duties
3. Damage to property exceeding $100,000
4. An oil discharge of 10,000 gallons or more—or the discharge of a hazardous substance in reportable quantity—into the navigable waters of the U.S. and the environment whether or not resulting from a marine casualty
5. Actual or constructive total loss of any inspected vessel
6. Actual or constructive total loss of any uninspected, self-propelled vessel of 100 gross tons or more.

In addition to notifying the Coast Guard when any of these casualties occur, the person-in-charge must make a written report as soon as possible to the officer in charge, marine inspection, at the port where the casualty occurred or nearest the port of first arrival. This report must be made on Coast Guard form CG-2692.

The required reporting in case of loss of life or injury resulting in incapacitation applies not only to ship's personnel, but also to others who may be on board, such as shipyard or harbor workers. However, the master does not need to report death or injury of such workers if the death or injury was not the result of a vessel casualty or a vessel equipment casualty. For example, if a longshoreman were to suffer an appendicitis attack on board the vessel and die, the death—not being the result of a vessel or equipment casualty—would therefore not have to be reported to the Coast Guard. If there is any doubt, a master should make a report.

Even if a death or injury that occurs on board is not required to be reported to the Coast Guard, the vessel will most likely be subject to the reporting requirements of the Occupational Safety and Health Administration (OSHA).[2]

Any serious marine incident requires that drug testing and alcohol screening be conducted as soon as possible but with a maximum time limit of two hours of the incident. If the vessel is on the high seas, the master may have to perform these required tests. Testing reports are completed on Coast Guard form CG-2692B (fig. 16).

FEDERAL DRUG AND ALCOHOL REGULATIONS

According to U.S. law, no one aboard who has a safety duty (i.e., a duty on a station bill) can have a blood alcohol content (BAC) over 0.04 percent and no alcohol can be consumed within four hours of standing a watch. If an on-duty mariner has a BAC of 0.02 percent, the person is not to be allowed to continue with his or her duties. A person under twenty-one years of age is considered intoxicated with a BAC of 0.01 percent.

A Coast Guard official, other law enforcement officers, or a marine employer (including the master) may direct an individual operating a vessel to undergo a chemical test when reasonable cause exists. Reasonable cause exists when the individual is involved with a marine casualty or when the individual is suspected of being in violation of the intoxication standards defined in 33 CFR §99.020 or §95.025.[3]

While aboard an inspected vessel, a crewmember and pilot or watchstander who is not a regular member of the crew

1. shall not perform or attempt to perform any scheduled duties within four hours of consuming any alcohol;
2. shall not be intoxicated at any time (0.04 percent BAC or 0.01 percent for any person under twenty-one years of age, or the effects of intoxication are apparent from the person's manner, behavior, disposition, speech, muscular movement, or general appearance as observed preferably by at least two supervisory persons);
3. shall not consume an intoxicant while on watch; and
4. may consume a legal nonprescription drug or prescription drug provided it does not cause the individual to become intoxicated.

A refusal to test will result in the presumption that the person was intoxicated. All tests or a refusal to test are to be logged in the official logbook and on form CG-2692B if the test is connected with a marine incident. Following an incident, the employer (the master is considered an employer as well) must make a determination as to whether the incident is—or is likely to become—a serious marine incident. If so, the employer (or master) must take all practicable steps to chemically test individuals directly involved with the incident. Persons directly involved include any persons whose order, action, or failure to act is determined to be a causative factor (or cannot be ruled out) in the events leading to or causing the incident. No alcohol is to be consumed for eight hours following an incident. After the incident, a BAC test must be administered to involved personnel within two hours. If the test cannot be administered within two hours, the vessel operator must log the reason the test could not be given. If any person refuses to provide a sample, this information must be logged in the vessel's official logbook.

In reaction to this legislation, some companies have decided to keep their ships dry, with no alcohol being allowed aboard at all. Other vessels now have some sort of breath alcohol testing device aboard.

Once a sample has been taken, a chain of custody must be established and maintained from the time of collection through the time of testing. If the specimen is not shipped immediately, it must be safeguarded during storage. Every effort should be made to minimize the number of persons handling the samples.

A master may be called upon to perform a postincident or for-cause drug and/or alcohol specimen collection. The Department of Transportation offers a certification for evidentiary testers, which is strongly recommended for proper specimen collection. The master's employer or union can arrange for it.

Collection of urine specimens should allow for privacy unless there is reason to believe that an individual may alter or substitute the specimen to be provided. The person making the collection, usually the master, should take every precaution to ensure the specimen is not adulterated or diluted during the process.

INTERNATIONAL SAFETY MANAGEMENT CODE (ISM)

Chapter IX of SOLAS is the international management code for the safe operation of ships and for pollution prevention—International Safety Management Code (ISM).

By July 2002, all vessels must be in compliance with the ISM Code, which is primarily codified in 33 CFR §96.100 et seq. Tankers have been in compliance since July 1998. Per MARPOL, vessels also must maintain a six-section shipboard oil pollution emergency plan (SOPEP).[4] Tankers must also maintain a vessel response plan. In addition, some states have supplemental requirements for contingency plans the vessel must maintain aboard.

One of the requirements of the ISM Code is that vessels maintain a binder or manual providing guidance to vessel personnel for various types of incidents and emergencies, part of a comprehensive safety management system (SMS). Vessels must have bridge procedure manuals that offer guidance in all types of at-sea emergencies as well as in-port guides for emergencies arising at anchor or alongside. For each port visited, manuals should list the names and telephone numbers used to obtain assistance in case of emergency, including the qualified individual (QI) at the company. A qualified individual is the person designated to handle postincident activities, mitigation efforts, and the media. The manuals will have the contact numbers for local Coast Guard offices, the National Response Center, police and fire departments, ambulances, agents, harbormasters, and so on. In addition to contact numbers, procedures for various contingencies should be outlined. Often, this is presented in a flow chart style. Below is a list of sections a comprehensive plan should contain:

1. Update sheets for recording corrections and insertions
2. Emergency notification persons and numbers
3. Procedures for vessel emergencies
    Collision
    Allision
    Grounding and stranding
    Flooding
    Fire
    Man overboard
    Steering casualty
    Mechanical failure
    Dragging anchor
    Pollution incident
    Abandoning ship
    Crowd control (if applicable)
    Medical emergency
    Helicopter evacuations
    Stowaway search and procedures
    Crew incidents and violence
    Bomb threat
    Sabotage
    Hijacking
    Terrorist activity

Piracy
In-port security plan
At-anchor security plan
At-sea security plan

These documents must be routinely updated to reflect changes in personnel or contact numbers. Most port state control agencies will review this document periodically.

ATTORNEYS AND INVESTIGATORS

It is inevitable that, in the course of a career, a master will be faced with various kinds of accidents involving the vessel and cargo, as well as accidents causing injuries to crew, passengers, and stevedores, often resulting in claims against the company. Opposition attorneys, investigators, cargo surveyors, and others may ask to see the logbook or bell book and may attempt to get statements from the master, the officers, or the crew. Under no circumstances, except by express permission from the company, should a master give any person a statement, either oral or written, regarding an accident, loss, or damage. No one should be permitted to interview any of the officers or crew or to see the vessel's logbooks, charts, or documents. No investigative persons should be allowed on board, and if on board they should be summarily escorted ashore. After an incident, an efficient gangway watch is imperative. Gangway watch personnel should verify everyone's identification and not let anyone aboard whose identity and purpose are questionable. The gangway should be in constant contact with the officer on watch.

Visitors may claim to be from the office, without giving specifics, implying that they are representatives of the company who owns the vessel. Investigators are persuasive talkers and are not under oath, so they may tell lies. They sometimes try to convince the master that, since the damages will eventually be paid for anyway, there is no reason why they should not get a statement or be allowed access to the logbooks. Unless such persons have unimpeachable credentials or are vouched for by the owner's representative known to you, investigators should be told nothing and should be escorted off the vessel.

Names of attorneys, their firms, and others representing the company should be logged along with the times they board and leave the vessel.

If it is necessary to talk to opposition attorneys—and this should be done only with the advice and consent of the company—statements should be carefully worded to avoid misunderstanding. Masters should state only facts, without offering any interpretations or opinions, and they should only sign papers after reading them over carefully. Under no condition should anyone sign any blank sheets, despite assurances that this will save time and trouble and that irrelevant lines will be crossed out. Many accidents now carry the potential for personal criminal liability, so many mariners have purchased license insurance to defray the cost of defending their licenses against a Coast Guard administrative suspension and revocation (S & R) hearing. Legal advice is recommended before speaking to anyone or signing anything.

COAST GUARD INVESTIGATIONS

The master should alert the crew that Coast Guard investigators may arrive in civilian clothes. Crewmembers should check for the green armed forces identification card that all military personnel are required to carry. A Coast Guard officer should not be offended if the gangway watch asks for identification. Indeed, it may indicate a level of awareness and compliance that indicates a well-run vessel.

There are two types of Coast Guard investigations, Part Four and Part Five. Anyone being questioned should ask the Coast Guard investigator which type is being performed. A Part Four type is a casualty investigation which is made to find out what happened. No criminal penalties can be brought as a result of a Part Four investigation; however, any information gathered by the Coast Guard can be presented to another law enforcement agency and can be incorporated into their criminal case. Under Part Five, answers to the same questions may result in a Coast Guard administrative hearing and the potential for criminal fines and jail time for certain incidents. The Coast Guard has the authority to Mirandize (read the rights to someone they are questioning) but rarely does so. Information gathered in any Coast Guard investigation may later be used by the FBI or EPA to pursue fines and criminal sanctions under their regulations.

Given the overlapping regulations of several agencies that will be involved in most major marine incidents, the potential exists for multiple violations from one incident. It is not impossible that the Drug Enforcement Agency (DEA), EPA, FBI, USCG, OSHA, and National Wildlife Service would all be interested in a major maritime accident, not to mention state agencies like the Air Quality Management District, Fish and Game, State Lands Commission, Sheriff's Department, and others.

Coast Guard investigators have the authority to write and to issue subpoenas on the scene. Failure to answer questions can result in jail time for contempt of court or for obstruction of justice. If a crewmember feels uncomfortable talking to a certain investigator, he or she should not refuse to answer questions, but rather request a different investigator, making it clear that there is no intent to impede the inquiry.

If the potential for criminal liability exists, a mariner has the right to plead the fifth amendment to prevent self-incrimination. However, in doing this, it may appear as if he or she is refusing to cooperate with the investigation. Crewmembers are advised not to speculate, and to simply state the facts in concise terms.

Most Coast Guard investigators are reasonable and will respond positively to questions and concerns. They can make clear a person's rights and explain which questions can be postponed until a lawyer is present. Persons being questioned can also tape the questioning. This may prove invaluable in a later hearing. Chapter 2, "United States Laws," provides more information on legal issues.

LOGBOOK ENTRIES

In cases of personal injury or accidents affecting the seaworthiness of the ship, such as fire on board, collision, or grounding, detailed entries should be made in the official log and in the deck logbook. In case of a serious accident, it is a good idea for a master to first make rough notes on a pad and then enter the details in the log in proper sequence after determining their accuracy. No one can be expected to remember every detail, so these should be written down as soon as possible after the occurrence, before events are forgotten. No entries in the logbook should be made haphazardly. If there is doubt about whether an event is significant enough to warrant entry, then the incident should be documented; if it happened, it should be entered in the log. The entire contents of a personal notebook may also be discoverable in any subsequent litigation.

If a casualty occurs, the owner, agent, master, or person-in-charge must see that all vessel records that might assist in investigating the casualty are retained and made available on request to Coast Guard investigating personnel. Such records would include deck and engine room logbooks, any electronic logs, bell books, charts, navigation workbooks, compass deviation cards, gyro records, cargo stowage plans, draft records, night order books, messages sent and received, GMDSS logs, VHF logs, crew and passenger lists, shipping articles, official logs, and so on.

One of the most revealing sources of information on vessel movements will most likely be the electronic chart display and information system (ECDIS). No one should attempt to erase or change the stored historical information in any way. The master should take every precaution to ensure other crewmembers do not tamper with the ECDIS.

In addition, if the vessel collides with or is in any way connected with an allision with a buoy or other aid to navigation under Coast Guard jurisdiction, the master must report the accident to the nearest officer in charge, marine inspection. A written report on CG-2692 is not required unless the accident results in one of the serious marine incidents or reportable marine casualties listed previously.

REPORTS, STATEMENTS, AND EVIDENCE

In case of an accident or casualty to the vessel or cargo—or of injury to a person—writing reports and statements and taking statements from witnesses can serve an important purpose in protecting the interests of both the master and the company. Masters inevitably will have to make statements and write reports covering a variety of accidents over the course of a career. They will be criticized by management if accident reports are not made promptly or if they are incomplete or inaccurate.

Many vessels now have ECDIS systems that track plotted contacts on a chart overlay. Most of these systems have a replay feature that allows the user to replay historical information. No one should be allowed to touch the ECDIS after a collision, as important evidence may be lost. No attempt should be made to erase data even if there is some suspicion that it may reveal that the fault lies with a member of the crew. Investigators often have an expert who can retrieve the data, or they may consider destruction of the evidence to be an indication of guilt.

All reports and statements should be completed as soon as possible to avoid rushing through them later. The master should start working on the paperwork early to ensure ample time to check it for accuracy.

Precision and validity are of the utmost importance, and small details are crucial. All reports and statements should be clear, neat, and legible, and a master must be meticulous with word choice. Proper and adequate reports and statements will go far toward protecting the interests of the company and will save the necessity of redoing them, or worse, retracting words at a hearing.

The company may require the use of special forms for reports on all accidents, even those that would not ordinarily require a comprehensive report or statement. If the company does not have special forms, then reports may be typed on plain paper in narrative letter format. If no company rules or instructions are available, the following notes may be useful.

Reports should be detailed, no matter how minor the accident, and should take into consideration that the recipients will be many miles away and the only details they learn will be from your reports. If special forms are to be filled out they should be completed as soon as possible after the occurrence, and all questions on the forms should be answered. If a question is not applicable, the preparer should draw a line through the space or mark it N/A instead of leaving it blank, so the reader knows it was not ignored. Although an officer designated by the master may make out reports, the master is responsible for their accuracy and should therefore check all reports before signing them. A copy of each should be put in the vessel's file.

In any case of an accident to the vessel or cargo or an injury to a crewmember, passenger, stevedore, or visitor on the vessel, the master should promptly obtain signed statements from witnesses, in their own handwriting, if practical, including their home addresses. If time permits, the handwritten statements should be typed and the typed copies signed by the witnesses. This is particularly necessary in cases involving personal injury. The witness making the statement should be given one of the typed copies. Taping or filming witnesses is especially helpful for eyewitnesses who can go to the scene and point out conditions or features of interest.

Photographs are also extremely helpful, when they are practical. They should be taken when the time of day and other such circumstances are similar to those relating to the incident.

After a serious accident, the company attorney may come on board to take statements from witnesses. The master should inform the crewmembers simply to tell the truth to the attorney. Through a misguided sense of loyalty a mariner will sometimes make an untrue statement under the illusion that he or she is helping the master or the vessel. Such statements, if found on cross-examination to be false, will harm the company's case.

The master's statement should include all pertinent details. A clear, concise, absolutely truthful statement will be the greatest assistance to the company's insurance department. Reports or statements should not be attached to the logbook.

When damage to the vessel or other property is the result of coming into contact with a dock, pier, bridge, or other fixed object, the company may want a damage report form.

Reports and statements should be filed with the company's insurance department when any casualties or accidents occur.

PROTECTION AND INDEMNITY SOCIETIES (P and I CLUBS)

Both at sea and in port, the vessel, cargo, crew, and passengers are subject to a variety of dangers. Marine insurance undertakes to indemnify the operating company against damage to or loss of the vessel or cargo and damage to other vessels. For protection against accidents and losses not covered by basic marine insurance, many shipowners have joined together in protection and indemnity societies, known as "P and I clubs." These clubs are owned by their shipowner members. Most P and I clubs issue certificates of insurance, which must be presented when entering port-state-controlled areas.

This type of insurance usually covers claims for damage to cargo during loading or discharging; third-party claims for liability to damaged cargo; crew and passenger sickness, injury, or loss of life; pollution liability; and damage to docks, cables, shore installations, aids to navigation, bridges, and other fixed or movable property. Some policies provide coverage for losses sustained due to stowaways or the rescuing of refugees. P and I clubs do not usually provide war risk insurance, hull and machinery insurance, or insurance for damage to cargo while the cargo is on board the vessel.

Marine insurance companies and P and I clubs will indemnify the shipowner only for damage and losses specified in the policy and only after the shipowner proves that such damage or loss has occurred. This is determined by surveys, entries in the log, reports submitted by the master, and statements of witnesses.

SHIPBOARD INCIDENTS

This discussion is by no means complete, as other incidents and accidents may occur. The master's reports should include a copy of any Coast Guard form that is made out and a copy of any notice of liability served on another vessel or received from any source. If surveyors' reports are made, they should also be included; however, surveyors will usually send their reports directly to the home office or local agent after the final version has been completed. A list of all the reports, statements, and other documents included should accompany the master's report. The master should retain a copy of the list and ensure all documents are enclosed before sealing the envelope.

The procedures manuals on many vessels have check-off sheets for various types of emergencies. Input from masters on improving or simplifying the documents will most likely be well received and welcomed by the appropriate shoreside manager.

Crew Related Incidents

The most common incident aboard ship may be crew related. The master is responsible for providing a safe and hospitable workplace for all aboard. Following are penalties for various crew offenses.

SHEATH KNIVES

Crewmembers may not carry sheath knives without the consent of the master.[5]

DESERTION

If a mariner deserts the vessel, he or she forfeits any part of the property or money left aboard and any part of earned wages.[6] Money, property, and wages forfeited may be applied to compensate the owner or master for any expenses incurred as a result of the desertion. The master shall surrender the balance to the secretary.[7]

REFUSING TO JOIN OR PERFORM DUTIES

For unreasonably neglecting or refusing to join the vessel, for absence without leave within twenty-four hours of the vessel's sailing, or for absence without leave from duties, the mariner forfeits not more than two days' pay or a sufficient amount to defray expenses incurred in hiring a substitute.[8]

QUITTING THE VESSEL WITHOUT LEAVE

For quitting the vessel without leave after the vessel has arrived at the port of delivery but before the vessel is placed in security, the mariner forfeits from his or her wages not more than one month's pay.[9]

WILLFUL DISOBEDIENCE

For willful disobedience to a lawful command at sea, the mariner, at the master's discretion, may be confined until the disobedience ends, and on arrival in port forfeits not more than four days' pay, or at the discretion of the court, may be imprisoned for not more than one month.

For continued willful disobedience to a lawful command or continued willful neglect of duty at sea, the mariner, at the discretion of the master, may be confined on water and 1,000 calories, with full rations every fifth day, until the disobedience ends. On arrival in port the mariner forfeits, for each twenty-four hours of continued disobedience or neglect, not more than twelve days' pay or, at the discretion of the court, may be imprisoned for not more than three months.[10]

ASSAULT

Violence and threatened violence aboard ship is not to be tolerated. The elimination of alcohol has done much to reduce acts of violence aboard ship, but incidents still occur. It is the master's responsibility to ensure a safe working and living environment for those aboard the vessel.

Violent persons should be removed from the vessel. For assaulting a master, mate, pilot, engineer, or staff officer, the mariner may be imprisoned for not more than two years.[11]

BARRATRY AND EMBEZZLING

For willfully damaging the vessel, or embezzling or willfully damaging any of the stores or cargo, the mariner forfeits from his or her wages the amount of the loss sustained and, at the discretion of the court, may be imprisoned.[12]

SMUGGLING

For smuggling that causes loss or damage to the owner or master, the mariner is liable for the loss or damage, and any part of the mariner's wages may be retained to satisfy the liability. The mariner may also be imprisoned.[13] This regulation is separate from federal drug and contraband laws. It is the master's responsibility to ensure no contraband is brought into any country from the vessel. This may mean conducting searches of staterooms and other areas, especially if there is cause to believe someone has smuggled material aboard. The master faces severe penalties if contraband is found aboard the vessel.

Vessel Accidents

By the time a person sails as master it is inevitable that he or she has experienced some sort of accident involving a vessel. Modern navigational tools such as RACON, GPS, ECDIS, advanced stress sensors and monitors, and other advances in technology have made the operation of vessels more precise and safe than ever, yet accidents still occur. As with other types of casualties, contingency planning and good management techniques can do much to lessen the occurrence of accidents aboard any vessel.

COLLISION WITH ANOTHER VESSEL

When two vessels collide, the following events should take place to accurately document the events and to assist the professional investigators in determining liability. A number of statements and reports will have to be completed, so both masters or officers assigned by them should start taking notes immediately. The master of each vessel, or their respective officers, will probably serve notice to the master of the other vessel (or the owner, agent, or company representative), declaring that the recipient's company will be held responsible for all damage sustained by the vessel of the master serving the notice. Depending on the company and the communications capabilities of each vessel, such notice may be handled by shore personnel. Each will request the addressee of the notice to acknowledge its · receipt. Most likely, the recipients will not do so, possibly even refusing to accept the notice.

Neither master will admit liability, even if the fault seems obvious; this is left to the companies' insurance departments. If a master chooses to acknowledge the other master's notice, he or she should admit only to receiving the notice, not to agreeing with any of the statements contained in it. If either master does sign the notice, the signature should be appended by a statement such as, "Signed for receipt of notice only. Fault or liability of any kind denied." Nothing else should be written on the notice because any additional statements may compromise a company's position.

A master is not obligated to sign or even to acknowledge the notice and should not do so if he or she is in doubt about what to do. A copy of any notice received should be sent to the insurance department immediately.

Masters should caution officers and crew not to discuss a collision or any other accident with unauthorized persons. No one should give out any information, and the master should not allow anyone except government officials to examine the logbooks.

If the vessel is in port the company attorneys will board soon after an accident to take statements from the master, the officer on duty, the crewmember who was at the wheel, the lookout, and any other person likely to have firsthand knowledge of the incident. Masters should always follow the advice of the company attorneys regarding any reports and statements.

In a U.S. port the Coast Guard will probably be on board before the attorneys and will want statements and possibly logbooks, bell books, the course recorder tape, and the ECDIS disk.

When several persons witness the same accident, each of them is likely to give a different version of how the accident occurred. The master should advise all witnesses to describe the incident truthfully in their own words, whether it affects the vessel adversely or not. It will be better for all concerned if no false statements are made.

If any witness is unsure of a detail or fact, it is important to say so. Precise statements of fact should be avoided if there is any uncertainty. Once a person is on the witness stand under cross-examination, the opposition's lawyers will quickly learn whether or not the witness is sure of the facts. A master should be sure the information in his or her statement, which may be used at a hearing or in court, can be substantiated by log entries or recording devices.

In the statement or report, a master should not comment on the possible incompetence of the ship's pilot. The master of the other vessel and the opposition's lawyers will take care of that.

A master should note in the logbook and in the statement the following items:

1. That he or she determined whether anyone was injured on all involved vessels
2. Communications conducted before and after the incident
3. Whether the other vessel was in need of assistance
4. That bilge soundings were taken hourly or more often, as necessary
5. The extent of known damage to the vessel
6. The names of witnesses, such as people who were on deck at the time

If a collision is imminent, the master should order people off the forecastle head and away from danger spots. If the vessel has a public address system, the imminent collision should be announced to the crew so they can prepare for impact. In a U.S. port, the master should notify the Coast Guard captain of the port as soon as possible, preferably by radio or satellite phone. In a foreign port, the agent should notify the local port authorities.

It is a moral and legal obligation of the master of a vessel to stand by and render assistance to the other vessel until such time as no further assistance is required—provided such aid does not endanger his or her own vessel or crew. The Coast Guard takes a very dim view of hit-and-run collisions. The master should always ask if assistance is needed, even if the damage appears to be slight.

The offer of assistance should be logged along with the other master's response, even if it is a refusal. However, should one master need help, the other should make every effort to provide whatever assistance is requested. The log should contain the date and the time when the master who requested aid states that no further help is required.

Each insurance company will require abstracts of the logbook and copies of the bell books. The masters must complete Coast Guard form CG-2692 (fig. 15). Federal law requires the master to make an entry regarding a collision in the official logbook, giving all particulars. This entry must be made as soon as practicable after the collision.

Following a collision, the master may be required to have a survey made by the American Bureau of Shipping or other classification society. The agent will make the necessary arrangements.

The master should check all reports relative to the collision, if made by another person on the vessel, before signing them. Electronically recorded data should be saved and photos and videos taken, if possible. Extra copies should be made of all messages sent and received pertaining to the collision.

ACCIDENTS THAT OCCUR WHEN ENTERING OR LEAVING DRYDOCK

Regardless of whether or not the shipyard has control of the vessel, if it touches another vessel or craft or the drydock itself, an accident report should be made out. Due to the close quarters in some drydocks, this type of accident occurs occasionally. If a vessel was using its engine, the master should make copies of the logbook and bell books covering the time period and show on a diagram the names of tugs used and their positions around the vessel. Several statements will be required: from the pilot, the officer on duty on the bridge, the crewmember at the wheel, and the lookout, if one was posted. Usually, however, the chief officer would be on the bow and a statement would come from him or her as well as from the crewmember on the bow. Statements will be required of anyone involved in the event or witnessing it.

ALLISIONS

When docking or undocking, vessels will occasionally strike the dock or pier with such force as to cause some damage to the dock and perhaps to dent a plate on the vessel. Quite often the dock or pier is in such dilapidated condition that if the vessel touches even lightly it will cause some damage. It is a common opinion among ships officers that a number of old docks and piers have been paid for many times over by claims allowed for alleged damage.

If a vessel strikes a dock, the master should check the condition of the dock and take photographs if possible. If a survey is held, he or she should pay particular attention to the condition of the dock in general and try to judge what its condition was before the accident. This information should be included in the report, which should be attached to any photographs taken.

If the case warrants it, the pilot may make a statement. If tugs were used, their names and positions around the vessel should be shown on a diagram. Copies of the log and bell books may need to be submitted to the insurance department.

In U.S. ports, damage by contact or allision with aids to navigation must be reported to the Coast Guard as soon as possible. It also should be reported to the company insurance department, giving the cause of such contact or allision. If in a foreign port, the agent should report the accident to the proper local authorities.

EXPLOSIVE ORDNANCE

Some coastal waters contain many forms of unexploded ordnance. If an object is snagged and cannot be immediately identified as a nonexplosive device, it must be treated as potentially explosive.

Following is the correct procedure if such an object is sighted:

1. Do not bring it alongside or aboard the vessel.
2. If possible, release the object and contact the nearest Coast Guard or navy unit.
3. Give the vessel's position, a description of the object, and its location.

If the object cannot be released by cutting the net or line the master should do the following:

1. Avoid any bump or shock.
2. Stream the object as far as possible.
3. Contact the nearest Coast Guard or navy unit and await instructions.
4. Position the crew as far forward as possible, keeping the house between them and the object.
5. Maintain steerageway as necessary to stay in the area until assistance or instructions arrive.

UNLABELED DRUMS

If any unlabeled drums or canisters are sighted, direct contact should be avoided; the sightings should be reported to the Coast Guard at their twenty-four-hour National Response Center reporting line: 800-424-8802.

GROUNDINGS

With the advent of continuous satellite navigation information, one would think groundings of GPS-equipped vessels using modern charts would be virtually eliminated. The Coast Guard has published warnings, however, about groundings that may have been "GPS-assisted." When planning voyages, mariners may lay tracks closer to charted hazards than they have in the past, relying on the increased positional accuracy offered by GPS. The weak link, however, is not with the GPS system, but with the charts. Most charts have yet to be updated using satellite survey techniques, and while the ship's GPS position is correct, the charted features are far less accurately positioned.

Other aspects of shiphandling, such as squat, have been overlooked by modern well-equipped vessel operators and have resulted in groundings. Navigators may forget to match the GPS datum with the chart datum, a chart may show outdated or sparse soundings, bottom contours can change, or the vessel could experience a casualty causing it to ground. While many advances have been made, grounding a vessel is still a very real concern and even a seemingly mild grounding can cause serious damage to the vessel.

At an Anchorage or Alongside a Dock

When anchoring or docking at a berth for the first time, a master should ask the pilot about the depth of water at low tide or check it on the chart or in the *Coast Pilot* or *Sailing Directions*. The ECDIS information should match other sources of data. The master should always consult these publications when approaching a place for the first time. In order to prevent the vessel from being ordered by the charterer to a wharf, dock, or anchorage where it cannot load a full cargo without touching the ground or resting on the bottom at low water, the "always afloat" clause is inserted in the charter party. This clause is usually worded in one of the following ways:

> . . . to proceed to _____, or so near thereto as she may safely get, always afloat, and being loaded shall proceed with all convenient speed to _____ or so near thereto as she may safely get and discharge her cargo, always afloat, in any safe dock, wharf, or anchorage.

> or

> That the cargo be laden and/or discharged in a dock or at any wharf or place that the charterer or his agents may direct, provided the vessel can safely lie afloat at any stage of the tide, except at such places where it is customary for similar sized vessels to safely lie aground.

If a vessel is ordered by the charterer or the charterer's agent to a wharf, dock, or anchorage that the master considers unsafe, he or she should immediately inform the charterer by notice of protest, giving the reason why it is considered unsafe. As an example, a berth may be considered unsafe due to incoming heavy swells that may affect the vessel, especially when there are only a few feet of water under the keel when fully loaded. If no change is made the master should immediately contact his or her own agent and the home office and then give the charterer or the charterer's agent another written notice of protest holding him or her liable for all damage the vessel may suffer as a consequence of carrying out the order. Copies of these notices, with a note of explanation, should go to the insurance department and to the vessel's agent, retaining a copy for the vessel's file. These notices should be sent by the fastest means available.

If the charterer does not rescind the order and no advice comes from the home office, and if the master thinks the vessel should not shift to such berth, he or she should not move it. Full details should be entered in the log, including the time not worked, if any, while the charterer or the charterer's agent decided what to do.

Company instructions should dictate which forms and reports are to be completed if a grounding should occur. Lacking such instructions, the master should inform the home office and the company agent as soon as possible after an accident and give them the following information:

1. Date and time of grounding and position or exact location in reference to a known object such as a lighthouse, and coordinates including datum. (To save time, the chart number should be included.)
2. Who was conning the vessel, who was on the bridge at the time, and what watch condition was set
3. Condition of the weather at the time of grounding: how clear, amount of fog, wind force, sea and swell, visibility, etc.
4. Drafts before and after grounding
5. Type of bottom
6. Soundings taken around the vessel, stage of tide at the time of grounding, and whether it was rising or falling
7. Any injuries or loss of life to crew or others
8. Damage to vessel and/or machinery
9. Any threat to the environment
10. Whether the vessel was in a dangerous position
11. Whether vessel was taking on water and where, the rate, and whether the situation was under control
12. The location and extent of any damage
13. Fuel and water on board
14. Water ballast on board and whether pumping it out (observing oil pollution laws)

15. Assistance at hand, required, requested, or ordered
16. If refloated, the date and time and whether the ship proceeded under own power
17. Coast Guard (or any other authorities) that have been notified
18. If there is or was any media attention

The master should notify the Coast Guard at the first port of arrival in the United States after the grounding and have Coast Guard form CG-2692 ready. There will probably be much to do, so an officer should be assigned to take notes on a scratch pad and put the notes in proper sequence before making a log entry. The master should make an entry in the official log, giving full details including the position, heading, and condition of the weather at the time of the grounding. Details like names, ratings, and document numbers of the officer on watch, the crewmember at the wheel, and the lookout should also be included. If statements from these people are necessary, it is advisable to get them as soon after the accident as possible. The statements should be signed by the persons making them and should include their home addresses.

The company insurance department will want a full account of the grounding and the cause. This should be in the statement, which should be detailed and concise, but not too long.

Included in the statement should be the protest at the first port after the grounding. A copy should go to the insurance department.

Reports and Statements after a Grounding
Copies of the following reports and statements should be acquired for the home office:

1. A statement from the officer on the bridge, taken as soon as possible after the grounding. If the officer was in any way at fault, his or her statement, if put off, may differ from the actual facts.
2. A statement from the helmsman. This also may change with time if the helmsman was in any way at fault; for example, he or she may have put the rudder over the wrong way at a critical time.
3. A statement from the lookout or any others having firsthand knowledge of the grounding
4. A statement from the chief engineer regarding the engine and the machinery: when and how long they were used in the attempt to refloat, any resulting damage, and so on
5. Signed abstracts of deck and engine logs
6. Signed copies of both bell books and any gear tests. The Coast Guard may want the logbooks and bell books for a while.
7. A record of bilge soundings taken after the vessel grounded. These should be taken often.

8. A diagram of soundings around the vessel at the time of grounding, showing the draft and the stage of the tide at the time

9. A diagram of soundings around the vessel at low water

10. Lists of deck and engine stores and equipment used in the attempt to refloat the vessel. Both lists should have the items marked "used" or "new," not "old." Fuel, lube oil, and freshwater should be shown on a separate report.

11. A statement of any deck or engine stores jettisoned, lost, or contaminated by water or oil so as to render them useless

12. The master's own statement giving a full description of events

13. Copies of all letters and messages sent or received relative to the grounding

14. Personal belongings lost by the crew and in what manner they were lost. This does not mean the crew will be reimbursed, but the list will be available if required. This list should be obtained promptly.

15. If a salvage agreement was made, the home office should be sent a copy. Lloyd's standard "no cure–no pay" agreement should be used.

In addition the master should give the home office the following information, much of which will be in the log:

1. Services rendered by tugs or other vessels, their names, hailing ports, nationality, and owners' names if available. If tugs were used, the agreement for their hire should be included.

2. Whether Lloyd's open form was ever agreed to

3. Dangers involved to the salvage vessels at any time

4. Weather conditions day by day

5. List of any injured, including members of the salvaging vessels, together with the injury reports and what efforts were made to get badly injured persons to a doctor or hospital. Statements from injured persons and witnesses should also be included, although these may be difficult to get at the time.

6. Names of surveyors who boarded and the organizations or classification societies they represent

7. Names, titles, and organizations of salvage masters or others who assist in any way

DRAGGING ANCHOR: CAUSING DAMAGE TO UNDERWATER PIPELINES, CABLES, OR OTHER VESSELS

Dragging anchor can cause damage to underwater pipelines, cables, or other vessels. Such accidents are always expensive and in some ports exact a fine and even criminal liability, especially in the United States. Damage to underwater cables may pose the threat of environmental damage as these cables are often filled with oil. The same issue applies to pipelines.

Generally if there is the least possibility of dragging, the prudent shipmaster will keep the engine at "hot standby," ready to maneuver on short notice. The master should enter in the night order book or leave word on the bridge, in writing, that bearings should be taken at specified intervals and that he or she should be called immediately if there is any indication that the vessel may drag. Watch officers should continuously compare visual and radar bearings with any electronic positioning devices aboard. Most electronic positioning devices also have anchor-watch alarms that can be set to a particular radius, and these tools should be employed as well. Some mates tie a rag to the top link in the wildcat to easily observe if the brake is holding. If the pawl is down, this is not an issue.

Sometimes, simply veering out more chain is the first step in preventing dragging. The circumstances of each case will dictate the best procedures.

If the vessel does drag and causes damage, the master will have to make a report and statements that should include the time he or she requested power on the engine, the time the engine was ready, and also what caused the vessel to drag and what was done to stop it. A line on the chart should show the course the vessel took while dragging, from its original position to where it fetched up or was brought under control, and any contacts it made with other vessels, craft, or buoys. The master will probably also have to make up Coast Guard form CG-2692. The officer on watch will have to make a complete statement of the circumstances of the dragging.

DAMAGE TO ANOTHER VESSEL ALONGSIDE A DOCK
DUE TO ALLEGED EXCESSIVE SPEED

Damage caused by excessive speed is sometimes called "wake damage," and it often occurs in narrow channels. It is a general rule, and a good one, for most ships to slow down when passing moored vessels. It is a regulation in most harbors that vessels must slow down when passing a dredge or similar craft working in or near a channel. The master should enter the reason for such "slow" bells in the bell book. Such an entry may well disprove a claim for alleged damage. If the master slows down or stops the screw to pass a fishing vessel, such precautions should be logged. This type of log entry can also be supplemented by supporting entries in the VHF logbook recording communications with the vessel that prompted the slowdown.

If any vessel, dredge, or other craft claims damage, detailed entries in the bell book will help determine the reason for a slow bell at the time of the alleged damage. Abstracts of the log and the bell book covering the time involved should also include the state of the tide and weather, including visibility, and any relevant communications.

Officers should make frequent notes in the bell book noting landmarks or aids to navigation to easily determine later where the vessel was at the time of any particular bell. In passing a vessel whose mooring lines are hanging slack or are otherwise inadequate, the watch officer should note that fact in the bell book, even if the moving vessel slowed down while passing. If the other vessel claims wake damage, the logging of the inadequacy of their mooring lines will help to defeat a claim.

Machinery and Equipment

Usually when equipment fails, the occurence is not considered to be caused by human error. Some quality managers, however, suggest that all casualties are the result of human error. If a piece of machinery breaks it indicates an error chain that was started by a human somewhere, perhaps in the design or manufacture of the part or possibly in its maintenance or use. The master should ensure that all activity on board is done "by the book," all maintenance is carried out as required, and all necessary parts and supplies are available to the departments that need them. Companies may frown on the master who orders twice as many parts and supplies as his predecessor, but this may indicate that the previous master was not maintaining the vessel to the same standards. Most vessels have a preventative maintenance plan and this should be strictly adhered to.

ACCIDENTS AND INJURIES DUE TO ALLEGEDLY DEFECTIVE MATERIAL

No matter how slight it may be, if an injury to a crewmember, passenger, stevedore, or other person on the vessel is caused by allegedly defective material, gear, or equipment of any kind, it is important to label and preserve the supposedly defective gear as evidence, if at all practicable to do so. On no account should an unauthorized person remove the gear from the vessel, nor should it be thrown overboard or destroyed. It should be saved, no matter how tempting it may be to toss it over the side. The master should not release it or show it to others until he or she receives instructions from the insurance department.

The master should take photographs (and even videotape if possible) of the allegedly defective part, particularly if for any reason the part cannot remain on board. These photographs should accompany the report to the company but should not be shown to anyone not connected with the company. No one else should take photographs without proper authority except government investigators making an official inspection or inquiry.

DEFECTIVE GEAR BELONGING TO STEVEDORES OR OTHERS

If an accident is caused by defective gear or equipment belonging to stevedores or others, the master should make every effort to keep that gear on board. If the owner of the equipment refuses to leave it aboard the vessel, this fact should be indicated in the report, which should include, if possible, a complete set of photographs of the equipment before the owner can remove it from the vessel.

If a line, chain, or sling parted, the report should note the type of cargo that was being lifted and an estimate of its weight. The winch should be inspected immediately by the chief engineer or one of the assistant engineers. The chief engineer is generally very concerned with the ship's winches and he or she will have them put in good order at the first sign of imperfection.

The chief officer should inspect the other gear and equipment involved, such as the runners and blocks. Opposing lawyers are experts at finding something wrong with equipment, especially if no inspections have been made.

If able to do so at the time, the injured person should prepare a statement showing how he or she came to be using the gear or equipment in question. Also, the master should get a statement from the person-in-charge and from witnesses, if any, with their home addresses. If a crewmember was injured or hospitalized and will be unable to continue working, the master will have to make up Coast Guard form CG-2692, a copy of which should be sent to the insurance department.

ACCOMMODATION LADDER ACCIDENTS

The accommodation ladder is often damaged by barges, lighters, launches, or other craft when the vessel is at anchor or made fast to mooring buoys and working cargo. This can cause a serious injury to anyone who is on the ladder at the time. The master should notify the stevedore foreman or person-in-charge, in writing, that the stevedore will be held responsible for any damage to the accommodation ladder or injury to persons on it caused by the stevedore's craft. The fact that the warning was given, and to whom, should be entered in the log. Generally, the stevedore foreman will have his or her own people raise or lower the ladder when there is a danger of its being damaged.

If alongside a dock, the master should be careful that the accommodation ladder does not become jammed against a bollard or other obstruction on the dock when the vessel surges or when the ladder moves along the dock with a falling or rising tide. This can damage the ladder considerably and cause injury to anyone on the ladder at the time. Rollers at the foot of the gangway are particularly dangerous if they are not fitted with a guard.

The gangway should be tended at all times by the gangway watch. A net should be rigged under the ladder and hand lines should be kept taut. If the ladder is not properly tended, a passing ship may cause the vessel to pull away from the dock and, if the ladder is not properly supported, cause the ladder to fall between the dock and the ship.

ACCIDENTS CAUSED BY BREAKDOWN OF MACHINERY OR EQUIPMENT

These accidents are not rare. The engineers may lose the plant while steaming into a channel or harbor, or a winch may fail when a stevedore is handling a sling of cargo. Losing the plant when underway in harbor may be the cause of various accidents—sometimes a collision—before the vessel can be brought under control. Computer casualties can also cause major incidents, if they happen at the wrong time and place.

The chief engineer should make a statement regarding the particulars of the breakdown, and the engineers on duty may also be required to make statements. If a cargo winch breaks down, the chief engineer's statement should indicate when the winch was last overhauled or repaired. Should the main engine fail and a subsequent hearing be held, as with any investigation, the Coast Guard will want the logbooks and bell book, course recorder information, and any other electronic or other recorded information.

BURSTING OF STEAM PIPES

This type of accident is infrequent. When a steam pipe bursts and no one is injured, a report is still required as it will be considered a reportable marine incident. It is important to retain the burst section of steam pipe on board for any investigation or until the insurance department or the Coast Guard takes custody of it or determines that it is no longer required.

BREAKAGE OF SHAFT

The master should prepare a statement of facts. If the ship is on time charter when this type of accident occurs, it will generally mean that the vessel goes off hire. It is therefore necessary that the date and time of the event and the position of the vessel at that time be accurate, as well as the date, time, and position of the vessel when taken in tow and the date and time the vessel arrives in port. The office and agent at the port of destination should remain fully advised.

The chief engineer will be required to furnish an account of fuel on hand at the time of the accident, at the times of arrival in port and departure, and at the time the vessel gets back to the position, or its equivalent, where the accident occurred. This information must be included in the statement of facts, which will probably be the only report required except for Coast Guard form CG-2692. Breaking the shaft may cause the loss of the propeller.

LOSS OF BLADE OR ENTIRE PROPELLER

When either a blade or the entire propeller is lost, the vessel will start to vibrate and the rpms will rise. The engineer on duty should cut down the rpms or stop, by which time the bridge should have put the telegraph on "stop" and called the master, if he or she is not already aware of the problem. If the vessel is not very deep, it may be possible to see what occurred by using a pilot ladder. Whoever goes down the pilot ladder should don a life preserver and safety harness. A message should go to the home office informing them of the accident, noting the weather at the time, the weather expected, and where the vessel is bound, if it is deviating from the original course. If the propeller has definitely struck something, this information should be included in the message and entered in the log and on Coast Guard form CG-2692. No one should speculate about uncertain facts.

If a blade is lost, it will be necessary to proceed to the nearest port with proper repair facilities. If possible, the vessel should proceed to a port in the general direction of the port of destination, if repair facilities are available and weather conditions are favorable.

If the entire propeller has been lost, the company may try to get assistance from a salvage tug or another company vessel, if one is close by, or they may leave it to the master to contact another vessel. In this respect, the Coast Guard automated mutual-assistance vessel rescue system (AMVER) can be of great help. Before accepting help from a salvage tug, the master should contact the head office. Salvage tugs often operate with Lloyd's open form, a "no cure–no pay" salvage agreement, and will request acceptance of this arrangement from the vessel in need of assistance. It may be cheaper to arrange for a set fee for towage rather than risk a salvage award against the company granted by a salvage arbitrator. The master should make an entry regarding the accident in the official logbook, giving the time, date, and position.

LINE IN PROPELLER

If a line gets caught in the propeller, the master should call a surveyor, preferably the American Bureau of Shipping (ABS) or Lloyd's, to check the blades and shaft. It is generally necessary to employ a diver to clear the line. The master should ensure and log that the shaft is stopped and brakes applied. If the crew is able to clear the line, a diver should check the blades and report the findings to the surveyor, who will then issue a seaworthy certificate if no serious damage is discovered. If the certificate cannot be issued before the vessel sails, the surveyor will make an entry in the log stating that the survey was made, noting the result, and explaining that the certificate will be sent to the vessel at a later date.

The master should then make a report describing how the line got caught in the propeller (e.g., line parted, tug let go too soon), the approximate amount of line caught, and the engine movement at the time. The report should show the times the diver started work, cleared the line, and departed. Also included should be the times the surveyor came on board and left, together with his or her name and organization, all in block letters.

LOSS OF ANCHOR AND CHAIN

If a vessel loses its anchor, the master should take cross bearings and/or activate the man overboard button on the GPS or ECDIS immediately to record the exact location. The report of the loss should include the following details:

1. Time, date, location coordinates and datum, bearings, and the number of the chart used

2. The type of anchor and amount of chain that was lost

3. Recording fathometer information

4. The cause of the loss. If another vessel was at fault, give its name, hailing port, nationality, owner's name (if available), and whether notice of liability was served.

5. Any injuries to crew or others, with reports and statements

6. Photos, if they are helpful

7. Wind, tide, and sea conditions at the time

8. Statements from the officers on the bridge and on the forecastle

Cargo Damage

Cargo damage is a constant problem. It will occur, it seems, regardless of how much care is taken to prevent it. Usually it is the chief officer who must write a statement and make a report giving the reason for the damage.

HEAVY WEATHER DAMAGE

If cargo is damaged by salt water, the chief officer should note the number of tarps used on each hatch and state that the hatches were properly battened down. If all facts are correct, the statement and report are to be countersigned by the master. The report may attribute the damage to heavy weather, but this is not an acceptable excuse unless a storm carried away a tarp or shoring, stove in some hatch boards, or caused cargo to shift.

The master should make up a log abstract covering the period of the heavy weather. The weather must have been extraordinarily heavy, not the rough weather usually expected on a voyage. The log should show what steps were taken to avoid heavy weather damage and to prevent laboring of the vessel, such as slowing down, changing course, or ballasting. These log entries will assist the insurance department in defending a claim for cargo damage. Any repairs to the vessel for damage attributed to the heavy weather on that voyage should be noted in the logbook and in the statement.

SWEAT DAMAGE

The log should show either the date the holds were ventilated or the reason they were not, such as heavy weather or other cause. Some vessels have electronic devices to record hold temperature and humidity. Many officer's fail to make log entries regarding ventilation of the holds, especially on vessels with blower systems. It is important to make a log entry when the ventilation system is turned on and again when it is shut down, including the reason for shutting down. On vessels with cowl ventilators, which must be trimmed by hand, the log should show each time they were trimmed, whether trimmed to the wind or backed to the wind, and why. The log should also show if the ventilator cowls are unshipped or covered for any reason. This also applies to hatches that are opened for ventilation.

PILFERAGE

When pilferage occurs, a statement is sometimes required from the chief officer and the officer who was on duty when the pilferage occurred or was discovered. The statement should indicate what precautions were taken to prevent pilferage, such as placing guards in the holds, keeping pilferable cargo in special lockers, and so forth. The marks and numbers of the missing cases and the location and manner of their stowage should also be included.

If pilferage occurs when the vessel is carrying military cargo, the cargo superintendent for the government may want a pilferage report signed by the chief officer or the master. Sometimes, because of the wording, such a report appears to be an acknowledgment of liability, and many masters refuse to sign it and will not permit the chief officer to sign it. However, the company may authorize the master to sign it if the following wording or a similar clause is added: "Acknowledgment of the pilferage, damage, or shortage reported herein is without prejudice to the contractual and legal defenses of the vessel and/or carrier."

The report should be prepared in duplicate and the master should keep a copy.

STEVEDORE DAMAGE

When stevedores or others working on the vessel cause damage to any part of the vessel or cargo, most companies require that a stevedore damage report be made up. (Although stevedore damage is stressed throughout this section, if any other party such as a drayman, repair gang, or others cause any damage to the cargo or vessel, the same reports should be made.)

Any damage caused by stevedores should be called to the attention of the stevedore foreman as soon as the damage occurs or is discovered, if the foreman is not already aware of it. The master should start a rough copy of the report as soon as the damage is known and make the required number of copies once the report is complete. He or she should take pictures when possible and save any broken items.

The stevedore may deny liability if the damage is not reported immediately. The master should be prepared to prove that the stevedores, who will most likely claim that the damage was already there, did the damage. The foreman should be requested to sign all copies of the report, admitting or denying liability, one copy being served on him or her. Most likely, the foreman will deny liability or refuse to sign, in which case the master should request that he or she sign the reports to acknowledge receipt of a copy. It is possible that the foreman will also refuse to accept a copy. If any such difficulties are encountered, a note to that effect should be made on the report and it should be taken up with the port captain or agent at once.

If possible, stevedore damage reports should be submitted before the vessel sails. If the damage is discovered after the vessel sails, the reports should be faxed or sent in from the next port. A copy should also be sent to the agent at the port where the damage occurred, with instructions to serve it on the stevedore.

Practically all vessel operating companies issue stevedore damage report forms, all of which have more or less the same items to check and questions to answer regarding the damage. When making up the report, if some of the questions do not apply, the master should draw a line through those spaces; this indicates that nothing has been missed or overlooked. One copy of the report goes to the home office, one goes to the stevedore, and one stays on board for the vessel's file. The master should follow the company's instructions regarding distribution, if they differ from those suggested here.

Deviation

Deviation means a departure from the usual route on a voyage. Deviation is justifiable for many reasons—for the purpose of saving life, to put a seriously sick or injured crewmember ashore, for urgent repairs, to restow cargo that has shifted and become a danger to the vessel, and so forth.

A deviation to the nearest port sometimes takes the vessel far off its course. For example, a vessel bound from the Panama Canal to Yokohama drops a blade at latitude 42°00'N, longitude 152°00'W. The vessel would proceed at slow speed to the nearest port, Honolulu. On completing repairs it would not return to the point of deviation but would take the regular route from Honolulu to Yokohama. The number of miles deviated would be the difference in distance between the point of deviation and Yokohama on the original track and the point of deviation and Yokohama via Honolulu. The extra fuel used would be computed using the known fuel consumption per mile. A statement of facts should be prepared giving full details of the deviation, including the fuel, freshwater, and lube oil consumed and the extra time and distance steamed.

If the purpose of the deviation was to put a sick or injured crewmember ashore or on another vessel, it will be necessary to make up Coast Guard form CG-2692. Also the master should enter details in the official log and the medical log and make up illness or injury reports, keeping the home office fully advised and notifying the agent at the port of refuge.

Customs form CF-26 (Report of Diversion, figure 1) must also be completed if the ship deviated to a U.S. port.

Fire

Fire at sea is one of the most dreaded of all marine casualties; all vessels must guard against it and also prepare to deal with it. Damage can be extensive, especially to cargo, not only from the fire itself but also from the water or other agents used to extinguish it. (See also "General Average" and "Particular Average" later in this chapter.)

In the event of a fire, the master or an officer should start taking notes as soon as possible. If in port, the report should include the names of all tugs and fireboats and the name and rank of the officer in charge of any Coast Guard detail or local fire department detail coming on board to assist.

Crewmembers can be very badly injured in a fire on board, so the master should try to avoid sending crewmembers into dangerous positions. Many people are too willing to take an unnecessary chance if given the opportunity.

The home office should be informed as soon as possible of the date and time the fire was discovered and its location on the vessel. If the fire is in a hold, the report should give the nature of the cargo. If the vessel is at sea, other information should be provided: the vessel's position and the weather conditions, whether the vessel is in any immediate danger, whether there are any injuries to crew or others, and whether assistance is required or at hand. Unless it is obvious that the fire can be extinguished almost immediately, the master should notify the nearest U.S. Coast Guard station, rescue coordination center (RCC), or foreign authority capable of rendering assistance. The Coast Guard AMVER system will, on request, indicate the nearest participating vessels. The master should then activate the GMDSS communications alerts if appropriate and keep a hard copy of any involved communications. When the fire is extinguished, the home office should be sent a general description of the damage to vessel or cargo. It may be advisable to send an initial report by telephone, followed by a more detailed report by fax.

The statement should give a full account of the fire, including when it was discovered and by whom, assistance rendered and by whom, when such assistance arrived, when the fire was extinguished, and the apparent damage to vessel and cargo.

If a Coast Guard fire-fighting detail was on board, the name and rank of the officer in charge should be recorded in the deck and official log and also on Coast Guard form CG-2692, which will have to be made up. The master should then make an entry in the official log giving all particulars.

In port, if the vessel has a shoreside phone, the gangway should have the phone numbers to local fire and police departments. The master of a vessel in port with a fire on board may be ordered by the port authorities to get underway, or the vessel may be towed away from the dock to a place where it will not be a danger to the port or to other vessels. The crew should be reminded to diligently tend the fire warps as the vessel's draft changes with cargo operations.

In U.S. ports, this order would usually be given by the Coast Guard COTP or a representative; however, the local port officials may also have the authority to have dangerous vessels moved. If this occurs, the master should enter full details in the log, including the name, rank, and official capacity of the person giving the order.

If the fire occurs at sea, the master should note protest on arrival in port. If the fire reached the crew's quarters, it is advisable to obtain a list of gear and clothing lost by each crewmember. This should be done as soon as possible. This does not necessarily mean that the company will pay for such losses, but the list should be available.

In addition to the master's own statement, the following papers will be required:

1. Signed abstracts of deck and engine logs
2. Lists from the chief officer and chief engineer stating which stores and gear were used, lost, or damaged by fire or water, and whether the items were new or used
3. Signed statements from officers and crewmembers who have any knowledge of the fire and the attempts to extinguish it, giving their names, home addresses, and document numbers
4. Signed statements, with home addresses, from any injured persons, and the same from witnesses to accidents causing the injuries
5. An injury report for every injured person regardless of how minor the injury may be
6. Coast Guard form CG-2692
7. Records of any postincident alcohol or drug testing, if required
8. Copies of all messages sent or received relative to the fire

Oil or Hazardous Materials (HAZMAT) Spill in Port

If an oil or hazardous materials (HAZMAT) spill occurs in port, it is likely to involve a fine, sometimes a hefty one, and possibly the potential for a criminal charge. Until any on-deck spills can be completely cleaned, oily portions of the deck should be roped off to prevent injuries due to slipping. It is advisable to post a notice at the gangway warning persons boarding that the deck is slippery. Longshoremen may refuse to come on board until a spill is cleaned up, especially if it occured at night.

Many ports issue special regulations regarding oil spills. The latest regulations should be on board; the agent can provide them if necessary.

Oil spills in U.S. ports must be reported to the National Response Center. This report may be made via the National Response Center's toll-free telephone number, 800-424-8802. Until recently, the report could be made to either the National Response Center or to the nearest Coast Guard unit. New regulations require that the report be made directly to the National Response Center except when this is not physically possible. In such a case, it is acceptable to notify the nearest Coast Guard unit, provided it is subsequently reported to the National Response Center as soon as possible. Failure to report an oil spill carries a fine, as does the spill itself.

The master should always try to mitigate the damage as much as possible and notify shoreside cleanup agencies or the contracted spill-response provider. For hazardous materials (HAZMAT) spills, it is necessary to include as much information about the substance as possible, such as its chemical name, UN number, manufacturer's name, and other pertinent information. The Emergency Response Guidebook and the material safety data sheet (MSDS) provide product information. Chemtrec (800-424-9300) can fax product information as well.

In some ports failure to report an oil spill is a criminal offense and may result in a fine and/or imprisonment for the master or other responsible officer. It is advisable to check regulations to see if the spill is a reportable incident that requires completion of CG-2692 and the administration of drug and alcohol tests.

Heavy Weather Damage to the Vessel

All repairs made to an American vessel in a foreign port are subject to a 50-percent duty. However, if such repairs are emergency repairs necessary to make the ship seaworthy, as in the case of damage caused by heavy weather, the duty may be remitted. Entries substantiating the heavy weather must be made in the logbook and abstracts of the logbook covering the period of the heavy weather must be submitted to the district director of customs. This is usually done by giving the abstracts to the customhouse broker or to the insurance department, depending upon company instructions. The abstracts may be typed on plain paper. It is rare that a statement is required; however, if damages are $25,000 or more or if the damage affects the seaworthiness of the vessel, Coast Guard form CG-2692 must be made up, and the master should note protest on arrival at the first port after the heavy weather.

If a statement is required, it should include the following:

1. Precautions taken to avoid damage, such as slowing down, changing course, heaving to, or ballasting
2. Wind direction and force and the state of the sea day by day; the time the heavy weather started and the time it moderated
3. Damage to vessel or cargo
4. Any injuries suffered by crew or passengers. This should be in the medical log and also in the official log if a crewmember is involved. Coast Guard form CG-2692, if required, and an injury report with the necessary statements should also be made up.
5. Any other information that may be of help to the insurance department

NOTE OF PROTEST

A note of protest (fig. 29) is a declaration or deposition by the master, made under oath, giving full particulars regarding heavy weather or other incidents that may have caused damage to the vessel or cargo. Its purpose is to state that the master and the crew performed their duties in protecting the vessel and cargo and that any damage sustained was not due to any fault of the vessel, its officers, or its crew but to circumstances beyond human control. The full extent of the damage may or may not be ascertained at the time protest is noted.

The master should always note protest after any accident such as a collision or grounding, even if there is doubt regarding whether a protest is necessary. Protest should be noted within twenty-four hours after arrival.

One copy of the protest should be given to the agent, one should be sent to the insurance department, and one should be kept for the vessel's file. In a foreign port, the consul will make the required number of copies.

Noting Protest in the United States

In the United States, protest is noted before a notary public. Very often the agent or customhouse broker will be a notary and may even help the master make up the note. If the notary does not have a printed form the master may make up a general form on the vessel.

Noting Protest in a Foreign Port

In foreign ports, protest is noted before the U.S. Consul, who will issue a special form. Department of State regulations require the master to appear personally before the consul. No witnesses are required. This duty may not be delegated unless the vessel operators furnish the consul with a written statement authorizing a vessel officer other than the master to note protest.

If there is no consul, protest can be noted before a notary public or a magistrate. If this is necessary, the master should consult the agent for assistance. It may be necessary to bring the logbook and several witnesses; the agent will determine how many. The witnesses must swear that the vessel encountered the conditions shown in the log and that the entries in the log are true facts. This may take several hours, as the logbook entries may have to be translated into the language of the country. See figure 30 for a sample form for noting protest before a notary or magistrate when no official form is prescribed.

Extending Protest

If further damage to the vessel or cargo is found after noting protest, the master may extend protest. For this, witnesses are required. When such action is taken, whether before a U.S. Consul or a notary, the master should bring the logbook and several members of the crew as witnesses. If the master deems it necessary to extend protest, he or she should advise the company before doing so. Figure 29 (page 2) is a marine extended protest.

MARINE INSURANCE AND AVERAGE

Many books have been written on the subject of marine insurance and average; this is a complicated field in the shipping and marine insurance industries and is a study in itself. A few highlights, and the master's responsibility in regard to reports and statements required, are given here.

In shipping and marine insurance terminology, "average" is a word meaning partial loss or damage sustained by a vessel and/or cargo during the course of a voyage. In marine insurance parlance, the voyage is often called a "maritime adventure." The origin of the word "average" (which in this sense has nothing to do with median or with mathematical averages) is said to be obscure, but legal historians assert that it derives from the Italian word *avaria,* meaning loss or damage.

For insurance purposes there are two kinds of average: general average and particular average. These terms indicate the character of the loss or damage and establish who bears that loss or damage.

General Average

General average is a voluntary sacrifice, deliberately made by the master, of the vessel's gear, equipment, stores, or cargo; it can also be a voluntary stranding of the vessel. It includes expenses incurred in time of peril to avoid or avert a greater danger or loss threatening the common adventure and is made for the safety and benefit of all interests concerned in the adventure. Such a voluntary sacrifice is an "act of man" and is called a *general average act;* the property sacrificed or expenses incurred are described as *general average loss.*

All such losses that arise as a result of sacrifices made or expenses incurred for the saving of the vessel and cargo constitute general average. These losses must be borne, in proportion to the value saved, by contributions from all interests benefited. These contributions are called general average contributions. In other words, the property saved must pay for the property sacrificed if the sacrifice was made to save the common adventure. This puts a great responsibility on the master, who alone has the authority to make the necessary sacrifices.

A peril must exist and must be one that threatens all the interests in the adventure. The danger must be such that there is no escape from it unless a sacrifice is made. The sacrifice must be reasonable, prudent, and made in good faith. That is, it should be made with due consideration for the good it will do. And finally, it must be successful—the peril or danger must be overcome and the vessel and cargo, or remainder of the cargo, saved.

Rule A of the York/Antwerp Rules gives a clear and definite picture of a general average: A general average act exists when, and only when, any extraordinary sacrifice or expenditure is intentionally and reasonably made or incurred for the common safety for the purpose of preserving from peril the property involved in a common maritime adventure.

The custom of general average is an old established rule of shipping, the origins of which date back almost 3,000 years to the Rhodian Laws of the Sea around 800 B.C. These laws were copied, with modifications, by many other countries in Europe and the Mediterranean. It was the custom at that time for merchants to accompany their goods on the voyage and to dispose of them en route or at the destination. Each merchant might have only a few casks, bales of goods, or skins of oil or wine.

Most of the ancient vessels were small and had very little in the way of decks or other protection from the elements. The cargo was stowed under whatever shelter was available, such as skins or an old sail. It is doubtful that there was much, if any, supervision of the loading, and even with the small amount of cargo carried, the vessels were probably overloaded. (It was not until several centuries later that some ports enacted laws to prevent overloading.) The vessels were safe enough in fair weather, but in heavy weather these small craft must have been extremely difficult to manage.

In time of peril, which was often, jettisoning cargo or spars was the usual remedy, and the master, after consultation with the merchants, would jettison what was most accessible or would do the most good. This practice would also be followed to lighten the vessel if it were chased by pirates, a common occurrence in the Mediterranean in those days. If the jettisoning served its purpose and the vessel made port, the owners of the remaining cargo, by prior agreement and the existing law of the time, reimbursed the owners of the sacrificed cargo for their loss in proportion to the value of their own cargo saved. If the vessel's spars or gear were jettisoned, they were paid for in a similar manner. At that time the procedure was called "coming into contribution." Today it is called general average.

THE YORK/ANTWERP RULES

Although the principles of general average are recognized by practically all maritime countries, the laws regarding them are not uniform. This lack of uniformity was recognized as the cause of long delays in settling claims. Today most general average claims are settled according to the York/Antwerp Rules. First adopted in 1864 by an international convention of shipowners, merchants, and others interested in the problem, the rules have been revised several times to bring them up-to-date, most recently in 1994.

These rules do not change the laws of general average in the maritime countries but they do furnish a common basis for the adjustment of general average. A clause in the bill of lading or charter party will usually provide "general average to be settled according to the York/Antwerp Rules 1994 at such port or place as may be selected by the carrier, and as to matters not provided in the Rules, according to the laws and usages of the port of destination." Occasionally the clause will omit some of the rules.

Some examples of general average include the following:

1. A voluntary jettison of cargo, ship's stores, equipment, or gear to lighten the vessel in order to refloat it. These must be thrown overboard, that is, jettisoned, not washed overboard. The mind and agency of man must be employed; it must be an "act of man." However, if craft are available and time, conditions, and weather permit, the goods should be put into boats or lighters. Cargo interests and underwriters may claim that the sacrifice of much, if not all, of the goods jettisoned was unnecessary and that the master was negligent or hasty in making the sacrifice. However, the master should not be hindered by the awareness of such future claims.
2. Expenses of discharging and lightering, if used
3. Cargo, ship's gear, stores, and equipment damaged by water or other agents or procedures used to extinguish a fire. This does not include cargo or ship's gear actually damaged by the fire itself; that would be particular average (defined later in this chapter). It also does not include damage due to smoke or heat, even if the smoke or heat is a result of attempts to extinguish the fire, rather than a result of the fire itself.
4. Cutting holes in the deck, hull, or bulkhead in order to get at a fire
5. Damage sustained by ship's engine, propeller, rudder, or other equipment, when used in a manner for which they were not intended in an attempt to refloat a stranded vessel
6. Fuel consumed in the attempt to refloat the vessel
7. Voluntary stranding for the good of all interests
8. Ship's material or cargo burned as fuel to reach a port of safety, provided it can be shown that the vessel sailed from the last port with sufficient fuel for the contemplated voyage. A sufficient supply does not mean a minimum supply or barely enough to reach the destination in good weather. It means the calculated supply necessary for the voyage plus a reasonable amount as a margin for safety considering the season of the year and the nature of the voyage.
9. Loss of an anchor and chain, slipped to avoid a peril
10. Damage by seawater to the ship or cargo in holds when hatches were opened to jettison cargo
11. Loss of freight caused by general average sacrifices
12. Sacrifice of ship's equipment. It must be shown that the gear or equipment was sacrificed or employed for a purpose for which it was not intended, such as using pumps for pumping water out of a stranded vessel if such water contained sand or other foreign substance.
13. Damage to boilers caused by using salt water in an emergency when the supply of freshwater would not enable the vessel to reach a safe port. The

master will have to show that he or she sailed from the last port with sufficient water for the contemplated voyage and give the reason why freshwater could not be made on the vessel

14. Damage to windlass, capstan, or winches that occurred during an attempt to pull the vessel off a strand

15. Putting into a port of refuge to avoid an immediate loss, or to repair damage suffered at sea, or to restow cargo that shifted in heavy weather. Expenses may include towage, pilotage, harbor dues, costs of discharging, warehousing, reloading when necessary, fuel consumed from point of deviation and return, and various other items.

GENERAL AVERAGE DEPOSIT OR BOND

When a general average has been declared, the carrier has a possessory lien on the cargo for its share of the general average. The lien is lost upon delivery of the cargo. It is not always practicable or desirable to hold the cargo on board or to warehouse it while waiting for the general average statement to be prepared, showing how much each interest owes, as this generally takes a long time. The average adjuster estimates what each party may have to pay, and the cargo is released to the owner or consignee on payment of a deposit, called a general average deposit, for which only one receipt is given. No copies are made. Refunds are made as required when the final exact settlement is determined. In place of a deposit the company may agree to accept a general average bond guaranteed by the cargo underwriters or by a bank.

It is not likely that the master will ever be called on to give a receipt for a general average deposit. If it should be necessary, no copies of the receipt should be made. All the information on the receipt is copied on the stub attached to the form.

GENERAL AVERAGE ADJUSTMENT

The adjustment of general average, or determination of the amount each interest must contribute, may be a lengthy and complicated job. It is generally handled by independent experts in the field, called average adjusters. The adjuster is supposed to be a fair and impartial arbiter specially trained in the work. The adjuster is expected to determine a disinterested adjustment that is fair and equitable, but unfortunately it is rarely satisfactory to all interests in the adventure and there are usually many complaints.

There is an immense amount of detail involved in the work of the average adjuster, depending on the nature of the cargo, the sacrifices made, and the expenses incurred. Several months may be required to complete the work, after which the adjuster will issue an average statement indicating how much each interest must contribute. The average adjuster will require the following documents:

1. Manifests of the cargo on board at the time of the accident
2. Copies of bills of lading for the cargo
3. Vessel's logbooks
4. Copies of protest noted and/or extended
5. Accounts of all expenses relative to the general average
6. List of ship's stores and equipment expended during and in connection with the accident

The adjuster notes on the manifest which lots of cargo may be released. Copies are given to the vessel, the agent, and others representing the company. The notes are usually made in color and a code is attached to or explained on the manifest. A typical example follows:

Red—Release cargo; general average contribution guaranteed by [name of bank]
Purple—Release cargo after obtaining consignee's signature on Lloyd's bond
Yellow—Deposit required
Blue—May release cargo as required; have security
Green—Release cargo.

When cargo is subject to general average, the master must not release any of it before checking against the coded manifest.

EXPENSE TO VESSEL DUE TO GENERAL AVERAGE SACRIFICE

The chief officer and chief engineer should make up lists showing all stores and equipment lost, damaged, or expended as a general average sacrifice in attempting to save the vessel or cargo. In case of fire, one list should show stores and equipment whose loss or damage was caused by the fire itself. Another list should contain stores or equipment lost or damaged in efforts to extinguish the fire. The latter should include bottles of CO_2 or other extinguishing agents expended, fire-fighting equipment damaged in extinguishing the fire, stores and equipment soaked beyond use or damaged by chemicals used to extinguish the fire, and tarps damaged or cut in an attempt to cover openings or ventilators or to smother the fire.

Still another list should show any necessary overtime authorized for the crew, mechanics, or stevedores in order to carry out the general average sacrifice. In performing a general average act, the master or officer in charge must use reason and prudence. In this emergency the master is the agent of the cargo owners, consignees, and underwriters as well as of the company, and he or she must do all possible to save them from loss. In authorizing overtime, the master should bear this in mind.

Particular Average

Particular average is a term applied to any accidental loss, less than a total loss of vessel and cargo, caused by a peril not of a general average nature. "Acts of God" are particular average. Accidental stranding, collision, loss of anchor and chain, and damage to vessel or cargo by heavy weather or fire are also losses described as particular average. The loss sustained is borne by the owners of the property damaged. It is said of particular average that the loss "lies where it falls." The other interests in the maritime adventure do not contribute to the interest suffering the loss.

The following should illustrate the difference between particular average and general average. Cargo damaged by fire is particular average, but cargo damaged by water, chemicals, or other means used to extinguish the fire in order to save the ship and the remaining cargo is general average. Damage caused by an accidental grounding is considered particular average. If a vessel accidentally collides with another ship and is badly holed, the damage to the ship and cargo due to the collision is particular average. If the vessel is then deliberately grounded in an attempt to prevent it from sinking (thereby saving the vessel and the remaining cargo), the resulting damage is general average.

SHIPBOARD ILLNESSES AND INJURIES

The frequency of shipboard accidents—many of which are avoidable—results in high costs in claims to the company and in pain and suffering to injured or sick crewmembers. Some vessels are found to be accident prone, and those in charge blame it on bad luck, even though other vessels in the same company and on the same run have far fewer accidents. Investigation usually proves that the accidents are not due to bad luck but to poor or nonexistent supervision or improper procedures. Additionally, despite the pre-employment physical exams required by most employers, crewmembers may have preexisting conditions that make them susceptible to injury or disease. Some countries check mariners for AIDS or HIV.

Safety

Many shipboard injuries can be prevented if proper care and attention is paid to accident prevention. Some typical causes of accidents are grease, oil, and other slippery substances on the deck or gangway; broken or improperly fitting hatch boards; open and unprotected hatchways in dark areas of the ship; broken or missing rungs on hold, tank, or pilot ladders; and broken gangway steps. But perhaps the most common cause, and the easiest to correct, is poor crew supervision or even rank indifference on the part of the officers. That places responsibility for practically all vessel accidents with the master, who is ultimately accountable for what happens on his or her vessel.

Most shipowners have an accident-prevention program supervised by a shoreside safety manager, and ISM requirements mandate procedure manuals and shipboard safety management systems. Circulars and pamphlets are issued dealing with accident prevention and safety. These should be kept on file, read by all crewmembers (including the officers), and discussed until they are thoroughly understood. Books on safety and accident prevention can be obtained from the Department of Labor and various other sources. The U.S. Coast Guard publication *Proceedings of the Marine Safety Council,* published monthly, should be obtained and read by all the officers and crew. It contains interesting and informative articles on safety and other matters of importance to mariners. If possible, the master should keep a file of back issues because they may offer interesting ideas that can be discussed at safety meetings.

An injured crewmember does not benefit the ship. Others must do his or her work; an officer must give medical treatment, sometimes for an extended period; there are forms to complete, statements to take, and letters to write regarding the accident. Finally, it is usually necessary to hold an investigation to learn the cause of the accident. All of these problems may have arisen because someone in charge failed to make sure that the injured person knew what he or she was doing and was working in a safe place, with safe and proper tools and personal protective equipment.

Foreign Medical Evacuation

Anytime an injured person has to be treated ashore, the issue of repatriation arises. If the medical facilities at the port are insufficient, the injured or ill mariner must be transported to the nearest appropriate facility for treatment. Most commercial airlines will not transport injured persons that have not yet been stabilized. There are several commercial firms specializing in foreign medical evacuations and insurance for this very expensive mode of travel. Mariners would be well advised to review their medical coverage and ensure it covers medical evacuations from overseas. Appendix E contains a list of firms specializing in air medical evacuation and travelers insurance.

Allowing Sick or Injured Mariners to Work

It is usually inefficient, dangerous to the mariner, and possibly expensive to the company for a sick or injured mariner to work, regardless of the type of illness or injury. It could cause a great deal of trouble for the officer who ordered the sailor to turn to, and it would probably require much correspondence on the master's part to explain why it was done. As soon as a mariner reports an illness or is reported ill, he or she should be taken off duty if the illness or injury is serious enough to warrant it. The master should never hesitate to consult a doctor via satellite phone. A day or two off duty at the onset of an illness may save time, from several days to a week or more, later on.

Injury and Illness in Port

While in port, if a crewmember, stevedore, or other person is injured in an accident, regardless of how it happened, it is of the utmost importance that the injured person be given first aid immediately and, if necessary, sent to a hospital or put under a doctor's care. Everything possible should be done for the injured person. Some docks and practically all shipyards have first-aid stations to which an injured person can be sent. When a vessel is in port, all relevant shoreside emergency medical service (EMS) numbers should be available to the watch.

All cases of injury to or illness of a crewmember, as well as any injury or medical treatment to persons on board who are not crewmembers, should be entered in the medical and official logs. Coast Guard form CG-2692 is required if anyone is rendered unfit for duty by an injury or illness. A copy of this report should be sent to the insurance department. In all cases of illness or injury to anyone on board, injury or illness reports should be made up for the company insurance department.

Injury and Illness at Sea

While at sea, if an accident causes a serious injury or a serious illness occurs, the master should seek assistance by radio or satellite communications from a passenger or navy ship having a doctor on board or from the contracted medical provider. Advice may be sought from the many hospitals in the various countries that supply radio medical advice through a system that is described later in this chapter. If it is advisable to transport the sick or injured person to a doctor, the Coast Guard AMVER system will, on request, send the names and positions of the closest participating vessels carrying a doctor. The GMDSS has urgency codes for the dissemination of medical emergency information and requests for assistance. Hard copies should be retained of all communications regarding the illness or injury, especially of any medical advice given by radio or satellite. The master should make frequent, detailed notes of any treatments given or standby personnel posted to monitor the injured or ill mariner.

Assistance by Aircraft

Helicopters may be used to evacuate sick or injured personnel or to drop needed supplies or trained rescuers. Generally, helicopters have an operational radius of about 150 to 300 nautical miles. Search and rescue (SAR) aircraft may also be used to drop supplies.

If the assistance involves a drop, usually the packages will be color coded to indicate their contents:

Red—medical supplies
Blue—food and water
Yellow—blankets and protective clothing
Black—miscellaneous equipment such as pumps, axes, compasses, rafts, EPIRBs, flares, and so on

Helicopter evacuation is a dangerous operation and should be attempted only in the event of very serious illness or injury. The *U.S. Coast Pilot* and the *International Aeronautical and Maritime Search and Rescue Manual* (IAMSAR) offer guidance for helicopter evacuation and vessels should be equipped with both publications. If arranging a helicopter evacuation, a rendevous point should be selected as soon as possible. In the early communications as much medical information as possible should be communicated and any changes in the patient's condition should be communicated as soon as they are noticed. At minimum, the following information should be sent to the rescue coordination center (RCC):

- Name and type of vessel and call sign
- Position of vessel and destination port, as well as last port of call
- Local weather, sea, and swell conditions
- How to identify the ship from the air, such as flags, smoke, and so on. At night, searchlights can be directed skyward until the aircraft gets close; then they should be secured so as not to blind the pilots.
- ETA to next port of call and course and speed
- Patient's name, age, gender, nationality, and language
- Patient's respiration, blood pressure, pulse rate, and temperature
- Location of pain or injury
- Nature of illness or injury, including apparent cause and related history
- Symptoms
- Type, form, and amount of any and all medications given
- Time of last food consumption
- Ability of patient to eat, drink, walk, or be moved
- Whether the vessel has a medicine chest, sick bay, or doctor aboard
- Whether a suitable clear area is available for helicopter evacuations
- Name, address, and phone numbers for the vessel's agent and head office
- Communications and homing signal equipment aboard
- Additional patient remarks, changes in any of the above conditions, and so on

In preparation for a helicopter evacuation, the patient should be moved as close to the pickup area as is feasible, as time is of the essence. The patient should be tagged with medical details including a list of medications given and when administered. The mariner's papers, passport, medical record, and other necessary documents should be in a package ready to be transported with the patient. The patient should be strapped in the stretcher face up, wearing a life jacket if possible. For hypothermic patients, it is imperative to hoist the person in a prone position because lifting such a patient in a vertical position could cause severe shock or cardiac arrest.

To prepare the ship, the master should ensure that the following actions are taken:

- Maintain a continuous guard on 2182 kHz or specified voice frequency.
- Advise the approaching aircraft as to the location of the pickup point so the pilot can make an appropriate approach.
- Select a suitable hoist area on the vessel. This space should have a radius of at least 50 feet and preferably is a clear space in the aft part of the vessel.
- Clear the helicopter operating area of debris or loose gear and secure all antennas above the area. Secure all running rigging.
- If the hoist is to be at night, illuminate the area and any obstructions for the pilots. Be sure the lights will not blind the approaching pilots.
- Place a pennant or windsock where it can clearly be seen by the helicopter pilot.
- Ensure that the bridge team has been well versed in the upcoming operation, and all hands have fully charged radios to keep communications between the deck and bridge uninterrupted. Given the high noise level anticipated during helicopter evacuations, voice communications may be impossible. Hand signals should be prearranged among the crew handling the evacuation.
- Charge the fire pumps and position fire-fighting equipment near the operating area.
- On tankers with inert gas systems, reduce the tank pressures to a slight positive pressure. Noninerted tankers should have tank pressures released within 30 minutes of commencement of helicopter operations. All tank openings must be secured. On gas carriers, all precautions should be taken to avoid gas emissions. On bulk carriers, surface ventilation should be ceased and all hatch openings should be fully secured.
- Change the vessel's course so the vessel rides easily and the wind is on the port bow. Try to choose a course that will keep stack gases clear of the hoist area. Reduce speed to the minimum required to keep control of the vessel and maintain steerageway. Once established, maintain course and speed.

Once the helicopter has lowered the basket, crewmembers should be cautioned to wait until it touches the deck before they touch the basket to avoid static shock. The trail line can be used to guide the basket to the deck, but it should not be secured to the vessel. This line will not cause shock. Crewmembers should never attempt to secure either the trail line or hoist cable to the vessel, nor should they attempt to move the basket without unhooking it from the hoist cable. The patient should be placed into the basket, with his or her hands clear of the sides. When ready for the hoist, a crewmember can signal the hoist operator by giving a thumbs-up signal. The patient, when ready and if able, can also signal by nodding.

Deviating for Medical Emergency

If expert medical attention is required due to an injury or illness at sea, or if there is any danger to life that could possibly be averted by proceeding to the nearest port, deviation would be justified. In fact, it is the master's duty to deviate if there is even a slim chance of saving a life by doing so. In the meantime the agent should be advised at the destination port, giving an estimated time of arrival. If there is no agent in that port, the port authorities should be notified so that a boat or ambulance will be on hand to transfer the sick or injured person to a hospital. A doctor may come on board with the authorities.

The master should send a message to the home office informing them of the deviation and the reason. Any time a serious incident occurs the home office should be notified immediately by radio or satellite communication, followed by a detailed hard copy reiterating what was contained in the initial report and any further information, including copies of the injury reports, statements, and photographs. Promptness in reporting serious incidents is particularly important; it will enable the insurance department to send an investigator to the vessel to take statements or depositions if necessary.

The agent at the port where the person was hospitalized should send the master a message containing the doctor's diagnosis, if it was not available before sailing. This is important, as a dishonest crewmember might later claim he or she was hospitalized for an entirely different reason, conceivably one involving an alleged injury or illness occurring several months before, which may or may not have been reported. This is another reason for making up reports for all injuries and illnesses, however slight, and also for entering them in the official log and medical log. Keeping such detailed records will serve the best interests of the company and may help defeat an expensive claim that could not otherwise be disproved. This is especially true of claims made by those who are known as "claim-happy" mariners. These records will also assist other crewmembers who are claiming fair compensation for legitimate injuries.

If it is necessary to deviate, a statement of facts should be made up giving the date, time, and position where the deviation commenced and the date and time the vessel returned to the same or an equivalent position. Data entered in the statement of facts should be substantiated by the entries in the log. (See appendix E for a list of companies providing medical evacuation and transport services and travelers insurance.)

Death of a Mariner

Instructions for handling the body of a deceased crewmember should be obtained from a medical doctor. If the cause of death was injury, photos may be helpful in preserving evidence. All details should be entered in the medical and official logs, as appropriate. The effects of the deceased should not be sold, as this is the court's responsibility. The items should be gathered and a detailed inventory should be taken. Legal obligations regarding wages and the effects of the deceased are found in 46 USC §10701. This is considered a serious marine incident and a CG-2692 should be completed.

Reports

In any case of injury or illness, regardless of the cause or how minor it is, the master should make up the required reports and obtain the necessary statements. Postincident drug or alcohol testing may be necessary. Even if a person who has no right to be on the vessel gets hurt while aboard, an injury report should be made up and an entry made in the medical log. Shore people working on the vessel are more likely to have accidents due to their inexperience and their lack of shipboard safety consciousness.

The master should start a rough injury report as soon as possible and type the final copies once all the facts are known. As soon as possible, the injured person should be requested to make a signed statement giving his or her version of how the accident occurred. It is important that the report be as complete as possible, omitting no detail that could be of some assistance to the insurance department.

The name and address of the doctor or hospital should be noted in the official log, medical log, and on the report, along with the diagnosis and treatment. If in a foreign port, the agent should have the diagnosis and prescribed treatment written in English. Copies of the diagnosis and the doctor's recommendations should be attached to the report.

When there is an accident on the vessel caused by tripping, slipping, or falling, the master and the chief officer should personally examine the scene as soon as possible after the accident, note the conditions, and take photos. Was there grease, oil, or other substance on the deck? Were lines, wire, dunnage, or hoses of any kind cluttering the deck at the scene of the accident; or were the lines faked down, wires coiled, dunnage stacked, and hoses safely out of the way? Findings should appear in the report and in the master's statement. If the accident occurred in the engine room, the chief engineer should accompany the master on the inspection.

The scene of every shipboard accident causing an injury should be photographed if possible. The date and the name of the vessel should be typed or block printed on the back of each photograph, and these should be sent in with the report. This is often overlooked.

Reports and statements should be completed as promptly as possible. If an injured crewmember is paid off in the port where the accident occurred, the report should be sent in from that port, if possible. It can be taken for granted that a crewmember, stevedore, or other person who was injured on the vessel, or asserts that he or she was injured, will put in a claim that will most likely be at the office of the insurance department before reports from the vessel arrive. If any additional information arises later, it can be sent in then.

When making up illness or injury reports, the master should give full particulars so that nothing is left in doubt. Important details are often missing, usually because the officer responsible put them off to a more convenient time or forgot about them until the end of the voyage, and then had to make them up in a hurry. Everyone involved should avoid such procrastination. The importance of making up reports promptly and forwarding them to the insurance department immediately after an illness or injury is discovered cannot be too strongly stressed.

Statements

The master should always try to get signed statements from witnesses to any accident causing an injury and from the injured person, regardless of how slight the injury may be. The statement should be dated and signed by the person making it and should include his or her home address and the name of the vessel. This is sometimes overlooked. A copy of the statement should be given to the person making it.

Statements should be obtained from all persons able to give any information on the cause of an accident as soon as practicable after the accident, while the facts are still fresh in their minds. A mariner will be more likely to correctly state the facts concerning an accident immediately after it happens and before being able to discuss it with others. If the statement is put off, he or she may discuss it with shipmates, probably with a "sea lawyer" or two, and perhaps with the injured person's lawyer. After that, the statement, if given at all, may differ widely from the actual facts.

Master's Statement

If the master can supply any information on the cause of an accident, he or she should also make up a statement. The master's statement is always considered important. It should state if he or she personally examined the scene of the accident and describe what was found; this is an important part of the statement. Any suspicious circumstances concerning the accident should also be included.

If any letters or notes were written to or received from others regarding an injury on the vessel, copies should be included with the master's statement. As a matter of policy, the master should be cautious about writing to others regarding an accident on the vessel unless requested to do so by the office. This also applies to interviews and statements, oral or written, requested by reporters and the like. The master should never discuss the facts except with company officials or government investigators and should never make a statement admitting liability. The insurance department will take care of that. When unauthorized persons, including reporters, request information or an opinion, the master should refer them to the office and should not offer an opinion one way or the other because of the probability of being misquoted.

If the master suspects the injured crewmember had been drinking or using drugs, the statement should mention this and describe any post-incident testing or collection performed. The report should not say a crewmember was drunk but should simply include whatever was indicated as BAC by the Breathalyzer (or, if unable to test, the reason why). The report should also indicate the crewmember's behaviors. Did the breath smell of alcohol? Was the crewmember staggering? Was speech incoherent or belligerent? Did the crewmember admit drinking too much or drinking just prior to the accident? If a required postincident test is not performed, it may cause a civil and or criminal penalty to be charged against the master. These are points that should be addressed in the master's statement. The same applies to those who were helping or working with the crewmember.

If the injured person has suffered similar injuries before, the master should bring it to the attention of the company, but should not mention the earlier accident in the report about the current injury. Some mariners make a habit—and a profitable one—of getting hurt on a vessel, and the alleged accidents may bear a surprising similarity.

If photographs, diagrams, or sketches are sent in with the report, the date and name of the.vessel should be shown on the back.

Medical Log

A medical log, which can be an ordinary ledger, should be maintained by the officer charged with first aid while the vessel is in service. All cases of injury or illness, however slight or minor, to a crewmember, passenger, longshoreman, or other person on the vessel should be entered in the medical log, along with the treatment given and any other pertinent data. The medical log must be signed by the person giving treatment; it is good practice also to have the ill or injured person sign the medical log.

A well-kept medical log will often save the company a claim and the master much correspondence. The master should make it a practice to read the medical log weekly. The entries should be legible—block printing them is one way to ensure this. Every case of injury to or illness of a crewmember must also be entered in the official log with the treatment given.

Hospitalized Mariners's Clothes and Effects

When a mariner is hospitalized in any port, his gear should accompany him; another crewmember can escort him to assist, if necessary. Taking the gear back to the United States on the ship should be avoided because while it remains on board, the vessel is responsible for its safety. If the hospitalized crewmember needs only a few items and wants to leave the rest on board with another mariner, the sick crewmember should be instructed to write a note naming the mariner who is to take charge of the gear and an itemized description of that gear. The mariner named should read and sign the note; otherwise the vessel may still be responsible for the gear. In any case, the master should take an inventory of all the gear and make a number of copies: one for the crewmember in the hospital, one to send with the report to the company, one to place with the gear, and one for the vessel's file. It is also likely that the consul and the agent will each want a copy.

If it is impractical to get the gear to the hospital or to put it ashore in charge of the agent, the vessel will be responsible for it. The master should lock the gear up in a safe place with a copy of the inventory attached.

It is important that the crewmember in the hospital gets the things he or she will need: toiletries, underwear, clothes, passport, and so forth. If not taken along, these items should be sent to the hospital, or if that is impractical, they should be left with the agent to be delivered later. Some books and magazines will be welcome, especially in a foreign port. Customs in most foreign ports will usually permit these things to be taken off the vessel. If there is any difficulty with customs, the consul's office can probably help in having the items cleared.

Mariners Examined by Private Doctors

Occasionally a crewmember will ask to see a doctor or dentist of his or her own choosing; this practice should be discouraged, and the master should recommend treatment by the doctor employed by the company or the agent at that port. Naturally, no one can prevent a person from going to a specific doctor. If hospitalization is necessary, the master should not waste time trying to contact the agent or home office, but should get the person to a hospital without delay.

If a mariner refuses the offer of treatment by a company doctor and consults a private doctor, these facts should be entered in the medical log, the official log, and on the illness or injury report, which is made up regardless of where treatment is provided. The bill for treatment by a private physician or dentist should be paid by the mariner. However, the master must not fail to offer a crewmember medical aid any time it is requested or required; this includes certain types of dental aid as well.

Bills for medical attention by private doctors or dentists should be returned to the mariner for payment and should not be signed by the master. If the bills must be paid before the vessel sails and the crewmember has no money, he or she should sign the official log for the amount as a draw. If the crewmember refuses to sign for the amount and local officials require that the bill be paid before the vessel sails, the master should make an entry in the official log that the crewmember will be charged with the amount. The mariner should be read the log entry and given a copy.

Any or all of the foregoing procedures may be disregarded if they are in conflict with the company instructions or union agreement.

Even if a mariner pays his or her own doctor bill, an injury or illness report should still be made up with a note to the effect that the crewmember paid the doctor. This fact should also be entered in the official and medical logs. The master should try to obtain a signed statement from the mariner stating that he or she refused the treatment offered and preferred to see a private doctor.

It may be difficult to get a report or diagnosis from the private doctor, especially if the mariner was treated for alcoholism or a sexually transmitted disease. The agent may need to procure the diagnosis, if possible. Failing that, the master should make an entry in the logs and on the report stating the reason why the diagnosis was not available.

Even after a mariner has seen a private doctor, if there is serious doubt as to the person's medical condition and concern that his or her health could be endangered by being at sea and away from ready access to professional medical attention, the crewmember should be sent to the company doctor. A mariner cannot be forced to accept medical treatment against his or her will, but the master has the right to require that the crewmember be examined for the protection of all aboard the vessel, and the mariner can be released if he or she refuses.

Medical Advice by Radio

It is the legal and moral duty and responsibility of the master of a vessel to seek medical advice by radio or satellite communications whenever the welfare of the crew or passengers requires it. Many countries offer medical advice by radio to ships, usually free of charge, so every master should take advantage of this service. The United States began a medical radio advice service in 1921; enough other countries have adopted similar services that the system now offers worldwide coverage. This system is often referred to as the medico system because messages sent through U.S. coast radio stations are prefixed "DH MEDICO." DH stands for "deadhead," a radio service term meaning that the message is free.

Most shipping lines also subscribe to commercial medical providers who stock the sick bay and offer twenty-four-hour medical advice to their clients by phone and/or fax. These numbers should be readily accessible to all who will potentially be providing medical treatment aboard. All officers should be familiar with calling procedures. One such commercial service providing free worldwide medical advice to ships is Centro Internazional Radio Medico (CIRM). It can be reached through the following:

Telephone—06-5923331-2

Fax—06-5923333

Telex—6 12068 CIRM1

Hydrographic Office *Publication No. 117, Radio Navigational Aids,* contains a listing, by country, of radio stations that will transmit medical advice by radio. The information in these publications is extracted from the *List of Radio Determination and Special Service Stations* published by the International Telecommunications Union, which may be consulted if more detailed information is needed.

Although radio medical advice is available worldwide, it is not actually an international system. Each country that offers medical advice by radio operates its own independent system with its own requirements. Masters should therefore consult one of the above publications before sending a medico message. For example, some countries insist that messages be sent in the official language of the country, while others will accept several different languages.

Messages regarding medical advice should be in plain language whenever possible, but in case of language problems, the signals from the medical signal code of the *International Code of Signals, Publication No. 102,* may be used. The medical signal code is also reprinted in chapter 12 of *The Ship's Medicine Chest and First Aid at Sea,* published by the U.S. Department of Health and Human Services.

All U.S. coast radio stations offer free medical message service to all vessels if the message is headed DH MEDICO and is signed by the master. Medical advice may also be obtained from any U.S. Coast Guard radio station. Messages to the Coast Guard will be handled either by a Coast Guard medical officer or by a hospital with which the Coast Guard has an agreement.

Commercial firms also offer medical advice by radio. Shipping companies may subscribe to these services for a fee. Such a firm will have its own doctors on duty twenty-four hours a day and will usually have its own communications facilities. The doctors at these companies are specially trained to deal with nonmedical personnel by radio, and they are aware of the limitations of shipboard medical treatment. Usually, they are also aware of the facilities available for evacuating a mariner from a ship in different parts of the world. A master whose company subscribes to such a service will of course obtain medical advice from that company whenever communications permit.

The more information and symptoms contained in a message, the easier it will be for the doctors to prescribe treatment. If a master requests medical advice by radio from any source, copies should be kept of all messages sent and received relating to the illness or injury.

SALVAGE

The law of salvage is peculiar to maritime law. In the United States, under common law, generally one owes no duty to render aid to another no matter how dire the circumstances nor how easy it may be to render that aid. At sea, the rules change. All mariners have a duty to render aid to a vessel in distress so long as doing so does not imperil the rescuing vessel, its cargo, or its crew. For thousands of years, laws have encouraged, though not required, risk-taking behavior for the benefit of an imperiled vessel. This is the law of salvage.

Nine hundred years before the Christian era, the Rhodian laws codified the concept of awarding monetary awards to volunteer salvors. Modern laws of all seafaring nations reflect an increasing trend toward encouraging voluntary assistance to property and vessels in maritime peril. Environmental concerns, now at a peak, also are reflected in strong public policy encouraging and rewarding voluntary salvors whose efforts prevent or mitigate environmental damage. Even where the vessel is considered a constructive total loss, salvors now have an incentive to mitigate environmental damage and will be entitled to a reward under the most frequently used salvage agreements. Another modern term is "liability salvage," the prevention or mitigation of harm to a third party, which saves the shipowner from third-party liability. Liability salvage has not yet been fully tested by the courts, as determining the value of what "could have happened" is a very gray area.

Deciding if Assistance Is Warranted and Master's Authority

Before requesting the assistance of a salvage vessel, masters must first determine if such assistance is needed. If time allows, it would be prudent to call the head office, the vessel's hull and machinery insurance representatives, and the company's P and I club before engaging the services (commercial or voluntary) of salvors or rescue tugs. Many owners and insurers have industry connections with salvage firms and could negotiate a better contract than could a master under duress. P and I clubs are especially interested in potential environmental and third-party liability, whereas the hull and machinery underwriters are interested in the vessel itself. With the advent of real-time communication found on most ships, it is more common for the owners and underwriters to contract directly with the salvaging company than for the master to make an on-the-spot agreement. Some underwriters require prior approval before being bound to pay for salvage services, and the master must be aware of any such insurance requirements. However, the master has the authority to bind the vessel and speaks for the ship and cargo owners. If the need for assistance is urgent, the master should not delay a request for aid in order to negotiate the terms of the salvage agreement. The master should never delay the request for assistance until the situation has worsened to the point that it becomes extremely difficult or impossible to provide aid. Ideally, some advice, guidance, and appropriate contact numbers should be available in the vessel's SMS plans.

Vessels requiring assistance should transmit either Mayday (for grave and imminent danger) or Pan-Pan (if life or the safety of the ship is in jeopardy) as a prefix to their message. Once salvage operations have commenced, a Securité message should be sent out periodically if the circumstances allow. Casualty reports should be made in accordance with the coastal state's requirements, if known, and the vessel's SMS plans.

The master has a duty to render his or her best efforts to minimize damage to the ship and cargo or harm to the crew and must exercise all due care to prevent or mitigate damage to the environment.

Refusing Assistance

Even if a vessel refuses assistance, the coastal state may impose assistance if it feels its shores or waterways are threatened. In addition, some commercial salvors have binders which contain phrases used to entice a vessel to hire them. Radio transmissions are usually taped by commercial salvage vessels, so communications must be made carefully and after as much consideration as the situation allows. If a vessel refuses assistance, the hovering tug may ask if the ship wants it to "just stand by." If the ship says "yes," the vessel may later be held to have hired the tug. This is a gray area and different courts and jurisdictions interpret salvage law differently. English courts and arbitrators are by far more conversant with salvage law than are U.S. courts.

Intervention by Coastal State Authorities

Most maritime nations are signatories to international conventions, or they have laws allowing interdiction by authorities to protect their coastlines and harbors. These laws usually allow the involved authorities to use their armed forces and/or to hire commercial salvors. In the United States, the Coast Guard has the obligation to protect the shores and waterways of the country. Under OPA '90, if the environment is being threatened by an actual or potential discharge of oil (all ships have fuel tanks and this statute is broadly interpreted), a federal on-scene coordinator (FOSC), usually a Coast Guard officer, will be appointed to coordinate rescue and cleanup efforts. This person, who supposedly shares the decision-making responsibility with the vessel owner and the involved state, will oversee and coordinate all efforts connected with the operation and may override the advice of the salvage teams and the master of the imperiled vessel. The United States may also intervene on the high seas under the Intervention on the

High Seas Act (IHSA) if the national coastline is being environmentally threatened. Other maritime nations, under the International Convention Relating to Intervention on the High Seas in Cases of Oil Pollution Casualties, 1969, and the Protocol Relating to Intervention on the High Seas in Cases of Marine Pollution by Substances Other than Oil, 1973, may intervene on the high seas if their coasts are threatened.

Engaging a Salvor

Once the decision has been made that assistance is needed, no time should be wasted in engaging a tug's services. If several vessels are available, the master or owner may hire more than one salvor if necessary but should be aware that each may submit a salvage claim. The hiring of a salvor does not relinquish the master of command of the vessel.

There are two primary methods governing the hiring of a salvage tug. If salvage services are rendered without an agreed form of contract, it does not prevent an assisting vessel from claiming salvage.

"NO CURE–NO PAY" AGREEMENT

The most common salvage agreement is the Lloyd's Open Form (LOF), which is a no cure–no pay agreement to render salvage services and to leave the amount of the salvage award "open" for determination at a later date when heads have cooled and retrospect may influence decisions. LOF provides reasonable terms for both vessel owner and salvor and sets forth the duties each owes the other. One of the benefits of LOF is that if the salvage attempt is unsuccessful, the vessel owes the salvor nothing. In the case of averted environmental casualties, the vessel owes the salvor expenses plus a bonus as discussed below. One of the features of LOF is that the vessel owner, by agreeing to LOF, agrees to salvage arbitration in London, which will be governed by English law.

LOF was revised in 2000 and was reduced from six pages to two (fig. 36). The form has gone through several iterations in the past twenty years in which critical language has changed, and professional salvors may ask to use a previous edition, such as LOF 1995 (fig. 37) or LOF 1980 rather than the current edition. One of the major changes in LOF occurred in the 1980 edition, which allowed the technically unsuccessful salvor of a full or partially full tanker to be awarded his expenses plus a bonus if he was partially successful or was somehow prevented from finishing the salvage. In LOF 1990 the language was again broadened to allow payments for partial success in the salvaging of any vessel that threatened environmental harm, and this broad language is seen in LOF 2000.

If a professional salvor requests an earlier edition of LOF, there is a reason for doing so. It would be advisable to consult with the vessel's underwriters (who would likely be bearing the brunt of any salvage award) prior to agreeing to any version of LOF.

In addition to LOF, there are other no cure–no pay agreements in use—the Japanese Shipping Exchange Salvage Agreement and the Scandinavian, Chinese, or German salvage agreements to mention a few. Generally, LOF is the most familiar form of agreement.

These agreements can be made orally by simply stating:

> "SS *vessel name* agrees to salvage services based on *Lloyds Open Form [1995, 2000, etc.]* a no cure–no pay agreement, at *GMT*, on *date*. Please acknowledge receipt by repeating back the foregoing. Master *name.*"

Appropriate entries must be made in the VHF and/or GMDSS log. It is probably prudent to send this message by INMARSAT telex so a hard, time-dated copy is available as a record of the agreement.

CONTRACT TOWING OR RESCUE TOWING

Contract or rescue towing is either a towage contract that stipulates a set hourly, daily, or job fee, or it is a time-and-materials-type contract. If a tug has agreed to contracted rescue, it has no right to claim salvage later unless it exceeded the scope of the original contract. Contract towage is not a no cure–no pay agreement; if a tug has agreed to a set fee for services, those fees must be paid regardless of the success of the venture.

Given the erosion of the strict no cure–no pay contracts and the increased concern over prevention of environmental harm, which is extremely difficult to value monetarily, many salvors prefer the contract for towage over LOF. There are several contract forms available, for example, the International Salvage Union–BIMCO Marine Services Agreement.

Working with a Salvage Team

Every effort should be made to work in harmony with the salvage team. Parties to a salvage operation are bound to use their best efforts to rescue the vessel and her cargo and to protect the environment. Most salvage operations will be orchestrated by a salvage master. The master and chief engineer should provide the salvage master with all requested plans, tables, vessel and cargo information, and any other information requested. Hiring a salvage team does not relieve the master of command. The master can call off the salvage efforts, provided a coastal state has not taken over the operation, but the salvors could still be entitled to a salvage award. In the United States, the Coast Guard will have primary jurisdiction over any marine casualty, but many other agencies, such as the EPA, FBI, U.S. Fish and Wildlife Service, and state agencies will be involved as well. One of the problems with such overlapping interests is that no one agency has knowledge of the entire legislative or operational picture, and most have no significant knowledge of marine salvage operations. When dealing with the authorities, a forthright approach as to the facts of the incident is best (See chapters on "Vessel Accidents and Incidents" and "United States Laws.")

The shipowner or operator should provide a knowledgeable media contact rather than siphon the master's attention away from the efforts at hand to deal with media attention.

After the Salvage Efforts

Salvage, by definition, is a voluntary undertaking rather than a contractual duty. For this reason it is highly unlikely a Coast Guard vessel could successfully win a salvage claim, rescue being their duty. However, there have been cases of military rescue teams being awarded salvage monies for going above and beyond the call of their ordinary duties. A ship's own crew is not prevented from claiming and being awarded salvage for rescuing their own ship if their actions were above and beyond what is normally expected of mariners. Similarly, if a tug hired to assist a ship into its berth goes above and beyond the scope of the originally contemplated contract due to some unforeseen event, it too may successfully claim salvage.

Courts are often more liberal in their salvage awards to professional salvors, those owners of specialized salvaging vessels that wait at trouble spots around the world to rescue distressed vessels. Several maritime nations have their own national salvage fleets, although with the decrease in vessel casualty rates this practice is diminishing. Courts usually hope to encourage capital investment and risk taking of this type, as all of society benefits by their presence.

In determining if a salvage award is warranted, the court must answer two questions:

1. Is it salvage?
2. If it is salvage, what is it worth?

IS IT SALVAGE?

For an event to be considered salvage three tests must be met. First, a vessel or goods carried on a vessel must be in maritime peril. There are many cases stretching this test. Courts have wrestled with questions concerning airplanes, what exactly is "maritime peril," when is a vessel not a vessel, and so on. Even a vessel drifting on a calm day was held to be in peril as it was not under control. The peril need not be imminent; otherwise salvors would wait for the situation to get really bad before taking action. Even the apprehension of peril has been held by courts to be "peril." The *degree* of peril is considered when establishing the actual dollar value of the award. The *existence* of peril is all that is needed to determine whether the event is considered salvage.

Second, the aid must be voluntary. Here, voluntary means the salvors had no preexisting duty nor a contractual duty to render the aid. A Coast

Guard cutter has a preexisting duty to render aid and generally will not be able to claim salvage. A contract salvor also cannot later claim salvage. Their crews, however, can, as contracts made between a salvaging vessel owner and the rescued party are generally not binding on the crew. As a general rule, being paid an hourly wage will not bar a mariner from claiming salvage against a third party, nor even against his or her own vessel in certain circumstances.

Third, the salvage effort must be successful in whole or in part. Generally, if the situation is made worse, the salvor will not be entitled to a salvage award. If the salvor contributed at all, even if only by standing by, the salvage effort is considered successful. Cooks have won salvage awards for making sandwiches for the salvage crew. Ships and crews have won awards for simply standing by during salvage operations. Modern no cure–no pay agreements now allow for some monetary compensation for the partial/thwarted mitigation of environmental damage—complete success is no longer a strict requirement.

WHAT IS IT WORTH?

Once these three tests are met, there is a legitimate salvage claim. The next question for the court is "what is the salvage effort worth?" Here, seven factors are considered by a U.S. court in order of importance. Traditionally there were six factors, called the Blackwall factors after a landmark salvage case; the seventh factor adds environmental risks, which are to be considered by the judge in making the salvage award.

Following are the six traditional Blackwall factors and the modern environmental element, to be considered in this descending order of importance.

1. Degree of peril to the rescued vessel
2. Value of the property salved
3. Risk to the salvors
4. Promptitude, skill, and energy displayed by the salvors
5. Value of the property used in the salvage
6. Time and labor spent by the salvors
7. Risk to the environment averted by the salvage effort

Unlike U.S. law, under LOF, the factors involved in a salvage award are governed by the International Convention on Salvage, 1989, Article 13:

The reward shall be fixed with a view to encouraging salvage operations, taking into account the following criteria without regard to the order in which they are presented below:

a) the salved value of the vessel and other property;

b) the skill and efforts of the salvors in preventing or minimizing damage to the environment;
c) the measure of success obtained by the salvor;
d) the nature and degree of the danger;
e) the skill and efforts of the salvors in salving the vessel, other property, and life;
f) the time used and expenses and losses incurred by the salvors;
g) the risk of liability and other risks run by the salvors or their equipment;
h) the promptness of the services rendered;
i) the availability and use of vessels or other equipment intended for salvage operations;
j) the state of readiness and efficiency of the salvor's equipment and the value thereof.

Salvage Award

The court will hear testimony on both sides. Obviously, the salvors will play up the factors and the owners/insurers of the distressed vessel will downplay the factors. The judge or arbitrator will then make an award.

Salvage awards are meant to encourage others to undertake risky rescue operations as well as to reward the salvors. The award is not based on the fair market value of the services rendered but is meant as a reward.

Usually the owner of any marine equipment used in the salvage operation is alongside the crew in pursuit of a salvage award but the owners of the salvage company, who were probably asleep during the whole operation, often get the largest share of the salvage awards. Masters of tugs and other vessels engaged in salvage operations are considered the agents of the owners and are usually free to exercise their best judgment regarding engaging in a salvage operation.

In 1804, Chief Justice Marshall, in discussing salvage awards in his opinion in *Mason v. The Blaireau,* said,

> The allowance of a very ample compensation for those services (one very much exceeding the mere risk encountered, and labor employed in effecting them), is intended as an inducement to render them, which it is for the public interests, and for the general interests of humanity to hold forth those who navigate the ocean.

Traditionally, awards have been based on a percentage of the total value of the salved vessel, her cargo, and freight (monies paid for the carriage of cargo). Percentages range from 2 percent (low-order salvage) to over 50 percent (high-order salvage). Any award over 50 percent of the value of the vessel is called a "moiety" and is very rare. In modern times, with the value of vessels, cargo, and freight skyrocketing, awards based on percentages often result in excessive awards, so courts consider strictly dollar values instead.

Judges are not bound by precedent in setting awards, as each case is different. Excessively large awards or awards that are drastically low can be appealed in federal courts. Salvage cases under LOF are submitted to binding arbitration in England.

For detailed information on salvage, the following publications should be consulted: *Peril at Sea and Salvage—A Guide for Masters,* International Chamber of Shipping, Oil Companies International Marine Forum, 1998; *Modern Marine Salvage,* William I. Milwee, Jr., Cornell Maritime Press, 1995; *The Nautical Institute on Command—A Practical Guide,* The Nautical Institute, 2000.

CHAPTER 5

Vessel Security

Incidents of terrorist attacks, smuggling, piracy, sabotage, barratry, stowaways, assaults, and other crimes aboard ship are escalating in frequency and severity worldwide. Masters of merchant cargo and passenger ships should see the recommendations and guidelines of IMO and other leading maritime agencies and experts that may pertain more specifically to their vessel, route, and cargo.[1]

Under the ISM code, by July 2002, all ships will be required to have a safety management system which should include a vessel security plan. As is true with vessel safety concerns, the ship's crew should be as prepared as possible to handle all sorts of threats to the vessel's and their own security. Masters should invest time in learning about vessel security so that they are prepared if the issue should arise.

HISTORY

Partly as a result of the terrorist hijacking of the Italian passenger ship *Achille Lauro* in October 1985, IMO formed a subcommittee to investigate the specific problems terrorism posed to merchant vessels. IMO's Maritime Security Committee passed a resolution entitled "Measures to Prevent Unlawful Acts Which Threaten the Safety of Ships and the Security of their Passengers and Crews" which was immediately and unanimously approved by the member countries.[2] While these are only guidelines, many countries, including the United States, have adopted them into their legislation and regulatory requirements.

In 1986, the Omnibus Diplomatic Security and Anti-Terrorism Act, based in large part on the IMO document, became law in the United States. Title 9 of this law constitutes the International Maritime Port and Security Act, which amended the Ports and Waterways Safety Act and mandated

97

security measures for passenger terminals and ports and the creation of security contingency plans. The Coast Guard's National Security Branch has been tasked with implementing these requirements.[3] The Passenger Vessel Safety Act was passed in 1993 and included further requirements. Due to varying degrees of implementation aboard passenger vessels, the Coast Guard has published new requirements outlining minimum security requirements for passenger vessels and terminals.[4]

Good security practices make good business sense. As awareness of international terrorism increases among the traveling public, so too will the expectation of security. Indeed, some passengers now inquire as to a carrier's security practices when planning sea voyages. Insurance companies, in assessing risk and potential legal liability, have a vested interest in a carrier's security practices as well.

Mariners should keep well apprised of the latest security information published in the *Notice to Mariners*, National Imagery and Mapping Agency (NIMA) broadcasts, and HYDROLANT and HYDROPAC warnings printed in *Notice to Mariners* as well as the antishipping activity section of Navigation Information Network (NAVINFONET), which contains the most recent five weeks of "Worldwide Threat to Shipping" messages from the Office of Naval Intelligence. NAVINFONET is a free service provided by the Marine Navigation Department of NIMA. It can be accessed via telephone modem from anywhere in the world and a variety of computer programs are available to extract data from the system.

NAVINFONET can be contacted as follows:

Marine Navigation Department
NAVINFONET STAFF
ST D 44
National Imagery and Mapping Agency
4600 Sangamore Rd.
Bethesda, MD 20816-5003

Contact numbers for data access can be found in *Publication No. 117.*

Information can also be gathered from the State Department's travel advisories.

The International Maritime Bureau has announced a new ship-tracking system, SHIPLOC, which has been available since late February 1999 and can be used by anyone with Internet access and a personal computer. The SHIPLOC transmitter, which is passively and remotely monitored, can be hidden aboard ship and its location not revealed for the crew's protection. It can be used as an antihijacking device as well as a remote monitoring device for the home office. Monthly rentals are presently under $500.

IMO SHIP SECURITY PLAN

Compliance with IMO resolutions requires both shoreside and shipboard security personnel and a shipboard security plan as part of an overall safety management system.[5]

A ship security plan should address any specific needs of a particular vessel, such as her design, manning, and route. In general, similar to the different watch conditions required by the STCW, the plan should specify different levels of security, each having its own particular requirements. The overall plan, per IMO guidelines, should include contingency plans for specific threats or warnings. Complete procedures for all potential threats and events, including a checklist of actions to take, should be included in the ship security plan.

The manual detailing the ship security plan should have a procedure for updating it, and the company should ensure there is a clear communication link between shipboard personnel and shoreside management so that any recommendations or improvements can be added to the manual. As with all other relevant corporate policies, the ship security plan would be a discoverable item in litigation.

Shoreside Security Officer

On shore, the IMO resolution calls for an operator security officer, a shoreside company-appointed executive who is responsible for developing and updating the ship security plan and for being the liaison with shipboard and dockside personnel. Many companies have a QI (qualified individual) who handles postincident activities, mitigation efforts, and media interfaces. It is likely that the QI will take over vessel security issues in many companies.

The operator security officer is responsible for ensuring that adequate training is provided and adequate security awareness is maintained. This will be reviewed during ISO/ISM compliance audits. Voyage planning should include security considerations as well as the usual weather and routing concerns, and the shoreside security officer should provide input to the voyage planning process. The responsibility should not end once the vessel leaves the dock. The shoreside security officer should stay updated on current international affairs in order to alert the vessel to any new security concerns along the route and provide useful information and advice. This corporate officer should have an intimate knowledge of security information resources and also of the vessel's characteristics, cargo, crew, routes, and ports of call.

Shipboard Security Officer

Aboard ship, the shipboard security officer should be assigned to implement and maintain the ship security plan. This person is the shipboard counterpart to the shoreside security officer. As part of his or her duties, the shipboard security officer should forward comments on shortcomings and recommendations regarding modifications of the plan to the appropriate shoreside security person. Such ideas may result from a shipboard safety meeting or from a suggestion dropped in a suggestion box. The shipboard security officer should encourage the crew to discuss security issues and offer ideas.

Under IMO guidelines and most countries' legislation, the operator security officer and the shipboard security officer each must have specific duties, and each can be held personally responsible should an incident occur. Given this unprecedented, legally mandated level of responsibility, it is imperative that vessel operators, unions, and employers of mariners provide professional training in shipboard security. Several European firms offer security training, and some United States companies are starting to offer the same. Commercial companies also provide various levels of security services.

In addition to the port-state-controlled ISM audits, a vessel should conduct its own internal audits to determine the level of compliance with internal policies.

SHIPBOARD SECURITY PRACTICES AND SEARCHES

The master and senior officers should encourage all crewmembers and shoreside employees to be aware of and report any abnormalities, even if they are only "gut feelings," to the shipboard security officer or master. The master should encourage communications from the crew and not chastise a crewmember if the report turns out to be unwarranted, as this would have a chilling effect on future reports.

As a general rule, ships must provide their own security. Port security personnel are not focused on the ship and instead are focused on the port facility. Even security personnel hired specifically for the vessel will not be as vigilant as crewmembers protecting their own ship.

Master's Searches

The master has the authority to search any space aboard the vessel at any time. Many vessels conduct random bag and luggage searches, depending on the port. Usually, a master waits for reasonable cause to search a specific stateroom; however, this is not strictly necessary. The master, being personally responsible for everything aboard, has the right to search all spaces of the vessel.

Maintaining Restricted Spaces

IMO guidelines have designated certain spaces as restricted areas, which must be constructed so as to deny entry to unauthorized persons. Effectively, this means these places must be fitted with working locks or some other mechanism to secure the space. IMO restricted spaces include the following:

1. Bridge
2. Radio room and communication area (this may be the bridge under GMDSS requirements)
3. Engine control station
4. Emergency steering gear room
5. Emergency generator room

HOSTILE AND UNAUTHORIZED BOARDERS

Unauthorized boarders, whether hijackers, pirates, or stowaways, pose a direct threat to the vessel and her crew. At minimum, they cause delay and additional expense. They can cause physical harm, illness, or even death to the crew; damage to the vessel and cargo; and damage or disruption to the port, adjacent waterways, or nearby vessels. Modern pirates and hijackers are better armed and stowaways are more desperate than in past decades, yet merchant ships have fewer crew and usually carry no armaments whatsoever to repel hostile boarders. The SMS of a vessel should include preventative measures and steps to be taken in the event of unauthorized boardings of various types. Drills should be designed to include hostile boarding scenarios. A special signal should be developed to alert the crew that the ship has been or is about to be boarded and crewmembers should have specific duties and stations during such an event. A prudent master should have communication equipment preprogrammed with pertinent contact and alerting information when entering waters known for hostile boarding of merchant vessels. This information can be found in *Publication No. 117, Radio Navigational Aids,* and in IAMSAR. The normal marine safety information received by vessels will offer various governmental warnings regarding recent hostile actions against shipping. This section will discuss various types of unauthorized boarders and offer suggestions and resources available to the master of a U.S. merchant vessel.

Prevention of Unauthorized Boarding in Port

Every vessel should maintain a rigorous gangway watch. No one should be‐ allowed aboard without authorization by an appropriate authority. The gangway is not the only place boarders gain access. Unpredictable roving rounds should include a check of areas not within view of the gangway, any dimly lit areas, cargo and stores hatches, RO/RO ramps, the stern, and the offshore side of the ship. Good lighting, unpredictable roving rounds, and highly visible, reliable communications will all serve to discourage would-be boarders. Crew and officers alike may become complacent in their rounds when nothing exciting has happened for weeks or even entire careers. The master must recognize that it is impossible to maintain a sense of high alert for days on end.

A guest or visitors log should be maintained scrupulously, including the person's name, identification number if appropriate, the reason for boarding the vessel, and the times aboard and away. Visitors and guests are never to be allowed to roam the ship unescorted. A vessel with a large number of crewmembers should have a crew list at the gangway watch station. Persons who are not members of the crew should be photographed and issued a pass. The film need only be developed if an incident occurs.

Shore or boarding passes and tickets should be checked carefully. Merchant mariner documents (MMDs) should be checked against crew lists, if the watch does not personally know the person. The passports of boarding personnel and passengers should be checked against their physical characteristics. (The *Achille Lauro* terrorists, all Arabs, used Norwegian passports in which the photos had not even been changed.)

The gangway watch should always have an immediate and continuous means of communication with the watch officer and should be required to check in following a preset schedule.

Inactive spaces should be locked and/or sealed.

Crewmembers must never rely on port security personnel—the ship must handle its own security.[6]

Prevention of Unauthorized Boarding while Underway

To prevent unauthorized boarding while underway, there is little most merchant vessels can do. Vessels should keep a vigilant radar and visual watch all around the vessel, not just ahead. Boarders typically board from astern, sneaking up in the radar's blind spot. When transiting waters known for hostile boardings, most vessels will be illuminated brightly.[7] Generally, lights facing away from the ship may ruin the boarders' night vision, making it difficult for them to see what is going on aboard the ship. If the ship's decks are illuminated, the boarders will have an easy time seeing what is going on aboard, but the crew will be peering out into darkness and will have a harder time spotting approaching vessels. Roving crew should try to stay in shadowed areas to avoid being a target. Operating companies should consider the purchase of low-light binoculars for vessels transiting hostile waters.

Crewmembers should be particularly wary of small craft paralleling a vessel's course and speed. Often, this shadow vessel is a decoy, so the crew should not focus all interest on that one vessel.

Ships should post roving patrols armed at a minimum with a whistle, radio, light, and nightstick. Some vessels charge their fire mains hoping to wash boarders off, if they are noticed in time. All hatches and doors should be secured from the inside except for the one door used by the watch, and it should be manned. Deadlights, if fitted, should be secured.

A well-patrolled vessel with lots of activity visible on deck may encourage some boarders to look for easier prey. However, many pirates are now armed with heavy assault weapons, and a roving guard with a nightstick or a fire hose will have little dissuasive effect.

Historically, most vessels have been unable to dispatch a distress call until after an incident has occurred. There is ongoing debate about arming the crews of merchant ships.

Seizing a lone crewmember has been used as a means of gaining control over the entire vessel. People off-duty should remain inside in a secured area. Persons who must go on deck should remain in constant communication with the bridge and should have several hideaway spots chosen beforehand, in case the vessel is boarded.

Hijacking

A hijacker is a person who intends to take command of the vessel and transport it to some other location, usually for political or religious reasons, or to steal the vessel and her cargo (sometimes also called piracy). A hijacking is similar to a terrorist attack in that the vessel is boarded and taken over, but no media attention is sought, unless the hijacking is for nonmonetary gain. The key difference is that the hijacker desires to keep the vessel underway and take it to a predetermined destination.

Piracy

Piracy is the taking by force of a vessel's cargo, cash, or other items of monetary value, or the stealing of the whole ship (sometimes called hijacking). Pirates are often seeking to raid the ship's safe and crew of valuables. It is wise not to broadcast information on the VHF or other nonsecure communication mode about cash receipts, payoff, or any other subjects involving valuable items that may be of interest to pirates. Crewmembers also should be cautioned not to discuss such topics ashore.

Pirates usually want as little media exposure as possible and ordinarily attack slow, easily boarded vessels that are unlikely to fight back. Piracy attacks have increased in number and severity over the last decades. In May 2000, a draft of an antipiracy code was presented to IMO's Maritime Safety Commission. It proposed standards of reporting, training, investigation, and cooperation among member nations in the tracking and apprehension of pirates. Also in May 2000, seventeen Asian countries adopted the Asian Anti-piracy Challenge and set forth a model action plan, which outlines antipiracy measures. (Antipiracy measures are described in the section on prevention of boarders.)

Terrorist Attacks

Terrorists are not pirates. Pirates are interested in monetary gain and want as little exposure as possible. Terrorists want as much exposure as possible and are usually fighting for some religious or political cause. While it is unlikely a cargo vessel will be the target of a terrorist attack (passenger vessels being more newsworthy), the prospect of a terrorist group seizing a tanker and threatening explosion or massive environmental damage is certainly within the realm of possibility.

Most merchant ships are not armed. There is great debate within industry circles as to the wisdom of arming merchant vessels with guns and other firearms, but as of yet, most commercial vessels remain largely unprotected. Some ships have a pistol stored in the master's safe, but this will probably prove ineffective against a zealous, well-armed, highly trained attacker.

Procedures if Boarded by Hostile Boarders

The vessel's SMS should have a detailed checklist or flow chart addressing actions to be taken in the event the vessel is boarded. Ideally, security drills would have exercised the crew for situations such as this, but few if any merchant ships conduct routine security drills. If a master suspects an imminent boarding or is being shadowed by a suspicious vessel, the nearest rescue coordination center (RCC) should be contacted and a safety "securité" alert should go out on VHF channels 16 and 70. If an attack does not occur, any urgency or safety messages should be canceled.

The following suggestions may help to resolve an incident:

1. Send a distress message if possible to the nearest RCC. Most GMDSS installations allow for the specification of hostile action in an automated distress call. Also contact local authorities, any nearby naval vessels, the Office of Naval Intelligence, the Maritime Administration (MARAD), and the Coast Guard, if possible. Sound the general alarm. A specific signal should exist indicating hostile boarding has taken place. The 1999 IAMSAR manual prescribes three remote push buttons to be located in the wheelhouse, master's cabin, and engine room that, when activated, send a preset attack alarm via satellite to alert authorities the vessel has been attacked.

2. In any communication include the name, official number, course, speed, last port, and destination of the vessel. Also include information on fuel reserves, if pertinent, and any hazardous conditions or cargo aboard the vessel. Include information on the vessel's available communications systems, including cellular phones, e-mail in staterooms, remote monitoring systems, and so forth. Also mention any injuries or health conditions aboard the vessel.

3. Try to determine who the terrorists are, what group they represent, and what they want. In the communications, transmit as much information about the attackers as is safely possible, including these items:

    Number of boarders, their gender, and their approximate ages

    Nationality and language spoken

    The group they represent and what their demands are

    Their level of sophistication

    Weapons they have and/or claim to have

    Communications systems used between the terrorists and outsiders

4. Explain noises and routine activities to the boarders to prevent them from reacting to something that is not a threat.

5. Do not fight back against armed intruders. In the past, pirates would simply tie up the crew and steal the money from the ship's safe. Modern pirates have no qualms about killing crewmembers who protest or struggle.

6. If armed law enforcement personnel arrive to resolve the situation, do not react to their presence or indicate their presence to the pirates. They may be dressed in civilian clothes to blend in with passengers or crew. Assist them in any way possible. Do not look at them, motion to them, or in any way reveal their presence.

7. Do not try to record the events unless you can do so safely. Make no effort to collect evidence of the pirate attack if doing so will draw attention to yourself. For example, do not attempt to take pictures or videotape unless you can do so safely.

Stowaways

The problem of stowaways has worsened as people become increasingly desperate in their efforts to escape war, famine, and financial and political unrest or simply to obtain a better standard of living. A stowaway is any person who obtains transportation without the consent of the owner, charterer, master, or person in command of any vessel or aircraft through concealment aboard such vessel or aircraft.[8] Later claims of refugee status will not change the original crime of stowing away, trespassing, and possibly other charges.[9]

Some stowaways intend to claim asylum, which will be dealt with later in this chapter, and some are simply criminals involved with trafficking drugs or other contraband. Modern stowaways are, by definition, not refugees. A refugee is a person who wishes to move to another country because of fear of persecution due to race, religion, political beliefs, or similar reasons.

Stowaways are a nuisance, a source of much trouble when found, and a source of danger to the vessel when not found. Stowaways in various parts of vessels have been the cause of fires due to careless smoking. Some have been found equipped with cooking gear and a supply of candles, matches, and several decks of playing cards. Stowaways hiding in the holds have been injured in various ways and have had to be hospitalized on arrival in port, at the expense of the vessel owner. If aliens, they must be sent back to the country from which they came, also at the company's expense. All of this points to the importance of thoroughly searching the vessel for stowaways.

Stowaway incidents have become increasingly newsworthy. Inevitably, if the media gets involved, local authorities will be much more thorough, international human rights groups may get involved, and the vessel will experience additional delays. With Internet and satellite communications growing exponentially and news being broadcast literally as it happens, what was once a relatively localized concern can become a global ordeal if not handled properly. Stowaways cause significant delays and additional costs; they may generate fines, adversely affect charter parties, and damage the ship or cargo, even unintentionally. Stowaways can also pose a significant health and safety risk to the crew if they are diseased or violent.

If stowaways are a concern, some vessels alter their sailing boards to reflect a less desirable port. The most desirable ports seem to be in North America or Europe. However, since many stowaways board with the collusion of port workers, this decoy may prove futile.

Stowaways are being found in increasing numbers, sometimes even outnumbering the crew. If there are numerous stowaways, a critical mass can be reached turning what was once a stowaway problem into outright piracy, especially if the stowaways are armed.

STOWAWAY SEARCH

Every possible precaution should be taken to prevent stowaways from taking passage on the vessel. Leaving from a port where stowaways are a likely possibility, the vessel should be searched thoroughly before leaving the dock and again immediately afterward. In high-risk ports, after the ship has sailed, the master may wish to anchor while still within the port and conduct a final search.

The best time to find stowaways is while the ship is still in port. If discovered after the ship has sailed, they become the ship's problem and the shipowner becomes financially responsible for the maintenance and repatriation expenses of the stowaways. Therefore, a thorough stowaway search should be conducted before the ship sails. Stowaways discovered before sailing should be immediately turned over to the local authorities with a full report of the incident.

A thorough stowaway search should include all open spaces not locked or otherwise secured, including cargo and machinery spaces. There are increasing reports of stowaways hiding in cargo containers and holds. Vehicles should be searched, including the trunks. Searchers should use all their senses during a search. They should listen for unusual sounds (breathing, coughing), notice unusual scents (smoke from cigarettes or cooking, urine, or feces) or look for garbage that is of an unfamiliar brand or in an unusual location. Crewmembers should search areas they are most familiar with so as to notice any abnormality. In the interest of safety, crewmembers should not search alone, and a means of communication should be established among all parties and the bridge. Searchers should carry, at a minimum, a flashlight, a nightstick, and a whistle. Most merchant vessels do not carry firearms; at most the master will have a gun in his safe. Some masters carry stun guns or mace with them aboard ship. Masters may want to consider the issuance of mace or pepper-spray to searching parties. Mace has the benefit of allowing the crew to spray and temporarily disable the intruder from several feet away, without having to make bodily contact.

There is now a device on the market that measures CO_2 content in containers and will allow a stowaway search of containers without having to break the door seal. The port authority or a ship's officer should ensure that before loading, all empty containers are checked and then sealed. Other available equipment includes infrared imaging equipment and other high-tech devices not normally carried aboard merchant ships.

If stowaways are found soon after leaving the dock they can more easily be sent back. If the vessel is only a few hours from the pilot station when stowaways are found, it may be worthwhile to return to the port where they boarded.

DISCOVERING A STOWAWAY

Once a stowaway is discovered, the master should notify the shipowners immediately with as many details as can be gathered. Most P and I policies cover financial loss incurred for the maintenance, removal, and repatriation of stowaways and some even cover the fines imposed by the disembarkation port. However, the policies often contain a provision that the underwriter may reduce or even reject a claim if it is determined that the ship did not take reasonable measures to prevent the boarding of stowaways. Regardless, the shipowner and the charterer (in some cases of container-bound stowaways) are still liable for all expenses. Additionally, costs incurred from a stowaway incident may be high but not high enough to meet the minimum deductible of a given policy, or the owner may not want to make a claim fearing adverse affects on future insurance rates.

If the stowaways are not returned to the port at which they stowed away, the agent at the port of destination should be notified.

When bringing a stowaway into the United States, the master should assemble all the details possible concerning the person: name, nationality, physical description, and photograph, if possible. All papers and other belongings should be taken and inventoried before a witness and given to the immigration officer on arrival. The master should also attempt to learn if any help was given to the stowaway by crew, passengers, or stevedores.

As the ship approaches the U.S. coast and before picking up the pilot, stowaways should be securely confined and precautions taken to make it impossible for them to get out through a porthole, kick-out panel, or other means. This usually means posting a crewmember on guard outside the room where stowaways are held. Stowaways have been known to jump over the side and swim ashore when the vessel was near a coast or proceeding upriver. If a stowaway escapes from the vessel, the company will be held responsible and may be fined. In all such instances the master should immediately notify the office or agent at the destination port and on arrival give all papers taken from the stowaway to the immigration boarding officer. In addition, the master should prepare a statement for the company and for the immigration officer, in case it is needed, explaining the precautions taken to prevent the stowaways from getting away. Ideally, the vessel's SMS will have a checklist and other procedures for the handling of stowaways.

When sending the arrival message, if not before, the master should mention that there are stowaways on board. On arrival, the boarding officers should be told about any stowaways. Some forms will require information about stowaways.

In some ports stowaways may be put in jail or may be held in detention by immigration, all at the expense of the ship's company. The immigration officer may order stowaways to be kept on board the vessel, in which case it is necessary to employ a guard all the time the vessel is in port. Stowaways have been known to escape from a vessel even with a guard on board. The vessel and master may be fined if a stowaway gets ashore.

If a stowaway is a U.S. citizen, the immigration officer will probably pass him but the company may want to file criminal charges. If he is a mariner, the Coast Guard will be interested. At any rate, he or she should be locked up and under guard until the master receives instructions from the office as to what is to be done.

It is poor policy for a master to let outside pressure from passengers, crew, or groups on shore have any influence on the treatment of stowaways. Many persons, having no responsibility in the matter, may plead for a stowaway's release while the vessel is in port. All suggestions from outsiders should be referred to the company office or agent or to immigration. Some entrepreneurial stowaways have also been known to offer to disappear at the next port—for a price.

The master should determine the port of embarkation and the nationality of the stowaway and prepare a detailed, written statement of the circumstances surrounding the incident. The master should look for clues that may reveal the true nationality of the stowaway such as language, religion, dental work (or lack thereof), tattoos or ethnic marks, signs of vaccinations, jewelry or religious emblems, types of food eaten, and so forth. If possible, a photograph should be taken and transmitted to the home office.

TREATMENT OF STOWAWAYS

If, after all precautions have been taken, one or more stowaways are found—they often travel in pairs—crewmembers should treat them humanely but should not pamper them. Unfortunately, it is sometimes necessary in dealing with stowaways to use force, either in self-defense or to subdue recalcitrant ones, especially when they are first discovered. However, the searchers should exercise great care to see that no unnecessary force is used on stowaways. They may seize the chance to sue the company for injuries received.

Sometimes when stowaways are found or make their presence known after the vessel is at sea, the passengers and crew will take up a collection for them. The master should not permit this, regardless of how harmless it may seem, because it only encourages the stowaways to try it again.

To date, there is no international convention regarding how stowaways are to be landed or repatriated; however, in 1996 IMO published nonbinding "Guidelines on the Allocation of Responsibilities to Seek the Successful Resolution of Stowaway Cases," which was distributed to member countries.

After stowaways have been discovered, the vessel's first scheduled port of call has been allocated by IMO to accept responsibility for them in accordance with the national laws of that country. If a case is unresolved by the time the ship sails, or if arrangements have been made for repatriation, or if the stowaway's presence on board endangers the vessel, this port is to consider allowing the stowaway to disembark and secure accommodations, at the expense of the shipowner. This first port of call is to assist in identifying stowaways, confirming their nationalities, and authenticating their documents, if possible; the port should also assist in the repatriation of the people. Ultimately, the burden falls on the shipowner to pay for the stowaways' meals, lodging, security, health, and repatriation.[10] Should stowaways claim asylum, the shipowner will be held responsible for their maintenance until the asylum case is resolved. Many port states refuse to accept stowaways, and there have been cases where stowaways have spent months, even years, aboard a vessel.

There have been several newsworthy cases of crews who allegedly mistreated stowaways, even throwing them overboard. Stowaways should be treated humanely; however, the master should make every attempt to disembark them as soon as possible for the safety of the crew and the vessel. Generally, a vessel will not divert from its regular route to disembark a stowaway unless the master has made formal arrangements with the target port to accept the person. If the stowaways pose significant health or security risks, the master may determine an alternate port of call specifically to deal with the stowaways' problems. Given modern health concerns such as autoimmune deficiency syndrome (AIDS), tuberculosis, and other communicable diseases ravaging developing countries, health concerns surrounding stowaways from these countries may become the paramount issues.

Stowaways are to be fed and housed, but no special treatment is required to accommodate religious or personal preferences. Although some masters have worked stowaways, it is considered extremely imprudent. The Immigration and Naturalization Service (INS) requires the owner, agent, master, charterer, or commanding officer of a vessel arriving in the U.S. with a stowaway to detain that person aboard the vessel until an immigration officer can complete an inspection of the person.[11] If necessary or prudent, stowaways may be handcuffed to prevent an escape in port or to restrain them.

Refugees

Acting under a legal duty to rescue life in peril at sea, the master may find that the vessel rescues not only imperiled mariners but, more commonly, refugees.[12] If refugees are encountered on the high seas, a master must take them aboard if their lives are in danger.

The Immigration and Nationality Act defines a refugee as a person who is "outside any country of such person's nationality . . . and who is unable or unwilling to return to, and is unable and unwilling to avail himself or herself of the protection of that country because of persecution or a well-founded fear of persecution on account of race, religion, nationality, membership in a particular social group, or political opinion."[13]

Refugee status is determined by the United States Immigration and Naturalization Service, not by the ship's crew.

The master should record the location where the person came aboard, or, if the vessel was at sea, the coordinates and the exact time the person was discovered and whether the vessel was in the territorial waters of any nation. The master should gather as much information as possible including the person's name, place and date of birth, nationality, occupation, documents in his or her possession, reason for requesting asylum or refugee status, health status, and so forth.

Unless the master receives advice to the contrary, the vessel should not deviate to return the refugees but should proceed to the planned destination. If the vessel has taken aboard refugees, the master should communicate the following particulars to the head office and the agent at the next port of call:

1. Name of the vessel, flag, and port of registry
2. Name and address of managing owners
3. Owner's agent at the next port of call
4. Estimated time of arrival at and departure from the next scheduled port
5. Exact date, time, and location of the rescue

6. Events leading up to the rescue
7. Number of refugees, including each person's full name, sex, age, date of birth, nationality, health status, and any family groups

Once the owners get this message, the United Nations High Commissioner for Refugees (UNHCR) should be contacted and UNHCR and the flag state will arrange for the refugees to be resettled. When the vessel arrives, the UNHCR is to take responsibility for the refugees for the resettlement process. Once the refugees have left the vessel, the vessel owners may make a claim for compensation for recoverable expenses (up to a $30,000 maximum) including subsistence on board ($10 per refugee per day), any fuel used during a deviation to rescue the refugees, communication expenses incurred during the rescue, any loss of hire caused by a delay in the refugees' disembarkation, and any additional port or agency fee due to the presence of refugees aboard.

Persons Claiming Asylum

The INS and the U.S. State Department are the lead agencies for an asylum issue. To claim asylum in the United States, an alien must have refugee status and must be at or within the borders of the country or must have arrived in the United States after having been interdicted on international or United States waters.[14]

SMUGGLING

In 1986 the United States passed the Anti-Drug Abuse Act, which increased the fines assessed against a shipowner whose vessel was found to have transported illegal drugs. However, given the potentially devastating financial result of steep penalties against a usually faultless carrier, since 1988 the U.S. Coast Guard allows owners to participate in the Carrier Initiative Program. The Carrier Initiative Program (CIP) of the U.S. Customs Service is aimed at private industry and offers a two-day antidrug-smuggling seminar for senior level managers, and a one-day seminar for midlevel managers and frontline personnel. Topics for the one-day seminar include the following:

Search techniques
Risk assessment
Concealment techniques
Document review
Physical and procedural safety
Personnel hiring
Drug source countries

Drug characteristics
Internal smuggling conspiracies

The two-day seminar adds these topics:

Legal issues concerning carrier liability
Penalty and mitigation procedures

Persons and companies desiring training should contact their local Customs Service.

Shipowners and carriers who sign an agreement with U.S. Customs agreeing to enhance security both in port and aboard ship will, should illegal drugs be found, have the degree of their compliance with the program considered as a mitigating factor in any proceedings against them. Owners whose vessels are engaged in trade with countries known for drug trafficking and who have received fines despite full compliance or those who feel it necessary to take extraordinary and expensive measures against drug trafficking can join the U. S. Customs Service's Super Carrier Initiative Program and receive assistance in reducing their exposure. (Chapter 11, "Customs," discusses this and similar situations in greater detail.)

BOMB THREATS

Any bomb threat should be taken seriously. Authorities should be notified and a search conducted. Searchers should look for anything out of the ordinary—packages or items that are not in their usual place or those that are shaped differently or are otherwise unusual.

Once a suspicious item is noticed, personnel should observe the following precautions:

1. Do not touch the item.
2. Do not use cellular phones, radios, or other electronics within 150 feet of the object.
3. Contact the appropriate shoreside security officer at once.
4. Contact the FBI, Coast Guard, port authority, VTS, and any appropriate state agency at once.
5. If the vessel is in port, evacuate at once.

If the vessel is at sea when the suspect item is found, there are several options:

1. Lock the space, don't touch the item, and wait until arrival at the next scheduled port so shoreside authorities can handle it.

2.   Divert to the nearest port that can handle such incidents.
3.   Evacuate the ship at sea.
4.   Evacuate to small boats if at anchor.

If the bomb threat is received by telephone, the person who answers the phone should try to keep the caller on the line for as long as possible and gather as much information as possible without interrupting the call. The Coast Guard bomb-threat forms provide the following suggestions. The exact words of the person calling should be noted.

1.   What does the bomb or device look like?
2.   When is it set to go off?
3.   Where is it?
4.   What kind of bomb is it?
5.   Why did you place the bomb?
6.   Who or what organization is responsible?

Caller's voice:

1.   Male/female?
2.   Intoxicated?
3.   Speech impediment?
4.   Accent?
5.   Scripted or ad lib?
6.   Recording?
7.   Voice altered by electronic device?

Background noises:

1.   Music?
2.   Children?
3.   Talk?
4.   Machines?
5.   Traffic?
6.   Airplane?
7.   Typing?
8.   Boating?
9.   Fan or vent?

SABOTAGE

Sabotage is the intentional damaging or disabling of the vessel or parts of the vessel. Unlike terrorists, most saboteurs have no grand cause to publicize and are usually not willing to give up their life to achieve their goals. Often, the saboteur is a disgruntled employee. Employers should screen candidates to the full extent allowed by law and should check all references. Aboard ship, a master should encourage friendly banter at mealtimes and in the lounges and should learn as much as possible about the people under his or her command. Deep psychological problems may be noticed early and simmering resentments diffused if the master pays attention to the personality traits of the people in his or her charge. While it is necessary for some officers to have passkeys, the master should restrict issuance of passkeys, especially grand masters, to those senior officers who have a direct need for the keys and are personally known to be reliable.

A vigilant deck watch will discourage attacks on the exterior of the ship. During rounds, crewmembers should check frequently over the side of the ship for bubbles in the water, unauthorized vessels, or any other suspicious activity. Chemical tankers and tankers carrying highly explosive or toxic cargoes should be aware of their increased vulnerability to an attack using fire and/or explosives.

Internal sabotage is a more realistic concern, as even the feeblest of minds can disable an engine by adding sand to lubricating oil or a contaminant to the fuel.

An increasing number of critical shipboard systems are computer controlled. The average American fourteen-year-old could probably disable a ship's computer systems in minutes. Merchant vessels, unlike naval vessels, are rarely designed with more than minimal security features. Merchant ship design provides easy access to antennas, backup battery systems, electrical cables, fuel and oil lines, food stores, potable water lines, and communications and navigation equipment, all of which are the master's responsibility to safeguard. Continuous observation and awareness and a happy, competent crew are often the best protections against internal threats.

For information on internal crew-related incidents, see chapter 4, "Vessel Accidents and Incidents."

CHAPTER 6

Communications

There are many texts available describing modern communications equipment and methods used aboard seagoing vessels. This chapter outlines general requirements only.

REPORTING REQUIREMENTS

While most vessels routinely communicate with their home office at least on a daily basis, some mention of the federal reporting requirements is in order.

The master of a U.S. flag vessel is to communicate with the owner, operator, agent, or charterer at least once every forty-eight hours. If the owner, charterer, agent, or operator of a U.S. flag vessel has not communicated with that vessel in forty-eight hours, he or she is required to immediately notify the Coast Guard and to use all available means to determine the status of the vessel.[1]

REGISTRATION OF EMERGENCY POSITION INDICATING RADIO BEACONS (EPIRBS)

For an emergency position indicating radio beacon (EPIRB) to be effective it must be registered with the National Oceanographic and Atmospheric Administration (NOAA). This registration expires every two years. For information or to receive a faxed registration form, masters can call 888-212-7283 or go to the NOAA Web site.

IMO STANDARD MARINE COMMUNICATIONS PHRASES (SMCP)

According to IMO's Marine Safety Committee, any officer in charge of a navigational watch must have the ability to understand and use the IMO standard marine communications phrases (SMCP) per STCW regulations.[2]

The SMCP tables are organized into four parts:

1. General spelling, positions, numbers, bearings, courses, distances, speed, time, and geographical names
2. Glossary of standard nautical terms
3. External communications phrases for distress, SAR, urgency, safety, pilotage, VTS, and other special situations
4. Onboard communications

Additionally, all officers must be able to speak English. The IMO Standard Ship Reporting System can be found in 33 CFR 161 Table 161.18(a). See figure 39.

AUTOMATED MUTUAL ASSISTANCE VESSEL RESCUE SYSTEM (AMVER)

The automated mutual assistance vessel rescue system (AMVER) is a voluntary worldwide service for vessels of 1,000 gross tons or more. U.S. law requires that the following vessels must report:

1. U.S. flag vessels of 1,000 gross tons or more operating in foreign commerce
2. Foreign flag vessels of 1,000 gross tons or more for which an interim war risk insurance binder has been issued under the provisions of Title XXI of the Merchant Marine Act of 1936

Most vessel participate using INMARSAT C or SITOR communications equipment. Information on AMVER and reporting can be found in *Publication No. 117, Radio Navigational Aids.*

GLOBAL MARITIME DISTRESS AND SAFETY SYSTEM (GMDSS)

All vessels were required to be in full compliance with the global maritime distress and safety system (GMDSS) as of February 1, 1999. GMDSS requirements apply to the following U.S. vessels on international voyages or on the open sea:

Cargo ships of 300 gross tons and over
Ships carrying more than 12 passengers

With the implementation of GMDSS, many vessels have done away with the radio officer's position. This places an additional burden on the vessel's deck officers. A GMDSS-equipped vessel must have two Federal Communications Commission (FCC) licensed GMDSS operators aboard. Usually the primary operator is the master, and the secondary operator is a senior deck officer. Like past ship stations, GMDSS stations must be inspected annually, usually by a qualified third party vendor. If the vessel is in compliance, a safety certificate will be issued. This certificate should be posted conspicuously. The GMDSS operators are responsible for operating and monitoring the communications and distress equipment aboard the vessel including the following:

1.   VHF radios including the digital selective calling features
2.   MF/HF radios
3.   INMARSAT A, B, and/or C systems
4.   Search and rescue transmitters (SARTs)
5.   EPIRBs
6.   Survival craft transponders
7.   NAVTEX and other marine safety information sources
8.   All associated printers
9.   Backup battery installations
10. GMDSS log[3]

Persons holding a valid FCC GMDSS operator's permit must also complete a USCG approved seventy-hour GMDSS course in order to be in compliance with STCW '95.[4]

One problem with GMDSS is the frequency of alarms received from vessels that are far too distant for the receiving vessel to offer assistance. During a normal four-hour bridge watch, it is not uncommon for the watch officer to receive over a dozen alerts, almost all of which are from vessels that are not even in the same ocean basin as the receiving vessel. The deluge of false alarms and distress alerts from remote areas has served only to desensitize watch officers. When a distress alert is received, the watch officer should allow at least five minutes to pass and observe if the alert is repeated or is answered by a shoreside rescue coordination center (RCC). After a suitable monitoring time, if no one responds to the alert, it should then be passed to a shoreside RCC via DSC or satellite communications. This practice will help eliminate the worldwide multiple forwarding of distress alerts.

Information on GMDSS can be found on the Coast Guard's Web site and includes the following:

- NAVTEX
- SafetyNET schedules (INMARSAT enhanced group calling system to disseminate maritime safety information)
- U.S. SAR areas
- NAVAREA charts
- Information on distress and safety calling channels
- AMVER
- International Ice Patrol
- Radiofacsimile and other marine safety broadcasts
- Digital selective calling information

REPORTS OF NAVIGATIONAL SAFETY INFORMATION

Masters should pass navigational safety information to governmental shore establishments. This may include information on the following:

Ice
Derelicts, mines, or other floating dangers
Casualties to lights, buoys, or other navigational aids
New (uncharted) or improperly charted wrecks, rocks, shoals, and so forth
Hostile action or action that may pose a threat to shipping

REPORTS OF HOSTILE ACTIVITIES

Ship hostile action reports (SHAR) should be sent to the National Imagery and Mapping Agency (NIMA) by whatever means is available. SHARs are used to disseminate information on hostile or potentially hostile actions against U.S. flag merchant ships. A SHAR is not a distress alert. SHARs can be reported by telephone to NIMA at 310-227-3147 or by telex at 898334. For a radio call to a shore radio station, the report should be formatted thus (station is PMO, ship is the T/S *Golden Bear* NMRY, date is August 21, 1996, at 1330 GMT):

XXX XXX XXX PMO PMO PMO DE NMRY NMRY NMRY
NRI TS GOLDEN BEAR 211330Z AUG 96
NIMA NAVSAFETY
BETHESDA MD
TELEX 898334
SHAR
CHINESE FREIGHTER HIT BY ROCKET FROM UNKNOWN LAND

BASED SOURCE WHILE TRANSITING STRTS AT 211200Z AUG 96 AT 03-14N 102-03E GUARDING COASTAL STATION (PMO) CAPT SMITH

ANTI-SHIPPING ACTIVITY MESSAGES (ASAM)

Anti-shipping activity messages (ASAMs) are used to report hostile actions against merchant vessels and are sent to NIMA as are SHARs. If a SHAR has been sent, an ASAM need not be sent as NIMA will generate and disseminate an ASAM as a result of the SHAR. The ship wishing to report hostile activity can file either the SHAR or the ASAM. ASAMs are distributed via the NAVINFONET system. All piracy, terrorism attacks, hostile actions, harassments, and threats while at anchor or at sea should be reported. Additional information can be obtained by contacting the following:

Marine Navigation Department
NAVINFONET Staff
ST D 44
4600 Sangamore Road
Bethesda, MD 20816-5003
301-227-3147

MARITIME ADMINISTRATION (MARAD) ADVISORIES

Maritime Administration (MARAD) advisories are issued by the Office of Ship Operations via the Marlinespike Electronic Bulletin Board System (BBS). MARAD advisories are published in the *Notice to Mariners* and on NAVINFONET, and MARAD can be accessed online. Information on the following is available:

Worldwide threats to shipping
Ready reserve foreign news
Treasury Department's office of foreign assets control
State Department travelers' advisories
Current maritime related legislation
Current press releases
Cargo preference
International and domestic marketing
Calendars of trade events
General public sales information
Special warnings

MEDICAL ADVICE

Publication No. 117, Radio Navigational Aids, outlines general procedures for obtaining medical advice by radio. Messages preceded by DH MEDICO indicate a request for or transmission of medical advice. The ITU List of Radiodetermination and Special Service Stations lists shore stations providing free medical message service to ships. These messages will normally be delivered only to hospitals or other facilities with which the SAR authorities have made previous arrangements.

Several commercial agencies provide subscription and pay-per-use medical advice services to vessels at sea. The best known is Radio Medico (CIRM), headquartered in Rome, Italy, which maintains 24-hour availability. It can be reached at:

Phone: 06-5923331-2
Fax: 06-5923333
Telex: 612068 CIRM I

REQUESTS FOR ASSISTANCE FROM U.S. NAVY

The following voice method should be used when hailing an unidentified naval unit for assistance:

"Any navy/air force/Coast Guard station guarding this net, this is T/S *Golden Bear,* emergency message follows:"

To reach the appropriate navy command center via telephone, section 4, appendix A, of *Publication No. 117* should be consulted for the phone numbers. To be truly useful, this publication must be updated via the *Notice to Mariners.*

To file a request for assistance via telex through an earth station, the following format should be used:

TO CINCPACFLT (for Pacific Ocean) or COMOCEANLANT (for Atlantic Ocean)

A. T/S *GOLDEN BEAR*
B. NMRY/1503249 (call sign and INMARSAT number)
C. LAT 09N, LONG 123E
D. 121345Z MAY 01 (date and time GMT, month, year)
E. SHIP BEING BOARDED BY PIRATES CASUALTIES ON DECK
F. REQUEST IMMEDIATE ASSISTANCE

CHAPTER 7

Shipping Articles

Shipping articles were created in part to stop the practice of shanghaiing sailors. In the past, sailors were occasionally drugged or kidnapped when too drunk to protest and put on ships to labor for months or even years under typically horrible conditions. Now, shanghaiing sailors is a scourge of the past, thanks to laws for the protection of mariners and the legal requirement for shipping articles—written agreements between master and crew.

BACKGROUND

Early legislation was confusing at best. In 1983, Congress enacted a partial revision of the laws pertaining to shipping in Title 46 of the *U.S. Code*.[1] Almost all of the statutes applicable to merchant mariners were repealed and then reenacted in revised form. Title 46 USC §10302 covers foreign and intercoastal articles. The new laws governing coastwise shipping articles can be found in Title 46 USC §10501. Regulations can be found in 46 CFR §14.

Shipping articles describe the written agreement between the master and the crew that covers the conditions and terms to which the crew will conform. Shipping articles also include particulars regarding the crew—ratings, wages, document numbers, social security numbers, dates of birth, and so forth. The articles give a description of the intended voyage, the ports of call, and the areas the vessel will travel, but they also usually include broad language indicating the vessel may sail anywhere in the world if necessary. Articles constitute a legal and binding document.

The top part of the articles form, containing the voyage details and the master's signature but omitting all crew signatures, is called the "forecastle card" and is posted under glass in the messrooms and sometimes also in a main passageway. If there are any riders attached to the articles, copies of the riders must also be posted as part of the forecastle card. The Coast Guard will supply CG-704 on request for use as a forecastle card.

The crewmembers sign articles on the bottom part of the form, which is confidential. Many companies provide individual articles on separate sheets for each mariner and most now use some form of computer program to generate their articles.

Shipping articles are divided into two classes: foreign or intercoastal, and coastwise. Articles are required by law and have different rules for each class. Stringent requirements apply to articles for foreign and intercoastal voyages; the rules are somewhat relaxed for coastwise voyages.

In the case of foreign or intercoastal articles, 46 USC §10304 shows the preferred format and wording of the articles. (See appendix A in this book for this form.) Coastwise articles are not subject to this section; they may be in any format and may use any wording desired, provided they clearly set out the nature of the agreement and they contain at least the minimum information specified by law.

On request, the Coast Guard officer in charge, marine inspection (OCMI), will supply the master with Coast Guard form CG-705A (fig. 13), Shipping Articles, which will be considered as a proper format to comply with the requirements of law. Any other form of shipping articles meeting the statutory requirements may also be used.

Shipping articles must, at a minimum, contain the following:

1. The nature and, as far as practicable, the duration of the intended voyage and the port or country in which the voyage is to end
2. The number and description of the crew and the capacity in which each mariner is to be engaged
3. The time at which each mariner is to be on board to begin work
4. The wages each mariner is to receive
5. Regulations about conduct on board and information on fines, short allowance of provisions, and other punishment for misconduct provided by law
6. A scale of the provisions that are to be provided to each mariner (this does not apply to coastwise articles)
7. Any stipulation in reference to draws and allotments of wages (foreign or intercoastal only; coastwise articles may not contain a provision on the allotment of wages)[2]
8. Other matters not contrary to law

Foreign or intercoastal articles must also include the text of the following section of federal law: "A seaman shall be served at least three meals a day that total at least 3,100 calories, including adequate water and adequate protein, vitamins, and minerals in accordance with the United States Recommended Daily Allowances."[3]

COASTWISE ARTICLES

Coastwise articles are required for a voyage "from a port in one state to a port in any other than an adjoining state." Shipping articles are not mandatory on a vessel that is making voyages solely between ports in the same state or between ports in two adjoining states. Shipping articles are required at all other times, and it is probably best to have the crew on articles even when it is not strictly required, in case the vessel is diverted while at sea.

Unlike foreign or intercoastal articles, coastwise articles may not contain a scale of provisions or any provision on the allotment of wages. All signing on and off is done solely by the master. Only a single copy of the coastwise articles needs to be made out.

When running coastwise, many of the crewmembers may remain on the vessel to make several voyages. In such cases, continuous coastwise articles can be used, the new crew being signed on as they are engaged.

FOREIGN OR INTERCOASTAL ARTICLES

Foreign or intercoastal articles are mandatory for a U.S. vessel (1) on a voyage between a port in the United States and a port in a foreign country (except a port in Canada, Mexico, or the West Indies) or (2) of at least 75 gross tons on a voyage between a port of the United States on the Atlantic Ocean and a port of the United States on the Pacific Ocean.

Voyages to Canada, Mexico, or the West Indies are referred to as "nearby foreign" and, because of their proximity to the United States, come under the rules for coastwise voyages. These requirements also do not apply to a vessel on which the mariners are entitled by custom or agreement to share in the profit or result of a voyage. These U.S. laws do not apply to foreign flag vessels.

The principal difference between foreign or intercoastal articles and coastwise articles is that under foreign articles, when any crewmembers are engaged or discharged in a foreign port, they must be signed on or off before a U.S. consular officer, whenever one is available. All engagements and discharges, whether or not before the consul, must be entered in the official log as well as on the articles.

The articles for a foreign or intercoastal voyage should be prepared in duplicate and the original retained on board as part of the vessel's permanent record.

ENGAGING A MARINER IN A FOREIGN PORT

When a mariner is engaged outside the United States on foreign articles, he or she must be signed on before the U.S. consul. Both the master and the mariner appear before the consul. If there is no consul at the port of engagement, the master may engage the mariner but should not have the person sign the articles. At the next port that has a consul, the consul must verify the crewmember's signature. The date of engagement shown on the articles should be the actual date that the crewmember was engaged, not the date that his or her signature was witnessed by the consul.

DISCHARGING A MARINER IN A FOREIGN PORT

When a crewmember is to be discharged in a foreign port, both the mariner and the master must appear before the U.S. consul if one is available. The release on the shipping articles is to be executed by both the master and the mariner in the presence of the consul. If no consul is available, then the release may be executed by the master and the crewmember alone.

Regulations allow the consul to excuse the master from personally appearing in the following circumstance: when the mariner to be discharged has been incapacitated by injury or illness; when his or her condition is such that prompt medical attention is necessary and cannot be furnished shipboard; and when the master cannot go with the crewmember to the consul's office without risk to the crew, the vessel, or the cargo.

In such a case, the master must send a written statement to the consul giving all the facts, including the reasons why he or she is unable to appear before the consul and the reasons why it is necessary to discharge the mariner. The statement should include an account of the wages due the mariner and should be accompanied by the cash to pay the wages due or, if the cash is not available, by an order to the owner for the amount due.

If the consul considers the statement satisfactory he or she may discharge the crewmember just as though the master were present. If the consul does not consider the statement satisfactory, he or she may refuse to discharge the mariner and may order the mariner returned to the vessel at the vessel's expense.

FAILURE TO JOIN IN A U.S. PORT AFTER CLEARING FOREIGN

If any of the crew fails to join the vessel when it sails from the last U.S. port after signing foreign or intercoastal articles, the master should not remove the person's name from the articles while the ship is at sea but should log the complete facts in the official log and have the crewmember's name removed from the articles by the U.S. consul at the first port. If there is no consul at the first port, the master should note that fact in the log and then remove the crewmember's name from the articles as in the case of any foreign discharge where there is no consul. The discharge should be marked with the date that the mariner failed to join, and full details should be entered in the official log. A crewmember who fails to board a vessel at the time specified on the articles he or she signed, without having given twenty-four-hours' notice of inability to do so, shall forfeit, for each hour's lateness, one-half of one day's pay; this is to be deducted from the mariner's wages if the lateness is recorded in the official logbook on the date of the violation.[4]

A crewmember who does not report at all, or subsequently deserts, forfeits all wages.

FAILURE TO JOIN IN A FOREIGN PORT

If a crewmember fails to join when the vessel sails from a foreign port, the master may have the person's name removed from the articles by the consul at the next port or, if it is likely that the crewmember will rejoin the vessel and the master will agree, the crewmember may remain on articles temporarily. In any case, the crewmember's pay should be stopped for the time he or she is off the ship. The master should communicate full details to the company and enter all the facts in the official log.

ALLOTMENTS

Usually at sign-on, a crewmember will indicate if he or she needs an allotment of wages. When on a foreign or intercoastal voyage, a mariner may designate that any part of his or her wages be paid by the shipping company directly to any of the following:

1. The mariner's grandparents, parents, spouse, sister, brother, or children
2. An agency authorized by the Department of the Treasury for the purchase of U.S. savings bonds for his or her account
3. A savings or investment account opened and maintained by the mariner in his or her name at a federally insured bank or savings and loan association[5]

An allotment to any other person or agency is invalid.

To be valid, an allotment note must be in writing and must be approved and signed by a shipping commissioner. Approval may be granted by the

U.S. consul, who performs the duties of shipping commissioner in a foreign port, and by the master, who performs the duties of shipping commissioner in a U.S. port.

VOYAGE DESCRIPTION

The voyage description is perhaps the most important part of the articles. It must set out the nature and probable duration of the voyage in clear and unambiguous terms. The voyage description is a binding part of the contract between the master and the crew. A mariner cannot legally be carried to sea against his or her will or be compelled to serve on a voyage other than the one described in the agreement that he or she signed.

The nature and duration of the voyage are described in the shipping articles. Any language that clearly describes the contemplated voyage may be used; however, the courts have held shipping articles to be invalid if they are so ambiguous or vague that they are not informative. For the guidance of masters, the U.S. Coast Guard has prepared the following examples of voyage descriptions.

Single Coastwise Voyage

From the port of Boston, Massachusetts, to one or more U.S. Gulf ports or places and such other coastwise ports or places as the master may direct and back to a final port or place of discharge in the United States on the Atlantic Coast north of Cape Hatteras, for a term of time not exceeding three (3) calendar months.

Series of Coastwise Voyages

From the port of Boston, Massachusetts, to one or more U.S. Gulf ports or places and such other coastwise port or place as the master may direct, for one or more voyages and back to a final port of discharge in the United States on the Atlantic Coast, north of Cape Hatteras, for a term of time not exceeding six (6) calendar months.

Foreign Voyage

From the port of New York, New York, to Antwerp, Belgium, and Rotterdam, Holland, and such other ports and places in any part of the world as the master may direct and back to a final port of discharge in the United States, excluding Alaska and Hawaii, for a term of time not exceeding six (6) calendar months.

Intercoastal Voyage

From the port of Philadelphia, Pennsylvania, to one or more ports on the Pacific Coast via one or more ports on the Atlantic and/or Gulf Coast and back to a final port of discharge on the Atlantic Coast for a term of time not exceeding six (6) calendar months.

Tramp Voyage

From the port of Galveston, Texas, on a tramp freighter (or tanker, as appropriate) voyage to ports in the U.S. Gulf and/or Caribbean Sea and/or South American and/or European ports and/or African ports and/or ports in the Far and Near East and/or Australia and such ports and places in any part of the world as the master may direct and back to a final port of discharge in the United States, excluding Alaska and Hawaii, not exceeding twelve (12) calendar months.

Voyage with a Confidential Destination

From the port of New York, New York, to a point in the Atlantic Ocean to the eastward of New York and thence to such ports and places in any part of the world as the master may direct or as may be ordered or directed by the United States government or any department, commission, or agency thereof and back to a final port of discharge in the United States, excluding Alaska and Hawaii, for a term of time not exceeding twelve (12) calendar months.

Employed Overseas for Long Periods

From the port of Hong Kong to Singapore and such ports and places in any part of the world as the master may direct and back to a final port or place of discharge for a term not exceeding six (6) calendar months; and from [latitude] and [longitude] to remain at offshore mineral and oil exploration sites or to proceed to, and remain at, offshore mineral and oil exploration sites off the Pacific Ocean coast of New Zealand and/or Australia for a term not exceeding twelve (12) calendar months.

SIGNING ON

Only a U.S citizen may serve as master, chief engineer, officer of a deck, or engineering watch aboard a vessel documented in the United States. If a documented vessel on a foreign voyage is deprived of a member of the crew for any reason, any position (except the position of master or radio officer) may be filled with a noncitizen until the vessel's return to a port at which, in the most expeditious manner, a replacement who is a citizen of the United States can be obtained. Each unlicensed mariner must be either a U.S. citizen or a documented alien admitted to the United States for permanent residence and aliens can comprise not more than 25 percent of the total number of unlicensed mariners aboard. If the vessel is operating with a construction or operating differential subsidy, then all of the crewmembers aboard must be United States citizens. Aboard passenger vessels receiving such subsidies, up to 10 percent of the crew may be noncitizens. Merchant mariners' documents will indicate the country of citizenship and should be checked when signing on crew.[6]

Regulatory language states that the crew must be signed on and off foreign or intercoastal shipping articles in the presence of a shipping commissioner; however, in 1980, Congress abolished the shipping commissioners, for all practical purposes, by passing an appropriations bill that prohibited the expenditure of any public funds for pay or administrative expenses in connection with shipping commissioners in the United States.

In U.S. ports, the duties of shipping commissioner now fall, by default, upon the master. In foreign ports, the U.S. consul continues to supervise the shipment and discharge of mariners.[7]

In order to guide masters in the shipment and discharge of mariners, the Coast Guard has prepared regulations to supplement the statutes.[8]

The Coast Guard has also issued a *Navigation and Vessel Inspection Circular* (NVIC 1-86) outlining the proper procedures. NVICs are updated periodically, at which time the existing NVIC is canceled and a new one is-sued. The latest version should always be on board.[9]

When the articles are opened, the master should sign and date the articles first, and then the crew should sign. After any of the crew-members have signed on, no changes may be made to the agreement without the written consent of each crewmember who has already signed the articles.

A rider is an attachment to the shipping articles that modifies or ampli-fies the printed form. If a rider is attached to the articles before the crewmembers sign on, it forms part of the original agreement, in which case it should be referred to in the main agreement form and also called to the attention of each crewmember before he or she signs the articles.

The law requires the master to have an agreement with each crew-member, but it is not necessary for every agreement to be the same. Occa-sionally, a master will sign on a mariner after the voyage has begun and will use a rider to modify the agreement for that crewmember only. For ex-ample, if a crewmember is hospitalized during the voyage and there is not enough time before sailing to obtain a regular company employee as a re-placement, the master might sign on a temporary relief mariner with a rider stating that he or she is engaged to serve only to the next port rather than for the duration of the voyage.

Many shipping companies are now printing and using shipping articles whereby each crewmember signs an individual agreement form rather than having the entire crew sign one agreement. This allows customized agreements for special circumstances, without the need for riders and therefore without confusion as to which terms of the agreement apply to a particular crewmember.

As with any contract, each crewmember signing the articles must do so freely and voluntarily with the knowledge of the terms of the agreement. It is therefore unlawful to sign on a mariner who is so intoxicated as to be unable to clearly understand what he or she is signing. Recent legislation mandates that the blood alcohol content of crewmembers aboard a U.S. flag vessel must not be over 0.04 percent, so drunkenness, not tolerated by any U.S. flag company, should not be a major issue during sign-on. If any mariner is unable to read the articles they must be read to him or her.[10]

Before each crewmember signs on, the person must present a U.S. merchant mariner's document properly endorsed for the rating in which he or she is to serve. This includes a food handler's endorsement for each member of the steward's department who is in any way engaged in the preparation or serving of meals. Each officer must also present a valid license in the proper grade. Each watchstanding deck officer must have a current radar observer and advanced radar plotting aid (ARPA) endorsement (if the vessel is so fitted) and each radio officer must have both a Coast Guard license and a current radio license issued by the Federal Communications Commission. Ship's surgeons, nurses, and pursers also must have valid merchant mariner's documents and USCG certificates of registry for the positions in which they intend to serve.[11] With the implementation of the Standard of Training, Certification, and Watchkeeping (STCW), additional documents are required to ship out.

The master should ensure that all crewmembers' documents and licenses will remain valid for the duration of the intended voyage. Documents that may be required, depending on the type of vessel, include the following:

1. U.S. merchant mariner's document—The MMD is now valid for five years and must be the newly issued credit-card-sized card with a color photo of the mariner. The card must be valid and properly endorsed. Check the citizenry notation.

2. USCG license—Licenses are valid for five years. Endorsements may or may not expire on the same date as the license. Radar endorsements rarely coincide with the license expiration date.

3. Certificate of registry—Staff personnel, such as doctors or pursers, must present valid certificates of registry.

4. STCW certificate—As of February 1, 2002, all mariners will be required to have a valid STCW '95 certificate when sailing foreign or offshore. Until then, STCW '78 certificates are acceptable.

5. FCC restricted radiotelephone operator's permit—The operator's permit is required of any person who will be using the vessel's VHF radios. The certificate is good for the lifetime of the holder and must bear the FCC seal on its face. An overly zealous USCG inspector could cause much disruption aboard the vessel if an officer is found to be without this permit.

6. FCC GMDSS radio operator license—Two GMDSS operators are required to be aboard while the vessel is at sea.
7. Preemployment drug and alcohol screens and fit-for-duty physicals.[12]

Documents often required by the shipping company (but not required by the Coast Guard) may be reviewed by the union or human resources personnel prior to sign-on, or this review may be the master's responsibility. These documents include the following:

1. Passport
2. International certification of vaccination[13]
3. Benzene card[14]
4. Respirator fit card[15]
5. Fit-for-duty slip

Even if a crewmember has been on the ship previously with the proper documents, the master should still insist that all crewmembers present their papers. Occasionally a mariner or officer will lose his or her documents and will try to sign on anyway, hoping that the master will not check. The crewmember cannot sign on without the proper papers. If time permits, the crewmember can go to the local Coast Guard office to apply for a duplicate or temporary document.

REPORTING THE SHIPMENT AND DISCHARGE OF MARINERS

After articles have been signed, a copy should be sent to the head office. Per 46 CFR §14.214, past requirements to complete form CG-735T are no longer in effect.

Dates of service on the vessel should not overlap. If a mariner has been discharged and reengaged, the mariner should be shown as a new crewmember on the date he or she joined after the discharge, not the date of the original engagement.

If a mariner's rating is changed, discharge papers should be made on the last date served in the old rating so that he or she can be engaged again on the date the new rating goes into effect. A second discharge should be made out for the mariner in this case, for the second rating. A crewmember cannot serve in two ratings on the same date.

From time to time additional persons may be on board the vessel, such as riding gangs, repair technicians, owner's representatives, and supercargoes. These people are not members of the crew for the purpose of shipping articles. They are not required to have mariner's papers, and their names are not entered on the articles. They are, however, added to the crew list, usually as "extra." Such people, who are not members of the crew but who are connected with the operation of the vessel, are not considered passengers; they are "persons in addition to the crew." The vessel's certificate of inspection specifies how many such persons may be carried.

DISCHARGING MARINERS

When a crewmember who holds a merchant mariner's document is discharged and paid any owed wages, the person should be issued a Certificate of Discharge to Merchant Seaman, CG-718A. Both the master and the mariner must sign the discharge. The original goes to the mariner, the yellow copy is for the ship or company records, and the white copy goes to the Coast Guard.

The master must pay the crewmember the balance of wages due when the crewmember is discharged or within two days of the termination of foreign or intercoastal articles, whichever is earlier.[16] This also applies to a crewmember on a foreign vessel while in a United States port and the U.S. courts are available to the mariner for enforcement of this regulation.

The discharges should be made up early on the voyage. The discharges sent in to the Coast Guard should be arranged in the same order as the names appear on the articles. Many masters incorrectly have crewmembers sign their discharges when they sign on. Then, if a mariner is not on board when the vessel pays off, his or her copy of the discharge is either sent to the office along with a wage voucher and any unclaimed wages or else mailed to his or her address on record. This commonly occurs when a mariner misses the ship or when one of the crew must be hospitalized. The master will then have all the white copies of the signed discharges. Of course, if a crewmember objects to signing a discharge that has not yet been completed, he or she cannot be required to do so.

While the above procedure is common practice, it is contrary to current law and regulation. Discharges are properly signed when a crewmember signs off the articles and signs the mutual release. U.S. Coast Guard NVIC 1-86 states that when a mariner is incapable of completing the release at the time of discharge in a foreign port, the certificate of discharge should be kept by the master until the end of the voyage and then delivered to the vessel's owner or agent along with the shipping articles. The mariner is to sign the discharge when he or she completes a mutual release and presents it to the company for payment of wages.

As previously mentioned, when a crewmember is discharged in a foreign port, he or she must be signed off in the presence of the U.S. consul, if there is one. If there is no consul at the port, the master may sign the crewmember off.

For each crewmember signed off, the official logbook entry as well as the articles should show the reason for the discharge. The usual reasons for discharging a crewmember as shown in the logbook and on the articles are as follows:

1. Mutual consent (sometimes abbreviated MC). A mariner may be discharged at any time, in any port, regardless of whether or not the agreement is completed, if both the mariner and the master agree to the discharge.[17]

2. Medical—not fit for duty (NFFD). When a crewmember is treated by a doctor and is declared not fit for duty, the master must decide if the crewmember should be discharged. This will depend upon how soon the person is expected to be fit for duty and how difficult or expensive it will be to obtain a relief. When a crewmember is hospitalized and cannot rejoin the vessel before sailing then he or she is unable to complete the agreement and should be signed off.

3. Failure to join. When a crewmember fails to sail with the ship and the person knew, or should have known, when the ship was departing, then the agreement has been broken and the crewmember may be discharged. To avoid argument, the sailing board should be properly posted sufficiently in advance so that all hands are aware of the sailing time. The board should be posted in strict accordance with the provisions of any applicable union agreements and a log entry should be made stating the time the board was posted and the exact language written on the board. Any subsequent changes should be logged as well.

4. Discharge for cause. A mariner may be discharged for cause in any port, but in a foreign port it is best avoided if possible. It will probably cost the company considerable expense to repatriate the crewmember to the United States and to send a replacement; in addition, it may be impossible to get a replacement before the ship sails. Unless the crewmember's conduct actually represents a danger to the ship, cargo, or persons, it is usually better to log each offense and then fire the person at the first U.S. port.

5. End of voyage. The voyage described in the shipping articles has been completed and the agreement between the master and the mariner has therefore ended.

It is important when making up the articles, the discharges, and other such forms that the mariner's name and document number be correctly entered. The crewmember's name should appear in full, not just the initials and surname (e.g., Pat Sean Jones, not P. S. Jones). The crewmember's document number should include the issue number, if any. If the number is 999-99-9999 D3, it should be written as such, not as 999-99-9999. The name and document number should be shown exactly as they appear on the mariner's document.

Forms should be checked carefully to see that the data entered on the various records all agree. Names of the ports of engagement and discharge should be written in full and not abbreviated (e.g., New Orleans, not N.O. or NOLA). Several spare pads of discharge forms should be kept on hand.

REPORTING CREW SHORTAGES
TO THE COAST GUARD

The required manning of U.S. merchant vessels is provided for by 46 USC §8101. Under this statute, a vessel for which a complement has been established, as shown on the vessel's certificate of inspection, is prohibited from being operated unless fully manned. If the vessel is deprived of the services of any of the required crew, the vacancies must be filled with replacements of the same or higher ratings, if available. Day workers may be able to fill these vacancies if the ratings can be covered.

The owner, charterer, or managing operator can be fined if the ship is operated with less than the required crew, except that the vessel may proceed on her voyage without all the ratings called for if all of the following terms are met:

1. Their services were lost without the consent, fault, or collusion of the owner, charterer, managing operator, agent, master, or person-in-charge, and
2. the master finds that the vessel is sufficiently manned for the voyage, and
3. replacements are not available to fill all the vacancies.

If the vessel sails shorthanded as permitted above, the master must report the cause of the shortage, in writing, to the nearest officer in charge, marine inspection (OCMI), in accordance with 46 CFR §15.725. This written report should contain the following information:

1. The name and merchant mariner's document number of each missing crewmember
2. A statement of the cause of the shortage
3. The port and the date on which the shortage occurred
4. A certification that no replacements of the same or higher rating were obtainable and that, in the master's judgment, the vessel was sufficiently manned to proceed safely

A copy of this and all completed forms should be retained in the vessel's file.

CHAPTER 8

Logbooks

With the increased reporting and record keeping requirements mandated by many recent regulations, the proper maintenance of logbooks is more important than ever. Masters should ensure that logs are kept in black pen with neat block letter entries and in twenty-four-hour time. In logs requiring copies of pages, red entries should be underlined to indicate the special status of the entry on the copies. Logs can prove to be invaluable sources of explanatory information in the event of an incident or mishap. Any falsification or critical omission from a log may render the entire log suspect and either damaging or useless. The master and the company will be better protected if every effort is made to ensure that all logs kept aboard the vessel are properly maintained.

LOGBOOK SECURITY

No unauthorized person should be permitted to read, examine, or take notes from the logbooks. All officers should be made aware of this. If a master has any doubt about whether a person should see the log, it is best to deny that person access to it. Insurance companies or others handling various claims will often send an investigator on board to take notes from the logbook. These investigators frequently assume a cloak of authority to suggest they have a right to examine the logbooks, and very often they are allowed access. Unless a person is known to be a representative of the company or has permission from the home office, no one should be allowed to see the logbooks. Anyone refused permission to see the logbook should be referred to the home office. (This does not apply to representatives of the Coast Guard, American Bureau of Shipping, National Cargo Bureau, or other government agencies. Such officials will have proper credentials.)

THE OFFICIAL LOGBOOK

There are few documents on the vessel that are as important to the master as the official logbook. It is required by law and must be kept in strict accordance with law and regulation.[1] The master is held personally responsible for the proper keeping of the official logbook and this duty should not be delegated to anyone else. If for any reason entries are made by another person, the master should check them carefully. All entries must be signed by the master and by a member of the crew as a witness, usually the chief mate. When an entry is made concerning a crewmember, the head of his or her department should also sign as a witness.

An official logbook is required on every U.S. merchant vessel making a voyage from a U.S. port to a foreign port (except a Canadian port) and on every vessel of 100 tons or more making an intercoastal voyage. An official log is not required on vessels in the coastwise trade or on vessels trading between U.S. and Canadian ports.

Official logbooks can be obtained from any Coast Guard OCMI. At the end of a voyage on which an official log is required, the log should be deposited with the nearest OCMI.

Manner of Making Entries

Entries in the official log should be written in black ink in a clear, legible, and careful manner. They should be in chronological order with not more than one line left blank between entries. Corrections should be made in the same manner as for the deck log—with a thin line drawn through the error and the master's initials accompanying the correction. Entries should never be erased or obliterated. It is best for entries to be block printed since the logbook may be read by an official who is totally unacquainted with the facts. No one should have to try to decipher any part of the log because of illegible entries.

Each entry in the official logbook is to be made as soon as possible after the occurrence to which it relates. If the entry is not made on the same day as the occurrence, then the entry must show both the date of the entry and the date of the occurrence. If the entry is about an event that happened before arrival at the final port of discharge, it must be made within twenty-four hours of such arrival. Each entry must be signed by the master and by the chief mate or another crewmember.

It is wise not to leave a line partially blank if the entries have stopped before using up a whole line. A line should be drawn from the last entry to the end of the blank line to prevent anyone from making unauthorized additions.

Failure to maintain the official logbook as required by law or failure to make a required entry is punishable by a fine. Making an entry more than twenty-four hours after arrival at the final port of discharge is punishable by a fine if the entry is about an occurrence that happened before arrival.

Required Entries

The following entries in the official log are required by 46 USC §11301:

1. Each legal conviction of a crewmember and the punishment inflicted
2. Each offense committed by a crewmember for whom it is intended to prosecute or to enforce a wage forfeiture, together with statements about reading the entry to the crewmember and the reply made to the charges
3. Each offense for which punishment is inflicted on board and the punishment inflicted
4. A statement of the conduct, character, and qualifications of each crewmember or a statement that the master declines to give an opinion about such conduct, character, and qualifications
5. Each illness of or injury to a crewmember, the nature of the illness or injury, and the medical treatment given
6. Each death on board, with the cause of death. If the deceased was a crewmember, the master must take charge of the mariner's money and property and must make an entry containing an inventory of that money and property and a statement of the wages due the mariner and the total deductions to be made from his or her wages. The master, the chief mate, and an unlicensed crewmember must sign this entry.
7. Each birth on board, with the sex of the infant and the names of the parents
8. Each marriage on board, with the names and ages of the parties
9. The name of each mariner who ceases to be a crewmember (except by death) and the place, time, manner, and reason
10. The wages due to a crewmember who dies during the voyage and the gross amount of all deductions to be made from his or her wages
11. The sale of the property of a mariner who dies during the voyage, including a statement of each article sold and the amount received for the property (see note)
12. When a marine casualty occurs, a statement about the casualty and the circumstances under which it occurred, made immediately after the casualty when it is practicable to do so
13. Recording of required conferences, such as the master/pilot predeparture or prearrival conference. These should specifically note what was discussed, such as expected under-keel clearances and escort tug conference. Most of these requirements can be found in 33 CFR. States also have their own requirements, which should also be recorded upon completion.[2]

Note: Item 11, while still law, is a holdover from the days when the master was allowed to sell the property of a mariner who died during the voyage. Current law requires that a deceased mariner's effects be given to the U.S. consul if the next port is a foreign port or be delivered as detailed in Coast Guard regulations if the next port is a U.S. port. The master is no longer allowed to sell the crewmember's effects.[3]

In addition to the items required to be logged by the statute cited above, the following entries must be made in accordance with Coast Guard regulations:

1. Weekly fire and emergency drills
2. Lowering each lifeboat to the water at least once every three months
3. Examining electric-power-operated lifeboat winches, motor controllers, emergency switches, master switches, and limit switches at least once every three months
4. Testing steering gear, whistle, and means of communication prior to departure from port. This is not the same as the test of steering gear, vessel control communications and alarms, emergency generator, storage batteries for emergency lighting and power systems, and main propulsion machinery (ahead and astern) that is required prior to entering into or getting underway in U.S. navigable waters.[4]
5. Drafts and load line markings prior to leaving port
6. The time and circumstances of at-sea opening and closing of watertight openings such as exposed cargo hatches; gangway, cargo, and coaling ports fitted below the freeboard deck; and port lights that are not accessible during navigation
7. Testing line-throwing apparatus every three months
8. Testing emergency lighting and power systems weekly
9. Timed load test of batteries for emergency lighting and power system every six months
10. Fuel oil data upon receipt of fuel on board: quantity received, name of vendor, name of the oil producer, and the flash point for the oil, which is certified by the producer
11. Visual inspection of cargo gear by a ship's officer at least once a month
12. Tests and inspections of all portable fire extinguishers, semiportable fire-extinguishing systems, and fixed fire-extinguishing systems annually

Offenses and Penalties

To assist the master in maintaining discipline on board the vessel, 46 USC §11501 specifies the following offenses, which must be logged, and the penalties for them:

1. For desertion the mariner forfeits any part of the money or property left on board and any part of earned wages.
2. For neglecting or refusing without reasonable cause to join the vessel or to proceed to sea in the vessel, for absence without leave within twenty-four hours of the vessel's sailing from a port (at the beginning or during the voyage), or for absence without leave from duties and without sufficient reason, the mariner forfeits from his wages not more than two days' pay or a sufficient amount to defray expenses incurred in hiring a substitute.

3. For quitting the vessel without leave after the vessel's arrival at the port of delivery and before the vessel is placed in security, the mariner forfeits from his wages not more than one month's pay.
4. For willful disobedience to a lawful command at sea, the crewmember, at the discretion of the master, may be confined until the disobedience ends, and on arrival in port forfeits from his wages not more than four days' pay or, at the discretion of the court, may be imprisoned for not more than one month.
5. For continued willful disobedience to lawful command or continued willful neglect of duty at sea, the crewmember, at the discretion of the master, may be confined, on water and 1,000 calories, with full rations every fifth day until the disobedience ends, and on arrival in port forfeits, for each twenty-four-hour continuance of the disobedience or neglect, not more than twelve days' pay or, at the discretion of the court, may be imprisoned for not more than three months.
6. For assaulting a master, mate, pilot, engineer, or staff officer, the mariner shall be imprisoned for not more than two years.
7. For willfully damaging the vessel or embezzling or willfully damaging any of the stores or cargo, the mariner forfeits from his or her wages the amount of the loss sustained and, at the discretion of the court, may be imprisoned for not more than twelve months.
8. For smuggling for which a crewmember is convicted causing loss or damage to the owner or master, the crewmember is liable to the owner or master for the loss or damage, and any part of his or her wages may be retained to satisfy the liability. The crewmember also may be imprisoned for not more than twelve months.

A crewmember who fails to be on board at the time specified in the shipping articles, without giving twenty-four-hour notice of inability to do so, forfeits one-half of one day's pay for each hour's lateness, provided the lateness is recorded in the official logbook on the date of the violation. A crewmember who does not report at all or who reports on board and subsequently deserts before the voyage begins forfeits all wages.[5]

The requirements for making entries relating to offenses and punishments are even more detailed than for other entries. These requirements must be followed exactly for the entries to be valid. If any offense becomes the subject of a legal proceeding and the entries have not been made exactly as prescribed, the court may refuse to receive the official logbook as evidence.

When an offense is committed, the master must make an entry, stating the details on the day of the offense. This entry must be signed by the master and by the chief mate or another crewmember. Before arrival in port (if the offense was committed at sea) or before departure (if the offense was committed in port) the master must read the entry to the offender, give the mariner a copy of the entry, and allow the person an opportunity to reply to the charge.

The master must then make another entry in the official log stating that the entry about the offense was read to the offender, and that a copy was given to him or her. The offender's reply should be logged word-for-word or should be handwritten by the person and included in—or attached to—the log. If no reply is made, the entry should so state.

The master should ask the crewmember to sign the entry that states the logging was read to him or her. It should be made clear that signing this entry merely confirms receipt and does not admit guilt. More than likely, the crewmember will refuse to sign, and the master should mark the log "refused to sign," sign it, and have a witness sign it as well.

Money, property, and wages forfeited for desertion may be applied to compensate the owner or master for expenses caused by the desertion. The remaining balance, if any, must be transferred to the secretary of the department under which the Coast Guard is operating, currently the Department of Transportation. All other forfeitures from the mariner's wages are retained by the shipowner.

Draws and Slop Accounts

The back of the official log provides a section for each crewmember to sign for cash draws and for credit purchases from the slop chest. The master should open an account for each crewmember as soon as he or she signs on.

If an error is made in entering an amount, or if the crewmember decides to change the amount, the master should not alter the figure already entered but draw a line through it and enter the new figure on the next line. Figures should never be altered after they are entered.

Most masters open the slop chest weekly. Prices of the items purchased by each crewmember should be summed and entered in the official logbook. On a long voyage during which many ports will be made, each person could be allotted two sections on opposite pages, one for draws and the other for slops.

Promoting a Crewmember

A crewmember who is promoted must be signed off the articles from the old rating and signed on in the new rating. An entry should be made in the official log for both events. If a crewmember is offered a promotion and refuses, it is wise for the master to enter that fact in the official log for his or her own protection.

Disrating a Mariner

Given cause, the master has the right to disrate a crewmember, subject to the provisions of any applicable union agreements. This is a very serious step that should be taken only after due consideration and after talking it over with the mariner's department head. Disrating is purely a corrective measure; it should never be used as punishment. A crewmember should be disrated only because of incompetency or almost complete inability to perform the duties of the rating. A person cannot be disrated below the next lower rating. To disrate a mariner in a foreign port, it is necessary to get the approval of the U.S. consul.

Disrating is seldom, if ever, done. The disrated mariner and the union will almost certainly dispute the action, possibly appealing to the courts. The master must then deal with the lost time and inconvenience of court appearances, with the chance that the disrating will not be upheld after all. It is doubtful whether the company will offer any help. If the crewmember's conduct does not actually endanger the crew or vessel, it is wiser for the master to log each breach of discipline and to sign the incompetent crewmember off at the first opportunity.

Items Often Neglected

Some common oversights and errors in keeping the official logbook are the following:

1. Failing to sign entries
2. Failing to have a witness sign entries
3. Failing to enter drafts and load line marks when leaving port, or omitting ports
4. Entering mean draft instead of position of load line mark
5. Omitting governing load line season from draft and load line entry
6. Omitting date and time of closing hatches and other openings before sailing
7. Failing to enter testing gear before sailing, or omitting the time
8. Failing to enter emergency drills, or making an inadequate entry
9. If weekly emergency drills were not held, failing to enter the reason why
10. Failing to make entries regarding injuries and illnesses to the crew and medical care afforded them, or entering them incompletely. The master should instruct the medical officer to notify him or her of the details as soon as possible after a mariner has reported sick or injured.
11. Omitting entries regarding mariners who leave the vessel for any reason before the end of the voyage, or making inadequate entries
12. Omitting wage accounts of such mariners
13. Failing to enter disciplinary loggings in detail
14. Failing to enter reading a logging to a mariner, furnishing him or her a copy, and the reply
15. Failing to log fuel oil taken and required data
16. Omitting weekly tests of the emergency lighting and power system

COMPANY LOG BOOK

For vessels that are not required by law to maintain official logbooks, the operating company may supply its own logs or records in whatever form it desires. These records will be considered to take the place of the official logbook and may be used for making the required entries. In this case, the records are not surrendered to the OCMI at the end of the voyage, but they must be kept on board available for review by a marine inspector for at least one year, except for separate records of tests and inspections of fire-fighting equipment, which must be kept with the vessel's logs until the certificate of inspection expires.

EXAMPLES OF LOG ENTRIES REGARDING CREW

For all log entries regarding crew, a date, time, and place must be included. If the vessel is at sea, the coordinates should be given as well as any other information that may be helpful, such as "approaching Hong Kong." The crewmember's full name, social security number, and rating or position should be included, along with a complete description of the offense and what penalties were incurred. If anyone ashore was involved or notified (e.g., consuls, medical personnel, police, or other authorities), this should be logged as well. The offending mariner must sign the entry after it has been read to him or her.

Manila, P. I.
5 Jan. 2000
1730

Elsa Turner, AB, 123-45-6789, was absent from duty without leave today from 0800 to 1700. For this offense Turner is fined by forfeiture from her wages one day's pay amounting to $_____.

/s/ Fletcher Christian   /s/ Karl Erlich
Chief Mate   Master

The above entry has been clearly and audibly read to Turner and a copy furnished her. Her reply to the charge was: "I have nothing to say."

/s/ Elsa Turner
/s/ Fletcher Christian   /s/ Karl Erlich
Chief Mate   Master

Boston, Mass.
6 Jan. 2000
1100

Watter T. Door, OS, 111-22-3333, returned to the vessel at 1000 stumbling and speaking incoherently. He had lost control of his bodily functions. He was tested for BAC, using _____ [machine description] at 1015 in accordance with the manufacturer's instructions. The test was administered by the master and

witnessed by the chief mate and deck delegate
_____ [give names]. The zeroing of the BAC test
apparatus was conducted at 1013 and was witnessed
by the master, chief mate, and deck delegate. After
three repeated tests, Door's BAC was shown each time
to be 0.05 percent, which is above the federal legal
standard of 0.04 percent BAC. Door was taken off articles as of 1030, 6 January 2000. All pay and allotments
stopped as of this date. Wages due are outlined below.
Because of his intoxication, Door was in no condition to
understand the logging that was read to him at this
time.

/s/ Sailor Mann	/s/ John Black	/s/ Frank White
Deck Delegate	Chief Mate	Master

Note: Normally this logging must be read to the mariner before departure from port. In this case, the master should wait until the crewmember
is sober enough to understand he or she has been let go. If for any reason
this cannot be done, the reason should be included in the log entry; otherwise the logging may not be valid.

Piraeus, Greece
21 Aug. 2000
1700

Wolf Larsen, AB, 123-45-6789, was absent from duty
without leave from 0800 to 1700. For this offense
Larson is fined by forfeiture from his wages one day's
pay amounting to $ _____.

/s/ O.T. D'Nied	/s/ J. Ripper
Chief Mate	Master

Position:
Lat. 07°22'N
Long. 123°14'W
Departure: Piraeus
22 June 2000
1130

Jane Doe, AB, 123-45-6789, failed to be on board when
vessel sailed for Barcelona at 1000. For this offense,
Doe is fined by forfeiture from her wages two days' pay
amounting to $_____. Agent at Piraeus instructed
that if Doe shows up to inform her that her transportation and all expenses involved in returning her to the
vessel will be charged to Doe and to have Doe sign a
statement to that effect. These instructions were con-
firmed by fax #20-192 at 1045. Agent told to notify U.S.
consul at Athens.

Wages due Doe as of 22 June 2000:

Earnings	$_____	
Wages due, 55 days	$_____	
Overtime	$_____	
Total earnings	$_____	$_____
Deductions	$_____	
Allotments (3)	$_____	

Draws	$_____	
Slops	$_____	
Social security	$_____	
Fed. inc. tax	$_____	
Unemployment ins.	$_____	
Fines	$_____	
Miscellaneous*	$_____	
Total deductions	$_____	$_____
Balance due	$_____	$_____

*This must be explained: union dues, child support, etc.
Doe's allotment stopped 22 June 2000. Doe's pay
stopped 22 June 2000.

/s/ Sailor Mann	/s/ Ethel Langer	/s/ Nate Foss
Deck Delegate	Chief Mate	Master

Note: The crewmember's allotment should always be stopped for the master's own protection. If the crewmember rejoins the vessel at another port, he or she can request that the allotment be reinstated.

Barcelona, Spain 28 June 2000 1800	Jane Doe, AB, 123-45-6789, rejoined vessel after failing to join at Piraeus on 22 June 2000. Doe's pay stopped from 23 June to 28 June 2000, inclusive. Doe instructed to turn to in the morning. The following bills, paid by agents at Piraeus and Barcelona, to be charged to Doe. Doe did not want her allotment reinstated. Pay to resume 29 June 2000.

Hotel and meals, Piraeus	$ 25.30
Taxi to airport, Piraeus	$ 7.50
Plane fare, Piraeus to Barcelona	$120.00
Hotel and meals, Barcelona	$ 35.40
Taxi to vessel, Barcelona	$ 15.00
Total expenses	$203.20

/s/ Sailor Mann	/s/ Ethel Langer	/s/ Nate Foss
Deck Delegate	Chief Mate	Master

29 June 2000 Barcelona, Spain 0900	The above log entries of 22 June and 28 June 2000, including list of expenses, have been clearly and audibly read to Doe and a copy of each given to her. She replied to the charges: "I guess I'll have to pay it."

/s/ Sailor Mann	/s/ Ethel Langer	/s/ Nate Foss
Deck Delegate	Chief Mate	Master

Note: When a crewmember misses the vessel and rejoins at another port he or she should not be logged for the time the vessel was at sea, but pay should be stopped for those days.

London, England	At 1000, Moe Stooges, AB, 123-45-6789, slipped on
20 Sept. 2000	deck. He complained of pain in his right knee and back.
1430	Stooges was sent to Mercy Hospital, Burdett Road, by
	taxi. Stooges returned to vessel at 1400 on 20 Septem-
	ber. He had a note from the doctor saying that he
	should be taken off duty for five days. Medicine was
	prescribed [record medicine], which was ordered
	through the agent. Witness to accident:
	M. Spike, Bosun
	2244 Maiden Lane
	Sailor Town, CA 94876

/s/ Mike Spike	/s/ John Black	/s/ Mathew Tanner
Bosun	Chief Mate	Master

Rotterdam, Holland	Moe Stooges, AB, 123-45-6789, returned to duty.
26 Sept. 2000	
0800	

/s/ Mike Spike	/s/ John Black	/s/ Mathew Tanner
Bosun	Chief Mate	Master

Note: In the above incident the details should be entered in the medical log, and Coast Guard form CG-2692 should be completed.

Position:	Bill Pyro, AB, 123-45-6789, set fire to his mattress
Lat. 07°22'N	while smoking in his bunk. Fire extinguished by wiper,
Long. 123°14'W	Joe Grease. Mattress and sheets damaged beyond re-
22 June 2000	pair. Pyro to be charged with cost of mattress and two
1130	sheets as follows:

1 innerspring mattress	$47.50
2 white sheets at $4.50 each	9.00
Total	$56.50

/s/ B.G. Eats	/s/ John Plimsoll	/s/ Frank Fair
Steward	Chief Mate	Master

Position:	The above entry has been clearly and audibly read to
Lat. 07°22'N	Pyro and a copy given to him. He replied to the charge:
Long. 123°14'W	"I must have fallen asleep."
22 June 2000	
1200	

/s/ B.G. Eats	/s/ John Plimsoll	/s/ Frank Fair
Steward	Chief Mate	Master

Bremen, Germany 4 Oct. 2000 0900	Harbor police came on board and reported that Joe Grease, wiper, Z-00001, was arrested at 0500.

Bremen, Germany 4 Oct. 2000 1700	Joe Grease, wiper, 123-45-6789, absent from duty without leave from 0800 to 1700. For this offense Grease is fined by forfeiture from his wages one day's pay amounting to $ _____. Grease not available to have logging read to him.

/s/ Mike Spike   /s/ Ilbe Watchin   /s/ Ima Goodmun
Crew Delegate   Chief Mate   Master

Hamburg, Germany 5 Oct. 2000 1500	Joe Grease, wiper, 123-45-6789, in custody of police at Bremen, taken off articles by U.S. consul, Hamburg, as of this date, 5 Oct. 2000. Pay stopped effective this date. Grease not available to have logging read to him. Allotment stopped 4 Oct. 2000. Wages due Grease:

Earnings
   Wages due, 118 days $_____
   Overtime $_____
   Total earnings $_____ $_____
Deductions
   Allotments (4) $_____
   Draws $_____
   Slops $_____
   Social security $_____
   Fed. inc. tax $_____
   Unemployment ins. $_____
   Fines $_____
   Miscellaneous* $_____
   Total deductions $_____ $_____
Balance due $_____
*This must be explained: union dues, child support, etc.

/s/ Ilbe Watchin   /s/ Ima Goodmun
Chief Mate   Master

Position: Lat. 07°22'N Long. 123°14'W 15 Nov. 2000 1600	Pintle N. Gudgeon, oiler, 222-33-4444, disobeyed a direct order from the chief engineer. Gudgeon was told to clean up spilled oil from the deck around the evaporator. She refused, saying: "That's not my job. Get the guy who spilled it to clean it up." For this offense Gudgeon is discharged for cause on arrival at the next port.

/s/ John Black   /s/ Frank White
Chief Mate   Master

Position: The above log entry has been clearly and audibly read
Lat. 07°22'N   to Gudgeon and a copy was given to her. She replied to
Long. 123°14'W   the charge: "You can't fire me. I'll see the union about
15 Nov. 2000   this."
1700

            /s/ John Black   /s/ Frank White
             Chief Mate   Master

Kingston, Jamaica   Signed off Pintle N. Gudgeon, oiler, 222-33-4444, dis-
18 Nov. 2000   charged for cause. Wages due Gudgeon:
1300

Earnings	$_____	
Wages due, 69 days	$_____	
Overtime	$_____	
Total earnings	$_____	$_____
Deductions		
Allotments (2)	$_____	
Draws	$_____	
Slops	$_____	
Social security	$_____	
Fed. inc. tax	$_____	
Unemployment ins.	$_____	
Fines	$_____	
Miscellaneous*	$_____	
Total deductions	$_____	$_____
Balance due		$_____

*This must be explained: union dues, child support, etc.

  /s/ Mike Spike   /s/ John Black   /s/Frank White
  Crew Delegate   Chief Mate   Master

Note: In this example, Gudgeon could also have been fined up to four days' pay for disobedience.

Kingston, Jamaica   Signed off Joseph Conrad, AB, 333-44-5555, mutual
19 Nov. 2000   consent. Wages due:
1400

Earnings		
Wages due, 69 days	$_____	
Overtime	$_____	
Total earnings	$_____	$_____
Deductions		
Allotments (2)	$_____	
Draws	$_____	
Slops	$_____	
Social security	$_____	_____
Fed. inc. tax	$_____	
Unemployment ins.	$_____	

Fines	$_____		
Miscellaneous*	$_____		
Total deductions	$_____	$_____	
Balance due		$_____	

*This must be explained: union dues, child support, etc.

Signed on Jack London, AB, 999-88-7777, as replacement.

/s/ Mike Spike	/s/ John Black	/s/ Frank White
Crew Delegate	Chief Mate	Master

THE DECK LOG AND REMOTE MONITORING

The deck log, or bridge logbook, is a continuous record of the activities of the vessel while in service, both at sea and in port. Some vessels use electronic deck logs that are maintained on computer disk. Some vessels also have ECDIS systems that record and store the vessel's movement information as well as the motion of other tracked contacts. Some passenger vessels have audio and video recording devices on the bridge, similar to the black boxes on airliners. These are called voyage data recorders (VDRs) in the maritime industry.[6]

GMDSS equipment keeps electronic logs of messages sent and received.

Voyage Data Recorders

Airliners have used black boxes for decades, but equipment offering the same sort of recording and monitoring aboard ship is relatively new to the maritime industry. Modern VDRs can record and play back information on personal computers for the reconstruction of incidents or simply to review an event or a watch. IMO is currently revising chapter 5 of the SOLAS Convention to require the fitting of VDRs by July 2002 on newly built passenger ships. Other passenger ships will be required to install VDRs by July 2004. Newbuildings over 3,000 gross registered tons will also have to be fitted, but the target date is unclear.

IMO is also working on VDR capability and testing requirements.[7] An IMO approved VDR must record the following:

1. Date and time, ideally taken from a source not on the vessel
2. Ship's position, speed, and heading
3. Wind speed and direction
4. Hull motion and stresses
5. Bridge and communications audio
6. Radar and ARPA information
7. Rudder and engine orders and responses

8. Depth soundings
9. Alarms
10. Watertight integrity/hull openings monitored
11. Watertight/fire door status

While most merchant vessels do not currently have VDRs, most vessels will be required to be so fitted soon. It is doubtful that such equipment will replace the paper deck log currently required to be maintained aboard all ships.

Paper Deck Logbook

All paper logs must reflect the same information that is being recorded by any electronic devices aboard. Some ships have engine room and position information streamed back to the head office using satellite uplinks. Many mariners feel Big Brother is watching, but the maritime industry still faces less remote monitoring than the airline industry. Undoubtedly, within the near future, continuous remote monitoring of vessels at sea will increase in scope and depth. Regardless of the logging method, the advice remains the same: entries should be concise, accurate, truthful, thorough, and timely.

It is very important to the master and to the company that the logbook be clear, complete, and correct. The book must reflect a true and accurate record of the voyage and of activities in port. It is the master's responsibility to see that entries are made of all important matters. A correct record of what took place on the voyage must be entered in sufficient detail to present a true picture.

All names and titles should be clearly and legibly block-printed. This includes pilots, Coast Guard officials, classification society surveyors, and others boarding the vessel. Generally, entries should be made in black ink, with these exceptions: arrival and departure times as well as confirmation of drills and testing of gear should be made in red ink and underlined, to emphasize their status on any copies being made.

If a statement of facts or a report is required, all the details should be taken from the logbook. All the facts must be straight and in order, thus precluding any argument at a later date and also avoiding much correspondence.

Masters should not make any entry of an important nature without due consideration and discussion with the officers acquainted with the facts. Many masters make notes regarding important events or casualties on a pad so that the entry can be arranged in proper sequence and made as letter-perfect as possible before it is inserted in the logbook. All officers should know that a careless entry that is not consistent with the facts, or an incomplete or untrue entry may, at the very least, reflect against the company's interests.

ROUTINE ENTRIES

Masters should not permit the officers to crowd too much on one page. If necessary, they can use the next page and head it with the same date or attach a supplemental sheet.

Entries relating to a check on mooring lines, bearings, decks, and tanks as well as to other duties of the officer on watch should not be mere formalities. The watch officers must report what was actually done, not what should have been done.

Entries regarding the following are of particular importance for the proper handling of various claims:

1. Damage to the vessel, environment, equipment, or cargo, and the cause
2. Actual precautions or security measures taken
3. Required meetings and conferences (e.g., prearrival, escort, safety, etc.)
4. Salvage or other assistance rendered or received
5. Reported injuries, if the company requires them
6. Touching or striking fixed, submerged, or floating objects
7. Resting on the bottom either alongside or at anchor
8. Touching bottom at any time
9. Any preventative or precautionary actions taken and the reason

DAMAGE TO OR BY THE VESSEL

The entry should include a description of the damage, if any, or a statement such as, "Damage unknown at this time." It should not include an opinion or speculation—only facts. The master should also enter the fact that bilge or tank soundings were taken, how often, and the results, as well as soundings around the vessel, if necessary, and the water depths found.

Damage of any kind to or by tugboats, barges, lighters, floating cranes, launches, or other craft alongside should be entered in the log, with the extent of the damage, if known. Also included should be the name or number of the craft involved, the state of the weather, and whether another vessel was passing at excessive speed. If the ship is damaged by another craft it will be practically impossible to get an admission of fault or responsibility from the person-in-charge of the other craft. It is important, therefore, for the master to note all facts in the logbook.

In the event of grounding or collision, the entry should include the position, full details of every maneuver made before and after the accident, every effort made to avoid the accident, and an account of damage sustained, as far as can be ascertained. In case of grounding, the entry should describe the efforts made to refloat the vessel, any stability calculations performed, and the names of tugs or other vessels assisting or standing by. If it becomes necessary to abandon the vessel, every effort should be made, short of endangering lives, to save the current deck, engine, and official logbooks and the current bell book.

Most vessels have various forms of electronic recording devices, and some passenger ships have sound and video recorders on the bridge. Watchstanders must understand the importance of consistency and thoroughness. Paper logs must match electronic recording devices, such as bell recorders and/or the ECDIS, GMDSS, and GPS logs, or the master will have a lot of explaining to do under less-than-favorable circumstances.

CORRECTIONS

No page should be torn or mutilated and no erasures or obliterations should be made. The master should correct errors in the logbook by drawing a single line through the incorrect entry and then initialing the correct entry. The incorrect entry should remain clearly visible; to render it illegible or to obliterate any part of it may lead to suspicion of falsification of the entry.

LATE ENTRIES

Late entries should be added at the end of the log entry for the watch, if possible, rather than trying to insert it with arrows and lines. Late entries can be headed "Late entry: 1955 open No. 2 hatch."

All of this may seem elementary, but it is surprising how often some officers forget to make the necessary entries.

WEATHER

At sea, the master should pay particular attention to entries regarding heavy weather. All efforts to avoid heavy weather damage should be logged, such as changing course, slowing down, or heaving to. The entry should note how the vessel is riding and whether or not she is shipping any seas, especially if it is necessary to have the crew on deck to secure gear or to repair damage. Most preprinted logs have no column for vessel motion, so it is imperative deck officers include this information as part of their signing out at the end of their watch.

Aboard freighters, deck officers often forget to enter the times of starting and stopping cargo ventilation fans along with the reason for stopping the fans, such as heavy rain or spray. On older ships that are not equipped with blower systems, the time of trimming, covering, or unshipping ventilators should be entered with the reason for these acts. The weather entries in the log must substantiate those regarding the fans. When at sea, entries regarding cargo ventilation should be made at least daily.

Even in good weather when there is no concern about damage to the vessel, weather entries must be made. Many lawsuits have been filed by crewmembers who claimed to have slipped on rain-slick decks on days when the logbook showed that there was not a cloud in the sky. Weather entries are equally important in port when many persons other than the crew may come aboard the vessel.

Vessels use various methods for recording the weather. Some use National Weather Service codes while others use abbreviations. It is helpful to deck officers for the master to clearly post the symbols and methods he or she prefers to use in the deck log.

Many officers overlook entering precautions taken during periods of low visibility, such as slowing down, closing all watertight doors, and sounding whistle signals. A Coast Guard investigator examining the logbook will rightly question an entry reading, "1030 thick fog set in," with no further details, nor will a vague entry such as "all precautions taken" suffice. Such an entry is of little value because it does not relate exactly what those precautions were. An investigating officer may have a different idea than the master of what constitutes all precautions.

DEVIATION AND DIVERSION

Whenever a master receives orders changing the vessel's destination, he or she should enter the time and position of the vessel when the message is received. This log entry, and perhaps also a copy of the communication, may have to be shown to the government authorities at the new destination. This is especially important if the change of orders comes by telephone; in the absence of a fax or telex, the log entry will be the only written proof of the diversion message.

PRATIQUE

At each port of call where the vessel must pass pratique, the master should enter the type of pratique granted along with the time.

CARGO, BALLAST, AND STABILITY

The log should contain full details regarding loading and discharging of cargo or ballast, including the number of longshore gangs required and the times they board and leave the vessel. Also included should be a record of the time and the reason for any work stoppage: equipment breakdowns, weather, stopping for meals or for the day, waiting for cargo or lighters, and so forth. This information may be required months later, and the successful settlement of a claim may depend upon an accurate entry in the logbook.

Many companies require that the vessel's stability, stated as so many feet of metacentric height (GM), be entered in the log upon sailing from each port. This entry should also be placed in the official log.

Some masters request that the vessel's rolling period be recorded in the log. This may be helpful in resolving claims as well as noting changes in the vessel's stability condition during a long sea passage.

END OF PASSAGE

At the end of each passage the master and the chief engineer should inspect the hull, rudder, and propeller (while it is being turned over, if possible) for damage of any kind. The results of this inspection should be entered in the log.

IDLE STATUS

If the vessel is laid up or otherwise put on idle status with less than the normal complement of personnel, the master should follow the company's instructions, if any, regarding the keeping of logbooks. Drafts should be taken daily and logged, and frequent inspections of the vessel should be made.

REPAIR STATUS

When a vessel goes into a shipyard or is laid up for repairs, the log of the previous voyage is usually continued unless the home office instructs otherwise. Entries should include the time work commenced each day and the time it stopped. If work is continued around the clock, that fact should be noted in the log. The master should enter in the log in block letters the names and titles of all officials, such as Coast Guard inspectors and American Bureau of Shipping surveyors, who board the vessel and who have any connection with the repair work. The draft should be taken and logged daily while the vessel is in the water, and weather entries should be made, particularly if any sandblasting, coating, or paintwork is being done.

OTHER LOGS

Although the deck logbook is the primary official record of the vessel's activities, there are various other documents, some required by law, that should receive similar care and attention. In the event of a casualty, many ship's records besides the logbook may be taken for use in an official investigation. If any occurrence on the vessel becomes the subject of a civil lawsuit, the plaintiff's attorney is sure to subpoena every paper that he or she can think of.

Bell Books

Whenever the vessel is maneuvering in harbor, an accurate record of engine orders must be kept in the bell book. On some ships, this is done electronically. The watch officers should also note in the bell book the name of the pilot and the time of boarding, the time the ship passes navigational marks, first or last line, when tugs come alongside, whether tug or ship lines were used, and so forth. Every detail that might possibly be referenced later should go into the bell book; unnecessary data can always be omitted later from the deck logbook. The old adage, "Not everything in the bell book should go into the logbook, but everything in the logbook should be found in the bell book," is still a good rule to follow. The bell book is used in making the deck logbook entry and must be kept with the same care as the logbook itself. Errors in the bell book should be corrected in the same manner as for the logbook. Many officers have a bad habit of making bell book entries in pencil instead of pen. The bell book should be kept in black ink just like the deck log.

When a vessel maneuvering in harbor reduces speed to avoid damage to other vessels or property, the reason for slowing down should be noted, such as "passing pipeline dredge." Whenever passing a vessel whose mooring lines are slack, that fact should be noted in the log. Vessels that suffer damage from passing ships because of the deficiency of their own moorings often claim excessive speed on the part of the passing vessel as the cause of the damage.

Medical Logs

Medical logbook entries are very important in proving the cause and extent of an injury or illness and the adequacy of treatment. The company will undoubtedly have report forms to be filled out in case of illness or injury to any of the crew. These should be treated as extensions of the medical log itself and should be complete and accurate in every respect. Personal injury cases often surface years after the alleged incident and may not come to trial for several years more. Especially important is the inclusion of any medical advice received by radio, phone, or fax. Copies of records pertaining to the illness or injury should be included if possible; if not, the entry should contain an indication of where the records are kept. Photos, where appropriate, are helpful as well. Medical logs should be maintained in the strictest of confidentiality.

Oil Record Book

The oil record book is required by federal law and by international agreement and must be current whenever a vessel enters a port.[8] The oil record book is scrutinized more often now than was formerly the case, particularly on tankers. In past criminal investigations, not making a required entry has been considered the same as making a false statement and has resulted in convictions. (See chapter 2, "United States Laws," for more information.)

National Invasive Species Act of 1996 (NISA)— Ballast Record Book

The National Invasive Species Act of 1996 requires that U.S. flag vessels and all vessels operating in U.S. waters maintain a ballast record book and report their ballasting activities.[9] The ballast log of a ship must contain the entries outlined in 33 CFR §151.2045.[10] Vessels will be subject to random boardings and inspections to ensure compliance.[11]

MARPOL Annex V—Garbage Log

All vessels must maintain a garbage log—a written record of garbage handling aboard ship.[12] It can be in any format as long as the requisite entries are made; many ships use a binder or bound notebook. The log must be prepared at the time of operation, certified as correct by the master, and kept aboard for two years. It must be available to the U.S. Coast Guard at any time. The following must be recorded for all garbage that is incinerated or discharged overboard, to another ship, or ashore:

1.   Type of operation (discharged overboard, incinerated, etc.)
2.   Date
3.   Location (name of port or coordinates and distance offshore, or name and official number of receiving ship)
4.   Amount of garbage in cubic meters
5.   For discharges at sea, a description of the garbage (floating dunnage, packing, ground paper or rags, victual wastes, incinerated ash, incinerated plastic residue, etc.)

Communications Logs

The master should keep copies of all radio, phone, telex, e-mail, or fax messages that are sent or received. Any that pertain to vessel casualties must be retained for examination by government investigators and company attorneys. Any that relate to possible civil claims may have to be produced in court at a later date. Otherwise, normal messages regarding routine company business should be retained until the end of the voyage and then either filed or disposed of, in accordance with the company's instructions.

Vessels must maintain a GMDSS log as well as a VHF log for routine radio communications.[13] Watch officers should enter the details of arrangements made with other vessels in the VHF log. For example, should there be an incident, a log entry stating "1025 VHF Ch. 13, passing arrangements made with the *Mary Maersk*" is not as helpful as the entry that says "1025 Ch. 13, agreed to port-to-port passing at 1.0 nm with *Mary Maersk*."

Course Recorder

If a vessel is involved in a collision the master can be sure that the government investigators will take the course recorder chart, and when they are done with it the attorneys for the other vessel will want it. The second mate should check the course recorder daily, correct the time and course settings if necessary, and note the date on the paper at the same time. It will be easiest if the course recorder is kept on GMT rather than local time. As each roll of course recorder paper is used up, the starting and ending dates should be written on the outside of the roll, and it should then be filed away with the completed logbooks and bell books.

Global Positioning System (GPS) and Position Logs

Most vessels maintain some type of a position log, even if only a spiral note-book. Such a log usually contains position information as well as course, speed, and leeway information. Ships also usually maintain informal anchor bearing logs. These logs are usually not signed by the watch officer and are often kept in pencil. Regardless, such a log may prove invaluable after some unforeseen incident.

There are many other logs, such as cargo logs, pumping logs, compass observation books, and chronometer rate books, which should all be maintained in a professional, neat, and orderly fashion.

CHAPTER 9

Documents and Certificates

Many documents and certificates of varying degrees of importance are necessary in the operation of a modern merchant vessel. One of a master's first duties on taking command should be to see that all the necessary documents are on board and current. Most vessels and shoreside managers now keep a database file on computer with the required documents sorted by expiration date.

The more important documents, except those required to be posted, should be carefully indexed and filed in an easily accessible place. It is a good idea for all these important papers to be kept in a single large binder with each certificate in its own clear plastic cover. This will make it easy to find individual documents or to carry the papers ashore if necessary. The less important documents that are seldom requested can be filed in a single file, suitably indexed.

The master should have a list showing the expiration dates of all the various certificates. The company's head office should keep track of the expiration dates and should arrange for renewals, but the master may have to remind them if an expiration date is near and no action is being taken.

CERTIFICATE OF DOCUMENTATION

Every merchant vessel, no matter what flag it flies, has a document that attests to the nationality and ownership of the vessel. This document is known as the certificate of documentation in the United States or the register in most foreign countries.

Formerly, U.S. oceangoing vessels were required to have one of two documents: a Certificate of Registry when in foreign trade or a Consolidated Certificate of Enrollment and License when in coastwise trade. The two documents have now been combined into a single one called a Certificate of

156

Documentation and referred to informally as the register. It is issued by the U.S. Coast Guard documentation office.

The certificate of documentation shows the vessel's name, official number, dimensions, owner's name and address, nationality, and details of the mortgages, if any. It shows the trades for which the vessel is documented. A vessel may not engage in a trade for which it is not documented, but a vessel may be documented for more than one trade and may change between those trades at will. U.S. vessels may be documented for any combination of the following trades:[1]

1. *Registry.* A vessel under registry may be employed in foreign trade; trade with Guam, American Samoa, Wake, Midway, or Kingman Reef; and other employments for which a coastwise license, Great Lakes license, or fishery license is not required.

2. *Coastwise license.* A vessel with a coastwise license endorsement may engage in the coastwise trade, the fisheries, and any other employment for which a registry or Great Lakes license is not required.

3. *Great Lakes license.* A Great Lakes license endorsement entitles the vessel to engage in the coastwise trade and the fisheries on the Great Lakes and their tributary and connecting waters; in trade with Canada; and in any other employment for which a registry, coastwise license, or fishery license is not required.

4. *Fishery license.* A fishery license entitles the vessel to fish within the fishery conservation zone and to landward of the conservation zone, and to land her catch, regardless of where caught, in the United States.

5. *Pleasure license.* A pleasure license entitles the vessel to pleasure use only.

No expiration date is shown on the certificate of documentation itself, but there should be a sticker attached to the back of the certificate showing the month and year of expiration. The certificate of documentation is good for one year only and must be renewed annually by the end of the month shown on the sticker. When it is renewed, the Coast Guard will send a new sticker to be attached to the back of the certificate. If any changes have to be made to the certificate of documentation, it must be sent to the Coast Guard documentation office.

There are very heavy fines for operating an undocumented vessel or one with an expired document, so a master should be sure the company is aware of the expiration date well in advance. Each day that the vessel is operated without a proper certificate is considered a separate offense.

When the vessel operates in the foreign trade, the local authorities in almost all ports will want to see the vessel's register. Many countries require the master to deposit the register with the government authorities while the vessel is in port. When the vessel is in the foreign trade and calling at U.S. ports, the agent will pick up the certificate of documentation and surrender it to U.S. Customs who will keep it until the ship clears outward. If the ship will be sailing within forty-eight hours, the certificate is normally not collected. If the ship is not clearing foreign but is going into the coastwise trade, customs will return the register when all the foreign cargo has been discharged. In some ports, customs may not collect the certificate at all.

CERTIFICATE OF INSPECTION (COI)

A certificate of inspection (COI) certifies that the vessel has been inspected by the Coast Guard and that it is in conformance with the applicable vessel inspection laws and regulations; it also sets forth the conditions under which the vessel may operate.[2] The vessel may not be navigated without a valid certificate of inspection except in two circumstances:

1. A vessel whose certificate of inspection expires at sea or in a foreign port may complete the voyage without a valid certificate if the certificate did not expire within the first fifteen days after the vessel left the last U.S. port and if the voyage will be completed within thirty days after the expiration date.[3]
2. The OCMI may issue a Permit to Proceed to Another Port for Repairs, form CG-948 (fig. 14).

The certificate of inspection is issued by the U.S. Coast Guard and is valid for two years. To renew the certificate the vessel will undergo an inspection, after which the marine inspector will issue a temporary certificate of inspection, valid for a limited time. The permanent certificate will usually be sent to the vessel within a few weeks. The certificate of inspection must be posted under glass in a conspicuous place.

A midterm inspection must be made between the tenth and fourteenth months following the date the certificate was issued. The initial inspection for certification and the midterm inspection must both be requested and scheduled in advance. Usually, two inspectors will be sent to a vessel, one for hull inspections and one for machinery inspections. If the vessel has any outstanding problems or CG-835s listed on the bridge card, those will usually be addressed first.

In preparation for a Coast Guard inspection, vessels and companies may request a copy of the inspection booklets used by Coast Guard inspectors when conducting their inspections. The booklet numbers are as follows:

Hull Inspection, 840A
Machinery Inspection, 840B
Barge Inspection, 840E
Drydock Inspection, 840H

Tankship Inspection, 840S

These booklets can also be downloaded from the U.S. Coast Guard Web site.

Sometimes the shipping company will request that changes be made to the certificate. In this case, amendment pages may be issued. These pages then become part of the certificate.

Bridge Record Card

Every vessel must have a bridge record card posted in the wheelhouse or chartroom. This card is for the use of Coast Guard inspectors and will most likely be checked whenever the Coast Guard comes aboard for any sort of inspection. Any time a vessel is issued a requirement to correct deficiencies, usually on Coast Guard form CG-835, the inspectors will note that fact on the bridge record card. When the deficiency is cleared, that also should be noted on the card.

CERTIFICATES OF CLASSIFICATION

When the American Bureau of Shipping first issues a classification for a vessel, two certificates will be provided to show its ABS class: a Certificate of Classification for Hull, and a Certificate of Classification for Machinery. The vessel must go through periodic surveys in order to maintain its class, but the certificates have no expiration dates and are good indefinitely unless ABS revokes or modifies the vessel's classification.

ABS CERTIFICATES OF SURVEY

ABS issues various survey certificates for hull surveys, machinery surveys, load line surveys, automation surveys, inert gas system surveys, tailshaft surveys, and other specific purposes. Although the ABS certificates are separate pieces of paper, the survey times usually coincide with the vessel's annual COI inspection. Some certificates are valid for more than one year; the tailshaft survey, for example, is valid for five years.

BUILDER'S CERTIFICATE

Also known as the master carpenter's certificate, the builder's certificate is signed by an official of the shipyard that constructed the vessel and certifies the name, year of completion, principal dimensions, international tonnages, and person or company for whom the vessel was built.

INTERNATIONAL SAFETY MANAGEMENT CODE (ISM) DOCUMENT OF COMPLIANCE AND SAFETY MANAGEMENT CERTIFICATE (SMC)

Both the ISM Document of Compliance and the Safety Management Certificate are issued by the vessel's classification society and are valid for five years. As of July 1, 1998, all oil and chemical tankers, gas carriers, bulk carriers, and passenger ships of 500 gross tons or more were required to have proof of ISM compliance. Other vessels are to be in compliance by July 1, 2002. Compliance will be assured by port state controls as well as audits. During the second or third year of the five-year period, a vessel must undergo a surveillance audit. Most U.S. flag vessels started to undergo these surveillance audits in the year 2000.

INTERNATIONAL LOAD LINE CERTIFICATE

The international load line certificate is issued by the American Bureau of Shipping on behalf of the U.S. Coast Guard under the provisions of the International Convention on Load Lines. It shows the maximum draft (stated in terms of minimum freeboard) to which the vessel may load in each season and load line zone of the world.[4]

The load line certificate is normally valid for four years but is subject to annual surveys, which must be endorsed on the back of the certificate. The annual surveys must be made within three months before or after the anniversary date of the original certificate issuance.

FREEBOARD ASSIGNMENT

The American Bureau of Shipping issues the freeboard assignment when the vessel is first surveyed to determine the allowable load lines. It shows the required freeboard for each of the seasonal load lines the vessel is assigned. This document is seldom asked for once the international load line certificate has been issued, as officials prefer to see the latter.

DEADWEIGHT CERTIFICATE

The deadweight certificate is usually a letter from a naval architect which is provided at the time of the vessel's construction. It certifies the vessel's full load summer draft, the displacement at that draft, the light-ship weight, and the resulting deadweight capacity.

TONNAGE CERTIFICATES

Most taxes and fees that are levied against vessels by various governments are assessed on the basis of net registered tons. The vessel's international tonnages, so-called because they are internationally accepted (except by the Panama and Suez Canals), are the gross tonnage and net tonnage shown on the certificate of documentation. Tolls for transit of the Panama Canal and the Suez Canal are also based on tonnage, but authorities at the two canals have their own methods of measuring tonnages; these are different from each other and from the international tonnages.

The vessel should obtain a Panama Canal tonnage certificate or a Suez Canal tonnage certificate before its first transit of either. The appropriate canal tonnage certificate must be presented to the boarding officer on each transit of either canal.

Originally the Suez Canal tonnage certificate was kept on board the vessel, like most other certificates. Each time the ship transited the canal the agent took the tonnage certificate ashore, showed it to the authorities, and returned it to the vessel.

For a while, the canal officials decided to keep all tonnage certificates ashore in their files. If a ship transited during this time, the certificate was taken ashore but was not returned to the vessel. If a vessel does not have a Suez Canal tonnage certificate on board, it is possible that the canal officials still have it in their files. In such a case, it would be prudent for the master to request the agent to return the certificate on the vessel's next Suez Canal transit; the authorities are once again allowing the certificates to be kept on board ship.

TONNAGE TAX RECEIPTS

Each time the vessel enters the United States from foreign it will have to pay tonnage tax. The "tonnage year" begins on the date of the vessel's first such entry. Tonnage tax receipts should be kept with the certificate of documentation as the customs boarding officer will want to see both on arrival. When the vessel receives the first receipt of a new tonnage year, the receipts from the previous tonnage year may be discarded.

STABILITY LETTER

Every U.S. vessel must have a letter from the Coast Guard certifying that calculations have been made showing that the vessel can be maintained in a satisfactory condition of stability. The letter must be posted under glass in the pilothouse. Any operating restrictions contained in the letter must be strictly observed.

GRAIN LOADING CERTIFICATE

Every vessel that carries grain in bulk must have a certificate of authorization prior to loading and a certificate of loading prior to sailing. These certificates are evidence that the vessel has complied with the grain stability regulations. The U.S. Coast Guard recognizes the National Cargo Bureau for the purpose of issuing these certificates. A tanker that has a grain stability letter does not need a certificate of authorization.

GRAIN STABILITY LETTER

When tankers load grain, they are generally exempted from complying with certain of the stability requirements of international and Coast Guard grain regulations. This is because the high compartmentalization of most tankers makes them inherently more stable and safer than dry cargo vessels for carrying grain. However, tankers still need a grain stability letter.

If the arrangement and structure of the vessel are such that the angle of list is less than five degrees (assuming a twelve-degree shift of grain with all cargo spaces slack and under the most unfavorable condition of loading), then the National Cargo Bureau will issue a letter so certifying. If a vessel has such a letter, it should be kept in a safe place, as it will save the time and expense of having to repeat the calculations should the vessel ever load grain again.

CARGO SHIP SAFETY
CONSTRUCTION CERTIFICATE

The American Bureau of Shipping issues a cargo ship safety construction certificate on behalf of the U.S. Coast Guard. It is issued under the provisions of the International Convention for the Safety of Life at Sea (SOLAS) 1974, and it certifies that the vessel is constructed in accordance with international standards for subdivision and stability; machinery and electrical installations; and fire protection, detection, and extinction. A supplement to the cargo ship safety construction certificate is required for all tankers and all cargo ships engaged in carrying oil. An attachment to the cargo ship safety construction certificate is required for all vessels and is endorsed upon completion of the mandatory annual surveys.

All three certificates are combined into one multipage form. The basic certificate and the supplement are good for a maximum of five years, provided the mandatory annual surveys are made and endorsed as required.

CARGO SHIP SAFETY EQUIPMENT CERTIFICATE

Issued by the U.S. Coast Guard under the provisions of SOLAS, the cargo ship safety equipment certificate attests that the ship is properly equipped with lifeboats, life rafts, life buoys, life jackets, fire extinguishers, fathometer, gyro compass, navigation lights and shapes, pilot ladder, whistle, and bell.

Any tanker or cargo ship engaged in the carriage of oil must also have a supplement to the cargo ship safety equipment certificate. Both the basic certificate and the supplement are valid for two years.

PASSENGER SHIP SAFETY CERTIFICATE

A passenger ship safety certificate is issued to passenger ships under SOLAS. It is the passenger ship equivalent of the cargo ship safety construction certificate and cargo ship safety equipment certificate.

FIRE EXTINGUISHER TEST AND INSPECTION CERTIFICATE

At a vessel's inspection for certification or midterm inspection, a private contractor is usually hired to perform the required annual test and inspection of all portable fire extinguishers and to replace or recharge the extinguishers as necessary. This is normally coincident with the vessel's COI inspection. At the completion of the work the vendor will issue a fire extinguisher test and inspection certificate, valid for one year, showing the condition of all portable fire extinguishers on board the vessel; this certificate is then shown to the Coast Guard inspectors.

The same is usually done, on the same or on a separate certificate, for the fixed carbon dioxide, halon, and foam extinguishing systems.

INFLATABLE LIFE RAFT TEST AND INSPECTION CERTIFICATE

The vessel's inflatable life rafts must be sent ashore annually for servicing by a company approved by the Coast Guard. The company will issue an inflatable life raft test and inspection certificate on its own form when the inflatable life rafts are returned to the vessel.

CERTIFICATE OF SANITARY CONSTRUCTION

The certificate of sanitary construction is issued by the U.S. Public Health Service at the time a vessel is built. It certifies that the vessel was constructed in accordance with Public Health Service regulations. This certificate is rarely, if ever, checked by authorities.

REGISTER OF CARGO GEAR

A register of cargo gear is required for every vessel equipped with masts, stays, booms, winches, cranes, elevators, conveyors, standing and running rigging, and other equipment used for loading and unloading. The vessel must keep records of the following:

1. An initial proof load test, disassembly, and examination of the cargo gear before it is placed into service
2. A proof load test, disassembly, and examination of the cargo gear every four years
3. Loose gear certificates, showing compliance with proof load test requirements for all chains, rings, hooks, links, shackles, swivels, blocks, or other loose gear used as cargo gear
4. Test certificates for wire rope
5. Annealing certificates for all wrought iron gear required to be annealed
6. Alterations, renewals, or repairs of cargo gear
7. Annual visual examination of cargo gear
8. Monthly inspection of cargo gear by ship's officer

Tankers need not have the cargo gear register for hose-handling and stores cranes but may instead request a "statement of fact" from ABS. Statements of fact are valid for one year and cost less than a cargo gear register certificate.[5]

GMDSS STATION LICENSE

The ship's GMDSS station license is valid for one year. Usually, testing, certification, and shore-based maintenance are conducted by a USCG-approved vendor. If the vessel is in compliance, a safety certificate will be issued. This certificate should be posted conspicuously.

INMARSAT ACCESS AUTHORIZATION CERTIFICATE

The INMARSAT access authorization certificate is required aboard vessels with satellite communications systems that utilize the INMARSAT satellites. Frequency allocations for satellite access are not shown on the ship radio station license; however, FCC regulations require the certificate to be displayed in the radio room or the GMDSS operating area along with the ship station license.

The access authorization certificate will be granted only after installation of the satellite communications system is complete and the system has been through its commissioning tests. These are a series of test transmissions and receptions made under the supervision of an authorized technician to verify that the equipment is operating correctly and is not causing any interference that would adversely affect the satellite communications system.

This certificate has no stated expiration date and is good as long as the satellite communications equipment is operating properly, unless revoked by INMARSAT.

BRIDGE-TO-BRIDGE RADIOTELEPHONY CERTIFICATE

Issued by the Federal Communications Commission (FCC), the bridge-to-bridge radiotelephony certificate verifies that the vessel complies with the Bridge-to-Bridge Radiotelephone Act. It must be renewed every year. This is strictly a U.S. requirement and it applies only to vessels within the navigable waters of the United States. If the certificate expires on a foreign voyage it will be impossible to renew it in a foreign port; the master must renew it at the first U.S. port. Some masters require their mates and any others using the VHF radios to clip their personal operator's license to the ship's certification.

CERTIFICATE OF FINANCIAL RESPONSIBILITY FOR WATER POLLUTION (COFR)

The certificate of financial responsibility for water pollution (COFR) is issued to the vessel operator by the Director of the U.S. Coast Guard National Pollution Funds Center. COFRs issued on and after July 21, 1994, are valid for three years. The certificate shows that the operator has posted a bond or otherwise demonstrated to the satisfaction of the Federal Maritime Commission financial capability to meet future obligations that may result because of pollution from the vessel.

If the operator is not the owner as shown on the certificate of documentation, then there should be a letter signed by both the operator and the owner acknowledging that the operator is responsible for the operation of the ship including any pollution control and cleanup. In the absence of such a letter, customs will want to know why the owner of the vessel and the person to whom the certificate of financial responsibility is issued are not the same. Many states and countries now require their own COFRs in addition to the federal COFR. These certificates have varying validity periods.[6]

CERTIFICATE OF INSURANCE OR OTHER FINANCIAL SECURITY IN RESPECT TO CIVIL LIABILITY FOR OIL POLLUTION DAMAGE

A certificate of insurance or other financial security in respect to civil liability for oil pollution damage is very similar in purpose to the U.S. Federal Maritime Commission's certificate of financial responsibility but it is an international certificate, required in non-U.S. ports, issued under the provisions of Article 7 of the International Convention on Civil Liability for Oil Pollution Damage, 1969. All ships carrying more than 2,000 tons of oil in bulk must have insurance or other acceptable security.

PROTECTION AND INDEMNITY (P and I) CERTIFICATE

Some foreign port state controls will ask for a protection and indemnity (P and I) certificate. This document is proof of the vessel's P and I coverage and supports the vessel's civil liability. It is issued by the P and I club.

INTERNATIONAL OIL POLLUTION PREVENTION CERTIFICATE (IOPP)

An international oil pollution prevention certificate (IOPP) is required on U.S. oil tankers of 150 gross tons and above and other vessels over 400 gross tons that engage in voyages to ports or other offshore terminals under the jurisdiction of other parties to MARPOL 73/78.[7] It is issued by the U.S. Coast Guard or a classification society under the provisions of MARPOL 73/78. It certifies that the vessel is equipped with pollution prevention equipment as required by international agreement. The IOPP will be issued after an initial survey when the ship is first put into service. Any supplements to the IOPP must remain attached to the certificate and if the supplement is changed, a new IOPP certificate must be issued. An attachment or supplement is necessary for the carriage of certain cargoes, such as noxious liquid substances. The IOPP is valid for four years, subject to annual surveys. A survey is required within a two-month window on either side of twelve months from the date of issuance and again at thirty-six months from that date. The survey is to ensure that the oily-water separator and associated pumps and piping systems remain satisfactory for their intended use.

U.S. COAST GUARD OILY-WATER MONITOR CERTIFICATE

A U.S. Coast Guard oily-water monitor certificate is valid for the lifetime of the oily-water monitoring system. It certifies that the system meets regulatory requirements.

SHIPBOARD OIL POLLUTION AND EMERGENCY PLAN (SOPEP)

MARPOL requires a shipboard oil pollution and emergency plan (SOPEP) for tankers over 150 gross tons and other vessels of 400 gross tons or more.[8] The SOPEP must have the following six sections:

- Introduction containing the text outlined in 33 CFR §151.26
- Preamble containing the explanation and use of the plan and describing how it relates to shore-based plans
- Reporting requirements including information on when, what, and to whom to report
- Steps to control a discharge
- National and local coordination contact information
- Appendices containing twenty-four-hour contact numbers, agencies, and officials in regularly visited ports

The SOPEP is usually prepared by the home office and, once prepared, is submitted to the Coast Guard for approval. Once on board, it is the master's responsibility to keep it updated with the most current contact numbers and other information. The SOPEP must, at a minimum, be reviewed annually, and a letter must be submitted to the Coast Guard stating that this review has been conducted.

VESSEL RESPONSE PLAN (VRP)

A vessel response plan (VRP) is required under OPA '90 on all tankers. It must be approved by the Coast Guard and is subject to audit.[9] Most states now require vessels, especially tankers, to have an oil-spill contingency plan. This requirement is already met by vessels complying with OPA '90 and other federal legislation but some states have their own requirements. Many overlapping and redundant requirements imposed by coastal states are currently being fought in the federal courts by industry groups and vessel owners and operators.

BALLAST PERMIT

Required by some states and usually purchased for a nominal fee, the ballast permit normally requires a vessel to report the quantity of ballast water to be released in a given port. The state requirement is in addition to federal ballast reporting requirements.[10] Given the passage of the National Invasive Species Act, it is likely that ballast water permits will become more expensive and more difficult to obtain as state and federal regulators wrestle with the problems posed by nonindigenous invasive species carried in ballast water.

DERAT

A derat form is a combination form which functions either as a deratting certificate or as a certificate of deratting exemption, as appropriate. In most foreign ports, the authorities will want to see the derat form. It is good for six months and can be renewed in almost any port in the world. This certificate is issued by the Public Health Service in the United States and by the port health officer in most foreign ports.[11]

If the inspector does not find any traces of rodent infestation, he will issue a certificate of deratting exemption. If he does find traces of rats, such as droppings, he will take measures to eliminate the rats, such as setting out rat poison or traps, and will then issue a deratting certificate. In some ports the inspector will not do the actual deratting; the master will be responsible for hiring a pest exterminator.

HAZARDOUS MATERIALS (HAZMAT) CERTIFICATE

The EPA issues a hazardous materials ("hazmat") certificate to vessels carrying such a material as a cargo. It is valid for one year.[12]

EQUIPMENT CERTIFICATES

The vessel should have equipment certificates issued by the American Bureau of Shipping for all ground tackle such as anchors, chain, connecting shackles, and so forth. The certificates show the manufacturer, markings, and the proof load that was applied during testing. There may also be equipment certificates for other pieces of gear, such as deck winches or hose-handling booms.

NOTICE OF PREFERRED FLEET MORTGAGE

When a preferred fleet mortgage is taken out on a vessel, a notice must be prominently posted in a conspicuous place. It usually contains language similar to the following:

> This vessel is covered by a preferred fleet mortgage dated [*date*] to [*name of bank*]. Under the terms of said mortgage, neither the owner, charterer, master, nor any other person has any right, power, or authority to create, incur, or permit to be placed or imposed upon this vessel any lien whatsoever other than liens for crew's wages or salvage.

Certificate carriage requirements change as quickly as the regulations change. This is by no means an exhaustive list.

CHAPTER 10

Crew Lists

Masters should have up-to-date crew lists available at all times. Some masters keep a copy of the crew list tucked inside the log. This is a poor practice as crew lists contain the crew's personal data. Crew lists should be maintained with the utmost confidentiality and treated like any other confidential personnel file. Once a potential offender is armed with a crewmember's social security number, home address, and next of kin, identity theft and credit fraud become distinct possibilities. Crew lists should be maintained under lock and key. If it becomes necessary to post a crew list, as a gangway control measure perhaps, then only redacted lists with personal data removed should be distributed. Gate guards should be given only redacted lists.

The officials in all foreign ports will require crew lists; U.S. Customs and the Immigration and Naturalization Service will require a crew list when the ship departs from the United States on a foreign voyage and when it returns; and many cargo terminals will want a crew list in order to check crewmembers in and out at the gate. This is especially true at military terminals; sometimes, more than one list will be requested. Some shipping companies will want masters to send the office a crew list from each port, either on immigration form I-418 (fig. 23) or on their own company form; or they may have a form for reporting only the changes in personnel without listing the entire crew. If there is much turnover among the crew, the department heads would probably appreciate receiving an updated crew list with each change.

Crew lists in almost all ports and countries should list the crewmembers in order of rank: deck officers (including the radio officer) first, followed by the unlicensed deck crew, the licensed engineers, the unlicensed engine crew, and finally the steward's department. Supercargoes, riding gangs, and other persons in addition to the crew should be listed at the end. The only exception to this arrangement is that upon arrival in the

United States, the list should be arranged alphabetically for the immigration inspector.

There are substantial fines for including persons on a crew list who are not crewmembers. Guests such as family members who are riding with the ship should not be given titles such as "librarian" in an effort to have them listed as crew. The newly enacted Illegal Immigration Reform and Immigrant Responsibility Act of 1996 has strengthened immigration regulations and increased penalties for violations.[1]

The master copy of the crew list should usually be typed on the vessel rather than in the agent's or broker's office. If it is done ashore there is a greater chance for misspelled names, errors in the document numbers, or other inaccuracies. As of February 1997, it is no longer necessary for customs to certify crew lists.[2]

CREW LISTS REQUIRED IN FOREIGN PORTS

Crew lists will be demanded by port officials in all foreign ports of call, and the agent in each such port will also want a copy. In many foreign ports the officials will want the crew lists to bear the ship's stamp in addition to the master's signature. The number of crew lists required at foreign ports varies greatly but is usually a half-dozen to a dozen, occasionally more.

Many countries are more liberal than the United States regarding forms and will accept crew lists prepared on the immigration form I-418, on company forms, or even on plain paper, as long as all the pertinent information is given. A few foreign countries require that the crew lists be on their own forms. The agent at the preceding port should be able to advise the master if this is necessary and obtain the blank forms. If the vessel does not have any forms and the crew lists are required immediately on arrival, the master can communicate the particulars to the agent at the port so the crew lists can be made up in advance.

VISAED CREW LIST

Some countries require a crew list to be on their own form and visaed by their consul at the last port prior to arrival in their country. (This is not the same visaed alien crew list required by the United States.) Not having the visaed crew list in a port where it is required will most likely cause the vessel to be assessed a fine. When traveling to a minor port, it is always wise to check on this with the agent.

VISAED ALIEN CREW LIST

A crew list must be visaed if there are aliens aboard who do not already
have U.S. entry visas in their passports, as may be the case for a vessel
with a non-U.S crew or a mixed crew. Usually, at the last foreign port of
call the ship visited before returning to the United States, the agent will
take the crew list to a U.S. Consul or U.S. Embassy and have a visa af-
fixed to the crew list. This crew list is made up in duplicate on the regular
form I-418, showing only those members of the crew who are nonresident
aliens. Registered aliens, for this purpose, are not considered nonresident aliens, and need not be listed. The names must be alphabetically arranged regardless of rating or department. The lists are taken to the U.S.
Consul's office at the last foreign port of call having one, where the consul
will visa the original crew list and keep the copy. The visaed alien crew
list is given to the immigration boarding officer on arrival at the first U.S.
port.

   When making up the alien crew list the master must put in column four
the date, city, and country of birth of each alien. If the alien has a passport,
the number, place of issue, and the issuing authority belong in column five;
if the alien does not have a passport, the master should write "none" in that
column.

   If the alien crew list cannot be visaed—for example, if there is no U.S.
Consul at the last port and the alien crew list has not been visaed in a previous port—that fact should be noted in the official log. The same applies if
the vessel is diverted to a U.S. port while at sea. If the logbook properly documents the reason the alien crew list was not visaed, the master can apply
for a waiver of visa upon arrival in the United States. Otherwise, there is a
fine for each nonresident alien brought to the United States who is not visaed on the alien crew list, unless that alien has had an individual visa issued and stamped in his or her passport.

RETURNING TO THE UNITED STATES

Before arriving at the first U.S. port from foreign, the master should generate a crew list with the names alphabetically arranged. The immigration
officer will use this list to check the names of the crew. The vessel will not
be cleared by immigration until this check is made. If the immigration officer uses the regular crew list, checking the crew may take considerable
time, whereas the alphabetically arranged crew list will greatly expedite
the process.

   The instructions on the reverse of form I-418 must be followed exactly.
For the immigration officer, this crew list does not need to have the

next-of-kin data filled in; only the name, rating, document number, nationality, date and place of birth, and, for non-U.S. citizens and nonresident aliens, passport numbers are required. The passport numbers for U.S. citizens and resident aliens should not be included. Instead, the list should contain the state of birth for U.S. citizens and the alien registration number for resident aliens.

If any crewmember was born in a foreign country but is a naturalized U.S. citizen, his or her citizenship should be listed as "U.S. (nat.)."

The master should also have two arrival crew lists arranged by rating for customs and extras for the agent and others.

U.S. customs and immigration officials in some ports will not accept photocopies. In ports where the officials do accept photocopies, the copy machine must reproduce the front and back of form I-418 onto the front and back of a single sheet of copy paper so that the I-418 can be signed on the back as required by regulation. Form I-418 is slightly wider than standard size 8½-by-11-inch paper, so the master should be careful the copy machine does not cut off any required information at the edges.

At least fifty sheets of blank crew list forms I-418 should always be on board. These are usually supplied through the office or the agent.

DEPARTING FOR FOREIGN PORTS

When a ship leaves the United States bound for foreign ports, a departing crew list completed on I-418 must be submitted to immigration, showing all crew changes. If crewmembers just joined the vessel, their landing permits should be attached to the departure crew list. Additionally, if any alien mariners were signed off, a copy of the completed form CF-408 should be attached to the departure crew list. Any desertions must be noted in the departure crew list. The master must ensure that personal effects and travel documents for any alien crewmembers remaining behind for medical reasons have been transferred ashore. The agent usually secures the necessary permissions for medical treatment, but the names of such crewmembers should be noted on the departing crew list.

PIER HEAD JUMP

If, after clearing for foreign at the last U.S. port of call, a member of the crew fails to rejoin or is hospitalized and it is necessary to get a replacement, the master should sign on the new crewmember just before sailing, making certain that he or she reads the details of the articles and any riders. The official log should contain all the facts. The name of the crewmember who did not join remains on the certified crew list but the new crewmember's name is not entered on the certified crew list.

The new crewmember's name and other data should then be added to the unofficial crew list and the name of the crewmember who failed to join should be deleted. As noted earlier, copies of the altered crew list should always be sent to the home office.

CHAPTER 11

Customs

While most import and export laws do not apply directly to the vessel, a general understanding of the role customs plays is vital to successful vessel management.[1] The Customs Service, a federal agency within the Treasury Department, was established on July 31, 1789, as the fifth act of the newly formed United States Congress. Originally designed as a revenue raising agency, the role of the Customs Service has expanded to include enforcement of drug laws. The focus of customs agents has become primarily enforcement-oriented and includes hazardous duties such as the seizure of contraband, illegal drugs, and weapons. Many customs officials carry firearms. Customs works with many other state and federal agencies and is often the enforcing agency in joint operations with the U.S. Departments of Agriculture and Health and Human Services as well as the Agricultural Marketing Service, the Food and Drug Administration, the Animal and Plant Health Inspection Service (APHIS), and more. Customs enforces regulations for the U.S. Treasury Department and other federal and state agencies at over 300 ports of entry in the United States and has attachés in twenty-five countries.[2]

The North American Free Trade Agreement Implementation Act, also called the Customs Modernization Act, became effective on December 8, 1993, with the goal of streamlining and automating the paper-based customs practices of past decades.[3] This was a statutory change, but customs regulations remained unchanged.

In February 1999, customs regulations were finally amended to properly implement the statutory changes brought about by the Customs Modernization Act. This act amended statutes governing the entry and loading and unloading of vessels in the United States. Prior to these amendments, the entry of both U.S. and foreign vessels had been governed by separate statutes, neither of which included elements concerning preliminary vessel entry or the boarding of vessels.[4] The act repealed and amended statutes to provide for the entry of vessels under the same statute.[5] One of the provisions of the amended law requires that a significant number of vessels be boarded to ensure compliance with the laws enforced by the Customs Service. Customs presently handles approximately 95,000 vessel arrivals annually.

Another provision of the Customs Modernization Act allows customs to electronically issue permits via the automated commercial system (ACS) to load or unload merchandise pursuant to an authorized data interchange system as an alternative to physical document presentation. ACS is a computerized tracking system used to track and monitor cargo, trading companies, and cargo manifests and to facilitate the customs process. It allows electronic filing of cargo manifests and electronic reporting of vessel arrival for carriers who have been granted approved filer status by customs.

Besides streamlining the paperwork, the new regulations also helped to free up customs agents for more thorough boardings and enforcement efforts. Two new concepts that emerged from the modernization act were "informed compliance" and "shared responsibility," which were based on the premise that in order to maximize voluntary compliance, industry needs to be aware of customs requirements. To this end, customs has prepared a series of informed compliance publications and videos outlining the new customs requirements, regulations, and procedures.

Most customs regulations include provisions for financial penalty and/or seizure of property or the vessel for regulatory violations. Mitigating factors such as the following may decrease the penalty:

1. Prior good record
2. Inexperience
3. Cooperation with customs officers, including voluntary disclosure of a violation
4. Contributory customs negligence

Aggravating factors, listed below, may serve to increase the assessed penalty:

1. Criminal violation relating to the subsequent transaction
2. Repetitive violations of the same restriction involved in the seizure
3. Evidence that the violation was intentional

Every vessel entering a U.S. port from a foreign port or place and subject to customs treatment must report arrival, make formal entry, and clear on departure. There are some exceptions to this procedure. U.S. vessels departing for a coastwise port with no foreign cargo, passengers, or baggage on board need not clear. For customs purposes, a U.S. vessel sailing between two U.S. ports but with foreign cargo on board is in the foreign trade and must enter and clear.

Masters and vessel owners may incur penalties for violations of U.S. customs laws, including violations committed by members of their crews. If masters take proper precautions, however, penalties may be avoided or reduced.

ENTERING THE UNITED STATES FROM FOREIGN PORTS

Most vessels submit cargo declarations electronically via fax or express delivery service before the vessel even arrives in port. The papers required for entering from foreign ports should be started as early as possible on the homeward voyage so as to be completed before arrival. Neatness and legibility are important. A few extra copies of all required papers should be prepared in case additional copies are requested.

U.S. Department of Agriculture and Animal and Plant Health Inspection Service

The U.S. Department of Agriculture (USDA) will usually board at the first U.S. port of entry to inspect food storage and preparation areas and garbage handling areas and equipment (such as incinerators) and will ask for a copy of the Ship's Stores Declaration (CF-1303, fig. 6). Usually, the USDA inspector is accompanied by the chief steward. User fees for the USDA inspection are collected by customs.

Deratting certificates are no longer required for vessels entering the United States. However, the Animal and Plant Health Inspection Service (APHIS) will still issue the certificate for a vessel needing it.

Vessels may be asked to dispose of items considered a health threat to the United States. Any pets on board must have complete vaccination cards; they will rarely be permitted ashore.

U.S. Public Health Service

The U.S. Public Health Service (USPHS) laws and quarantine regulations require that masters of vessels arriving from foreign areas immediately report by radio to the quarantine station (usually via the agent) any deaths that have occurred among passengers or crew, and any illnesses reported during the fifteen days prior to arrival having one or more of the following symptoms:

1. Temperature of 100°F or greater accompanied or followed by rash, jaundice, or glandular swelling which has lasted over forty-eight hours
2. Temperature of 100°F or greater which persisted for two days or more
3. Diarrhea (three or more loose stools or a greater than normal number of loose stools in a twenty-four-hour period)[6]

Reporting Arrival

Within twenty-four hours after arrival, the following vessels must report arrival:

1. Any vessel from a foreign port or place
2. A foreign vessel from either a domestic port or the high seas
3. A U.S. vessel carrying bonded merchandise or foreign merchandise for which entry has not been made
4. Any vessel that has visited a hovering vessel or that has received merchandise while outside the territorial sea

Such arrival should be reported by any means of communication to the district director of customs or to the customs boarding officer assigned to the vessel.[7] Usually, arrival is reported by telephone by the agent. If the carrier is an ACS approved filer, arrival reports may be made electronically.

For customs purposes, the time of arrival is considered to be the time when the vessel first comes to rest, whether at anchor or at a dock, in any harbor within the customs territory of the United States. The time of departure is the time when the vessel gets underway and proceeds on her voyage without thereafter coming to rest in the harbor from which she is departing.

If a vessel that has arrived from a foreign port or place departs or attempts to depart from a customs collection district without report of arrival or without making entry as required, the master will be subject to heavy penalties. The vessel may be subject to arrest, seizure, and forfeiture.[8]

Reporting Arrival, Entering, and Clearing on Board

If a passenger vessel operating on a regular schedule arrives in port at night between 5 P.M. and 8 A.M. or on a Sunday or federal holiday and plans to sail that same night (or Sunday or holiday), the vessel may report arrival, make entry, and clear on board. This avoids the need to make entry at the customhouse and is allowed in order to expedite the sailing of passenger vessels, which have short in-port stays.[9]

In order for the customs boarding officer to receive the report of arrival, accept entry, and issue clearance on board the vessel, the owner, master, or agent of the vessel must have made advance application for this service and filed a bond in accordance with customs regulations.

Boarding Officers

When a vessel arrives at the first U.S. port from a foreign port of call, a customs officer, usually accompanied by an immigration officer, will board at the first dock. At subsequent ports only the customs officer will board, and then only if the vessel is carrying inward foreign cargo or inward-bound passengers for landing. The Department of Agriculture no longer routinely boards every vessel arriving from a foreign port, so there may or may not be a USDA boarding officer, either at the first port or at subsequent ports.

Under federal law, the master of any vessel who obstructs or hinders any officer who is lawfully boarding the vessel for the purpose of enforcing any of the revenue or navigation laws of the United States is liable for a heavy fine.

Persons Boarding or Leaving the Vessel

Customs regulations state that prior to clearance by the customs boarding officer, no person may board a vessel arriving directly from a place outside of U.S. Customs territory without permission from the customs boarding officer or the district director of customs. However, the pilot, Coast Guard officers, immigration officer, health officer, an inspector of the Animal and Plant Health Inspection Service of the U.S. Department of Agriculture, the vessel's agent, or a consular officer may go aboard. No one may go ashore except the above named officials and the master or other authorized officer, who may go ashore to report arrival or to make formal entry.

At the first port of entry from a foreign port and at subsequent U.S. ports, if inward foreign cargo is on board either for discharge or in transit, the crew and passengers should be informed that no one is permitted to go ashore until the vessel has been cleared by customs. The vessel must also be cleared by immigration at the first port. (See chapter 12, "Immigration," for more detailed information.) Permission for the crew and passengers to go ashore may be given soon after the customs officer boards but no one should be allowed ashore until that permission is given. A watch should be posted at the gangway to see that these rules are enforced.

Mail

Federal law requires that a vessel arriving at a U.S. port with mail on board cannot make formal entry or break bulk until all mail has been delivered to the nearest post office. Generally, however, the agent makes arrangements with customs to permit passengers to land and work to start. Merchant vessels very rarely carry mail these days and it is unlikely a master will encounter this situation.

Preliminary Entry

Merchant ships usually make preliminary entry in order to obtain customs clearance to start working cargo immediately upon arrival. By filing an application on CF-3171 (fig. 9), a vessel may request preliminary entry by radio. The request for preliminary entry is usually dropped off at the customhouse by the agent, the form is signed as approved by customs, and the agent notifies the vessel that it is cleared for preliminary entry and may unload upon arrival.[10] Making preliminary entry does not excuse the master from also making formal entry at the customhouse.

If the vessel has on board any inward foreign cargo, passengers, or baggage and the master wishes to load or discharge any cargo, passengers, or baggage before making formal entry, preliminary entry must be made. The granting of preliminary vessel entry by customs upon or subsequent to the arrival of the vessel is conditioned upon the presentation to and acceptance by customs of all forms, electronic or otherwise, comprising a complete manifest. Presentation is done by submitting a cargo declaration on CF-1302 (fig. 4) and CF-3171 (fig. 9), or the electronic equivalents, no less than forty-eight hours prior to the arrival of the vessel. The CF-3171 will also serve as notice of intended date of arrival. If a voyage takes less than forty-eight hours, the port director may allow for the presentation of the requisite forms within less than forty-eight hours prior to arrival. Additionally, customs must receive the vessel's ETA.

Formal Entry

Despite clearly worded regulations, actual practices for formal entry vary around the United States. Some ports rarely perform formal entry procedures aboard a vessel while others do it routinely. Technically, formal entry must be made at the customhouse within forty-eight hours after arrival, Sunday and holidays excepted, for the following vessels:

1. Any vessel from a foreign port or place
2. Any foreign vessel from a domestic port
3. A U.S. vessel carrying bonded merchandise or foreign merchandise for which entry has not been made
4. Any vessel that has visited a hovering vessel as defined in 19 USC §1401(k) or that has received merchandise or passengers while outside the territorial sea[11]

Under certain circumstances, U.S. vessels arriving in ports of the United States directly from other United States ports must make entry. Entry of such vessels is required when they have merchandise aboard that is being transported in bond or when they have unentered foreign merchandise aboard. For the purposes of the vessel entry requirements, merchandise transported in bond does not include bonded ship's stores or supplies. While U.S. vessels transporting unentered foreign merchandise must fully comply with the usual formal entry procedures, U.S. vessels carrying no unentered foreign merchandise but which have bonded merchandise aboard may satisfy vessel entry requirements by making a required report of arrival and presenting a completed CF-1300 (Vessel Entrance or Clearance Statement, figure 3). Report of arrival as provided in 19 CFR §4.2 and submission of CF-1300 satisfies all entry requirements for the subject vessels.

Papers that will be required for customs and other boarding officers when entering should be readily available. Documents required upon boarding are these:

1. Certificate of documentation or register
2. Load line certificate
3. International tonnage certificate and tonnage tax receipts
4. SOLAS certificate
5. Certificate of financial responsibility
6. Clearance from the last port
7. Any bills of health issued at the foreign port or place from which the vessel arrived

INWARD FOREIGN MANIFESTS

The documents required for entry are collectively called the "inward foreign manifest." Every vessel arriving from a foreign port must present an original and one copy of the manifest to the boarding officer.[12] Masters failing to produce a manifest to customs will incur a penalty.[13] If the vessel will proceed to another U.S. port with inward foreign cargo or passengers remaining on board then an additional copy of the manifest will be required to be certified as the traveling manifest.

The following forms (the inward foreign manifest) are required upon entry and are to be completed in triplicate:

1. CF-1300—Vessel Entrance or Clearance Statement (fig. 3)
2. CF-1302—Cargo Declaration or electronic equivalent (fig.4)
3. CF-1303—Ship's Stores Declaration (fig. 6)
4. CF-1304—Crew's Effects Declaration (fig. 7)
5. CF-226—Record of Vessel Foreign Repair or Equipment Purchase (fig. 2); U.S. vessels must file a foreign repairs declaration, indicating any repairs that were made abroad. A negative declaration on form CF-1300 is required if no repairs were made.
6. I-418—Crew List (fig. 23)
7. I-418—Passenger List, to include extras and stowaways (fig. 23)

Any document that is not required may be omitted from the manifest if the word "none" is inserted in spaces sixteen, eighteen, and/or nineteen of the vessel entrance or clearance statement (CF-1300). For example, a tanker would not have a passenger list since tankers are prohibited by law from carrying passengers.

Besides the two copies of the manifest required by law (three if a traveling manifest will be required), the district director of customs may require additional copies for local use. Customs regulations state that a reasonable amount of time is to be allowed vessel personnel for the preparation of these additional manifests. In actual practice, it is much better to make up extra manifests before arrival so that they are ready if they are requested.

The master, the purser, or a licensed deck officer may enter the vessel by appearing in person at the customhouse, or the required documents, properly executed by the master or authorized officer, may be delivered to the customhouse by the vessel's agent or other personal representative of the master. The latter procedure is almost always followed—it is very rare for a master to personally enter the vessel at the customhouse. Regardless of who enters or clears a vessel, the master is still personally responsible for any statutory penalties that may apply.

If the vessel has on board any alcoholic liquors or any merchandise (sea stores excepted) that is prohibited from importation into the United States, there is an additional penalty of a fine and/or imprisonment.

Under certain circumstances when the customs office is closed and the vessel cannot provide the required forms within the prescribed time, the port director has the discretion to perform formal entry not only aboard vessels at the time of arrival, but at other locations and outside of normal business hours.

If a vessel will remain in port for at least forty-eight hours, customs will retain the vessel's certificate of documentation and return it prior to sailing. This ensures the vessel clears outbound properly.

A master may have to send the original vessel documents ashore, as customs generally will not accept photocopies. The agent should provide a receipt for any permanent documents taken ashore to the customhouse in order to enter or clear or for any other reason. Photocopies of all these documents should be kept in the vessel's files for replacing the original should any document be lost. If any of these documents are lost the master will have to explain to the issuing agencies why they were not properly safeguarded.

Some foreign ports no longer issue clearances. If that is the case at the vessel's last foreign port, the master should ask the agent for a letter stating that the officials at that port do not issue clearances. This letter may need to be presented to customs in the United States in lieu of a clearance. If the vessel arrived via the Panama Canal, the canal clearance should accompany the clearance from the previous foreign port.

Upon making entry, any master who presents any forged, altered, or false document or paper, knowing the document to be false and not so revealing to the customs officer accepting entry, is subject to a fine and/or imprisonment. This is in addition to any forfeiture to which the vessel may be subject.

Vessel Entrance or Clearance Statement
The vessel entrance or clearance statement (CF-1300, figure 3) combines and replaces earlier forms CF-1300, CF-1301, and CF-1378.

Cargo Declaration
The cargo declaration (CF-1302, figure 4) is a list of all inward foreign cargo on board. Merchandise should be described on the cargo declaration in the order of its discharging and loading ports. For example: a vessel loads cargo at Cebu, Kobe, Nagoya, and Yokohama for discharge at Honolulu, New Orleans, Savannah, and New York. All Honolulu cargo is listed in order of ports of loading: Cebu for Honolulu, Kobe for Honolulu, etc. The same is then done for New Orleans cargo, then Savannah cargo, and finally New York cargo. These sheets are then made up into complete sets in order of ports of discharge with the cargo for discharge at Honolulu on top. These complete sets should be checked against each other to make certain the sheets are in the same order in all the sets. After checking, the sheets should be numbered consecutively.

Each sheet of the cargo declaration must show the port of loading and the port of discharge in the appropriate blanks. Load and discharge ports are sometimes omitted when the sheets are made up (see "Optional Cargo" later in this chapter) if the discharge port is unknown.

When inward foreign cargo is containerized, each bill of lading is to be listed in the column headed "B/L Nr." in numerical order according to bill of lading number. The number of the container that contains the cargo covered by that bill of lading and the number of the container seal will be listed in column six opposite the bill of lading number. The number of any other bill of lading for other cargo in that same container must appear in column six immediately under the container and seal numbers. Only the cargo covered by the bill of lading listed in the column headed "B/L Nr." is to be described in column seven.

The quantity of each shipment of cargo should be stated either in column eight or column nine of the cargo declaration, as appropriate. Column eight is the gross weight in either pounds or kilograms. Column nine is the quantity expressed according to the unit of measure specified in the tariff schedules of the United States.[14] Only one of the columns should be used.

For containerized or palletized cargo, customs officers will accept a cargo declaration that has been prepared on the basis of information furnished by the shipper. If the cargo declaration covers containerized or palletized cargo only, the following statement may be placed on the declaration: "The information appearing on the declaration relating to the quantity and description of the cargo is in each instance based on the shipper's load and count. I have no knowledge or information which would lead me to believe or to suspect that the information furnished by the shipper is incomplete, inaccurate, or false in any way."

If the cargo declaration covers both conventional cargo and also containerized or palletized cargo, the abbreviation SLAC (shipper's load and count) may be placed next to each containerized or palletized shipment on the declaration and the following statement placed on the declaration:

"The information appearing on this declaration relating to the quantity and description of cargo preceded by the abbreviation SLAC is in each instance based on the shipper's load and count. I have no information which would lead me to believe or to suspect that the information furnished by the shipper is incomplete, inaccurate, or false in any way."

The appropriate statement, if one is used, should be placed on the last page of the cargo declaration. Wording similar to shipper's load and count may be substituted, but customs will not accept vague expressions such as "said to contain" or "accepted as containing."

Each shipment listed on the cargo declaration must show the name of the person or company to whom it is consigned. If the shipment is consigned "to order," the declaration should say so.

If the vessel loads cargo for the United States at foreign ports, the agent, customs broker, or company representative at each loading port will put the bill of lading on board. In the case of general cargo, they may also make up the cargo declaration, omitting the date of arrival. If this is not done, then the cargo declaration will have to be made up on the vessel, getting the required particulars from the bills of lading. Cargo declarations are usually made up on board in the case of tankers, ore carriers, or other bulk cargo vessels.

When a bundle of completed cargo declaration sheets is placed on board in a foreign port, the master should check to see that they are for his or her vessel and double-check the data in the upper part of the forms. It is not uncommon for people to insert a wrong name for the vessel or the master. It is a good practice for the master to type this information on a blank declaration beforehand for the cargo clerk to copy.

When the cargo declaration is typed, it should be neat and legible, with at least one blank line between each entry so that the form will be easily readable. Customs officers may refuse to accept sloppy or illegible declarations.

If the cargo declaration has been omitted from the manifest because the vessel arrived in ballast with no cargo on board, the word "none" should be inserted in block sixteen of the vessel entrance and clearance statement. However, should the vessel have solid ballast, it must be shown on the manifest, stating the type and quantity and where stowed, for example: "350 tons iron ballast (ingots), in No. 3 hold" or "250 tons sand ballast on deck, to be discharged at sea."

Ship's Stores Declaration

Federal law requires that goods which are to remain on board the vessel as ship's stores or sea stores must be listed separately from merchandise which is to be landed. Such items must be listed on CF-1303, Ship's Stores Declaration (fig. 6). Customs regulations allow less than whole packages of sea or ship's stores to be described as "sundry small and broken stores."

Ship's stores are goods that become part of the ship's equipment for use on board in the running of the vessel; sea stores are goods for consumption by the crew or passengers. Fuel, paint, mooring lines, and so forth are ship's stores. Cigarettes, soft drinks, liquor, and other slop chest items are sea stores.

If more ship's stores or sea stores are found on board than are listed on the manifest, or if any ship's stores or sea stores are landed without a permit, the goods are subject to forfeiture. If any sea stores or ship's stores are landed, they will be treated as imported merchandise with the appropriate customs permit.

Crew Member's Declaration

A crewmember's declaration form (CF-5129, figure 10) must be filled out by each crewmember before arrival in the United States. This declaration must list all items procured abroad, regardless of how they were acquired, and the cost, or the fair market value, if the item was not acquired by purchase. It is the master's responsibility to see that crew curios are manifested and that each crewmember lists his or her curios. All costs or values are to be stated in U.S. dollars. If a crewmember has no goods to declare, he or she must still submit a CF-5129 with the notation "none" or "nothing to declare" on the face.

Articles acquired exclusively for use on the voyage that will not be landed in the United States and items which have previously been entered and cleared through customs need not be declared. If there is any doubt whether an item should be declared or not, the crewmember should be told to declare the item and to clarify the matter with the customs boarding officer on arrival.[15] If a crewmember has declared an item that he or she intends to keep on board the vessel and that will not be landed in the United States, the notation ROB (remain on board) should appear after the item on the declaration. Any undeclared or undervalued items that are found are subject to forfeiture and the master and the owner of the goods are each liable to a penalty equal to the value of such goods. If the value exceeds $500, the vessel is also subject to forfeiture.

Liquor, tobacco products, and other articles withdrawn from a U.S. bonded warehouse as vessel supplies are, by law, intended only for the crew's use on a voyage. If the master or any other officer or crewmember brings any of these articles back to the United States as personal baggage, the articles must be declared to a customs officer. If they are not declared, the articles will be subject to forfeiture and seizure and, additionally, the person not declaring the articles could incur penalties equal to the value of such undeclared articles.[16]

Notices should be posted in the crews' and officers' messrooms informing all hands of the importance of declaring everything. If the master or the vessel is fined because a crewmember fails to declare a curio, the master is entitled to collect the amount of the fine from the crewmember at fault.

Crew's Effects Declaration

The crew's effects declaration (CF-1304, figure 7) is a list of all articles acquired abroad by ship's officers and crewmembers. These articles are known as crew curios. Before a U.S. vessel arrives from a foreign port, each crewmember must fill out CF-5129, Crew Member's Declaration.

After each crewmember has submitted a signed declaration, the master uses the crewmembers' declarations to make up CF-1304, Crew's Effects Declaration. The crewmembers should be listed on the crew's effects declaration in order by rating. The serial number from each crewmember's declaration belongs in column seven. If a crewmember has nothing to declare, "none" should appear in place of the serial number.

In lieu of describing the articles on CF-1304, the master may instead furnish a crew list form I-418 (fig. 23) endorsed as follows: "I certify that this list, with its supporting crew member's declarations, is a true and accurate manifest of all articles on board the vessel acquired abroad by myself and the officers and crewmembers of this vessel, other than articles exclusively for use on the voyage or that have been duly cleared through customs in the United States."

On this crew list each person's shipping article number should appear opposite his or her name and, in column five, the serial number of the crewmember's declaration or the word "none."

Any mariner or passenger who has a foreign-made article that has already been cleared or that was purchased in the United States, such as a camera, sextant, or binoculars, may register the article with customs before leaving the United States. This is done by taking the article to any custom house and filling out a registration slip, CF-4455, which will then be signed and stamped by a customs officer.

Upon returning to the United States, the registration form is proof that the article has already been properly entered into the United States and is entitled to be brought ashore free of duty. Registered articles need not be declared on CF-5129. For the article to be eligible for registration, customs officers usually require that it have a serial number or similar unique identification.

If either the master or the vessel has been fined because of misconduct of a crewmember, such as smuggling contraband or failing to declare crew curios, and the crewmember is no longer available for recovery of the fine, the agent may apply to customs to have the fine remitted. They will want to see logbook entries or other proof that notices were posted advising the crew to declare all curios, that the master searched the vessel for contraband before arrival, and that the master took all reasonable precautions to prevent smuggling.

Crew List

Crew lists are to be prepared on form I-418 (fig. 23) in accordance with regulations of the Immigration and Naturalization Service. Instructions for completing crew lists are printed on form I-418.[17]

Passenger List

Passenger lists (I-418, figure 23) are also to be completed in accordance with immigration regulations. On the last page of the passenger list the master must sign the certification that is on the back of form I-418. If the vessel is carrying any baggage that is not accompanying a passenger, that baggage and the marks or addresses on the packages must be manifested on the last page of the passenger list under the heading "unaccompanied baggage."

The Traveling Manifest

If the vessel is to proceed to any other U.S. ports after the first port of arrival with inward foreign passengers or cargo remaining on board (residue cargo), an additional copy of the manifest will be required for use as a traveling manifest. The manifest is assembled and taken to the customhouse when making formal entry, at which time the customs officer will certify the complete set as the traveling manifest, called the "traveler." The traveler will be returned to the master when the vessel clears. It must be shown to the customs boarding officer at each port when making preliminary entry and the agent will take it to the customhouse when making formal entry. The master can pick it up again when clearing. This is repeated at each port until all the inward foreign cargo has been discharged and all inward passengers have been landed. At that port the traveler is surrendered to customs. No one may make any changes on the traveler once it has been certified.

Post Entry

If, after the cargo declaration and crew's effects declaration are submitted and formal entry has been made, a discrepancy is discovered between the merchandise manifested on the declarations and the merchandise actually found on board the vessel, the error must be corrected by submitting CF-5931, Discrepancy Report and Declaration (fig. 11). The master should report the shortage or overage to the agent, customs broker, or company representative, who will prepare the post entry.

Customs charges a small fee for a post entry but there are no penalties provided that the discrepancy was the result of a nonnegligent clerical error or a typographical mistake and there has been no loss of customs revenue to the United States. Failure to submit a post entry may subject the master to a heavy fine. If the same vessel or agent repeatedly has similar manifest discrepancies, the customs officer may attribute it to negligence and refuse to allow it as clerical error.

A post entry need not be submitted if the only discrepancy is an error in the marks or numbers listed for packages and the marks or numbers actually on the packages, provided that the quantity and description of the contents of the packages is correct.

Discrepancies in the manifested quantity of bulk petroleum products must be reported on CF-5931 if the difference exceeds 1 percent.

Foreign Repairs or Equipment

The owner or master of every U.S. vessel arriving from a foreign port must declare all equipment, parts, or materials purchased and all repairs made outside the United States upon arrival. This declaration is made on CF-226 (fig. 2) and is required regardless of whether the expenditures are dutiable or not. The declaration must be shown to the customs boarding officer on demand and must be presented as part of the original manifest when making formal entry.

If no foreign repairs or purchases were made on the voyage, the master should submit a CF-226 with "none" typed on the face. If any foreign repairs or purchases were made, then the declaration will probably be made up by a customs broker or other person who specializes in customs regulations because of the detailed paperwork that will be required to document the cost of the repairs or purchases and to support any claims for remission of duties.

For any equipment, repair parts, or material purchased outside the United States, or any repairs made to a U.S. vessel outside the country, the vessel is liable to a duty of 50 percent of the cost of the equipment or repairs. (Labor cost is included in the cost of foreign repairs, but not the cost of any repair work done by regular members of the ship's crew.)

For purposes of assessing duty on foreign repairs or purchases, the following places are not considered to be outside the United States: American Samoa, Guantanamo Bay Naval Station, Guam, Puerto Rico, or the U.S. Virgin Islands.

If the vessel remains outside the United States for two years or more, then only foreign repairs or purchases made during the first six months after leaving the last U.S. port are dutiable.

If the vessel is compelled to have foreign repairs made or to purchase foreign equipment due to stress of weather or other casualty, and if the repairs or equipment are necessary to secure the safety and seaworthiness of the vessel to enable her to reach her port of destination in the United States, then the duty may be remitted. "Casualty" does not include repairs or purchases necessary due to ordinary wear and tear; however, if any part is serviced or repaired immediately before leaving the United States and the part then fails within six months of the servicing or repair, the failure will be deemed to be a casualty.

If the equipment, parts, or materials were produced in the United States, purchased by the vessel owner in the United States, and installed by residents of the United States or by regular members of the crew, the duty may be remitted, even though the work is done in a foreign port.

Duty will be remitted if the equipment, parts, materials, or labor were used as dunnage for cargo, for packing or shoring of cargo, for building temporary bulkheads or similar devices to control bulk cargo, or to prepare tanks to carry liquid cargo. Preparing tanks for carriage of liquid cargo does not include permanent repair or alteration.

If the repairs are for damage caused by heavy weather, the master may need to prepare abstracts of the deck log covering the periods of heavy weather. The damage will, of course, have been entered in the logbook and protest noted at the first port of call after the heavy weather. Copies of these abstracts and protests may be necessary to have the duty remitted. A copy of such protest should always be sent to the insurance department from the port where the note of protest was made.

Estimated duties or a bond should be submitted on CF-301 prior to departure of the vessel. If the master or owner fails to declare, enter, and pay duty on such expenditures, or makes false statements in connection with such declaration, it will subject the vessel to forfeiture or the owner to a monetary penalty up to the value of the vessel.[18] To avoid this, masters should declare all costs of labor, repairs, and purchases for the vessel that are associated with a debt incurred or a payment made outside the United States, even if it is believed that the cost is not subject to a duty. Masters should include all such foreign repairs and purchases even if they were not made while the vessel was under his or her command.

Fees

In addition to collecting U.S. Department of Treasury fees, customs officers have the authority to collect fees on behalf of other federal and state agencies. Usually, fees are handled by the port agent, but the master must retain the receipts and should understand the various fees assessed against his or her vessel.[19]

TONNAGE TAX

The tonnage tax on vessels was established by the third act of Congress on July 20, 1789. Every merchant vessel entering a U.S. port from a foreign port is liable to U.S. Customs for payment of tonnage tax as follows:

1. If the vessel is coming from any foreign port in North America, Central America, the Caribbean, the coast of South America bordering on the Caribbean Sea (considered to include the mouth of the Orinoco River), or the high seas adjacent to the United States or to any of the above locations, the tonnage tax is $0.09 per net registered ton.
2. If the vessel is coming from any other foreign port, the tonnage tax is $0.27 per net registered ton.

Other tonnage tax rules are as follows:

1. No vessel will be required to make more than five tax payments at either rate in a tax year.
2. No vessel will be required to pay more than a combined total of $1.80 per net registered ton per tax year.
3. A tax year starts with the date of the vessel's first tonnage tax payment and ends exactly one year later, at which point the tax year begins again with the vessel's next arrival from a foreign port.
4. If the vessel arrives with cargo or passengers loaded at different ports to which different tax rates apply, tonnage tax will be collected at the higher rate.

Tonnage tax does not apply to the following vessels:

1. A vessel that arrives in distress
2. A vessel that comes into port for bunkers, sea stores, or ship's stores only and that transacts no other business (including receiving orders) and departs within twenty-four hours
3. A passenger vessel making three trips or more per week between a U.S. port and a foreign port
4. A vessel entering directly from the U.S. Virgin Islands, American Samoa, Guam, Wake Island, Midway Island, Canton Island, Kingman Reef, or Guantanamo Bay Naval Station
5. A vessel engaged exclusively in laying or repairing cables

A vessel that calls at a U.S. port for orders only must pay tonnage tax.

USER FEES

Vessels engaged in foreign trade must pay user fees upon entry. These fees are paid on a per-voyage basis as follows:

1. Vessels arriving from Mexico or Canada are charged $100 per voyage up to a maximum of $1,500.
2. Vessels arriving from any other foreign port are charged $397 per voyage up to a maximum of $5,955.
3. Vessels arriving from St. Croix, USVI, are not charged user fees.

SPECIAL TAX AND LIGHT MONEY

A U.S. vessel entering from a foreign port is liable for an additional $0.50 per ton special tax and $0.50 per ton light money if any vessel officer is not a U.S. citizen. This does not apply if the vessel is making her first arrival in the United States from a foreign or intercoastal voyage and all the officers who are not citizens are below the grade of master and are filling vacancies that occurred on the voyage. The master must be a U.S. citizen in any case.

U.S. DEPARTMENT OF AGRICULTURE (USDA)

Customs will collect a $61.75 fee on behalf of the USDA for all vessels arriving from a foreign port (except from Canada) up to a maximum of fifteen times per calendar year.

U.S. IMMIGRATION AND NATURALIZATION SERVICE (INS)

Customs will collect a visa waiver fee on behalf of the U.S. Immigration and Naturalization Service from each vessel arriving from a foreign port unless either the crew list is visaed or each person aboard has a personal visa in his or her passport.

RECEIPTS

The master should keep all original receipts for customs fees as well as receipts for fees paid to customs on behalf of other agencies. Customs officials will want to inspect the original tax receipts upon boarding. Without original receipts, a vessel that has already paid maximum taxes may be charged again.

Overcarried Cargo That Has Been to a Foreign Port

Outward foreign cargo which has been at a foreign port but was overcarried and brought back to the United States must be manifested, even though it is of U.S. origin. If the cargo was overcarried by mistake and will be returned to the intended foreign port of discharge, the master should note on the cargo declaration: "Undelivered—to be returned to original foreign destination."

Residue Cargo for Foreign Ports

If a vessel calls at a U.S. port with inward foreign cargo on board that will be retained for discharge at a foreign port, that cargo must still be manifested on the cargo declaration. If the vessel clears directly for a foreign port from the first U.S. port of arrival, the cargo retained on board may be declared by inserting the following statement on the outward cargo declaration: "All cargo declared on entry in this port as cargo for discharge at foreign ports and so shown on the cargo declaration filed upon entry has been and is retained on board."

If any of the cargo originally manifested to remain on board has subsequently been landed, then the outward cargo declaration must list each item that has been retained on board.

If the vessel will proceed to any other U.S. ports, then the vessel must follow the same requirements previously mentioned for sailing coastwise with inward foreign cargo (see "Inward Foreign Manifests," this chapter).

Sealing Sea Stores and Curios

When a vessel arrives from a foreign port or when a vessel in foreign trade arrives from a domestic port, the customs boarding officer may, if he or she thinks it necessary, seal the storeroom containing sea stores or ship's stores not necessary for immediate use. The officer may also require all crew curios that are to remain on board, for which duty has not been paid and no permit to land has been issued, to be placed in one locker or storeroom, which will be subsequently sealed.

In practice, U.S. Customs officers do not usually bother to collect and seal the curios or to seal the storerooms, particularly if the vessel is not carrying passengers and therefore has only a modest inventory of slop chest goods. If the customs officer does require the curios to be collected and sealed, they should all be securely tied, wrapped, or boxed, and the owner's name should be printed on each package.

Once a storeroom has been sealed by customs, the seal may not be broken without permission from customs until the vessel has departed port and dropped the pilot. If a seal is broken at sea while proceeding coastwise, the master must notify the customs boarding officer at the next port so that he can reseal the storeroom.

Each crewmember will be permitted to keep out 50 cigars, 300 cigarettes, or 2 kilograms of smoking tobacco, or a proportionate amount of each, and 1 liter of alcoholic beverages for use in port.

Lightering Offshore

A ship that enters the United States after visiting a vessel on the high seas is considered to have come from a foreign port or place if any export cargo from the United States is transshipped to the vessel on the high seas or if any cargo received from the vessel on the high seas is brought into the United States. Therefore, if a vessel lighters to or from another vessel in international waters, the master will have to enter and clear the same as if the vessel had called at a foreign country.

Arriving Intercoastal via the Panama Canal

The Canal Zone of the Panama Canal is a foreign port or place and vessels that call at the Canal Zone will have to enter and clear upon their return. Merchandise imported from the Canal Zone is treated the same as merchandise imported from any other foreign country. However, a U.S. vessel sailing between two U.S. ports that merely transits the canal without transacting any business in the Canal Zone will not be required to enter and clear. The vessel will, however, be required to report arrival to customs because of such transit.

If the vessel did no business in the canal but the crew or passengers purchased curios from the line handlers on the vessel during the transit, then each crewmember or passenger will have to submit a Crew Member's Declaration, CF-5129 (fig. 10), or Customs Declaration, CF-6059B (fig. 12), as appropriate. The master must then make up a Crew's Effects Declaration, CF-1304 (fig. 7), and contact the agent before arrival to request the services of a customs officer to clear these curios.

Harbor of Refuge

Vessels arriving in distress or those arriving to take on bunkers, sea stores, or ship's stores only, need not enter and clear provided they will depart within twenty-four hours without having landed or taken on any passengers or merchandise except such bunkers or stores. However, the master, owner, or agent must report the dates and times of arrival and departure and the quantity of bunkers, sea stores, or ship's stores taken on board. If any ship's business is transacted other than as excepted above, the vessel will have to enter and clear. This includes signing crewmembers off and on. If the vessel is in port over twenty-four hours, the master must surrender the last clearance and enter and clear again.

CLEARING FOR A FOREIGN PORT

The following vessels are required to clear before departing from the United States:

1. All vessels departing a U.S. port bound for a foreign port or place
2. All foreign vessels departing for another port or place in the United States
3. All U.S. vessels departing for another port or place in the United States that have merchandise on board that is being transported in bond or foreign merchandise for which entry has not been made
4. All vessels departing for points outside the territorial sea to visit a hovering vessel or to receive merchandise or passengers while outside the territorial sea, as well as foreign vessels delivering merchandise or passengers while outside the territorial sea

Before clearance is granted to a vessel bound for a foreign port, the port director will verify compliance with respect to the following matters:

1. Accounting for inward cargo
2. Outward cargo declarations
3. Documentation
4. Verification of nationality and tonnage
5. Verification of inspection
6. Inspection under state laws
7. Closed ports or places
8. Passengers

9. Shipping articles and enforcement of Seamen's Act
10. Officer's competency certificates (STCW certificates)
11. Medicine and slop chests
12. Load line regulations
13. Carriage of United States securities, etc.
14. Carriage of mail
15. Public health regulations
16. Inspection of vessels carrying livestock
17. Inspection of meat, meat-food products, and inedible fats
18. Neutrality exportation of arms and munitions
19. Payment of state and federal fees and fees due the government of the Virgin Islands
20. Orders restricting shipping
21. Estimated duties deposited or a bond given to cover duties on foreign repairs and equipment for vessels of the United States
22. Illegal discharge of oil
23. Attached or arrested vessel
24. Immigration laws

Application to clear before departing for a foreign port is made by filing a Vessel Entrance or Clearance Statement, CF-1300 (fig. 3), at the customhouse along with other required documents. Necessary information may also be transmitted electronically. As with entry, this can be done by the master, purser, or licensed deck officer, or by the agent or other personal representative of the master. If the vessel will be in port less than twenty-four hours, it is usual to enter and clear at the same time. Clearance will be granted either on CF-1300 or electronically.

A vessel clearing outward must clear for a particular named port; no vessel may clear for the high seas except a vessel that will visit another vessel on the high seas for the purpose of transshipping export or import merchandise bound from or to the United States.

Clearance may be denied under various circumstances if the vessel is not in compliance with applicable navigation laws. A U.S. vessel will not be issued a clearance to a foreign port unless it is properly documented and has a valid certificate of inspection or, in lieu of a certificate of inspection, a permit to proceed to another port for repairs, Coast Guard form CG-948 (fig.14).

The clearance is valid until midnight of the second day after issuance; if the vessel does not depart before that time, the master will have to get the clearance extended. The agent can do this. If the voyage is canceled after clearance is granted, the reason for cancelation must be reported in writing and the certificate of clearance and any related papers returned to customs within twenty-four hours after the cancelation. The certificate of clearance must be filed in a safe place; the officials at the first foreign port will very likely want to see it.

No vessel, American or foreign flag, may sail directly foreign without a foreign clearance. This includes vessels in the foreign trade sailing coastwise on a permit to proceed. Sailing foreign without clearance will result in a heavy fine being imposed on the vessel the next time the vessel calls at any U.S. port. If a vessel is sailing coastwise and the owners desire to divert to a foreign port, the master will have to put into a U.S. port to clear. As expensive as this may be, there is no alternative to this procedure.

Diversion

If after departure a vessel is diverted to a port other than the one named in the clearance, the master should telex the agent at the departure port with instructions to notify customs of the diversion and file a notice of diversion on form CF-26 (fig. 1). If the diversion is from one foreign port to another foreign port, no customs notification is necessary.

A vessel whose final destination is not known may clear for a named port "for orders" if the vessel is in ballast or if any cargo on board is to be discharged at a port in the same country as the port for which the vessel is clearing.

Outward-Bound Cargo Declaration

All outward-bound cargo must be manifested on CF-1302A, Cargo Declaration Outward with Commercial Forms (fig. 5). Copies of bills of lading or equivalent commercial documents must be attached to the cargo declaration along with any export declarations that may be required by regulations of the Department of Commerce. If any such export declarations are required, they should be provided by the customs broker or by the shipper.

At a minimum, the outward cargo declaration must show the following:

1. Name and address of the shipper
2. Description of the cargo, the number of packages, and their gross weight
3. Name of the vessel
4. Port of loading
5. Intended foreign port of discharge

If the bills of lading or equivalent documents that are attached to the cargo declaration describe the cargo by showing on their face the information required by columns six, seven, and either eight or nine of the cargo declaration, the information does not have to be repeated on the cargo declaration provided the cargo declaration makes reference to the bills of lading with a statement such as "Cargo as per attached commercial documents."

Cargo declarations for containerized or palletized cargo may be prepared using the shipper's load and count under the same rules already described for preparing CF-1302.

If, when the vessel is ready to depart, a complete outward-bound cargo declaration is not ready, or all the required export declarations are not ready for filing, customs may accept an incomplete manifest if a bond is on file in accordance with customs regulations and if the appropriate box is checked on CF-1300.

The master or agent must deliver a complete set of foreign cargo clearance documents no later than the fourth business day after vessel clearance.

Crew List

As of February 1997, customs no longer certifies crew lists. This change is reflected in customs regulations 19 CFR §4.9(b) and §4.68. However, customs and immigration will need to see the departure crew list, reflecting any crew changes. (See chapter 10, "Crew Lists," and chapter 12, "Immigration.")

Stores List

The master will need to submit a stores list showing ship's stores and sea stores, the same as is required for arrival.

Certificate of Documentation

Customs will want to see the certificate of documentation to verify that the vessel is documented for registry (foreign trade) or, if bound for the Great Lakes, has a Great Lakes license endorsement. They will also verify the tonnage, nationality, and ownership of the vessel.

Certificate of Inspection

No U.S. vessel required to be inspected may be granted a clearance unless it has a valid U.S. Coast Guard certificate of inspection or, in lieu of a certificate of inspection, a permit to proceed to another port for repairs, Coast Guard form CG-948.

Shipping Articles

The customs officers in some ports will want to see the shipping articles before granting clearance in order to ascertain that the vessel has a full complement as required by the certificate of inspection and that the vessel has complied with the laws respecting shipment of mariners.

SAILING COASTWISE WITH RESIDUE FOREIGN CARGO OR PASSENGERS ON BOARD

If a vessel will discharge any of the inward-bound foreign cargo or passengers at any U.S. port other than the first port of arrival, then one copy of the manifest must be certified as the traveling manifest at the first port of arrival. Before a vessel can proceed from one U.S. port to another with residue foreign cargo or passengers on board, the master must obtain a permit to proceed from the district director of customs. The permit to proceed is applied for by submitting CF-1300 in triplicate. If no inward-bound foreign cargo or passengers will be discharged at the next port, the master should note that fact on CF-1300 by inserting the words "to load only" in parentheses after the name of the port to which the vessel is to proceed.

One copy of the permit to proceed will be attached to the traveling manifest and the other will be given to the master. The original will be retained by customs. The traveling manifest, with the duplicate permit attached, will be returned to the master. If the vessel's certificate of documentation is on deposit with customs, it will also be returned at this time.

Customs regulations call for a traveling crew's effects declaration, along with the unused crewmembers' declarations for items that remain on board, to be placed in a sealed envelope and given to the master for delivery to the customs boarding officer at the next port. This procedure may not be followed in all ports. In any case, it is easier for all concerned if the master tries to clear all the crew curios at the first port of arrival, even if the items will not be landed until a subsequent port.

Upon arrival at the next port the master must report arrival and make entry within twenty-four hours by delivering to the district director of customs the vessel's documentation certificate, the endorsed permit to proceed, the traveling manifest, the traveling crew's effects declaration and remaining crewmembers' declarations, and an abstract manifest for that port consisting of the following:

1. A new vessel entrance or clearance statement
2. A cargo declaration of all cargo for discharge at that port
3. A passenger list of all passengers to be landed at that port
4. A crew's effects declaration in duplicate of all unentered articles acquired abroad by officers and crew remaining on board
5. A ship's stores declaration in duplicate

If no inward-bound foreign cargo or passengers are to be discharged at that port the cargo declaration and the passenger list may be omitted from the abstract manifest if it includes the following statement in the remarks section of the vessel entrance or clearance statement: "Vessel on an inward foreign voyage with residue cargo/passengers or no cargo or passengers for discharge at this port."

Preliminary entry may be made in the same way as entry for the first port of arrival, and the same procedure is followed for each subsequent U.S. port. The traveling manifest is surrendered to customs at the final port of discharge, except that if inward-bound foreign cargo remains on board for discharge at a foreign port, the traveling manifest will be surrendered at the final port of departure from the United States, if it is different from the final port of discharge. If the vessel proceeds from one U.S. port to another via an intermediate foreign port, the traveling manifest is not surrendered when clearing for the foreign port if the vessel still has foreign cargo on board for discharge at a subsequent U.S. port.

The traveling crew's effects declaration is surrendered at any port from which the vessel will depart directly for a foreign port.

DIVERSION BETWEEN U.S. PORTS WITH INWARD-BOUND FOREIGN CARGO

If, while en route between two U.S. ports on a permit to proceed, the vessel receives orders to divert to a U.S. port other than the one named in the permit to proceed, the papers must not be changed in any way. In such a case, the agent should request the office of the district director of customs where the permit was issued to telephone the district director at the new port in advance of the vessel's arrival to report the diversion. If the phone call is made after arrival in the new port, the vessel may be subject to a penalty; therefore, it is important that the first district director be requested to make the call in ample time before the vessel's arrival.

OPTIONAL CARGO

Inward-bound foreign cargo is sometimes shipped without a U.S. discharge port being designated in the charter party or bill of lading, or the documents may show several optional ports, one or more of which will be designated as the discharge port or ports. There is usually a clause in the bill of lading or the charter party calling for the discharge ports to be designated before the vessel reaches a certain position or by a certain date. As soon as the port is known it should be entered on the manifest. When the vessel arrives at the first U.S. port, the discharge ports for all cargo to be discharged on that coast must be designated.

If a vessel arrives on either the Atlantic or Pacific Coast with cargo for the opposite coast or the Great Lakes, or if a vessel arrives on the Great Lakes with cargo for the Atlantic or Pacific Coast and the discharge ports are not yet known, customs will accept a cargo declaration that shows such cargo as destined for "optional ports, Atlantic Coast" or "optional ports, Pacific Coast" or "optional ports, Great Lakes" as appropriate. At the first port on the next area, all discharge ports for the optional cargo must be designated.

SAILING COASTWISE WITH OUTWARD-BOUND FOREIGN CARGO

A vessel that has loaded cargo or passengers at a U.S. port for discharge at a foreign port must clear on a permit to proceed in order to depart for another U.S. port. This is done by filing a vessel entrance or clearance statement in duplicate, the same as when applying for a permit to proceed coastwise with inward-bound foreign cargo. The statement should show all previous loading ports if the port from which the vessel is to be cleared is not the first port where outward-bound foreign cargo was loaded.

An outward-bound cargo declaration must also be filed in accordance with the same rules that apply when clearing for a foreign port.

VESSEL IN COASTWISE TRADE TOUCHING AT FOREIGN PORT

A U.S. vessel on a voyage between two U.S. ports may also call at intermediate foreign ports to load or discharge merchandise or passengers. A permit to proceed or clearance must be obtained at each U.S. loading port for the foreign ports at which the vessel is intended to touch. An outward-bound cargo declaration must be submitted, but it need only show the cargo for a foreign destination. The master must also submit a complete coastwise cargo declaration describing all merchandise that is to be transported to U.S. destinations via the foreign ports.

TRADE WITH NONCONTIGUOUS PORT

"Noncontiguous territory" means all of the island territories and possessions of the United States. A vessel that is not required to clear but is transporting merchandise from the District of Columbia or any state of the United States to any noncontiguous territory including Puerto Rico, or from Puerto Rico to any other noncontiguous territory, must, if required by Department of Commerce regulations, submit a complete manifest along with shippers' export declarations before departing. Alternatively, a bond may be posted if the documents are not ready before departure.[20]

A U.S. vessel that arrives at a port in any state of the United States, the District of Columbia, or Puerto Rico from a port in a noncontiguous territory other than Puerto Rico will not be required to make entry, but the master must report arrival within twenty-four hours and must submit a cargo declaration to the customs boarding officer on arrival and to the district director of customs at the customhouse within forty-eight hours. If the vessel proceeds to another port in any state, the District of Columbia, or

Puerto Rico, the master must submit a cargo declaration the same as for a vessel proceeding to another port with inward-bound foreign cargo on board, but no permit to proceed will be required.

FINES AND PENALTIES

When a vessel owner, master, or person-in-charge has become subject to any penalty for violation of the customs or revenue laws of the United States, the vessel may be held for payment and may be seized to pay the penalty.

Manifest Penalties

If the customs officer finds that unmanifested merchandise is on board or has been discharged from the vessel prior to making entry, a penalty equal to the domestic value of the merchandise—up to a maximum of $10,000—may be incurred. The merchandise is also subject to forfeiture if it belongs to the master of a vessel, the vessel owner, or any officer or crewmember.

Masters who unload unmanifested merchandise could also incur a penalty for unloading without a permit. This permit is obtained from customs during the preliminary entry process.

If masters of vessels describe merchandise on a manifest and that merchandise is not found or located on the vessel, a penalty of $1,000 may be imposed.

The vessel owner or anyone else directly or indirectly responsible for any discrepancy may be liable for the penalties. However, if customs has cited the master of a vessel for a violation, the burden is on the master to prove that someone else is responsible for the violation.

Under certain conditions, masters may be permitted to explain manifest discrepancies. In such cases, masters may be able to avoid penalties for the filing of false or incorrect manifests.

Loading and Unloading Penalties

If merchandise is loaded on or discharged from a vessel without a permit, masters of vessels will incur a penalty equal to the value of the merchandise. The merchandise will also be subject to forfeiture and, if the merchandise is worth more than $500, the vessel will be subject to forfeiture. Furthermore, anyone else involved in the loading or discharging of the merchandise will also incur a penalty equal to the value of the merchandise. A permit to unload does not permit the unloading of unmanifested merchandise. If unmanifested merchandise is unloaded, the master will incur a penalty.[21]

Controlled Substances

The master of a vessel may incur substantial penalties if unmanifested controlled substances are found aboard the vessel.[22] The amount of the penalty is determined by the kind of substance found:

- Heroin, morphine, cocaine, isonipecaine, or opiates—$1,000 per ounce
- Smoking opium, marijuana, and hashish—$500 per ounce
- Crude opium—$200 per ounce

Clearance of the vessel may be held up until the penalty is paid or satisfactory bond is given for payment of the penalty. Additionally, the vessel may be subject to seizure and possible forfeiture.

How to Avoid Penalties

The penalties assessed against masters may be remitted or reduced if it can be proven that (1) neither the master nor the vessel owners had knowledge that narcotic drugs were on board, and (2) both the master and the vessel owner exercised the highest degree of care and diligence in taking precautions to prevent violations by the other officers and crewmembers.

It is the master's responsibility to decide what precautions are reasonably sufficient to guard against smuggling and other illegal acts that may be committed by crewmembers. Some things customs considers when determining penalties are the following:

1. Did the master post warnings around the ship warning crewmembers against smuggling and advising them of the possible penalties? Was this information read to crewmembers who cannot read or understand English?
2. Did the master order frequent searches of the vessel by trustworthy department heads acting as personal representatives of the master?
3. Did the master provide a reliable gangway watch while in port? Was it maintained at all times by responsible crewmembers who were told to keep all unauthorized persons from boarding the vessel and to permit only authorized loading and unloading of merchandise and crew's effects?

Precautions should be especially strict when returning to the United States after visiting a port where narcotics are readily available. If it is impossible to take the above precautions, the master can still avoid or reduce penalties by showing he or she exercised the highest degree of care and diligence by taking other actions.

Anti- or counter-smuggling information and training for masters and ship's crew can be obtained at all U.S. ports by contacting local customs port directors. The training can be narrowly or broadly tailored to meet the needs of individual vessels or masters.[23]

If a master locates narcotics or suspects narcotics activity, he or she should notify customs immediately. If narcotics are found and it is necessary to move them, they should be moved carefully to preserve fingerprint evidence. Such narcotics should be given immediately to customs upon arrival.

CHAPTER 12

Immigration

The immigration officer boards at the first U.S. port of entry. He or she will require a crew list arranged in alphabetical order; the visaed alien crew list if there are any nonresident aliens in the crew who do not have an appropriate U.S. visa on their passports; and one set of completed Crewman's Landing Permit, form I-95AB (fig. 21), for each nonresident alien. If the vessel is carrying passengers, the immigration officer will require an Aircraft/Vessel Report, form I-92 (fig. 19); an Arrival/Departure Record, form I-94 (fig. 20), for each alien passenger except resident aliens and lawfully admitted immigrants; and a passenger list.

The immigration officer will check each crewmember and passenger in person against the crew list and the passenger list. This process will be considerably expedited if the lists are prepared, in accordance with the printed instructions, with the names alphabetically arranged, surnames first. This is different from the practice at most foreign ports, where crew lists are prepared in order of rank. The immigration officer should be given a comfortable place to work and a ship's officer should be detailed to assist in getting the crew assembled as quickly as possible. The crewmembers should bring their merchant mariners' documents and passports with them. Resident alien crewmembers will also have to show their alien registration receipt card, form I-551 (known as a green card).

By immigration and customs regulations, neither passengers nor crew are permitted to go ashore until they are cleared by the immigration boarding officer and until the vessel is cleared by customs. The vessel is subject to a fine if these rules are not strictly observed. It is therefore advisable for the master to post a notice warning the crew and passengers that any person causing the vessel to be fined by going ashore prematurely will be required to pay the vessel's fine.

SIGNING ON ALIENS IN FOREIGN PORTS

It may save the master and the company great expense and inconvenience if the master avoids signing on nonresident aliens in foreign ports. Many such aliens have merchant mariners' documents and social security numbers, and they can show discharges from American vessels. However, these documents mean nothing to an immigration officer, who may still refuse to admit an alien or may give him or her a D-1 permit which involves a lot of red tape. Sailing shorthanded is definitely preferable to signing on a nonresident alien in a foreign port. If, despite all efforts to avoid it, it is necessary to sign on a nonresident alien to fill a vacancy as called for in the certificate of inspection, the master should make certain the person is a licensed mariner and has papers, such as an STCW certification, to prove it. Even so, there is a possibility that the person will be detained on arrival in the United States. If the nonresident alien is not a licensed mariner, the immigration officer may order him or her detained on the vessel and deported. It may then be necessary to employ a guard to watch the person all the time the vessel is in a U.S. port.

THE VISAED ALIEN CREW LIST

If there are any nonresident aliens in the crew, it will be necessary to make up an alien crew list in duplicate on form I-418 (fig. 23). This crew list must be visaed by the U.S. consul at the last foreign port of call before sailing for the United States. Usually, the agent will bring the crew list to the U.S. Consul or U.S. Embassy and a visa will be attached to the crew list. If the master is unable to do this—for example, if there is no U.S. Consul at the last foreign port or if the vessel has sailed for a foreign port and receives orders at sea to divert to a U.S. port—an entry in the official log should explain the circumstances. The duplicate copy of the crew list is kept by the consul. Registered (resident) aliens should not be on this list; they should be on the regular crew list. The alien crew list, visaed or unvisaed, is given to the immigration boarding officer on arrival at the first U.S. port. If the list was not visaed when it should have been, the immigration officer may ask to see the entry in the official log that explains why.

CREWMAN'S LANDING PERMIT

Before arriving at the first port in the United States, the master should prepare form I-95AB, Crewman's Landing Permit, for each nonresident alien crewmember whose name appears on the visaed alien crew list. The completed forms are given to the immigration officer when he or she boards the vessel. The immigration officer will classify each such nonresident alien according to D-1 or D-2 status.

The conditional landing permit designated D-1 is good for a maximum of twenty-nine days, but it restricts the alien and the master in the following ways:

1. The crewmember's passport must be surrendered to the master for safe-keeping.

2. The crewmember must sail with the vessel from every port in the United States unless he or she has advance permission in writing from the master or agent to join the vessel in another U.S. port.

3. The crewmember must sail with the vessel when it leaves the United States.

4. The crewmember may be reexamined by immigration at any time during the period of admission and for certain causes may be returned to the vessel under an order of detention as though he or she had been detained on arrival.

5. The crewmember may not be discharged or paid off without written permission in advance from immigration. For each violation of this requirement, the vessel will be liable to the district director of customs for a penalty.

The D-2 permit grants the alien crewmember a conditional permit to land temporarily for a period not to exceed twenty-nine days if the immigration officer is satisfied that the alien crewmember intends to depart within twenty-nine days as a crewmember on another vessel or as a passenger by any means of transportation. Aliens in this category may be paid off. If the vessel remains in the United States for more than twenty-nine days, the D-2 landing permit will have to be extended.

The immigration officer will stamp the front of each nonresident alien's landing permit D-1 or D-2 according to the category assigned. Once the crewmember's papers have been inspected, the landing permit will be stamped with the date of arrival. The landing permit, not the passport, should be carried ashore.

Request for D-2 Status

The immigration officer should be requested to grant D-2 status to all alien crewmembers in order that the payoff may be completed without having a backlog of wages due. Should the request be refused, the agent should make written application to the immigration officer in charge of the district for a D-2 type of admission. If this application is refused in the port of arrival, additional written requests may be made at subsequent ports. If these are also denied, the master should, to avoid keeping a backlog of wages, request permission to pay wages to the alien even though he or she may not be discharged. Such permission is seldom granted, but it is worth a try. If it is granted, the alien must sail with the vessel or the vessel will be fined.

DRAWS AND WAGES

Since the holder of a D-1 permit cannot be paid off, he or she will most likely ask for a draw and will probably want as much money as possible. This is a difficult position for the master and discretion should be used in granting such draws. If the alien receives a draw close to the total amount owed he or she may leave the ship and not return. The Immigration and Naturalization Service may take a dim view of a large draw payment to an alien holding a D-1 permit.

Should such a situation arise, the master should consult the company's attorneys or payroll department for advice as to the procedure to follow.

Holding back an alien's pay presents a small problem in accounting, as the amount represents unclaimed wages which may have to be paid a voyage or two later. The master should follow the company's instructions for dealing with this situation. If the company has no special instructions, the master should give the mariner a voucher showing the wages due and make a note in the official log of the reason why the mariner's wages are being withheld. The master may also want to type a brief note on the face of the voucher.

PAYING OFF A FOREIGN CREWMEMBER

A completed Application to Pay Off or Discharge Alien Crewman (I-408, figure 22) and all relevant landing permits must be presented to the immigration officer for every alien crewmember being discharged. Once the crewmember is cleared to depart, he or she will be issued a D-2 permit.

DESERTION

Federal law requires that the owner, agent, or master of a vessel immediately report to immigration, in writing, any case of an alien crewmember illegally landing or deserting in a U.S. port. This report should include the alien's name, nationality, passport number, personal description, time and circumstances of the landing or desertion, and any information or documents that might aid in apprehending the alien, specifically including any passport or personal documents that the alien surrendered to the master.

The master or the agent should notify immigration by telephone as soon as the alien is discovered missing. This telephone notification should be followed by a written report as soon as possible, but definitely within twenty-four hours. Despite the immediate telephone call to immigration, the written report is still required by law.

DETAINEES

Instead of issuing a D-1 or D-2 permit, the immigration officer may prohibit shore leave of any kind and may issue a detention order requiring the master to detain an alien on board the vessel. If the immigration officer prohibits shore leave, he or she will stamp "Permission to land temporarily at all U.S. ports is refused" on the crewman's landing permit and return it to the master. Immigration will also issue a "notice of detention" to the master listing the detainees.

Alien passengers as well as crewmembers may be detained. The master may need to employ a special guard to see that detainees do not go ashore. The vessel is liable for a substantial fine if detainees go ashore, even if they return to the vessel.

REPORTING CHANGES IN CREW

Immigration regulations require that every vessel departing from the United States submit form I-418 showing all changes in the nonresident alien crew. The first line of the form should have the caption "Arrival Crew List, form I-418, filed at [U.S. port of arrival]."

Under the heading "Added Crewmen" should be a list of the names of all nonresident aliens who were not members of the crew when the vessel last arrived in the United States. For each such person the form I-94 or I-95AB that was given to the crewmember at the last arrival in the United States should be attached or, if the person has no such form, a newly executed form I-95AB.

Under the heading "Separated Crewmen" should be a list of all nonresident aliens who were members of the crew when the vessel arrived in the United States but who will not be departing with the vessel. For each such crewmember, the list should show the person's nationality, passport number, port and date of separation, and the reason for the failure to depart. If an application to pay off or discharge an alien crewmember was granted subsequent to arrival, the triplicate copy of form I-418 should be attached.

If there have been no changes, the master should endorse the I-418, "No changes in nonresident alien crew upon departure." Immigration officers usually do not require this form from U.S. vessels that had no nonresident aliens on board on arrival and that do not have any nonresident aliens on board upon departure.

MEDICAL TREATMENT OF NONRESIDENT ALIEN

If a nonresident alien requires medical treatment and the person was refused a conditional landing permit or was issued a D-1 landing permit, the master will have to apply to immigration for permission to land the person. The Immigration Service will not give the alien a D-2 landing permit in such a case; instead, the mariner will be paroled into the custody of the agent or a company official. The crewmember must have a form I-94, which the immigration officials will endorse to reflect the terms of parole.

The master, agent, or an official of the company will have to sign a guarantee for the mariner's medical expenses and other related expenses. When medical treatment or hospitalization is completed, the ship's company is responsible for departure of the alien from the country.

INWARD PASSENGERS

Some cargo vessels are equipped to carry up to twelve passengers. For immigration and customs purposes, a passenger is any person carried on board a vessel who is not connected with the operation, navigation, ownership, or business of the vessel, and as such must be shown on a passenger list, completed on form I-418.

The passengers' names must be listed in alphabetical order, family names first. If stowaways are discovered, their names should be put on a separate list marked "stowaways"; the name of the port where each one stowed away should be included. The immigration officer will require two copies of the passenger list at the first port of arrival. It is advisable to have some extra lists and to keep one for the vessel's file.

The death of a passenger must be noted on the passenger list along with the cause of death. Of course the home office and the agent at the port of arrival should be notified immediately.

Before sailing from a foreign port it is advisable, if any of the passengers are aliens, for either the master or the agent to check their passports and visas. An alien passenger whose passport lacks a proper visa may be refused permission to land by the immigration officer. This means that the company may have to return the alien to the port where the person embarked and the vessel may be subject to a fine.

An alien passenger may be detained for reasons other than lack of a proper visa. If the immigration officer issues a detention order on the passenger, the master should notify the company office or agent immediately. It may be necessary to employ a guard to see that the detained passenger remains on board.

For information on stowaways, see chapter 5, "Vessel Security."

Regulations of the Immigration and Naturalization Service are found in 8 CFR. Federal statutes pertaining to immigration are contained in 8 USC.

CHAPTER 13

Accounting

Very few merchant vessels carry pursers these days. Therefore the master, or an officer directed by the master, must prepare the vessel's accounts—payrolls, wage vouchers, portage, etc. Regardless of who handles the accounts, the master is responsible for their accuracy.

After the shipping articles have been opened, the names of the crew should be entered in the official logbook, the slop chest account book, and the payroll. It will make the job easier if the names are entered in the same sequence on each of these forms. Most masters enter the names on all forms in the same order as they appear on the shipping articles and on the crew list.

ACCOUNTING FORMS

Various forms of payroll records and wage vouchers are used by different companies. Computer software is also available for the master's use. All are basically the same although some may include space for additional items, such as company insurance, union benefits, and other deductions.

For accounting purposes the master should have on board the following forms, books, and information:

1. Cash receipt book or similar form
2. The port and date where each crewmember was engaged and, if different, the port and date where the crewmember joined. This information is necessary in case transportation must be paid.
3. W-4 forms showing social security numbers and tax exemptions claimed. Each crewmember should fill out this form the day he or she joins. An ample supply of blank forms should be on hand.
4. A sufficient stock of blank wage vouchers

5. An ample supply of blank payroll forms
6. Pay scales showing wages, overtime rates, and any special payments that may be called for under union agreements
7. Copies of union agreements and working rules with the latest amendments and clarifications
8. Accounting instructions and a supply of any special forms required by the company
9. Treasury Department form 1078, Certificate of Alien Claiming Residence in the United States (fig. 24)
10. An ample supply of overtime sheets for each department
11. Several blank official logbooks
12. If on foreign or intercoastal articles, the amount of any allotment for each crewmember and when payable
13. The current rate for social security (FICA) contributions and the amount of income that is taxable
14. The current tax rate for state unemployment insurance. This varies by state and is often changed. It is generally a small amount, payable to the state in which the vessel is registered.
15. Current tax withholding tables
16. An ample supply of earnings statements or similar forms. These show the total earnings, taxes, other deductions, and the balance due for each member of the crew. It is copied from the payroll and a copy is given to each crewmember on payoff.
17. Subsistence and room allowance rates (board and lodging). These rates are usually on the pay scales and are always in the union agreements.
18. Amount of deductions for company insurance and other benefits
19. Master's cash statement (portage) forms
20. Slop chest statement and inventory forms

Copies of all completed accounting forms (papers, vouchers, letters regarding any payment of wages) should be made for the vessel's file. The name of the vessel, date, voyage number, and port should appear on all forms and papers generated.

ORDERING CASH

In order to give draws and to pay the crew off at the end of the voyage, the master will need to have sufficient cash on hand. The company will probably specify how cash is to be ordered and possibly how much the master is to carry. The maximum amount of cash allowed on board may be set by the company's insurance policy. Aboard the vessel, the combination to the safe should be known only to the master. Some ship companies keep the combination on file in the office; in that case, the chief officer should be instructed to obtain the combination from the office by radio if the master should become incapacitated.

As a security measure, the master should refrain from discussing cash orders or other financial transactions over nonsecure communications systems, especially VHF radios.

When ordering cash the master must specify the breakdown, that is, how the total amount is to be apportioned among the various denominations of currency. Some companies establish a standard breakdown for given amounts, so cash could be ordered "$30,000 standard breakdown." At payoff time, when the crewmembers have a lot of money to carry home with them, they will want mostly large bills, like fifties and hundreds. When receiving a draw during the voyage they will want smaller bills, mostly twenties. A mariner going ashore after banking hours may find that no one will accept or change a one-hundred-dollar bill.

Money is generally delivered in a sealed bag. The usual procedure is for the master to break the seal, count the money, and sign the receipt in the presence of the delivery guard. The guard will want the master's signature on several copies of the receipt and will undoubtedly want each copy to be stamped with the ship's stamp. The master should get two copies of the receipt, one for the ship's file and one to send to the company along with the master's cash statement.

It sometimes happens that the guard will not allow the seal to be broken until after the master signs the receipt. In this case, the master should insert the words "one bag said to contain" in front of the dollar amount on the receipt and make a note stating that he or she was not allowed to count the money. After signing the receipt, the master must count the money as soon as the guard has turned the bag over and report any discrepancies.

As a security measure, the master should handle financial transactions in a locked room with a reliable gangway watch posted.

ADVANCES

An advance is not a draw. An advance is money advanced to the mariner before it has been earned and such payment is prohibited by law. A master may not do any of the following:

1. Pay a mariner wages in advance of the time when the mariner has earned the wages
2. Pay advance wages of the mariner to another person
3. Make to another person an order, note, or other evidence of indebtedness of the wages, or pay any other person for the engagement of the mariner when payment is deducted or is to be deducted from the mariner's wages.[1]

Should a master pay a crewmember from wages yet to be earned, the person may claim the amount to be due him or her at sign-off as the amount would appear to be missing from the sign-off wages. Additionally, wage advances, being legally void, may not then be deducted from a sailor's pay should he or she become injured during the voyage and entitled to payment for the full voyage. Interestingly, this regulation also applies to a foreign vessel within the waters of the United States.

DRAWS

After the beginning of a voyage, a mariner is entitled to receive from the master, on demand, one-half of the balance of wages earned and remaining unpaid at each port at which the vessel loads or delivers cargo. This is called a "draw." Most crewmembers do not request half of their wages but instead draw spending money for shopping in port. A demand may not be made before the end of five days from the beginning of the voyage and not more than once in five days nor more than once in the same port on the same entry. However, union agreements may call for a draw at specific intervals regardless of why or how long the vessel is in port.

If the master does not comply, the mariner is released from articles and entitled to the entirety of his or her wages.

In practice there is no reason to restrict the crew to only one draw during an extended stay in port or to limit draws only to ports where cargo is to be worked; such a policy would certainly result in hard feelings between the master and the crew. Most masters will give a draw every five days or every week during a long port stay.

Although the mariner is entitled by law to draw half of the balance of earned wages that remain unpaid, most companies allow the crewmember to draw the entire balance of earned wages, less deductions. For obvious reasons it is poor policy to allow a crewmember to draw all of his or her gross wages before deductions, or to overdraw. Nevertheless, mariners will sometimes ask to overdraw, and some masters allow a crewmember to overdraw in special circumstances.

Before a mariner is entitled to a draw, he or she should have earned at least the amount necessary to pay the next allotment, if any, as well as previous draws, slops, taxes, and other deductions. If a crewmember is allowed to overdraw and he or she misses the sailing, the master may be responsible for the amount overdrawn. It is, however, entirely the master's responsibility if, under special circumstances, he or she permits a crewmember to overdraw.

If the master makes an error entering a draw in the official logbook, the error should not be erased or changed in any way. A line should be drawn through the entire entry, a new entry made on the next line, and the correction initialed. The log should always include the date when the draw was made.

Union agreements usually call for the draw to be made in U.S. currency. If foreign money is used and the agent does not supply a conversion table, the master should make one up and post copies on the bulletin boards. The rate of exchange used should also be entered in the official log. Even though a draw may be made in foreign money, the crew should sign for the equivalent in U.S. dollars. In order to simplify the accounting as much as possible, it is much better to deal in U.S. currency only.

PAYROLL

Wages in most shipping companies are now paid based on a thirty-day month: a mariner's monthly salary divided by thirty is the daily pay. Under this most agreeable system there are actually twelve months and five days in each year. Some companies use a 365-day year: the monthly salary multiplied by twelve and divided by 365 is the daily pay. The union agreements or company instructions will specify how daily pay is to be calculated.

On the voyage homeward, the master should total up the draws for each person as shown in the official logbook. These should be double-checked and then entered in the proper column of the payroll. When the slop chest has been closed for the voyage, the master must check and total the slop chest account book, if one was used. This book or a printout of the file should not be destroyed but should be kept with the voyage file. The totals should be entered in the proper column of the payroll and in the official log.

The crew is usually anxious to know how much is to be deducted for draws and slops at the end of the voyage. They will appreciate it if they can find out the totals as soon as the master has calculated them. When on a foreign or intercoastal voyage, federal law requires the master to give each crewmember an accounting of wages and deductions forty-eight hours before he or she is paid off or discharged.

The master should start the payroll in ample time so that it can be completed before arriving at the payoff port. Early on the return voyage, or even on the outward voyage if time permits, the data that will not change should be entered: names, ratings, social security numbers, starting dates, wages per month, tax exemptions, and, when completed, draw, allotment, and slop chest amounts. These figures can be entered on a rough or pencil copy or on a spreadsheet draft of the payroll, from which the required number of finished copies will be printed. The rough pencil copy, or one of the typed copies, is completed in pencil as soon as it is known when to close the payroll. This is generally midnight on the day of arrival.

It is preferable to complete a rough copy in pencil—there will probably be some erasures—and to transfer the figures to the original sheet after it is checked and balanced, taking care not to transpose any of the figures; this is a common error. Some companies may require several extra copies showing only the base wages earned by each person. These are for the unions who may require the information to calculate welfare, pension, and vacation benefits. The extra copies may be photocopies, but they must be legible.

If the port of payoff is definitely known, the master can estimate the day of arrival and, if time permits, make a payroll for that day and for a day later, in case weather delays the vessel. These may be rough copies but both should be balanced; then, when the master is sure of the arrival day, the figures from the appropriate copy can be entered on the original payroll. Again, care should be taken to avoid transposing any of the figures. This method, although it involves some extra work, will save time eventually and avoids the rush of making up a new payroll if the vessel is delayed. Most companies employ computer software that simplifies the entire task.

Before balancing the payroll, all the figures should be checked and rechecked. The social security numbers and tax exemptions should be checked against the W-4 forms. The overtime should be carefully checked and, if there are several sheets per crewmember, the sheets for each person should be stapled or clipped together.

Some companies not yet using computer programs require that the payrolls be entirely typed. Others, more practical, require that only a few items be typed, such as names and ratings, social security numbers, starting dates, and base pay. Needless to say, the payroll, if typed, should be checked before typing and checked against the rough copy after typing. Some companies do not use a master payroll at all. Instead, only individual wage vouchers are submitted.

CHANGE LIST

It may be necessary to make up a change list after the payroll is completed. The total for each person is broken down to the highest denomination of bills and change. When completed, the lists should be balanced.

Some masters adjust the amount of taxes withheld so that the balance due each crewmember comes out to an even dollar amount so that there is no need to worry about small change. (There is no objection to this procedure, since it can be accomplished by an adjustment of fifty cents or less.) On a large payoff, these masters may even adjust the amount to the nearest twenty or fifty dollars.

PORT PAYROLL

The port payroll, if used, covers the period between paying off for the voyage just completed and opening articles for the next voyage. Some companies require that discharges are to be made up each time there is a payoff in port. Most masters sign on the crewmembers who will remain for the next voyage at the same time they sign off the crew for the completed voyage. This eliminates the necessity for a port payroll.

OVERTIME

For many mariners, depending upon the union contract, over 35 percent of their total income is paid for overtime. It is imperative that the master, chief mate, and bosun understand the collective bargaining agreement in detail.

Overtime Sheets

Overtime support sheets issued by the different companies vary in form but all require essentially the same data. The department heads should check and correct the overtime sheets for their departments every week or so to be sure there is no overlapping of hours except as permitted by the union agreement, that times and total hours are correct, that work performed is clearly described, and that the overtime claimed is according to the agreement.

Many crewmembers will have several overtime sheets. When a sheet is full it should be totaled and double-checked. If the total on one sheet is carried forward to the next sheet, that fact should be noted on both sheets. When a crewmember has more than one sheet, they should be numbered and stapled or clipped together.

Disputed Overtime

If a crewmember turns in overtime that the master does not believe is payable he or she should dispute it by drawing a single line through the disputed entry and writing a brief note explaining why it is disputed. The master must not obliterate the entry or make it unreadable and should not include the disputed overtime in the total hours and should not pay it. The mariner's copy of the overtime sheet is proof that a claim was submitted for the overtime in case the crewmember later wants to file a grievance against the company.

Just because a mariner has written in overtime does not mean that it should automatically be paid. Some mariners do not know their agreement very well and will claim overtime when it is not payable, and occasionally the master may even encounter a crewmember who is actually trying to cheat.

Extra Earnings on Overtime Sheets

Extra earnings, such as division of wages, extra meals, and passenger money are shown on the payroll or wage vouchers if columns are provided. If there are no columns for these payments, they should be itemized on the overtime sheets. For example:

Totals:	Straight overtime (3 sheets)	$1,025.58
	Extra meals, see letter	$ 14.50
	Passenger money, see letter	$ 52.50
	Division of wages, see letter	$ 138.25
	Grand total	$1,230.83

The total should then be entered in the overtime column of the payroll.

All overtime appearing on the payroll or on a voucher should be supported by overtime sheets; each sheet should be signed by the crewmember, the appropriate department head, and the master.

OTHER PAYMENTS

Many union contracts allow for additional payments to be made to mariners for additional or unexpected duties or risks. Each contract is different and it would be wise for the master and chief mate to invest the time necessary to thoroughly understand the union contract. Detailed records should be kept to facilitate resolution of any disputed additional wages or bonuses.

War Zone Bonuses

The payroll form may have a column for bonuses. If there is more than one, the bonuses may be grouped together and the total sum per person entered. All details should be given in a supporting letter. War zone bonuses are sometimes broken down as follows:

Area bonus—This bonus calls for wages to be increased, usually by a given percentage, for every day that the vessel is within a war zone. The war zone is usually defined by agreement between the operating company and the crew unions. Area bonuses have been as high as 100 percent.

Harbor attack bonus—This is a payment, provided under some agreements, whereby the crew will receive an additional sum if they are in a harbor where any vessel is attacked. This is in addition to the area bonus.

Vessel attack bonus—This bonus is paid if the vessel itself is attacked. It is either in addition to or higher than the harbor attack bonus.

Ammunition bonus—This generally calls for an extra payment to the crew for each day that the vessel is carrying more than a specified amount of ammunition. The supporting letter should give the dates the ammunition cargo was loaded and discharged, the amount of ammunition (usually in tons), and the number of days it was aboard.

Promotions

If a crewmember is promoted during the voyage, the person's name should appear on the payroll twice, once for each rating. It will be easiest for both the master and the accounting department if the two entries appear on adjacent lines on the payroll. Dates must not overlap, either on the payroll or on the discharges.

Nonwatch Pay

Nonwatch pay should not be added to the base pay but should be entered in a separate column unless instructions from the company state otherwise.

Linen Money

Some union agreements require the crew to be paid a certain amount when they are not issued clean linen as often as stipulated in the agreement. This sometimes occurs when, on a long voyage, the vessel calls at ports that do not have adequate laundry facilities. This payment is seldom necessary if a little foresight is used, but if it must be made, a supporting letter may be required to explain the circumstances, naming the ports where the laundry could not be done and giving any other reason why the clean linen was not issued.

Division of Wages for Missing Crewmember

When a member of the crew is missing—because he or she failed to join on sailing, was hospitalized, could not obtain the required rating, or is on board but is ill and laid up— the crewmembers who temporarily take over the work either divide the missing crewmember's wages or receive overtime. This most often affects the steward's department or the watchstanding licensed officers. If an unlicensed watchstander is missing or laid up, a day-worker is usually put on watch and no division of wages is necessary. This, of course, should be in accordance with any union agreement. The master should write a supporting letter explaining the facts, showing the crewmember's wages per month, the number of days he or she was missing (with dates), to whom the money was paid, and the amount. It can either be paid by voucher or added to the overtime of the crewmembers involved. If the latter occurs, it should be explained on the overtime sheet.

Passenger Money

Some dry cargo vessels carry up to twelve passengers. The union agreement may require that one or two passenger utility people be added to the steward's department according to the number of passengers on board for the voyage, or that a specified sum of money per passenger per day be paid to the crewmembers in the steward's department who attend the passengers.

As a general rule, only one passenger utility person is carried and if the agreement calls for an additional person, the company, in lieu of taking on a second crewmember, will divide the required sum among the crew who are sharing the work.

The section of the agreement pertaining to passenger money should be thoroughly understood. The logbook should note the dates, ports, and times the passengers embark and disembark. A supporting letter should show the number of passengers carried, the times, dates, and ports of embarkation and debarkation, rate per day per passenger, number of days on board, total amount payable, names and ratings of the crewmembers, and the amount of money each will receive. This sum can be paid by voucher or added to the overtime if a column is not provided on the payroll. If the latter occurs, it should be explained on the overtime sheet.

Extra Meals Served

The union agreement may specify that crewmembers in the steward's department who prepare and serve meals to persons other than the crew will receive an extra payment for each such meal served. The procedure varies in different companies but definite instructions are generally issued regarding extra meals. A supporting letter is required to show the total number of extra meals served, the charge per meal, and the total amount, as well as the names and ratings of the crewmembers who share the amount and how much each person will get. Some companies issue meal chits that must be signed by the person receiving the meal, in which case a supporting letter is usually not necessary. These amounts can be placed in a spare column on the payroll or added to the overtime sheet with an explanatory note.

Penalty Cargo

The union agreement may call for the crew to receive extra pay if the vessel is carrying a particularly noxious or dirty cargo. These penalty cargoes are listed in the agreements. The payroll may have a column for this; otherwise, a supporting letter is required showing the date the cargo was loaded, the type of cargo, the date and port at which it was discharged, and the total number of days it was on board. This information should also be in the logbook.

Dirty Work

An extra payment is provided for crewmembers who are required to perform especially unpleasant work such as entering boilers or working on sewage disposal machines. Jobs qualifying as dirty work, if any, will be specified in the applicable agreement.

Mariner Receiving Pay of Higher Rating

The union agreement may stipulate that under certain circumstances a crewmember will receive the pay for the next higher rating instead of the usual pay rate. For example, when more than a certain number of passengers are carried on a cargo vessel, the second cook might receive chief cook's pay during the time the passengers are on board. The difference may be entered on a separate line of the payroll, paid by voucher, or added to the crewmember's overtime with an explanatory note, depending upon company instructions. The master may have to write a supporting letter giving the number of passengers carried, the days they were on board, and the dates of embarking and disembarking.

This is not a promotion as such and need not be entered in the official log. Usually the agreement provides that the crewmember is not actually being promoted to the higher rating, but only that the person is receiving the higher rate of pay temporarily. The master should abide by the union agreement or company instructions if they differ from the above.

PAYROLL DEDUCTIONS

Nothing upsets a person faster than a mix-up about pay. Masters must ensure that any payroll deductions are correct and timely, especially allotments. Taxes should be taken out according to published schedules. Any complaints regarding pay should be looked into immediately.

Allotments

When on a foreign or intercoastal voyage, a crewmember may designate that the shipping company pay any part of his or her wages directly to any of the following:

1. The mariner's grandparents, parents, spouse, sister, brother, or children
2. An agency authorized by the Department of the Treasury for the purchase of U.S. savings bonds for the mariner's account
3. A savings or investment account opened and maintained by the mariner in his or her name at a federally insured bank or savings and loan association[2]

An allotment to any other person or agency is invalid.

To be valid, an allotment note must be in writing and must be approved and signed by a shipping commissioner. The U.S. consul may perform the duties of shipping commissioner in a foreign port, and the master may perform the duties of shipping commissioner in a U.S. port.

Federal Withholding Tax

Federal withholding tax for all employees is levied on wages and overtime and also on extras such as bonuses of all kinds, extra meal money, passenger money, and wages for missing crewmembers. The tax is not levied on payments made for transportation or subsistence (while in drydock, for example).

W-4 FORM (EMPLOYEE'S WITHHOLDING ALLOWANCE CERTIFICATE)

A column on the payroll and a space on the voucher will be headed "Tax Exemptions" or "Tax Status" or the like. The number of tax exemptions and the marital status claimed by the crewmembers on the W-4 form are entered here. Check to see that the W-4 forms have been properly made out. If a crewmember is incapable of writing legibly it will save time and trouble to have the form typed or printed and then signed by the person. The date and signature must be on each form.

A resident alien fills out the W-4 form and also Treasury Department form 1078, Certificate of Alien Claiming Residence in the United States (fig. 24), which should be attached to the W-4 form. The resident alien must have a registration card showing proof of legal entry into the United States. Merely claiming residence or showing that he or she had previously paid full taxes is not sufficient proof.

State Unemployment Insurance

An unemployment tax up to a stated amount is paid by each member of the crew, including all aliens. This tax is levied by the state in which the vessel is registered but the entire crew pays this tax regardless of where their homes might be. For example, a crewmember whose home is in New York and who works on a vessel that sails between New York and Texas but is registered in Wilmington, Delaware, will pay the unemployment tax of Delaware. The tax varies from state to state and the amount is changed from time to time. It is levied on the same amounts that are used in computing social security deductions as shown on the payroll or voucher.

Social Security (FICA)

Social security deductions are levied on all wages, overtime, and other payments except subsistence and lodging.

As mariners often change vessels and companies, and social security contributions are deducted for each voyage up to the maximum amount, it follows that many mariners will overpay their social security contribution. In this case they can apply the amount of overpayment against their federal income tax. The total amount of social security paid each year will appear on the W-2 form, Wage and Tax Statement, which is issued by all companies to their employees. Crewmembers who change companies often will receive a number of W-2 forms.

Some companies periodically issue a form showing, as far as can be ascertained, the amount of social security and unemployment insurance tax already paid by each member of the crew while working for that company.

If this information is not available for any member of the crew the master must assume that the full amount of taxes is due. Once a crewmember has paid the maximum tax due, no further deductions are made.

While working for a company the employee does not receive any credit for social security deductions paid while employed by another company. The crewmember is liable for the maximum social security amount on wages earned while working for the current company regardless of what may have been withheld by another company. Any excess amounts withheld will be applied to the person's income tax as explained above.

VOUCHERS

Vouchers are essentially IOUs from the company to the mariner and they should be handled with the same care and scrutiny as any other payroll document. There are various types of vouchers. In all cases, the master should make copies for the office and for the vessel's files.

Transportation

Transportation is usually paid and signed for on a voucher separate from the payroll; some companies include a column for transportation on the payroll. Travel fares are not subject to withholding, social security, or unemployment insurance taxes. The usual procedure when transportation is payable is to have the agent ascertain from the ticket office the fare and the length of time the journey will take, then determine the pay and subsistence the crewmember will receive. Wages, subsistence, and transportation are all paid at the same time.

If the agent pays for the transportation, he or she may want a travel voucher or a letter from the master authorizing the transportation charge to the company.

The master must clearly understand the transportation clauses of any applicable union agreement and keep an accurate list of where each person joined the vessel. In some companies the master will not pay the crewmembers' transportation; instead the company or the agent will make travel arrangements for them and will pay the fares directly to the airline or other carrier.

Vouchers Not Paid by Master

When a member of the crew fails to join for any reason, a wage voucher is made up and either given to the agent or forwarded to the accounting office, depending upon the company's instructions. The master should not give any money to the agent, instead providing only the voucher, which should show that the balance has not been paid and is due to the mariner. However, the master should sign the voucher authorizing payment.

If the voucher is given to the agent, the master should also provide instructions regarding payment. If the crewmember turns up after the ship sails, the agent should either pay the wages and have the mariner sign the voucher as a receipt, or give the mariner the voucher to present to the operating company for payment. Which procedure is used will depend on the company's policy. The master should keep several copies of the voucher, including one for the vessel's file.

Wage Vouchers

A member of the crew who is paid off before the end of the voyage may be paid by wage voucher. Like other forms, these vouchers will vary with the different companies, but the items included are more or less the same. A crewmember who is paid off after signing on is paid by voucher, but the person's name should be included in the payroll with a note in the signature column stating that he or she was paid by voucher. Vouchers used in paying off crewmembers not on articles (such as people who have quit before signing on), vouchers for overtime which was disputed but has since been determined to be payable, and similar vouchers are called miscellaneous vouchers. All paid vouchers should be kept in a safe place.

The master should make a sufficient number of copies of vouchers to provide one for the mariner, one for the vessel's file, and the required number, usually no more than two, for the accounting department. When a crewmember has been paid off in a foreign port, regardless of the reason, the U.S. consul will require a record of the figures shown on the voucher.

If a crewmember fails to join in any port and the vessel sails before the vouchers can be made up, the agent and/or operating company should be advised by radio or telephone of the amount the crewmember is owed and that the allotment, if there is one, should be stopped. The master should make an entry in the official log of any such failure to join, regardless of the reasons, and include the crewmember's wage account.

The voucher should include overtime but not disputed overtime. The latter should not be paid until settled at the port of payoff or by whatever procedure the company uses. The master should be sure he or she has the W-4 form, which should have been made up when the crewmember shipped. It could be very disconcerting to find, after a crewmember has failed to join, that there was not a W-4 form for the person. If this should happen, "1" should be given as the number of exemptions claimed. The crewmember's social security number would be on the articles and on the crew data card, which should also include the exemptions, but if the articles have not been opened and a data card has not been made up, "not available" should be written in the space provided for the social security number.

Vouchers should be filed as soon as they are paid. A lost or misplaced voucher may be the master's responsibility.

The master should maintain a rough list of miscellaneous vouchers and add new vouchers to it as they are made up. This list should show the voucher number, name and rating of the crewmember, and balance paid. These vouchers should be numbered consecutively and, on the cash statement or settlement, shown as "miscellaneous vouchers, numbers __ to __ as per attached list."

Vouchers shown on the payroll for crewmembers who have signed articles but were paid off and signed off or who failed to join before the end of the voyage need not be included in the above list, but a separate list of such vouchers should be made for the master's own protection.

The miscellaneous voucher list can be made up as follows:

SS *Seven Seas* Voy. 95
Miscellaneous Vouchers

No.	Name	Rate	Balance Paid
1.	U. Esceegee	AB	$1,229.00
2.	W. Turn	OS	528.00
3.	W. T. Door	Oiler	671.20
4.	B. Floatin	Oiler	1,232.00
5.	I.C. Rust	Bosun	835.30
6.	U. Stier	OS	497.90
7.	I. Steu	Cook	104.90
8.	N. Bowditch	3/M	1,083.80
9.	C. Speed	OS	677.00
10.	E. Sperry	AB	823.20
	Total		$7,682.30

THE SLOP CHEST

Federal law requires that every vessel on a foreign or intercoastal voyage, except a voyage to Canada, Bermuda, the West Indies, Mexico, or Central America, must have a slop chest. The slop chest must contain sufficient clothing for the voyage for each crewmember, including everything necessary—boots or shoes, hats or caps, underclothing, outer clothing, foul weather clothing—and also a complete supply of tobacco and blankets.[3] These requirements have not changed in decades and most slop chests carry additional items for the convenience of the crew.

When taking command of a vessel in operation, the master should have the slop chest inventoried, if possible, before permitting anything to be sold. This is often a good job for the cadet, if there is one aboard.

When coastwise, most masters use a plain ruled notebook for a slop chest account book and have each mariner sign for slop chest purchases when they are made. Some vessels have computer-generated forms or spreadsheets. At payoff, the total of each crewmember's purchases is entered on the payroll and on the wage voucher.

On a foreign voyage the slops should be entered and signed for in the official log. Some masters have the crew sign a slop chest account book for individual purchases made during the voyage and then have them sign the official log only for the total at payoff. Other masters have the crew initial the official log for each slop chest purchase at the time it is made and also sign for the total at payoff. The latter is probably the better procedure. Whether in a slop chest account book or in the official log, all sales to a crewmember should be initialed at the time of the sale. This applies only to slops sold on credit. A mariner need not sign for the purchase when paying with cash because the purchase price will not be deducted from wages.

It seems inevitable that there will always be a shortage in the slop chest accounting at the end of the voyage. Usually the shortage is small and most likely due to failure to enter a sale in the account book. When slop chest supplies are received, they should be checked carefully, although it is seldom that an error is made at that time. If a shortage is found when supplies are received, it should be reported and noted on the delivery invoice.

The slop chest form (it varies with different companies) shows the quantity and cost of merchandise on hand from the previous voyage, items received during the present voyage, items sold during the voyage, and merchandise on board at the end of the voyage. The master probably will not have a chance to check this form before sailing, but it should be checked at the first opportunity.

Several price lists should be posted on the bulletin boards and in the slop chest room, and one copy should be put in the slop chest account book. If possible, the master should keep a running inventory and, on a long voyage, check the slop chest several times against the running inventory.

After the slop chest has been opened for the last time on the voyage, the master should take a complete inventory, which should balance with the running inventory. The account book should then be checked for overcharges and undercharges and the accounts entered on the payroll.

The master must never charge the crew more than the amount shown on the slop chest price list regardless of how much of a shortage occurs. Federal law requires that slop chest goods be sold to the crew at a profit not exceeding ten percent of the reasonable wholesale value at the port where the voyage began.

If any profit is realized from the slop chest account, it is distributed in accordance with company policy. The profit may be retained by the company, kept by the master as compensation for handling the slop chest, kept by another officer who handles the slop chest, donated to a crew recreation fund, or handled in a similar manner. If the company has no policy, it is recommended that the master simply sell slop chest goods at cost. The book-keeping will be simpler and the crew will appreciate it. Slop chest profits are usually very small anyway.

MASTER'S EXPENSES

The master should keep an accurate account of all money paid out on company business, backing up the account with receipts whenever possible and with notes when it is impossible to get receipts. The total should be entered on the cash statement and the original sent along with the statement. The master should retain a copy of the completed expense account for the vessel's file. Master's expenses should be kept to a minimum.

For accounting purposes, most companies prefer to have supplies requisitioned through the company or agent rather than purchased through the master. Occasionally, time does not permit the normal procedure, for example, if the vessel has just received a change of orders and is about to sail and the master must buy charts for the voyage. Some companies give the master a fixed monthly allowance to spend on incidentals, without prior office approval.

MASTER'S CASH STATEMENT (PORTAGE)

The master's cash statement, also known as the portage, is a statement showing all cash transactions for the accounting period. It includes the beginning balance, all cash received, all cash paid out, and the ending balance. The master should start a rough cash statement at the beginning of the accounting period and record all receipts and expenditures as soon as they are made. This will avoid any cash transactions being forgotten. Needless to say, the cash statement must agree exactly with the actual cash on hand or the master will be liable for any shortage. At the end of the accounting period the final copy can be typed from the rough record.

Whenever there is a change of masters, the outgoing master should prepare a cash statement in quadruplicate. The outgoing master and the incoming master each must sign the statement after the new master has counted the cash and verified that the amount on hand is correct. One copy goes to each master for his or her personal records, one goes into the vessel's file, and one goes to the accounting department at the end of the accounting period.

This chapter outlined the traditional method of paying mariners, still practiced by some shipping companies. In other companies, the crew is paid by check issued aboard ship or from the home office. In these cases, of course, the company instructions should be followed.

CHAPTER 14

Ocean Bill of Lading

The ocean bill of lading, abbreviated "B/L," is a very important commercial shipping document. It is the basic document between shipper and carrier, and between shipper and consignee. Like many commercial documents, the B/L is usually printed in such small type that it is difficult and tedious to read. Nevertheless, the master should read carefully all the terms and conditions on the B/L issued by the company.

A bill of lading is issued by the company when a cargo is loaded on a vessel. The master's copies will list the cargo loaded on the vessel, including the weights, descriptions, loading ports, and destination ports. If there is any discrepancy between what is shown on the B/L and what is listed on the cargo manifest or cargo plan, the information shown on the B/L should be used, as it is more likely to be correct.

The signed B/L serves several definite purposes in connection with the carriage of goods by sea.

1. It is the final signed receipt from the carrier, both for the goods shown on the B/L and for the condition of those goods. In the United States, both the Harter Act of 1893 and the Carriage of Goods by Sea Act of 1936 (COGSA) require the carrier to issue a B/L as receipt for the goods.
2. It describes the nature, quantity, weight, and packaging of the goods, and any identifying marks or numbers.
3. It represents the contract of carriage (affreightment), defining the terms and conditions of carriage between the carrier and the shipper.
4. It is the document of title for the goods shown on the B/L. If it is made out "to order" it is negotiable and the goods shown on the B/L may be sold by endorsing and delivering the B/L to another party.
5. It determines the respective responsibilities of the carrier, the shipper, and the consignee. It enables the shipper to arrange insurance against damage or loss for which the carrier is not liable.

226

TYPES OF BILLS OF LADING

It is common practice to issue multiple original bills of lading, often three, for the same cargo. In such a case, the B/L will contain a stipulation such as the following:

"In witness whereof the master has signed three bills of lading, all of this tenor and date, one of which being accomplished, the others stand void."

All of the originals are negotiable, but the cargo will be delivered to the person who first presents a valid B/L at the discharge port. This is not done so that the shipper can sell the same cargo to more than one person; it is done to ensure against any possible unreliability of mail service. Usually several originals will be sent to the same consignee by different means.

In addition to the original bill of lading, a great number of nonnegotiable copies may also be issued. The number varies greatly according to the company and trade. These copies, marked "nonnegotiable" on their faces, are distributed to interested parties. The master should make certain that he or she receives copies of all bills of lading covering the cargo on board. Copies may be sent to company agents or consignees at ports of discharge via ship mail, that is, in envelopes containing cargo papers given to the master before sailing. The envelopes bear the names of the discharge ports and may be marked with the agent's or consignee's name. These envelopes must be turned over to the agent or appropriate person at the various ports.

Straight Bill of Lading

A straight bill of lading shows that the goods are consigned directly to a person or firm. It is stamped to indicate that it is a "straight bill of lading, not negotiable." The goods will be delivered only to the person or company named in the B/L.

"To Order" Bill of Lading

The "to order" bill of lading is negotiable and, because it permits full flexibility of negotiation, is the most common type used. It is written "to order" or "order of" a person, bank, or firm, or to the order of the shipper, who then temporarily retains title to the goods. Since the B/L is negotiable, the title to the goods described on the bill may be transferred to another party by endorsement of a signed original bill of lading. A negotiable B/L may be resold several times, each successive holder becoming the owner of the goods described in the bill.

The final holder of the original B/L, or the agent on his or her order, may claim the cargo at the port of destination by surrendering the B/L. The agent or the final holder of the B/L is entitled to receive the cargo in the condition noted on the B/L and, in some instances, must pay any freight due the carrier. When one of the original bills of lading is presented to claim the cargo, the others become void. This is stated on the B/L.

Through Bill of Lading

A through bill of lading is issued when goods are to be sent by two or more carriers and the shipper wishes the first carrier to make arrangements for the complete journey. The first carrier may issue a through B/L and under-take to make all the arrangements necessary to see that the goods reach their final destination. A through bill of lading may be either straight or to order. The cargo, having been handled by different carriers, should be checked for possible damage or shortage when received and before it is de-livered to an on-carrier. The through B/L should contain a clause limiting the issuing carrier's liability for cargo damage to the period that the cargo is actually under the carrier's control. The issuing carrier's liability should end when the cargo is passed on to the next carrier. If there is no such clause, the carrier issuing the through B/L could conceivably be held re-sponsible for damage occurring during any part of the cargo movement. If a vessel is an on-carrier under a through B/L, the previous carrier should be notified in writing of any damage or shortage, and such exceptions should also be entered in the logbook and on the exception lists. Cargo carried on board the vessel should be carefully checked on discharge; any damage or shortage should be noted and a receipt requested. If the cargo is in good shape, the receipt should so state.

Unclean Bill of Lading

A bill of lading that bears exceptions of any kind is termed "unclean," "dirty," "foul," or, in some ports, a "claused" B/L. In this book such a bill is referred to as an "unclean" B/L.

An unclean B/L might not be accepted by banks or others when finan-cial transactions concerning the B/L are involved. The bank sometimes re-quires that the shipper furnish a letter of guarantee holding the bank or other party free from any claims arising from a B/L on which exceptions are noted. The shipper may be reluctant to do this. Sometimes a letter of in-demnity is offered to the carrier, promising to indemnify the carrier for any claims if it will omit the exceptions and issue a clean B/L. If a master is ever asked to accept a letter of indemnity in lieu of noting exceptions on the B/L, he or she should refuse and refer the other party to the office. The decision to accept such a letter is solely the responsibility of the company. (See next section, "Letter of Indemnity.")

If a master knows the B/L to be incorrect, he or she should not sign it un-der protest unless the company instructs it. The master's signature on a B/L usually means that the B/L has been accepted as correct; to sign under protest puts the master in the position of both accepting and disputing the same document. If a master believes the B/L to be in error, nothing requires him or her to sign it. The master should insist that the discrepancy be identified and the B/L corrected. To avoid delay to the vessel, the office may instruct the master to sign (possibly under protest) a B/L known to be inaccurate. In such a case, the master should abide by the instructions from the company; responsibility for the consequences is the company's.

LETTER OF INDEMNITY

Shippers dislike unclean bills of lading; it is difficult to clear them through a bank, to make other financial negotiations, or to arrange the kind of insurance that is so necessary in foreign commerce. Moreover, an unclean B/L is difficult to sell to another party.

This has caused the occasional practice among shippers of requesting a clean B/L in place of an unclean one in return for a letter of indemnity given to the company, agent, or master. The letter states that in consideration of being given a clean B/L, the shipper indemnifies the carrier and the master against all risks and claims arising from the exceptions that made the B/L unclean. This practice, although occasionally used, has been said to be legally void and unenforceable. Unless financial or other adequate security is provided with the letter, there is no assurance that the company will not suffer a loss if the shipper sells the B/L to another party, thereby passing the title of the cargo to a party who may be unaware of the exceptions and the letter of indemnity.

The final holder of the B/L, as owner of the goods shown thereon, would hold the vessel's company responsible under the terms expressed in the B/L and, in the absence of any exception, would expect the goods to be delivered in the condition described on the B /L. A master who signs a B/L for so many parcels "in good order and condition," knowing that this is untrue (having accepted a letter of indemnity), issues a commercial document with a gross misstatement on it, which may be considered fraud. In the event a suit is brought against the master's company, the letter of indemnity is useless.

The acceptance of such a letter of indemnity is entirely up to the company or charterer. If such a letter is offered in a port where the master customarily signs bills of lading, it should be refused, as acceptance would commit the company to an agreement that might cause much trouble and expense. If the agent or the shipper insists that the master accept the letter, then the master should notify the home office, make certain to communicate all the facts, and wait for approval from the company. A long-distance telephone call or a radio or satellite message will be much cheaper than a heavy claim. If the decision is left to the master, it should be turned down.

MASTER'S SIGNATURE ON BILLS OF LADING

In the liner trades it has become very rare that the master must personally sign the B/L. In modern shipping practice it is customary for an official in the company freight department to sign the B/L for the master. However, when carrying bulk cargoes, it may be required that the master sign the B/L. There may be a great many copies, all for the same cargo, and they are generally brought on board to be signed only a few minutes before sailing.

In such cases it is sometimes permitted to use a rubber stamp signature on the nonnegotiable copies after signing a number of them by hand. Any changes in these bills of lading, typed or written, must be initialed by the master on each B/L. On a few of the bills of lading where changes have been made, a full signature may be required.

When a vessel is under time charter, the charterer may request that the master sign a letter which authorizes the charterer or the charterer's agent to sign a B/L on the master's behalf. An example of such a letter follows:

SS *Seven Seas*
World Shipping Co.
New York, NY
To whom it may concern:

You, as agents, general agents, and all subagents appointed by you at all the vessel's ports of call, are hereby authorized to enter into and do all things necessary for the proper execution and signing on my behalf, in my name, and as my agent, bills of lading, passenger tickets, and other documents for the carriage of goods and passengers on board the SS *Seven Seas*. This authorization shall remain in full force and effect as long as you continue to act as agent for the above vessel, unless sooner terminated by me or whomever shall go for master.

Date
Yours truly,
Master

Sometimes at tanker terminals, a blank B/L is brought aboard for the master's signature soon after docking, before loading has even begun. The terminal personnel may tell the master that this will avoid delay to the vessel in that they can fill in the figures after the ship has sailed; the vessel will not be held up while shore figures are calculated. This is accepted practice in some companies where the vessel and the terminal are both owned by the same company or where the vessel is time chartered to a company that also owns the terminal. The master should verify with the shipowner or time charterer, as appropriate, whether or not this practice is acceptable. In all other cases the master should refuse to sign a blank B/L unless the company instructs otherwise. Signing the B/L acknowledges receipt of the cargo listed on the B/L. This could prove embarrassing if the terminal short-loads the vessel and then presents a B/L with the master's signature on it showing that a full cargo was delivered.

With packaged goods it is possible to ascertain by actual count exactly how many packages of each type of cargo are on board. This is not true of bulk cargoes where the tonnage of cargo on board must be determined by deadweight survey or, in the case of tankers, by ullaging. In these cases there will always be a difference between ship figures and shore figures. Most shipping companies instruct their masters to dispute the B/L only if the difference between ship and shore figures exceeds a certain allowance, usually one-half or one-quarter of one percent.

PARCELS OF HIGH VALUE

If a master must sign a B/L for very valuable parcels whose contents are shown on the B/L but cannot be readily verified, one of the officers should check the packages to see that they are intact and no one has tampered with them. If possible, the weights should also be checked. In one instance, ten cases were described on the B/L as containing 100 boxes of high-speed computer chips. When opened on the dock at the discharge port, the cases were found to be full of neatly folded and boxed pieces of burlap—and old burlap at that! Before signing the B/L the master should get a report from the officer making the check. The B/L may be designated as "said to contain" certain articles.

As a matter of caution and good practice, all packages of high value should be checked regardless of who signs the B/L.

In preparing and signing a B/L in any port, the master should exercise the utmost care in order to protect the best interests of the company. The quantity or count as shown on the dock receipt or mate's receipt should be the same as that supplied by the shipper, who may have been the person who prepared the B/L. If the count or weight appears to be less than that given by the shipper, a note should be added to the B/L, " ___ cases (or other unit) in dispute, if on board to be delivered"; the master should make a note in the logbook and make certain that any other exceptions are noted on the B/L. When the B/L is signed and given to the shipper, it is an acknowledgment that the goods shown on the B/L have been received in the quantity and condition stated, which, if no exceptions are noted, may be described as "in good order and condition."

In some ports the shipper may flatly refuse to make, or allow the master to make, any exceptions on the B/L. In such a case, the master should not sign the B/L until the matter has been referred to the office for resolution.

If the vessel is in a foreign port and the master is requested to sign a B/L written in a language he or she does not understand, the B/L should be translated, in writing, by the agent, or better still, by the consul's office or someone else not interested in the cargo. A supply of the company's B/L blanks should be kept on board and these should be used whenever possible. In the event of a claim regarding the cargo, the B/L with its notes of exceptions (or lack of them) and its description of the cargo may be of major importance.

When signing a B/L or documents of any kind, the master should be sure, before committing the company to any agreement, that everything is in order and that he or she understands the documents. The master should not sign an antedated or postdated B/L, or an unclean B/L as a clean one even if a letter of indemnity is offered, unless so instructed by the company.

CHARTER PARTIES

The B/L, as noted before, is a contract of carriage for the cargo described. If the vessel is chartered, then the charter party, particularly if it is a voyage charter, will also contain clauses that constitute a contract of carriage. If a vessel is chartered to load a cargo and a B/L is then issued for that cargo, the B/L does not create a new contract and does not end the contract created by the charter party.

The company will certainly want the charter party to take precedence and may instruct the master to insert a note in the B/L stating that the B/L is issued under the terms of a charter party and that the charter party is to take precedence. If there is a contrary clause in the B/L (one stating that the B/L is to take precedence), the master should refer the matter to the company for clarification before signing the B/L.

CHAPTER 15

Charter Parties

A charter party is a contract by which a shipowner agrees to lease, and the charterer agrees to hire, a vessel or all or part of its cargo space, on terms and conditions set forth in the contract. Unless expressly prohibited from doing so by the terms of the charter party, the charterer is generally allowed to enter into subcontracts with other charterers.

The main types of charter parties are the bareboat charter party (also known as a demise charter), the time charter party, and the voyage charter party. There are several general forms for each main type of charter party and many modifications of those general forms.

The master should be familiar with the basic characteristics of the different types of charter parties. Charter party agreements are often negotiated by telex and satellite messages between the shipowner and the charterer or broker while the ship is at sea. Unfortunately, many shipping companies are careless about informing their masters of the provisions of particular charter parties, especially if the vessel is in the tramp trade and is making a series of voyage charters for different charterers.

Most charter parties are preprinted documents with blanks where the shipowner and charterer fill in particulars such as the name, dimensions, and capacity of the vessel; demurrage rate; laytime allowed; freight or hire rate, and so on. Shippers of large quantities of bulk cargo have charter parties with special titles such as Fosfo, Baltimore Grain Charter Party, Gencon, and Intertanktime.

Shipowners and charterers may, and usually do, have clauses added, deleted, or amended to suit their particular needs. These added or amended clauses may be handwritten or typed, and they are especially important. In cases of lawsuits where a preprinted clause and an added clause conflict, the courts generally hold that the added clause takes precedence.

If the vessel is chartered, it is of the utmost importance that the master read the charter party carefully, especially the added clauses, until it is thoroughly understood—no simple feat considering that charter parties can be many pages of fine-print legalese. The master should see that the officers, especially the chief officer, are informed of the more important provisions of the charter party, and it can do no harm for them to read it as a matter of information and instruction.

The master should make notes of clauses referring to time allotted for loading or discharging and compute the laytime allowed. It is important to note the type of units given in the charter party—the clause on loading may specify a certain number of long tons or short tons per day and the clause on discharging may specify metric tons, or vice versa. The correct unit must be shown on the time sheet.

The important clauses may be checkmarked for quick reference. If any refer to dates of notification of ETA to consignee, charterer, or charterer's agent, the master should make a note of the day the message is to be sent and be sure to send it.

If the ship is chartered the master should try to obtain a complete list of the charterer's agents, including street addresses and phone, telex, and beeper numbers in all ports the vessel is likely to make. Charterer's instructions should state the procedures for sending ETAs to the charterer or the charterer's agents. If no such instructions are available, the agent should be advised at least seventy-two hours before arrival.

BAREBOAT CHARTER PARTY

By this type of charter, the shipowner leases the entire vessel, and the charterer has the same responsibility as an owner for operation of the vessel. In other words, the charterer becomes a ship operator by using a rented vessel rather than building or buying a vessel. The charterer becomes the owner *pro hac vice* (owner for a time). The shipowner has, for the period covered by the charter party, relinquished control of and liability for the operation of the vessel. Provisions of modern environmental laws may allow certain types of liabilities to penetrate through to the owner. The charterer pays all expenses—fuel, stores, provisions, harbor dues, pilotage, and so forth—and employs and pays the crew. There may, however, be a clause in the charter party stating that the master and the chief engineer must be approved by the shipowner.

The charterer is responsible for the upkeep, preservation, and safety of the vessel. Before delivery to the charterer, the vessel is surveyed by representatives of both parties, and the same is done on redelivery. The charter party will specify that the vessel must be redelivered in the same good order and condition as when delivered, ordinary wear and tear excepted. On redelivery, the owner's representatives, usually a port captain and a port engineer, may check the logbooks for information pertaining to groundings, collisions, or other damage.

Fuel oil and lube oil in the vessel on delivery are usually paid for by the charterer at the current price in the port of delivery; fuel oil and lube oil remaining on board on redelivery are paid for by the shipowner at the current price in the port of redelivery.

Although a bareboat charter party is written for a stipulated period of time, it should not be confused with a time charter party, whereby the shipowner rents out the cargo space but does not relinquish control of the vessel.

The provisions of a bareboat charter party are not of paramount importance to the master. The charterer employs the master and operates the vessel as the owner would.

TIME CHARTER PARTY

By this charter, the charterer hires the vessel and its entire cargo-carrying capacity for a specified period of time and for a specified sum per day (called "hire"), payable at designated intervals. All the proper cargo space, including that for deck cargo, is at the charterer's disposal. This is sometimes referred to in a charter party as the "full reach and burden" of the vessel and the charterer invariably assumes it to include any mast or deck lockers available and probably a locker or two in the mate's room as well.

The shipping company is responsible for the physical operation of the vessel, and it employs the master and the entire crew. It also pays for the stores and provisions and the upkeep and repair of the vessel. In other words, the shipowner puts at the charterer's disposal a fully equipped vessel and operates it for the charterer's benefit.

The charterer usually pays for fuel, tugs, pilots, harbor dues, stevedoring expenses, and entering and clearing fees, but generally does not pay expenses pertaining to the crew, with the exception of crew overtime related to the cargo. The charterer pays for any fuel in the vessel on delivery and the shipowner pays for any fuel in the vessel on redelivery, both at current market prices at the port, unless otherwise agreed.

In this type of charter party, unlike a voyage charter party, there is no mention of laytime, dispatch, or demurrage, unless the charterer subcharters the vessel to another shipper on a voyage basis. In that case, it is the master's responsibility to the time charterer to see that the provisions of the subcharter are complied with and that the subcharterer's interests are protected, so long as they are not in conflict with the interests of the master's company. A subcharter does not alter the responsibilities between the shipowner and the original charterer.

REPORTS REQUIRED BY THE CHARTERER

On a time charter the master may be required to send the charterer deck and engine room log abstracts, engineer's passage reports, port activity reports, and periodic radio or satellite reports giving position, speed, and weather. All of these should be sent promptly as requested by the charterer, just as they would be sent to the home office. If reports are to be made on special forms provided by the charterer, the master should request a supply before sailing. The charterer may instruct the master that arrival and departure reports for all ports should be submitted on completion of the voyage. These reports should not be put off until the end of the voyage but should be completed as soon as possible after the vessel arrives or departs from a port of call and the pertinent details are known. If the job is postponed until the end of the voyage the master will have to consult the logbooks and many other papers to get the required information.

The master is responsible first to his or her own company but should also look out for the best interests of the time charterer regarding outturn of cargo and quick dispatch.

Performance Warranties

Performance warranties, which are written into a marine charter, are the charterer's way of guaranteeing the performance of the vessel. There are various types of performance warranties, but most specify speed and the discharge or loading rates for cargo. When a vessel can't meet any of the stipulations of a performance warranty, full details should be placed in the appropriate logs. Masters and other senior personnel aboard the vessel should be made aware of these provisions of the charter party.

SPEED

Under a time charter party, the shipowner generally warrants that the vessel can maintain a certain speed. If, due to weather or any other reason, this cannot be accomplished, the reason should be noted in the logbook. For example, "heavy weather, unable to maintain speed" or "in adverse current (named, such as Gulf Stream), unable to maintain speed." An entry claiming inability to maintain speed due to heavy weather should be substantiated by the weather section of the logbook and any other supporting weather documents.

Watch officers should log the wind force and direction at least once each watch; most time charter parties excuse the vessel from maintaining her warranted speed if the wind force exceeds a specified level (commonly Beaufort 5). If the vessel cannot maintain speed, except due to heavy weather or other reason excused by the charter party, the shipowner will have to pay the charterer a penalty. On the other hand, if the vessel consistently exceeds her warranted speed the charter party may provide that the shipowner is entitled to a bonus from the time charterer.

FUEL CONSUMPTION

Since the time charterer pays for the fuel, the shipowner will also have to warrant that the fuel consumption will not be higher than a certain figure, generally stated in tons per day. If the vessel's fuel consumption exceeds the warranted consumption, the shipowner will have to pay for the extra fuel used, unless, as with speed, the extra fuel consumption is due to weather or other excepted reasons beyond the shipowner's control.

DISCHARGE RATE

The owner of a tanker or other self-discharging vessel must guarantee the discharging ability of the vessel. It is generally agreed that a tanker should be capable of maintaining at least 100-psi discharge pressure at the manifold or some other mutually accepted standard.

Failure to meet any of the vessel's warranties can result in the shipowner's having to pay heavy penalties to the time charterer; therefore, the master should ensure that a full explanation is given in the logbook any time the vessel fails to perform as warranted.

Crew Overtime for the Account of the Charterer

Crew overtime in connection with the cargo is generally for the account of the time charterer and should be kept on a separate sheet. Instructions from the company should specify what overtime, if any, is to be charged to the charterer. In making up these sheets it will greatly facilitate the eventual settlement between the company and the charterer if the master describes the overtime work in detail, with a breakdown of each specific operation.

Off Hire

A time charter party contains a clause known variously as the "off hire" clause, the "breakdown" clause, or the "cesser of hire" clause. This clause states the following: "In the event of loss of time from deficiency of stores or crew, breakdown of machinery, stranding, fire, or any damage preventing the working of the vessel for more than __ hours, the payment of hire shall cease until she is again in an efficient state to resume her service."

The time allowed is usually twenty-four hours. If a vessel is broken down longer than the period allowed in the charter party, then the vessel is off hire for the entire time it is out of service, not just for the time in excess of the allotted time. In addition to breakdowns, off hire includes periods when the ship is withdrawn from service for drydocking or overhaul.

Deviation

While at sea on a time charter, if the vessel develops engine trouble or any other fault that forces her to deviate to a nearby port for repairs or other assistance, it is usually taken off hire from the time of the breakdown until the time it returns to the geographical position where the breakdown occurred and from which the voyage will be resumed. If the route from the port of refuge to the destination port is such that the vessel will not return to the place where the breakdown occurred, the vessel is taken off hire from the time of the breakdown to the time it reaches a position where it is the same distance from the destination as it was when deviation commenced.

The master should log the exact time and position of the point of deviation—as well as the amount of fuel oil, diesel oil, lube oil, and water on board at the time—and notify the home office in detail regarding the incident. If the charterer has an agent at the port of refuge, he or she should be notified, and also the master's own agent, if one is in the port. Logbooks, both deck and engine, should carry complete reports of the deviation.

At the earliest opportunity in the port of refuge, the master should make a note of protest before the U.S. consul or a notary public; if the latter, the agent should make the necessary arrangements.

A statement of facts should be drawn up, covering the period from the time the breakdown occurred and the deviation commenced to the time the vessel returned to the point of deviation and the voyage was resumed or it may be faxed upon completion of the voyage. The master and the chief engineer should sign this statement. It is generally sent to the home office from the first port after the voyage is resumed. A typical statement of facts is shown in figure 31 for a vessel under time charter bound from New York to Casablanca. The vessel lost a blade in latitude 39°40'N, longitude 70°00'W, and returned to New York for repairs.

VOYAGE CHARTER PARTY

This is a charter party for the carriage of a full cargo, not for a period of time, but at a stipulated rate per ton, net barrels, or whatever the customary cargo measurement may be, called "freight." The charter party is for one voyage only, between named ports or to ports to be named on arrival in a given area. This is the most frequently used charter party and most commodities and trades have a particular type to suit their purposes.

In a voyage charter party, the charterer assumes no responsibility for the operation of the vessel but generally pays stevedoring expenses in and out. A statement to that effect will be included in the charter party.

The master is particularly concerned with voyage charter parties because of the laytime, dispatch, demurrage, and canceling clauses and because of the necessity of tendering the notice of readiness to load or discharge. In this type of charter, the charterer contracts to provide a cargo on a particular voyage and must load and discharge the cargo at a given rate per day. The charter is generally for bulk cargo (stipulated in tons or cubic feet for dry cargo and in tons or net barrels for liquid cargo) and is usually for the entire carrying capacity of the vessel.

When the full capacity of the vessel is chartered, the charterer must pay freight based on a full cargo even if he ultimately supplies less than a full cargo. In that case, the charterer must pay freight on the cargo loaded, and he must also pay "dead freight" (at the same rate) on the difference between the cargo loaded and the cargo that could have been loaded. On tankers, the charterer may sometimes supply a cargo, which, due to its light density, fills up all of the cargo tanks but does not bring the ship down to her maximum legal draft. Although the ship is full, the charterer will still have to pay dead freight on the difference between the cargo tonnage actually loaded and the tonnage that would have put the ship down to full draft.

Occasionally a voyage charterer may contract for less than the full cargo capacity of a vessel if the freight rate offered is high enough to satisfy the shipowner. In this instance the charterer will have to pay dead freight only if the cargo supplied is less than the amount contracted for.

On freighters, if the entire carrying capacity is to be used and is stipulated in tons, the stowage should be carefully watched to make certain that all available space is utilized. If the broken stowage is not kept to a minimum, the master may find that the vessel is full and there is still some cargo to be loaded, an evidence of poor stowage for which the charterer may try to hold the vessel responsible or may claim that the wrong cubic measurement was given in the charter party.

Laytime

When the vessel on a voyage charter is in port, the expenses of the shipowner continue. At the same time, the loading or discharging is controlled by the charterer who, if not held to a definite number of days to complete this work, can make the stay in port long and expensive for the shipowner. For this reason the charter party will specify a definite number of days for loading or discharging of cargo, or it may specify a certain quantity per day to be loaded or discharged.

The time allowed is called laytime (or lay days) and is stipulated in the charter party as working days, weather working days, running days, and excepted days, all of which are explained later in this chapter. Many charter parties now state the allowed laytime in hours (e.g., working hours, running hours, etc.). The term "laytime" is preferable to "lay days" because many charter brokers use the phrase lay days to refer to the time period during which the shipowner must present the vessel to the charterer for loading (see "Readiness and Canceling Dates" later in this chapter).

If the charterer loads or discharges the cargo in less time than the allotted laytime, dispatch money is earned at a specified rate per day or per hour saved. If it takes longer to load or discharge than the allotted laytime, the charterer must pay demurrage at a set amount per hour or per day. Both dispatch and demurrage may become the cause of much disagreement; the vessel's logbook can play an important part in resolving such disputes.

TYPES OF LAY DAYS

Working days are those days during which work is normally done in the port concerned, the number of hours worked per day depending on the custom of the port. Eight hours is normal in most ports. Sundays and holidays are excepted if they are so recognized. In some Latin American and Mediterranean ports, "saints' days" are celebrated locally, and it may be difficult to get work done on these days. Most port guides list holidays for various countries and ports. The charter party may stipulate "Sundays and holidays excepted unless worked," sometimes adding "only hours worked to be counted."

Running days (also called "consecutive days"), if without qualification, are days of twenty-four hours. All days are counted, including Sundays and holidays and days of bad weather, even if no work was done, unless expressly stipulated to the contrary in the charter party.

Weather working days are the normal working days in the port concerned, excluding those days when, because of foul weather, it would be unreasonable to expect loading or discharging of cargo. If the vessel is working at an anchorage, this may include days when it is impossible to bring lighters or barges to the ship or to keep them alongside due to swell, sea, or surf; these are sometimes called "surf days."

Excepted days are those days during which no work can be done because of a fault in the vessel, such as a breakdown of boilers or machinery, with consequent loss of power to the winches or cargo pumps; fire in any part of the ship, if it interferes with loading or discharging of cargo; or any other stoppage of cargo work that is not the fault of the charterer. Full details should be entered in the logbook. Excepted days are not counted as used laytime.

Demurrage

A very important clause is the demurrage clause, which states that if the charterer does not complete loading or discharging within the laytime allowed by the charter party, the delay must be paid for at a stipulated sum per day or per hour or pro rata part thereof. Unless otherwise provided in the charter party, demurrage starts from the time loading or discharging should have been completed. All days are counted, whether or not cargo is worked, including Sundays, holidays, and days not worked due to bad weather or other reasons. Once a vessel is on demurrage, the time runs consecutively unless otherwise provided in the charter party. Demurrage will be suspended for any period during which the charterer is prevented from working because of any fault of the ship, such as machinery breakdown.

In the tanker trades, the charter party will specify a discharge rate, usually stated as either the pressure to be maintained at the ship's manifold, or a maximum time period for discharge of an entire cargo. If the vessel does not maintain the stated pressure, then any additional discharging time used due to the vessel's failure to maintain her warranted pumping rate will not count against the charterer as used laytime and demurrage will not be payable. If the vessel maintains the required pressure and the discharging still takes longer than the stipulated time, the delay will usually be considered to be due to excessive back pressure in the shore pipelines, for which the charterer is responsible, and demurrage will be payable.

Dispatch Money

A clause in the charter party usually stipulates that the shipowner will pay the charterer dispatch money at a set rate per day or pro rata for laytime saved in loading or discharging. The amount is usually one-third to one-half of the demurrage rate. When making up the time sheet, it is important to note whether the charter party provides that dispatch money is payable for all time saved or for all working time saved and to calculate the dispatch money accordingly.

Time Sheet

This is an abstract showing the times of all cargo operations, the laytime used, and the number of hours for which dispatch or demurrage is due. Time sheets (or laytime statements) are not standard and vary greatly by company and trade. Some are printed forms issued by the company, shipper, or consignee. If no form is provided, the one shown in figure 33 may be used, altered as necessary. In some companies, the master will not prepare the time sheets; instead, these will be made up by someone in the home office using the master's log abstracts. The log must substantiate the time sheet. If necessary, as is often the case, explanatory notes may be added. If the master's time sheet differs in fact from that of the charterer's agent, both should be checked. It is not always necessary that the vessel's copy (the one made up by the master or the chief officer) be signed by the charterer's agent, unless it is required by the company, but a copy should be given to the charterer's agent as well as to the vessel's agent and the home office. A copy should be placed in the vessel's file. The master will probably be required to sign the time sheet made up by the charterer's agent. It should be checked for accuracy before signing and a copy kept for the vessel's file.

Disputes often arise regarding laytime and the amount of dispatch or demurrage due, and settlement is negotiated between the shipowner and charterer. To fully protect the company's interests, the master should be sure that the logbook entries in regard to all cargo operations are accurate. Before signing the charterer's time sheet (even if it seems correct), it may be advisable for the master to append to it the following note: "Signed without prejudice to any of the terms, conditions, and exceptions of governing charter party."

This is especially necessary if the charter party does not stipulate a definite amount of laytime or the number of tons per day to be loaded or discharged. Some charter parties deal in rather vague terms such as "according to the custom of the port," "vessel to be loaded or discharged as customary," or "with reasonable dispatch." These terms are much too indefinite and, if they do appear, the master should get an interpretation from a responsible party connected with the company.

Readiness and Canceling Dates

A voyage charter party usually stipulates that the shipowner will present the vessel to the charterer or the charterer's agent at the loading port within certain dates. This is commonly a period of three days to a week. Some charter parties refer to this interval as the "lay days"; however, this term is easily confused with the lay days allowed the charterer for loading or discharging (see "Laytime" earlier in this chapter).

The first day the ship is to be presented is called the "readiness date." Though not obligated to accept the ship before the readiness date, the charterer may do so if the cargo is ready and a berth is available. If the charterer does accept the vessel early, under the provisions of the charter party, laytime starts on the day of acceptance, just as it does when the ship is on schedule. It is obviously to the shipowner's advantage to have the vessel accepted early, if possible.

The last day of the window of acceptance is called the "canceling date." If the vessel is not presented and the notice of readiness is not tendered by a certain time on the canceling date, the charterer has the option of canceling the charter party by giving notice to the shipowner. Missing the canceling date is a very serious affair; the shipowner will probably have spent many thousands of dollars in fuel and other operating expenses in getting the ship to the loading port. If the ship is late, the charterer will almost surely cancel the charter party, although he or she will not necessarily charter another vessel in place of the one rejected. Instead, the charterer may offer the shipowner a new charter party with new terms that are considerably less favorable than those in the original contract.

The Notice of Readiness

When on a voyage charter it is the master's responsibility to advise the charterer or the charterer's agent, in writing, as soon as the vessel is in all respects ready to load or discharge. This advice is given in the form of a notice of readiness presented (tendered) to the charterer or the charterer's agent. Usually, prior to arrival a message is sent informing the charterer of the ETA and advising that the vessel will be ready to work cargo. In some cases when a vessel is to load and it is expected at a definite hour, the company or the agent at the port may tender the notice. This is especially likely if the vessel is to go directly alongside on arrival and is not required to be granted pratique or to clear customs. The agent should advise the master if this was done.

Before the notice of readiness may be tendered, the vessel must have arrived at the place for loading or discharging as stipulated in the charter party or as near thereto as it can safely get, and the vessel must be actually ready to load or to discharge cargo at the specified time. These requirements may be modified by the terms of the particular governing charter party.

At the discharge port the master should tender the notice without delay. Generally, the charter party will contain a clause stating, "laytime is to commence __ hours after written notice has been given that the vessel is ready to discharge, whether in berth or not at the place ordered." Sometimes the charter party stipulates that the notice can be tendered during designated office hours only. The time allowed may vary. Some charter parties may require that the notice be tendered by the master only; with others, notice may be tendered by master, owner, or agent. The time allowed between tendering the notice of readiness and the start of laytime gives the charterer time to make the necessary arrangements for discharging the cargo. However, the clause may include "unless charterer commences to discharge before the __ hours have elapsed," in which case laytime usually commences when the discharging begins.

The date and time the notice is tendered should be entered in the logbook. If for any reason the notice cannot be tendered after arrival, the reason should be entered in the logbook. If the vessel must anchor to await a berth, the master should send the agent a message instructing him or her to tender a notice of readiness on the master's behalf. Even if this is done, when the ship finally goes alongside, the master should still try to have the charterer's agent sign the notice made up on the ship.

The notice may be prepared by the agent and presented on board for the master's signature. There may be up to ten copies. The master should be sure to obtain one copy for the vessel's file and one for the home office. If there is uncertainty as to whether the agent will prepare the notice, it is a good idea for the master to make it up before arrival, omitting the date and time, which can be filled in when it is tendered.

Generally, a notice of readiness is required by the terms of the charter party. If there is no one to receive it, the facts should be logged and an attempt made to tender the notice when the charterer or the charterer's agent shows up, leaving the original date and time on the notice. If the charterer or his agent refuses to accept the tendered notice, claiming that the vessel is not in all respects ready to load or discharge, an entry should be made in the log, noting the reason for the refusal. The company should be advised of the facts at once. In the absence of other instructions from the company, the master should direct the agent to employ a surveyor to inspect the vessel and inform the charterer or the charterer's agent that this is being done. On the master's time sheet, laytime should be counted from the time stipulated in the charter party as though the notice had been accepted and signed when tendered. Following is a typical notice of readiness, which may be changed in any way deemed suitable:

Seven Seas Steamship Corporation
NOTICE OF READINESS
To whom it may concern:

The SS/MV _____, under my command, now at _____, is as of _____
hours this _____ day of 20___ ready in all respects to load/discharge a cargo of
_____ in accordance with the charter party dated _____.

Master
Accepted at _____ hours, _____ 20_____.
Signed: _____
Title: _____

Arrived Ship

When on a voyage charter and a notice of readiness must be tendered, it is important that the master accurately determine the arrival time. For charter party purposes, arrival at the bar or pilot station is not necessarily considered arrival time at a port. Generally, arrival is taken to mean the time when the vessel is moored in the harbor proper, at the terminal designated in the charter party, or at any place where vessels normally wait for a dock to load or discharge. If a dock or berth is named in the charter party and is available, it is generally taken that the vessel must be made fast to that dock or berth before it is considered to have arrived. It is up to the charterer to secure the dock or berth. If the berth is not available, the vessel is considered to have arrived when it is made fast to a waiting berth or anchored at a place where vessels customarily await berths. Many masters use the time that they ring "finished with engines" as the time of tendering the notice of readiness.

The vessel on arrival must be ready in all respects to load or discharge in accordance with the terms of the charter party. This means that the vessel must be ready to work without delay, even if it is not at a dock or berth; otherwise the charterer may refuse the notice of readiness, claiming that the vessel is not ready when in fact there is no berth ready. A tanker in ballast docking at a loading berth usually is considered to have arrived, even though it may not be able to load cargo until it has discharged ballast, as long as the vessel is otherwise ready to load. In that case, the master should tender the notice as soon as the vessel is all fast in the loading berth; however, the time spent deballasting and drying or cleaning the ballast tanks will not count against the charterer as used laytime.

If, as often occurs, the vessel must first load or discharge other cargo and then shift to the berth called for in the charter party, laytime does not commence until the vessel has arrived at that berth and the notice has been tendered. When possible, however, the agent will tender the notice a day before the vessel shifts, so that when it arrives at the specified berth the vessel will start work immediately and laytime will begin. If the berth to which the vessel is to shift is not available, the notice of readiness should be tendered as soon as cargo operations at the first berth are complete and the vessel is ready to shift.

The above guidelines may be modified by the relevant charter party and, in some cases, by the custom of the port. If there is doubt as to whether or not the vessel has arrived under the terms of the charter party, it is best if the master tenders the notice of readiness. It is better to tender early rather than late.

If the master tenders the notice early, laytime will not start until the time stipulated in the charter party even though the notice may have been presented sooner; at least the charterer will have been officially advised of the vessel's presence in the port and readiness to work cargo, and the master can always tender another notice at the proper time.

If the master tenders the notice late, laytime will not start until the specified number of hours after the notice has been tendered, even though it properly should have begun some hours before.

If the cargo to be loaded requires special fittings and the charter party stipulates that the charterer is to bear the expense of the fittings and their installation, laytime begins when the installation work is started. However, if there is inward-bound cargo remaining in some of the holds and the charter is for all of the space, laytime generally begins after the inward-bound cargo is removed and the holds are cleaned, even though the charterer may have started on the fittings in the space available before the inward-bound cargo was completely discharged. This may cause some dispute, so it is important that all times used, both by the vessel in discharging and by the charterer in installing the fittings, are accurately logged.

PREPARING HOLDS

With some dry bulk cargoes, the vessel must prepare the holds. This means opening the hatches and spreading tarps or other cloths, if necessary, to protect cargo in the tween decks. Holds must be cleaned, bilges and rose boxes covered, and drain pipes plugged and cemented where necessary. Some companies hire shore gangs to do this work if time permits. If done by the crew, the master is responsible for its completion in time to commence loading or discharging as soon as the vessel is made fast. Any doubt about whether it will be necessary to prepare the holds before arrival should be resolved by asking the company or agent for instructions. Uncovering the hatches or preparing holds may be overtime work for the crew. If so, they are likely to take their time doing the work, a contingency not to be overlooked. Generally, the home office or agent will send a message in ample time, letting the master know that the vessel must prepare the holds.

STEVEDORE DAMAGE WHEN UNDER CHARTER

If, as is usual under a voyage or time charter party, the charterer pays the stevedores, the master or the chief officer should ascertain who has the authority to sign reports of any damage that may be done by stevedores to the vessel or to the cargo. When such damage is discovered, or as soon thereafter as possible, the stevedore's foreman should be notified in writing, and copies of the notice should be sent to the charterer or the charterer's agent and to the master's company. If the damage is not discovered until after the cargo is out but was apparently sustained during cargo operations the same procedure should be followed.

In either case, a full accounting must be made on a stevedore damage report. If no printed forms are on board, a typewritten form is acceptable. Generally this is not a standard form, each company printing its own, but the information called for is practically the same on all versions. Copies, as complete as possible, should go to the stevedore and to the charterer or his agent, and the required number should go to the master's office, keeping one copy for the vessel's file.

The master should try to get the stevedore's representative to sign a damage report either admitting or denying liability. It is quite likely that he or she will refuse to do this and may even refuse to accept a copy of the report. The charterer or the charterer's agent should also be requested to sign the report, as the charter party usually contains a clause holding the charterer responsible for stevedore damage. All details should be entered in the log.

Some charterers issue "instructions to the master"; these usually include a note on stevedore damage which specifies that the charterer is not responsible for damage to the vessel unless notified by the master at the time the damage occurs and that the master is to cooperate with the charterer and the charterer's agents in giving prompt written notice to the party causing such damage. The instructions may go on to say that claims against stevedores for repair costs are often rejected on the grounds that the damage was not called to the attention of the stevedore when it occurred.

It is apparent that unless the stevedore or the charterer assumes liability for the damage, the master's company will have to pay for the repairs, which will undoubtedly call for explanatory letters from the master and from the chief officer.

SIGNING DAMAGE LETTERS

Some charterers instruct their agents to present the master with a letter to sign prior to sailing, stating that notices of responsibility have been served on stevedores and other third parties for damage caused and that copies of such notices are attached or that the vessel has been inspected under the master's supervision and that no damage has been observed. A typical letter is shown below.

Certificate of Satisfactory Loading/Discharging
Port_____Date_____
SS *Seaworthy*
To whom it may concern:

This is to certify that the loading/discharging of my vessel was conducted under my supervision and in accordance with my instructions and to my satisfaction. I further certify that no damage was done to my vessel while loading/discharging this cargo for which the stevedores or others may be liable or responsible.

_____
Master, SS *Seaworthy*

Masters should be wary about signing such a letter, as damages caused by stevedores may not be noticed until a later date. Furthermore, it is common for a vessel to arrive one day and sail the next, or even the same day, having worked cargo continuously. Under these circumstances, a thorough inspection would be impractical. A master's signature on such a letter might force the company to pay for repairs that rightly should be borne by the charterer's stevedore. If the master is pressured into signing such a letter, he or she should insist that the following, or a similar note, be added: "Signed without prejudice, in case stevedore damage or other damage, not noted at the time due to fast turnaround or for other reason, is discovered after sailing."

Some companies issue a form letter including the qualifying note, to be given to the charterer or the charterer's agent after the master fills in the name of the vessel, the charterer's name, the port, the date, and his or her own signature.

It sometimes occurs that stevedore damage or other damage is repaired at the expense of the party causing it or at the charterer's expense. In such cases the damage report should still be made out but a note appended as follows: "Damage by _____ at _____ repaired for their account."

DUNNAGE

When the cargo is discharged, the master should ascertain to whom the dunnage, if any, belongs. The consignee may claim the dunnage for the charterer and may try to discharge it with the cargo. Because of the cost of dunnage, this could be a very important item if the vessel is to load another cargo that requires dunnage. If the charterer prepares the holds, he is usually allowed to use any dunnage already in the vessel.

CHAPTER 16

Panama Canal

A t midnight on December 31, 1999, pursuant to the Panama Canal Act of 1979, the United States Panama Canal Commission relinquished control and operation of the Panama Canal, and authority over all Panama Canal operations was turned over to the Panama Canal Authority of Panama.[1] Most operating requirements remain the same as when the canal was under United States control. The provisions of 35 CFR, although no longer officially in effect, provide useful guidance to vessels transiting the canal. Additional information and regulations can be obtained by contacting the Panama Canal Authority directly or via the company's agent.[2]

VESSEL CHARACTERISTICS AND REQUIREMENTS

The maximum dimensions overall, including bulbous bow, for vessels acceptable for regular transit of the canal is a length of 289.56 meters and a beam of 32.31 meters; passenger and container vessels may have an overall length of up to 294.13 meters. The maximum length overall for integrated tug-and-barge combinations is 274.32 meters and the maximum beam is 32.31 meters. A beam of up to 32.61 meters may be permitted with prior permission.

The maximum aggregate overall length for non-self-propelled vessels, including accompanying tugs, provided the tugs lock through with the vessel, is 259.08 meters with a maximum beam of 30.48 meters.

Maximum allowable height for any vessel transiting the canal is 57.91 meters, measured from the waterline to the highest point. Maximum allowable height may be increased to 62.48 meters with prior permission.

Maximum permissible draft for canal transit is 12.04 meters freshwater when the level of Gatun Lake is 24.84 meters or higher. This may be reduced depending on the level of Gatun Lake. Draft limitations are also dependent on vessel design and handling criteria. For vessels in ballast, minimum draft tables can be found in *Sailing Directions Publication 153*. On a vessel with excessive draft, list, or trim, or one that is over her marks, the master may have to sign a release to the Panama Canal Commission and employ an extra tug for part of the canal transit. A vessel with a list exceeding ten degrees will not be allowed to transit the canal. A vessel with a list of between three and ten degrees may be allowed to transit, but only at her own risk and at the discretion of the canal authorities.

If there is any doubt concerning a vessel's suitability, it should be clarified directly with the marine director at Balboa.

RELEASE FROM LIABILITY

Masters will be required to execute a "form of undertaking" to release the canal authority from liability in case of accident and to indemnify the authority for damages sustained in the following instances:

1. When a vessel transits at less than the minimum drafts, has a list in excess of three degrees, or is so loaded or trimmed that maneuverability is adversely affected
2. When a vessel has protrusions
3. When visibility from the vessel's navigation bridge presents a hazard
4. When the vessel's chocks, bitts, or other equipment do not meet canal requirements
5. When a vessel transits on a one-time delivery with an extreme beam exceeding 32.31 meters
6. When the vessel is to be docked, drydocked, or berthed by a canal pilot

RADIO COMMUNICATION AND ETA

Estimated time of arrival (ETA) should be reported to traffic management at least forty-eight hours in advance, earlier if possible. *Sailing Directions Publication 153* contains a detailed list of questions, reproduced later in this section; responses to these should be included with this initial contact. When approaching from the Pacific, vessels must report their speed and their actual time of passing Punta Mala or latitude 07°28'N to the signal station at Flamenco Island on VHF channel 12. Vessels approaching from the Atlantic side shall report twelve hours prior to arrival at Cristobal any change of one hour or more in the expected time of arrival.

Vessels arriving at either coast are to communicate with Panama Canal signal stations on VHF channel 12 and maintain a continuous watch on this channel while awaiting transit. Once in transit, a continuous watch on channels 13 and 16 is required.

Sailing Directions Publication 153 Reporting Requirements

The ETA message should be in the following format, with each item identified by a heading from the phonetic alphabet. The word "negat" should be used after each item that can be answered "no," "none," or "not applicable."

ALPHA—The Panama Canal identification number of the vessel.

BRAVO—Estimated date and time of arrival, port of arrival, and request for canal transit if desired.

CHARLIE—Estimated draft upon arrival, in feet and inches, fore and aft, in tropical freshwater (density 0.9954).

DELTA—Any changes in the vessel's name, country of registry, structure, or use of tanks that have occurred since the vessel last called in Panama Canal waters.

ECHO—Will the vessel dock at Balboa or Cristobal? What is the reason for docking? If it is for cargo operations, fuel, or water, give the tonnage involved in each case. Is there any reason the vessel will not be ready to transit upon arrival? What is the reason?

FOXTROT—The nature and tonnage of any deck cargo.

GOLF—If the vessel is carrying any explosives or dangerous cargoes in bulk, state the correct technical name, quantity (in long tons), United Nations number, and the International Maritime Organization class for each dangerous cargo carried. If the vessel is a tanker in ballast condition and not gas-free, state the correct technical name, United Nations number, and International Maritime Organization class of the previously carried cargo.

HOTEL—If the vessel is carrying any packaged dangerous goods other than explosives, state the International Maritime Organization class and the total quantity (in long tons) within each class.

INDIA—Quarantine and immigration information:

1. Is radio pratique desired?
2. The ports at which the vessel has called within fifteen days preceding its arrival at the canal
3. All cases of communicable disease aboard and the nature of the disease or diseases, if known
4. The number of deaths that have occurred since departure from the last port and the cause of each death, if known
5. The number of passengers disembarking and their port of destination
6. The number and ports of origin of any stowaway and a brief description of the identity papers of each stowaway
7. The number, kind, and country of origin of any animals aboard. Are any animals to be landed?

8. The country of origin of all meat, whether carried as cargo or as ship's stores

9. Has the vessel called at a port in any country infected with foot-and-mouth disease or rinderpest during its present voyage? Countries considered to be infected are:

   a. All countries east of the thirtieth meridian west longitude and west of the international date line, except Australia, Channel Islands, Fiji, Greenland, Iceland, Japan, New Zealand, Northern Ireland, Norway, Republic of Ireland

   b. All countries of South America

   c. Curacao (the leeward islands of the Netherlands Antilles)

   d. Martinique

   e. Cuba

   f. Guadaloupe

10. Specify whether the vessel has a valid deratting certificate or a deratting exemption certificate issued within 180 days prior to arrival.

The exact format and requirements of this message are changed from time to time; the master should check the latest Panama Canal regulations for the current requirements. The master can send this message directly to the navigation division of the Panama Canal or to the agent with instructions to pass it to the canal authorities.

Changes in ETA

A vessel approaching the Panama Canal from the Atlantic must report by radio, at least twelve hours prior to arrival, any change in ETA of one hour or more. A vessel approaching from the Pacific must report the time of passing the latitude of Punta Mala and the speed being made good.

DOCUMENTS REQUIRED ON ARRIVAL

The following Panama Canal forms must be ready for presentation to the boarding officer on arrival:

1. Ship's Information and Quarantine Declaration (fig. 25), 1 set
2. Cargo Declaration (fig. 26), 1 copy
3. Crew List for Incoming Vessels (fig. 27), 2 copies
4. Passenger List (fig. 28), 2 copies

In addition, the following is required for vessels berthing at Cristobal or Balboa:

1.   Stores list, 1 copy (ship's forms allowed)

The following documents must always be available on board for inspection:

1.   Panama Canal tonnage certificate (only if transiting canal)
2.   Clearance from last port
3.   Ship's certificate of documentation or register
4.   Derat or deratting exemption
5.   FMC oil pollution certificate

The master may be asked for a copy of the ship's plans (general arrangement, engine room, capacity, midship, etc.) for admeasurement purposes. The boarding officer almost never requests the plans, but the regulations require that they be available. They are not required if the vessel is calling at a canal port but is not going to transit the canal.

In addition, the following documents must be available for inspection if requested by the boarding officer:

1.   Ship's log
2.   All ship's documents pertaining to cargo, classification, construction, load lines, equipment, safety, sanitation, and tonnage
3.   SOLAS and IOPP certificate, for ships carrying dangerous cargo in bulk
4.   STCW certificates for officers and crew, if the nation of registry has implemented the convention standards

COMPLETING CANAL FORMS

Forms used at the canal are sometimes changed. Generally, if the old forms have already been made up, they will be accepted. When a vessel receives new forms the master should destroy the obsolete ones. If the vessel is bound for the Panama Canal and there are no canal forms on board, the master should have the company request several sets from its agent at the canal, time permitting. In some U.S. ports the company's local agent may have a supply. At the canal, the boarding officer will give the master a set for the vessel's next transit, but the master should have the agent at the canal supply the vessel with several additional sets as well as a copy of the latest canal regulations.

Most of the forms are self-explanatory and simple to fill out. The master should start making them up early on the voyage, especially the cargo declaration form, which may take a little time. Many of the items can be filled out before arrival. A few details, such as date and time of arrival, draft, and fuel must be entered after arrival.

TRANSIT

Transit through the fifty-mile-long canal usually takes about nine hours. Arriving vessels are to anchor in designated anchorages and await boarding officials. Overboard waste discharge, other than potable water, is prohibited in the canal opening area. Admeasurement will normally be done at anchor but may be done during transit. Vessels making their maiden transit and arriving after 2000 will be measured the next day. The canal authority may dispatch vessels through the canal in the order they see fit. Generally, priority passage will be given to warships, passenger vessels with accommodations for fifty or more passengers, vessels carrying mail, or vessels on fixed schedules. Normally, ships scheduled for priority transit will transit within twenty-four hours of arrival. Vessels may also be "booked for transit," which means that prior to the vessel's arrival, a specific date for transit has been assigned by the canal authorities. Vessels arriving ahead of schedule may not normally transit prior to their scheduled date once booked for transit. Fog conditions between September and December may suspend night transits.

The following items apply to Panama Canal transit:

Mooring lines. Vessels should have six mooring lines, each 250 feet long with five-foot eyes, at the ready fore and aft.

Hull protrusions. Nothing should protrude from the hull or the master may be asked to sign a waiver.

Navigation gear. All navigation gear will be checked prior to transit. The master should ensure that the vessel's compass deviation cards are current and accurately reflect the vessel's deviation.

Steering light. All vessels over 100 meters in length must have a blue steering light installed along the centerline near the stem that is clearly visible from the bridge.

Signal flags. A pilot assigned to a vessel for transit will be given a schedule number. For northbound transits, ships shall fly "H" under the international numeral pennant corresponding to the assigned schedule number. For southbound transits, ships shall fly "H" over the numeral pennant. Preference ships shall fly "Z" under the schedule number and display a blue light at night.

Personnel on duty. The master must be on the bridge and a ship's officer and qualified mariner are to stand by on the forecastle whenever the vessel is entering or leaving a lock; is underway in Gaillard Cut; is docking, undocking, or getting underway; or is anchoring, mooring, or shifting berth. At all other times when a vessel is moving in canal waters, the master or a qualified representative must be on the bridge. The chief engineer is to be on duty in the engine room while the vessel approaches and passes through the locks and until lockage is complete and the vessel is clear of the lock walls. The chief engineer is also to be on duty in the engine room while the vessel is transiting Gaillard Cut, docking or undocking, getting underway, anchoring, mooring, or shifting berth.

Anchors and mooring equipment ready. During transit, the vessel's anchors must be ready for letting go and her mooring equipment must be energized and ready to work.

COLREGS and Inland Navigational Rules. While in transit, the International Regulations for Preventing Collisions at Sea (72 COLREGS) shall be observed; however, warning and whistle signals must conform with the Inland Navigational Rules Act of 1980. Additional rules and modifications, including speed limits for various portions of the canal, may be found in the Panama Canal rules.

PANAMA CANAL PILOTS

Unlike normal pilotage conditions where a pilot has an advisory capacity, while under Panama Canal pilotage, the vessel's navigation is under the exclusive control of the Panama Canal pilot and a master's helm command will not supersede the navigational commands of the pilot. The canal pilots carry their own GPS units, which are connected to laptop computers and are linked to a canal vessel movement tracking system. If so equipped, the pilot will probably request an outlet and the use of a desk or counter that faces forward, preferably near the centerline of the vessel.

Pilot Boarding

Pilot ladder posts must be at least 120 centimeters (approximately 4 feet) off the deck. Pilots normally board inside the breakwater at a point north of Mole Beacon on the Atlantic side and in the merchant vessel anchorage, seaward of buoys 1 and 2, on the Pacific side.

TUG AVAILABILITY

A Voith-Schneider (cycloidal) tractor tug will assist the vessel into the locks and may lock through with the ship. It usually makes up near the bow and uses tug lines.

CANAL CLEARANCE

Before sailing from the canal the master will be given a canal clearance. This is usually delivered to the vessel when the transit is completed and the pilot disembarks. This clearance is given to the officials at the next port, if required. If the next port is a U.S. port, customs will want the clearance.

CHAPTER 17

Suez Canal

The Suez Canal was opened for navigation in 1869. From Port Said on the Mediterranean Sea, the canal extends south roughly 100 miles to the city of Suez and on to the Red Sea. Approximately twenty-five thousand ships transit the canal each year under the guidance of the Suez Canal Authority (SCA). Due to its unique location and the absence of locks, the canal can be widened and deepened any time it becomes necessary. The canal has no locks because the two connected seas have approximately the same water level. Most of the canal is restricted to one-way traffic; however, there are many passing bays along its length and the canal cuts through several lakes, which are used as convoy passing areas.

Heading southward, a vessel will transit the main body of the canal, Lake Timsah, the Bitter Lakes, and on to the Gulf of Suez. The eastern side of the canal is bordered by the northwestern part of the Sinai Peninsula, and the western side of the canal is the eastern extent of the Nile River Delta. On the northwestern edge of the canal, off Lake Timsah, is the Ismailia Canal, which connects the capital city of Cairo to the Suez Canal.

DIMENSIONS

Masters should consult the most recent *Notice to Mariners* corrections to *Publication 172* and the SCA Rules of Navigation for the most up-to-date canal and vessel dimension information.

Canal Dimensions

Width: Typical cross section of the canal shows a channel width of approximately 119 meters between the 20-meter depth curves, and some areas have been widened by 50 meters. There are areas with widths of 104 meters listed in the SCA Rules of Navigation.

Depth: Except for areas noted on the chart, the canal was dredged to a depth of 20.5 meters in 1994.

Currents: Peak currents usually occur 50 minutes after high and low water at both Port Said and Port Tewfik. Between Port Said and Great Bitter Lake, tidal currents may reach 1 knot, or even 2 knots with a strong prevailing wind. In the southern part of the canal, current averages of 1.5 knots and 2.5 knots during spring tides are rather common. Between the Port of Suez and the Bitter Lakes, the north current is called the flood and the south current is called the ebb. In summer the ebb usually lasts longer than 6 hours; in winter the flood dominates.

Buoyage: The west side of the canal is marked with kilometer posts from Port Said High Light to the port of Suez. Where there are two channels, a suffix of E or W will denote which channel is being marked.

Given the double-ended nature of the canal, in order to conform with IALA buoyage conventions, the direction of buoyage reverses at km 4.0 and km 2.8E at approximate latitude 31°13.5'N. To the north of this position, in Port Said, the port hand buoys are on the east side of the channel and the starboard side buoys are on the west side. South of these positions, the buoyage is reversed.

Vessel Dimensions

Maximum permitted dimensions: Beam, 74.67 meters (with no length restrictions); draft (fwd), 9.75 meters; draft (aft), 11 meters. (Generally, vessels with smaller beams will be allowed deeper drafts. Other beam/draft combinations can be found in the Beam/Draft Tables available from the SCA or the vessel's agent.)

Wide vessels: Vessels with a beam over 71 meters may be allowed transit by special request. Those with a beam over 74.67 meters may be permitted passage under special SCA conditions.

Deep vessels: Vessels with a draft between 15.2 meters and 17.06 meters must conduct a satisfactory sea trial at either Bur Said Roads or the Port of Suez before making their first passage at that draft.

Ballasted vessels: Vessels with a beam of 74.67 meters and draft of 9.75 meters forward and 11 meters aft will be permitted to transit.

Other vessels: Vessels with a beam over 64 meters and with similar drafts to the ballasted vessels listed above will be permitted transit only during calm weather with a beam wind of 10 knots or less. (ULCCs and VLCCs will not be allowed to transit if there is a beam wind of over 10 knots.)

DOCUMENTS

The following documents must be readily available aboard vessels requesting transit:

Suez Canal tonnage certificate
Certificate of registry
Statistical declaration
Extract from any of the vessel's official documents and information concern-
    ing her type and cargo
Declaration concerning the use of double-bottom tanks and the lower part of
    high tanks
Declaration concerning vessels in ballast
Declaration concerning state of navigability
The last classification certificate issued
Crew lists
Any other information relevant to the vessel's transit

Vessels arriving at the canal for the first time should call the respective signal station and give their call sign and Suez Canal file number. Approaching the roads, vessels are required to give their international call sign. The SCA Ismailia may be contacted directly through "SUQ."

PRETRANSIT PREPARATIONS

Prior to transit, all vessels must have their ladders, booms, boats, and derricks stowed such that they do not protrude from the sides of the vessel. Vessels shall have at least six flexible, floating mooring lines with eyes (four on vessels with constant tension mooring winches). Bow anchors must be ready for letting go. Prior to transit, a gear test should be conducted to ascertain the readiness of the propulsion gear, steering, engine order telegraph, and rudder angle and rpm indicators, and to ensure that the VHF and radar are in good working order. Vessels in ballast must fill ballast tanks per SCA instructions. Vessels will be required to provide or hire mooring boats to run out mooring lines as prescribed by the SCA. Transiting vessels are monitored by the Suez Canal Vessel Traffic Management System (SCVTMS). The SCVTMS continuously monitors all transiting vessels' positions and distances from other ships via three computerized tracking radars, television cameras, and a voice communications network.

Transit through the canal will require U.S. charts 56100, 56081, 56082, 56083, and 62193 or the British Admiralty equivalents. Transit generally takes between 11 and 14 hours, including anchoring. Although sections of the canal have been doubled for one-way traffic, there may be occasions when a vessel will be instructed to tie up to the bollards on the canal banks. Areas where the canal has been widened to allow such tie-ups are called "gares."

TRANSITING INFORMATION

Transit information can be found in *Publication 172, Sailing Directions (En Route)*. However, regulations change frequently; up-to-date information should be sought via the vessel's agent or directly from the Suez Canal Authority (SCA). The manual is available on CD-ROM.[1] All vessels seeking transit must be approved by the SCA and must be represented by an agent.

The Convoy System

Transit through the canal is done with a convoy system, with groups of ships departing at prearranged times so they pass in the Great Bitter Lake area. The southbound convoys (N1) consist of three groups—A, B, and C. Sometimes a second southbound convoy (N2) is formed, but several types of vessels are prohibited from joining this second convoy.

Group A:
>   Made up of vessels in Port Said
>   Vessels enter the canal at the south end of the harbor
>   Speed of transit 7.6 knots

Group B:
>   Made up of third- and fourth-generation container vessels; VLCCs in ballast; vessels with drafts over 11.6 meters; LPG, LNG, and non-gas-free vessels (loaded or ballasted); and LASH vessels over 35,000 Suez Canal gross tons (SCGT) anchored in North Anchorage north of Port Said
>   Speed of transit 7.6 knots
>   Vessels should enter the buoyed approach fairway of the East Channel in position 31°22'N, 032°23'E, known as km 135, and proceed via Port Said east branch.

Group C:
>   Made up of vessels in South Anchorage that will enter through Port Said West Channel in time to join group B at km 17

Vessels prohibited from joining the second southbound convoy are the following:

Single-bottomed tankers carrying liquid bulk chemicals
LNG and LPG vessels
Warships
Vessels carrying deck cargo in excess of regulations
Vessels with a beam over 45 meters or a draft exceeding 11.5 meters
Vessels over 90,000 SCGT

Tankers, single- or double-bottomed, carrying bulk liquid chemicals with a
−23°C flash point

SOUTHBOUND CONVOY SCHEDULE

Vessels of groups A and B must be in the Port Said anchorage by 1900 and
must have been declared ready for transit by their agents. Convoy N1 will
proceed to the canal entrance at 0100, and vessels may join the convoy until that time. Vessels under 5,000 tons follow behind group B and may join
as late as 0600. Group A will proceed as soon as the last vessel of the northbound convoy has entered the east channel at km 17. Vessels of group B,
containerships at the lead, enter the channel at km 135 as soon as the last
vessel of the northbound convoy has passed. From km 17 the convoy proceeds with group A in the lead and has free run until the Bitter Lakes,
where they anchor on the west side of the channel through Great Bitter
Lake. Once the northbound convoy has passed the Bitter Lakes, the southbound convoy proceeds, this time with group B leading.

NORTHBOUND CONVOY SCHEDULE

The northbound convoy consists of two groups, A (parts 1 and 2) and B. The
speed of transit is 7 to 7.6 knots for both groups.

Group A1:
   Third- and fourth-generation container vessels, LPG and LNG (both
   loaded or non-gas-free), and LASH vessels over 35,000 SCGT
Group A2 :
   Loaded tankers and heavy bulk carriers (draft over 11.6 meters or LBP
   over 289.7 meters)
Group B:
   Other vessels anchored in the Suez anchorages

By 0100 vessels must have arrived at the anchorage and be declared ready
for transit by their agents. By 0300 vessels in group B must have arrived in
the waiting area southeast of Newport Rock Channel and be declared ready
for transit by their agents. At 0615 the leading vessel of group Al enters at
km 160. Group B follows with a cutoff time of 1130. The northbound convoy
usually proceeds without stopping via the east channel off El Kabrit, the
east channel through Great Bitter Lake, the east branch at Deversoir, the
east channel through Lake Timsah, the east branch at El Ballah, and then
from km 17 through the east channel to the Mediterranean Sea.

Prearrival Information

The SCA requires four days advance notice from vessels that wish to join a
transiting convoy. Notice may be sent to "SUQ" directly via radiotele-

phone, telex, or INMARSAT or, as is more common, via the agent.[2] This message should contain the following:

Name
Call sign
Nationality
Type
Draft on day of transit
Suez Canal gross tonnage (SCGT)
Deadweight tonnage

All vessels must send the following required message to SCA via "SUQ" or the agent at least 48 hours prior to arrival. The 48-hour prearrival message should contain the following:

Type, nationality (flag), vessel's name and former name
Suez Canal gross and net tonnage
International gross registered tonnage, net registered tonnage, and deadweight tonnage
Owner's and charterer's name
Whether the vessel intends to transit or stay in a harbor, and the length of the stay
ETA Port Said (southbound) or Suez (northbound)
Date of last transit and changes to particulars if any (if none, state "particulars—no changes")
Nature and quantity of cargo
Quantity and IMO class of any dangerous cargo
Number and nationalities of crew and passengers

Upon approaching from seaward, the Harbor Office (HP1) should be contacted on VHF channel 16. Contact should be made as follows:

Fifteen miles before arrival at fairway buoy of Port Said, or
Five miles before arrival at separation zone buoy no. 1 off Port of Suez.

The arrival message should contain the following:

Position
Vessel's name and call sign
Suez Canal official number and code number
Suez Canal gross tonnage and deadweight tonnage
Draft
Whether the vessel is loaded or in ballast
Nature of cargo

Any defects concerning the safety of navigation

In addition, if the vessel is transiting for the first time, the message should contain the following:

Date of building
Whether a Suez Canal tonnage certificate is held and, if so, its date of issue
Call sign or official number
Length overall
Beam
Type of engines

Once inside the harbor, pilots and radar guidance stations can be reached as below:

Port Said Pilot Vessel and Radar Guidance
    Outer Harbor   HP2   Ch. 12
    Inner Harbor   HP3   Ch. 13
Port Suez Pilot Vessel and Radar Guidance
    Outer Harbor   HP2   Ch. 11
    Inner Harbor   HP3   Ch. 14

Notice of cancelation or alteration must be given at least 24 hours in advance to avoid a fine. Vessels arriving without prior booking may be allowed to join the convoy if space allows.

TRANSITING REGULATIONS

Whenever a vessel transits the canal, the master has tacitly agreed to all regulations contained in the SCA manual. The pilot will provide this manual, if the agent has not already provided one. The master must be thoroughly familiar with all canal regulations.

Speed: Normal speed in the Suez Canal per SCA regulations is 7–7.6 knots. If the vessel handles badly at this speed, it should be adjusted accordingly. Due to narrow channel and shallow water effects, it is generally prudent to slow down when entering a narrower portion of the canal to maintain good steerage control. Careful speed management is also required when passing a dredge or moored vessel, and the master must ensure his vessel's speed is slow enough not to cause the moored vessel to carry away off her moorings. Due to the large volume of water displaced (relative to the width and depth of the canal) when a vessel is underway, there is a maximum hull speed all vessels will reach, regardless of engine rpms.

Grounding: Should a vessel go aground while in the canal, only SCA officials can direct the refloating operation. If a collision appears imminent, under SCA regulations, the master must not hesitate to run his vessel aground if in so doing he can avoid a collision.

Steering: Only hand steering is permitted in the canal. Great care should be taken, as the canal banks are not always symmetrical with the dredged channel. Great care should also be taken if the vessel is experiencing a beam wind as she could be blown against the lee shore.

Communications: Ships must be equipped on the bridge with VHF radio that has channels 6, 8 through 17, 71, 73, and 74.

Day and Night Signals

The pilot will carry the canal regulations and signal book for use by the master during transit. Night signal lights should be hoisted at the foremast head or where other vessels can best see them. At night, when a vessel is made fast, she should display one red light aft. During night transits, vessels must keep their searchlight on, show their regulation lights as required, and keep a lookout forward.

The searchlight shall be mounted at the bow along the axis of the vessel and must illuminate the canal clearly 1,500 meters ahead. This searchlight must be of a gastight type aboard tankers that are not gas-free. Two shore electricians must be embarked to operate the searchlight. Vessels are also required to have lighting capable of illuminating a 200-meter diameter around the vessel as well as their funnels.

The following day/night signals are excerpts from the SCA manual:

"I need a pilot."
   Flag G under a black ball / Three white lights in a vertical line. If proceeding from port to sea or changing berths, this signal should be raised 30 minutes prior to departure from the dock. If transiting the canal, it should be hoisted about two hours before the first vessel enters the canal.
"A pilot is en route to you."
   Flag U above flag A / White rocket or UA in Morse code via signal lamp
"Follow pilot boat; too rough for boarding here."
   Flag U above flag F / White flare or UF by Morse code signal lamp
"Pilot vessel cannot go out."
   Flag U above flag I / Red rocket or UI by Morse code signal lamp
"Tanker carrying bulk petroleum (flash point 23° to 49°C)."
   Flag B over one ball / Two red lights over white light
"Vessel carrying explosives."
   Ball over flag B / White light over two red lights

Sound Signals

The International COLREGS sound signals shall apply in the canal. The only other allowed signals are the following:

Five or six short blasts, repeated at rapid intervals, to indicate the ship is reducing speed and may have to stop or make fast

One prolonged blast to attract attention

Other signals as described in the most recent SCA manual

PILOTAGE

Pilotage is compulsory for all non-Egyptian vessels over 300 SCGT when entering, leaving, or shifting berth in canal waters or in Port Said or Port Suez harbors. Pilots are employed in four stages during various segments of canal transit. Some vessels may carry additional pilots. Once a pilot is on the way to the vessel, an anchored vessel should bring her cable to short stay and be ready to make way for the canal entrance upon the embarkation of the pilot. Vessels moored to docks should similarly prepare their vessel for a speedy departure once the pilot is aboard. A spare cabin shall be made available to the pilot. If one is not provided, additional pilotage fees may be levied. The master should apprise the pilot of any maneuvering characteristics and peculiarities of the vessel. The pilot's duties commence and cease at the entrance buoys of Port Said and the port of Suez. Pilots serve in a strictly advisory capacity and the ultimate responsibility for the handling of the vessel lies solely with the master.

ESCORT TUGS

Vessels greater than 70,000 Suez Canal net tonnage (SCNT) will be required to have at least one escort tug. Vessels less than 70,000 SCNT may be required to have a tug at the discretion of the SCA. Vessels requiring tugs must have ready two polypropylene emergency towlines of 16-inch circumference to connect the stern of the ship to the tug during stopping operations. The lines should be long enough to allow a distance of about 50 meters between the stern of the vessel and the bow of the tug. The lines should be eye-spliced to fit in the quick-release hooks on the tugs. On the vessel, the lines should be made fast to the port and starboard stern bitts with the eyes hanging over the stern about 2 meters from the water' s surface, lashed with break-free rope stoppers, to break loose when necessary.

CHAPTER 18

Foreign Ports

Only general information on foreign port requirements can be provided. The first port of call in a foreign country usually requires the most papers.

When approaching a foreign port for the first time, the master should check the sailing directions and the company port information file for special port requirements and also to see if it is necessary to notify the harbormaster, captain of the port, or other authority regarding the vessel's ETA, draft, or other matters. Generally, giving the ETA to the agent is sufficient as he or she will notify the required authorities, but a few ports insist on a message directly from the ship. The *Guide to Port Entry*, published by Shipping Guides Ltd. of England, is especially useful for paperwork requirements, and it also has diagrams of many docks in all parts of the world.

AGENTS

In most ports—probably all foreign ports—the company will appoint a local agent. The agent's job is to represent the master, the vessel, and the company and to see that the vessel's stay in port goes as smoothly as possible. The agent will order tugs, pilot, and line handlers; arrange transportation and medical treatment for the crew; coordinate repairs and stores deliveries; make required reports to port authorities; advise the master of special local laws or regulations; enter and clear at the customhouse for the master; and generally assist the master with in-port business.

Many companies supply their masters with a book listing the agents to use at each port where their vessels normally call. If the vessel is ordered to a port where the company does not have an agent, one should be appointed without delay. A radio message should be sent to the master, giving the agent's name and all contact information.

265

If the vessel is chartered, the charterer may appoint an agent also. Many times the shipowner and charterer will use the same agent; if not, the master must be sure to keep the charterer's agent informed of the vessel's ETA and of any particulars affecting the charterer's business.

At some small ports there may be only one agency available and it may be associated with the cargo terminal. In such a case, where the agency is not truly independent, the master must be especially careful to see that the company's interests are properly protected, particularly in the event of a dispute between the vessel and the terminal.

The master should give the agent a daily update of the vessel's ETA beginning three or four days before arrival, or as soon as possible after departure on a short voyage. If there are any port requirements, such as crewmembers needing to see the doctor or charts to be purchased, the master should advise the agent early enough to allow time to make arrangements. It may be difficult or impossible to obtain some services or products on weekends or holidays. The master should be sure to radio the agent to supply the local national flag on arrival, if the vessel does not already have one; many governments are very sensitive regarding the display of the courtesy flag.

In all foreign ports the agent will want the figures for fuel, water, and draft on arrival and on sailing; an ETA for the next port; crew lists; and passenger lists. The master should check with the agent to determine whether a notice of readiness, if required, has been prepared.

The agent should meet the ship on arrival and should assist the master with customs, immigration, quarantine, or other local authorities. The agent is the best person to advise the master on the delicate matter of gratuities to government officials.

Before the agent leaves the ship, the master should obtain a telephone number so the agency can be called in case of emergency. Most large agencies maintain a twenty-four-hour answering service; if not, the agent's cellular phone and home number are necessary alternatives. If the master goes ashore, the chief officer should have these numbers. If any emergency or serious difficulty arises, the master or chief officer should not hesitate to call upon the agent for assistance.

If the master is asked to sign any document written in a foreign language that he or she does not understand, the agent should translate it.

In the event of a serious emergency, such as a badly injured crewmember, the master may have to put into a port where the company does not have an agent and when there is not time for the company to appoint one. The master should appoint his or her own agent if one is available and if the local authorities advise it. Often a ship without an agent is subject to delays that cost far more than an agency fee.

An agent hired by the master will probably want a letter of appointment from the master. This is simply a signed and dated letter addressed to the agent, stating that the master is appointing the person as the local agent to represent the master and the vessel. The appointment is binding upon the company and is the agent's assurance of being paid. Of course, the master should communicate full details to the company as soon as possible.

If the vessel needs fresh provisions in port (and the ordering of stores is the responsibility of the master rather than the company's purchasing department), it is prudent to allow the agent to handle the order. In many ports, ship chandlers will board the vessel as soon as it is tied up, looking for business. Their stated prices are usually high, and the prices shown on their bills may be even higher than those shown on the price lists. Some chandlers may offer the master commissions, presents, kickbacks, or a percentage of the order. Such offers should be politely refused.

The agent probably knows most of the local ship chandlers and will give the order to the one found to be most reliable. An agent may want to rotate orders among the various ship chandlers. This will prevent anyone on the vessel from using influence in placing the order. In some ports the agent may have a contract with a firm of ship chandlers; if this is the case, prices for an order placed through the agent may be lower than prices for an order placed directly with the chandler.

Most agents are very professional, but some will do only the minimum work necessary to obtain their fee. The master should not hesitate to tell both the agent and the company if there is a problem with the agency's service. If the master is especially dissatisfied, a different agent can be requested for the vessel's next call at that port. Most ports have several agencies and it is a simple matter for the company to change agents if they wish to do so. The master should also compliment an agency for good service; a good agent can be of tremendous assistance to the master and the company.

Agents can offer much valuable advice but, as always, the responsibility for any decision made is the master's.

CLEARANCE

On entering some ports the master must produce a clearance from the last port of call. On entering the first U.S. port from a foreign port, the master must produce a clearance from the last foreign port. Depending upon the practice in each port, this clearance may be issued by customs, the harbormaster, or the harbor police. The agent will bring it on board before sailing. If the departing port does not issue clearances, the agent should furnish the master with a letter stating that fact. The letter is given to the authorities at the next port in lieu of the clearance.

QUARANTINE

The quarantine officer, sometimes called the sanitary or health officer, boards the vessel in the first port of call in the country. Bills of health are very rarely required anymore but if a vessel calls at an infected port, it may be necessary to get a bill of health from the consul of the country the vessel will visit next and, in some cases, for subsequent ports in other countries. The agent in the infected port will know what is required.

The quarantine officer may want to see the derat certificate and may ask for a maritime declaration of health. This is an international form, usually printed in the language of the country with an English translation. It deals with such items as ports visited by the vessel in the previous three months, dates of sailing, and reports of any sickness aboard that is suspected to be contagious. It requires a yes or no answer to several questions about any sickness currently on board or occurring during the voyage. The quarantine officer may want a crew list, passenger list, and stores list.

The health officer may also want to see the shot records of the crew and passengers. If anyone on board does not have a shot record, has one with an outdated vaccination, or lacks various shots, the health authorities may require the person to receive the shots at that time. If the crew's shot records are collected, the master should be sure to return them before the vessel pays off.

In practice, due to the great advances made worldwide in eradicating various diseases over the last several decades, shot records are very rarely called for and shots are seldom required. Most mariners do not even carry shot records anymore.

CREW LISTS

Crew lists are required in all foreign ports. These must be given to the customs, quarantine, and immigration officers when they board. The agent always wants a copy and the terminal may want one for the gate guard. A half-dozen to a dozen crew lists will be required in most ports. Sometimes officials other than those noted request copies. Most countries require the master to sign several of the crew lists. Social security numbers, next-of-kin, home addresses, and other personal information, if at all possible, should be omitted from crew lists given to noncompany personnel.

PASSENGER LISTS

In all foreign ports, at least two passenger lists will be required and it is advisable to have a number of extra copies. The list should indicate which passengers are landing and which are in transit; in some ports two separate lists may be required. It is helpful but not necessary to use form I-418 (fig. 23); ordinary paper will do, unless the country requires special forms. For each passenger, the list should include the full name, sex, age, nationality, passport number and country of issue, port of embarkation, and destination.

The immigration officer may want to see the passports of the passengers in transit. If so, it is a good idea to collect these passports in advance, so that if the vessel enters port at night it will not be necessary to awaken the passengers. Usually if the passports are available, the officials will not require the master to wake the passengers. If the officials do want to see the passengers, it is sometimes possible to make arrangements for them to return during daylight hours rather than disturb the passengers' sleep.

STORES LISTS

A stores list is required in all ports except free ports. Be especially careful that the quantities shown for cigarettes and other tobacco products, alcoholic beverages, ship's weapons and ammunition, and narcotic drugs in the medicine chest are accurate. All tobacco and alcohol products in the slop chest, and therefore belonging to the ship, should be shown on the stores lists. All tobacco and alcohol in the crew rooms and belonging to the crew should be shown on the crew's effects list.

Customs will probably seal the slop chest. The master must not under any circumstances break the seal or sell any tobacco or alcohol to the crew, no matter how long the vessel stays in port, without written permission from customs. If the vessel's stay is especially long, the agent can apply to customs to open the slop chest and reseal it after the allowed sales.

VISAED DOCUMENTS

Some countries require that crew lists, passenger lists, stores lists, and manifests be visaed by their consuls. Some countries also require that the crew list be on a special form, issued by them, which must be procured from and visaed by their consul, usually at the last port prior to arrival in the country. When a special crew list or other forms must be visaed, the agent or broker should attend to it. Regardless of who gets the required visas or makes up the forms, it is the master's responsibility to see that it is done and that the papers are on board before sailing, or if not ready before sailing, that the agent or broker knows where to send them. Some countries fine the vessel if the visaed papers are not on board as required, or they impose a fine for each member of the crew omitted from the visaed crew list.

In large ports, special customhouse brokers are employed to make up these papers. They are familiar with the numerous details, understand the language, and have current information on any changes in the rules and regulations of these countries. They also have a supply of necessary forms.

IMMIGRATION

The immigration officer usually comes on board soon after docking or anchoring, or possibly before, if the vessel passes through locks. He or she may want to see the passports of any passengers whether landing or not. The master should be sure to ask whether shore passes are required and, if so, whether they must be collected and returned before sailing. The immigration officer will want a crew list and passenger list.

CUSTOMS

The customs officer boards the vessel at each port except free ports. However, if the vessel leaves the free port and enters a customs port or area, it will be necessary to observe customs rules in regard to stores lists and crew declarations. Often what is termed a free port may be only a section or area of the port proper. The customs officer will require stores lists and a crew's effects declaration and may seal up excess cigarettes and other tobacco products, spirits, and perhaps some other goods of high duty value. It is possible that he or she will want to count the cartons of cigarettes and bottles or cases of alcohol products.

In some countries one or more customs officers may be assigned to the vessel and stay on board all the time the vessel is in that port. They should be given a comfortable room, allowed to eat in the officers mess, and receive courteous and considerate treatment.

The customs boarding officer will want to see the register (certificate of documentation), the load line certificate, and perhaps also the safety equipment, STCW certificates, and other internationally required documents. If the vessel is required to enter at the customhouse, it may be necessary to send these certificates ashore with the agent. In some ports the customs boarding officer will take the register, giving a receipt for it. The master should be sure to get the register back before sailing and check to see that it is the correct one.

The customs boarding officer will want copies of the stores lists, crew's effects list, crew list, passenger list (if any are on board in transit), list of passengers landing, cargo manifest, and possibly the clearance from the last port.

TONNAGE TAX

At the first port of call in some countries, the master may have to pay a tonnage tax (also called tonnage dues or light dues) for which the customs officer will provide a tonnage tax receipt. This receipt may be good for a certain length of time during which the vessel may call at other ports in that country without the payment of additional tonnage tax, or it may be good for a definite number of calls over a stated period. The period of its validity dates from the day the tonnage tax receipt is issued. The receipt should be kept in a safe place; the master may have to produce it on arrival at subsequent ports in the same country. If it is taken up by the agent or by the customs officer, the master should make certain it is returned before sailing. The customs officers at each port in that country may want to see it.

CREW'S EFFECTS LISTS

Before arriving at the first port of call in any country, the master should make up a crew's effects list. This list must show the cigarettes, other tobacco products, alcoholic beverages, and items of high duty value (such as cameras, radios, and jewelry) owned by the crew. Other than tobacco and alcohol, the rules are usually rather vague regarding just what must be declared. It is best to tell the crewmembers that if there is any doubt about whether or not an item is declarable, they should declare it.

Each country has its own rules regarding the amount of tobacco or alcohol products that may be kept out by the crew for personal use. A common allowance is two hundred cigarettes (one carton) or an equivalent amount of other tobacco products, and one quart or liter of spirits per person. A few countries require that all tobacco or alcohol products over the allowed amount be collected and stored in a sealed room or locker; however, this practice is rare nowadays. If it is necessary to place any of the crew's personal belongings under seal, each person should write his or her name on the packages placed under seal.

SEARCHES

Although it is unusual for a merchant vessel to be searched these days, practically all customs agencies do maintain teams of searchers for use when the need arises. Some ports may occasionally pick vessels at random to be searched in order to verify compliance with customs laws. They are especially likely to give a particular vessel a complete search if they have ever had any trouble, such as smuggling, with that ship in the past, even though there may have been a complete change of crew in the meantime.

These searchers, either because they are ex-mariners or have long experience, are very thorough and rarely miss concealed articles. The vessel is subject to a fine, sometimes a heavy one, and crewmembers and even the master may be jailed if any undeclared articles or contraband are found. If any of the crew is suspected of drug smuggling, the searchers will very likely bring with them dogs that are trained to sniff out drugs of all types.

CUSTOMS SEAL

The customs laws and regulations in all countries should be strictly followed, particularly in regard to customs seals. Once a customs seal is on a locker or room, no one must break the seal or tamper with it. If the vessel is to proceed to another port in the same country, the seals should be left intact until permission is given, in writing if possible, to break them at sea after leaving the first port. The only time a seal may be broken without permission is when the vessel leaves her last port of call in a country, is outside port limits, and has dropped the pilot. The customs laws in all countries are very strict about this, and a seal broken without authority may result in a very heavy fine. It is not worth taking a chance.

TRADITIONAL COURTESIES

In all ports, foreign and domestic, officials should be treated courteously and with consideration. Above all, no one should argue with them. Generally they will have the last word and it may turn out to be an expensive one for the company and a troublesome one for the master. Becoming familiar with local social customs could help prevent difficult situations.

Gratuities to Officials

Gratuities of some kind, usually cartons of cigarettes or bottles of whiskey, are generally given to the officials in most foreign ports. Usually the master keeps a few extra cartons of cigarettes, which are not shown on the stores list, for gratuities. The officials may help themselves when they inspect the storerooms. If there is doubt about what gratuities should be given, the master should consult the agent about the local customs. Sometimes the agent will also expect a gratuity, but it is the master's decision whether to give one.

SHORE LEAVE

Union agreements often contain a clause specifying that if shore leave is denied crewmembers, they may claim overtime for the number of hours of shore leave they were denied, unless the master has a letter from a government authority stating that shore leave was prohibited by law, regulation, or government order. The crew may claim that shore leave was denied if a launch is not provided as called for in the agreement.

When the vessel arrives at the first port of call in any country, it must generally comply with various formalities before any crewmembers or passengers will be allowed ashore. These include granting pratique and immigration and customs clearance. If the vessel arrives at night, these formalities may not be completed until the following morning. If the vessel must anchor, the agent will usually be on the job and have a shore-leave launch waiting.

In some cases, the immigration and customs officers will give permission for people to leave as soon as pratique is granted, unless passes have to be made up. In other cases, the vessel may remain at anchor for several days awaiting a berth. Even though pratique may have been granted, customs and immigration may not clear the vessel until it docks. Regardless of this, the crew might claim overtime for the time they were not able to go ashore while the vessel was awaiting clearance. Such overtime should be disputed.

On arrival at a port where the vessel may have to remain at anchor under the above conditions, it is important for the agent to get a letter from customs, immigration, or other authority stating the reason why shore leave was prohibited.

SHORE LAUNCH

In some ports the vessel may anchor or tie up to buoys, making it necessary for the crew to use a launch for shore leave. The master should make up a boat schedule as soon as possible after arrival and post it on the bulletin boards. The agent should give a copy to the boat operator and another to the launch office at the landing. Usually boats are run every four hours, at the change of watch, with possibly an extra boat on the 4 to 8 watch for the steward's department.

DANGEROUS OR FLAMMABLE CARGO

What the master thinks is safe cargo may not be considered so by the local port officials. Should the authorities consider any of the cargo dangerous and/or flammable, they may require the master to run out hoses at each hatch or area where such cargo is stowed. They may also have a detail from the fire department stand by with equipment as long as the vessel is in port with that cargo on board. The master should check with the agent as to whether it will be necessary to fly the "bravo" flag during the day and display a red light at night. The vessel may be fined for not doing so if it is required. The master should also ask about any other local requirements.

DUNNAGE AND SCRAP

In many foreign ports, junk dealers will board to buy dunnage, old line, tarps, scrap metal, and other such items. Shipowners generally issue instructions regarding this, and the master is usually permitted wide discretion. If, in the absence of instructions to the contrary, the master considers it to be in the best interests of the company to get rid of dunnage or junk, it should be done through the agent and the proper receipts obtained.

U.S. CONSUL

Most major foreign ports have a U.S. consul. The consul's office performs various services for U.S. vessels and mariners. If any mariners are shipped or discharged in a foreign port, they must be signed on or signed off before the consul, if there is one in the port. The consul will also make arrangements for the repatriation of destitute mariners. If the master desires to note protest because of some extraordinary occurrence on the voyage, the consul's office will accept the protest.

Federal law requires the master to deposit the register (certificate of documentation) with the U.S. consul or vice consul upon arrival in a foreign port, if there is a consul or vice consul in the port. The consul will return the register when the vessel receives clearance from the port authorities, provided the master has complied with the law regarding shipment and discharge of mariners.

The federal courts have ruled that arrival at a foreign port means an arrival for ship's business that requires an entry at the customhouse. The master will not be required to deposit the register if the vessel calls at a foreign port only incidentally—for example, to obtain orders—and the local officials do not require the vessel to enter at the customhouse. The master will have to deposit the register if the vessel is required to enter, regardless of the purpose for entering port.

The consul's office may have a form for the master to complete. The consul is required by law to make reports to the Secretary of Commerce of mariners shipped or discharged before the consul and the wages paid them, the registered tonnages of U.S. vessels calling at the port, the number of their crew and the number who are U.S. citizens, and the nature and value of the cargo.

SAILING OR DEPARTURE PERMIT

In some ports the vessel cannot depart until the immigration officer, harbor police, or other local authority has issued a permit. The master may have to show or give this permit to the pilot before the vessel can sail, so it should be kept in a handy place. This is for local use and is not the same as the clearance.

CHAPTER 19

Flag Etiquette

Flags should always be maintained in good condition; they should never be flown at night (unless lighted) or flown in inclement weather. No country's flag should be allowed to touch the deck or ground. If a flag is becoming tattered, it may be possible to cut off the frayed edge and rehem the flag, but this is usually an indication that the flag should be replaced.

COURTESY FLAG

When entering a foreign port it is customary to fly the national flag of the host country from a halyard, usually on the starboard side. In many ports, flying the courtesy flag is required by law. In certain countries the officials are very sensitive about this and the vessel may get a rough reception or even a fine from the authorities if the courtesy flag is not properly flying on arrival. If there is a question as to which edge is to be flown on top, it is helpful to know that the manufacturer's tag is usually sewn to the top edge or top corner. Some flags, such as the British flag, look symmetrical but do indeed have a top and a bottom edge.

When the vessel receives orders to a foreign port for which the master does not have a flag, the agent at the previous port may be able to supply one. If the vessel is diverted at sea and is unable to obtain a courtesy flag before arrival, the master should radio the agent to have one available on arrival.

THE COLORS

The American flag is to be flown from sunrise to sunset from the highest centerline halyard when near land or falling in with other ships. When the first line is passed, or anchor let go, the flag is to be shifted to the centerline flagstaff at the stern. In port, military and government-owned vessels fly the Union Jack at the foremast. If both the colors and the Jack are flown, they should be raised and lowered in unison. The flags should be raised briskly and lowered slowly, in a ceremonious manner. While most merchant mariners never expect to participate in naval ceremonies, the occasion may arise. Merchant ships under government charter routinely convoy with naval vessels and masters should be aware of proper flag etiquette and custom.

Dipping the Colors

When passing close aboard a U.S. naval vessel or a naval vessel of a recognized nation, it is a courtesy to dip the ensign. This should be done only when passing close enough that the honor is visible from the other vessel's bridge. The colors are lowered to half-mast. This will be matched by the saluted naval vessel. Once matched at half-mast, the merchant ship hauls the colors back to the peak, and the honored naval vessel then does the same.

Displaying Colors at Half-Mast

When displaying the colors at half-mast, the flag should first be raised to the peak, then lowered to half-mast. Before lowering the colors, the flag should again be hoisted to the peak before being lowered.

VISITING DIGNITARIES

Should the master be notified of an official visit by military personnel, the vessel should be readied to pay appropriate respects. If tradition calls for the ship to show a flag representing the visitor's rank, it should be flown on the inboard halyard.

When the master and/or other officers visit a foreign naval vessel, unless the practices of the host nation dictate otherwise, upon boarding they should stop at the quarterdeck, remove their hats, and come to attention—right hand over heart—facing the host nation's flag. The officers should then identify themselves, request permission to board, and state the nature of their business.

DRESSING SHIP

When dressing ship, flags should be displayed from 0800 until evening colors. Traditionally, a string of international signal flags was run from the waterline forward, over the masthead, and to the waterline aft, with several flags being allowed to touch the water from both ends. Flags and pennants should be strung together in the traditional order, not haphazardly. The navy strings two flags to one pennant. The traditional sequence, which is most pleasing to the eye, is: AB2, UJ1, KE3, GH6, IV5, FL4, DM7, PO 3rd repeater, RN 1st repeater, ST0, CX9, WQ8, ZY 2nd repeater.

Shipping Articles

AGREEMENT FOR FOREIGN OR INTERCOASTAL VOYAGE

Title 46, *U.S. Code,* Section 10304 provides that the form of the agreement required by section 10302 of this title shall be in substance as follows:

United States of America

[Date and place of first signature of agreement]: _____

It is agreed between the master and seamen of the _____, of which _____ is at present master, or whoever shall go for master, now bound from the port of _____ to _____ [here the voyage is to be described, and the places named at which the vessel is to touch, or if that cannot be done, the general nature and probable length of the voyage is to be stated].

The seamen agree to conduct themselves in an orderly, faithful, honest, and sober manner, and to be at all times diligent in their respective duties, and to be obedient to the lawful commands of the master, or of an individual who lawfully succeeds the master, and of their superior officers in everything related to the vessel, and the stores and cargo of the vessel, whether on board, in boats, or on shore. In consideration of this service by the seamen to be performed, the master agrees to pay the crew, as wages, the amounts beside their names respectively expressed, and to supply them with provisions according to the annexed scale.

It is agreed that any embezzlement, or willful or negligent destruction of any part of the vessel's cargo or stores, shall be made good to the owner out of the wages of the person guilty of the embezzlement or destruction.

If an individual holds himself or herself out as qualified for a duty which the individual proves incompetent to perform, the individual's wages shall be reduced in proportion to the incompetency.

It also is agreed that if a seaman considers himself or herself to be aggrieved by any breach of this agreement or otherwise, the seaman shall present the complaint to the master or officer in charge of the vessel, in a quiet and orderly manner, who shall take steps that the case requires.

It also is agreed that [here any other stipulations may be inserted to which the parties agree, and that are not contrary to law].

In witness whereof, the parties have subscribed their names to this agreement on the dates beside their respective signatures.

Signed by _____ , master, on the _____ day of _____ , two thousand and _____ .

Signature of seaman:_____
Birthplace: Time of service:
Age: Months:
Height: Days:
    Feet: Hospital money:
    Inches: Whole wages:
Description: Wages due:
    Complexion: Place and time of entry:
    Hair: Time at which seaman is to
Wages each month: be aboard:
Wages each voyage: In what capacity:
    Amount of draw: Shipping commissioner's
Amount of monthly allotment: signature or initials:
Conduct qualifications: Allotment payable to:

Note: In the place for signature and descriptions of individuals engaged after the first departure of the vessel, the entries are to be made as above, except that the signature of the consul or vice consul, customs officer, or witness before whom the individual is engaged, is to be entered.

Figures: Sample Forms

FIG. 1   283

DEPARTMENT OF THE TREASURY
UNITED STATES CUSTOMS SERVICE

REPORT OF DIVERSION

Approved through 5/31/96
OMB No. 1515-0071

19 CFR 4.91 (a) and (b)

1. PORT WHICH GRANTED CLEARANCE OR PERMIT TO PROCEED	2. NATIONALITY *(American or Foreign)*

3. NAME OF VESSEL	4. RIG	5. DATE

⌐   CUSTOMS PORT DIRECTOR   ⌐

∟   ⌐

6. NAME OF PORT TO WHICH CLEARED	7. DATE OF CLEARANCE

8. ACTUAL/EXPECTED PORT OF ARRIVAL	9. DATE OF ARRIVAL

PLEASE NOTIFY THE PORT DIRECTOR AT THE PORT OF ARRIVAL. (The port director will act only when timely notified under section 4.91(a), and 4.91(b), of the Customs Regulations.)

AND/OR

GRANT RELIEF FROM ANY PENALTY TO WHICH THE MASTER, OWNER, OR AGENT MAY BE LIABLE UNDER 46 U.S.C. 91 OR 19 U.S.C. 1445.

10. REASONS

11. REPORT SUBMITTED BY	12. TITLE *(Owner, Master, or Agent)*	13. DATE

14. PENALTY CASE NUMBER	☐ Port ☐ District	15. AMOUNT OF PENALTY $

16. PENALTY ASSESSED AGAINST	17. SECTION OF LAW VIOLATED

18. RECOMMEND THAT THE PENALTY BE   ☐ Remitted   ☐ Mitigated to $

19. CUSTOMS PORT DIRECTOR BY	20. DATE

21. PURSUANT TO THE AUTHORITY CONTAINED IN 19 U.S.C. 1618 OR 46 U.S.C. 7, THE ABOVE PENALTY IS   ☐ Remitted   ☐ Mitigated to $

22. SIGNATURE OF CUSTOMS PORT DIRECTOR BY	23. DATE

NOTE: No notice of remission will be furnished. If no notice is received within 30 days, the petitioner may presume that penalty has been remitted.

PAPERWORK REDUCTION ACT NOTICE: The Paperwork Reduction Act of 1980 says we must tell you why we are collecting this information, how we will use it, and whether you have to give it to us. We ask for the information to carry out the Customs Service laws of the United States. The form is used by vessel owners, masters, or agents when requesting a diversion of the vessel or to petition for relief from penalties as a result of an unlawful diversion or both. The use of this form is mandatory.

Statement Required by 5 CFR 1320.21: The estimated average burden associated with this collection of information is 5 minutes per respondent or recordkeeper depending on individual circumstances. Comments concerning the accuracy of this burden estimate and suggestions for reducing this burden should be directed to U.S. Customs Service, Paperwork Management Branch, Washington DC 20229, and to the Office of Management and Budget, Paperwork Reduction Project (1515-0071), Washington DC 20503.

Customs Form 26 (090298)

Form Approved, OMB No. 1515-0082—See back of form for Paperwork Reduction Act Notice.

DEPARTMENT OF THE TREASURY
UNITED STATES CUSTOMS SERVICE

RECORD OF VESSEL
FOREIGN REPAIR OR EQUIPMENT PURCHASE

19 CFR 4.7, 4.14

1. FUNCTION OF THIS DOCUMENT (Mark only one)

☐ DECLARATION
(Complete Items 1 through 16 Only)

☐ ENTRY
(Complete Items 1-15 and 19-25)

ITEMS BELOW FOR ENTRY ONLY; DO NOT USE FOR DECLARATION

18. ENTRY NUMBER AND DATE

CUSTOMS USE ONLY

2. OWNER NAME AND ADDRESS

3. REPRESENTED LOCALLY BY

4. VESSEL NAME

5. NAME OF MASTER

19. NAME OF PRINCIPAL AND SURETY

6. PORT ARRIVED FROM

7. VOYAGE NO.

8. U.S. PORT OF ARRIVAL

9. PORT CODE

10. ARRIVAL DATE

20. BOND NUMBER

21. BOND AMOUNT

11. LOCATION (City and Country) AND DATE OF REPAIRS ETC. AND SAILING DATE FROM THAT COUNTRY

12. DESCRIPTION OF WORK PERFORMED INCLUDING IDENTIFICATION OF MATERIALS/EQUIPMENT PURCHASED

COST IN FOREIGN MONEY

13. Material, Parts or Equipment

14. Labor

22. EXCHANGE RATE

23. ENTERED U.S. COST

24. DUTY @ 50% ENTERED COST IN U.S. MONEY

15. TOTAL AMOUNT DECLARED

15a. Material, Etc.

15b. Labor

ITEMS BELOW FOR DECLARATION ONLY, DO NOT USE FOR ENTRY

16. CERTIFICATION OF MASTER

AS MASTER OF THE SAID VESSEL, I HEREBY SUBSCRIBE TO THE DECLARATION STATEMENT ON THE BACK OF THIS DOCUMENT.

17. CUSTOMS USE ONLY

I have examined the vessel's log, which indicates:

☐ The undeclared repairs or purchases which I have listed on the back of this declaration.

☐ No undeclared repairs or purchases

25. CERTIFICATION OF MASTER OR AUTHORIZED AGENT OF THE OWNER

I HEREBY SUBSCRIBE TO THE STATEMENT RELATIVE TO AN ENTRY ON THE BACK OF THIS DOCUMENT.
(Mark Box "A" or Box "B")

☐ A (full and complete)   ☐ B (incomplete)

A. SIGNATURE

B. TITLE

C. DATE

A. SIGNATURE

B. TITLE

C. DATE

A. SIGNATURE

C. SIGNATURE

D. TITLE

E. DATE

Customs Form 226 (052196)

FIG. 3   285

DEPARTMENT OF THE TREASURY
UNITED STATES CUSTOMS SERVICE

VESSEL ENTRANCE OR CLEARANCE STATEMENT

OMB No. 1515-0060

☐ ENTRANCE   ☐ CLEARANCE

Customs Directive No. 3120-017   Trade Code (see back).

1. Manifest Number	2. Port of Arrival	3. Date & Time Of Arrival / Departure	4. Vessel Operating Draft (in feet and inches) (see back for instructions)

5. Nationality, Name and Type of Vessel (see back for instructions) | 6. Vessel Built at/Year | 7. Name Address & Phone No. of Ship's Agent

8. Name & Country of Owner | 9. Name & Country of Operator (see back for instructions)

10. Gross Tonnage	11. Net Tonnage	12. Port Arrived From / Departed For	13. IMO#/ Official #/Call Sign (see back for instructions)

14. List All Dock Locations (continue on back if necessary)

15. Particulars of Voyage (Previous and Subsequent Ports of Call; underline where remaining cargo will be discharged.) (continue on back if necessary)

16. Brief Description of Cargo

17. ☐ Check if Incomplete Manifest for Export   ☐ Check if Complete Manifest filed for export
☐ Check if Licensed Cargo Loaded

18. Number of Crew	19. Number of Passengers	20. List All Carriers on Board by SCAC Code

21. Tonnage Mark ☐ None   ☐ Submerged   ☐ Not Submerged | 22. Bunkers; Type, Barrels, Value

23. Load Line Expires	24. Solas Certificate Expires	25. Passengers Allowed Per Coast Guard Certificate	26. Number of Passengers Embarking/Disembarking

27. Cert. of Fin. Resp. No. (Oil Pollution) and Exp. Date	28. Cert. of Fin. Resp. (Passenger Death/Injury)	29. Cert. of Fin. Resp. (Passenger Transportation Identification)

30. PURPOSE OF ENTRANCE OR CLEARANCE

☐ D (Discharge Foreign Cargo)   ☐ X (Export Cargo On Board On Arrival)   ☐ L (Lade Cargo For Export)

☐ F (Foreign Cargo To Remain On Board (FROB))   ☐ N (No Cargo Transactions)   ☐ Y (Military Cargo For Discharge)

31. Print and Sign Name of Master, Authorized Agent or Officer, Date

FOR CUSTOMS USE ONLY

32. Customs User Fee Paid Up* ☐	33. APHIS User Fee Paid Up* ☐	34. Tonnage Tax Paid Up* ☐

35. Cash Receipt, CF 368 or Transaction No	36. Total Fees Collected	37. Port Entered / Cleared, Time and Date

38. Customs Officer Remarks

39. Signature and Title of Officer Receiving Entry/ Granting Clearance

☐ CHECK BOXES ONLY IF FEES NOT COLLECTED   Customs Form 1300 (0100)

(left margin, rotated) Attach CF 1002 Certificate of Tonnage Here

Continued on next page

FIG. 3—*Continued*

INSTRUCTIONS

Trade Codes: Please enter the code that best describes the arriving or departing vessel

(1)	Foreign In Ballast
(2)	Foreign Bulk
(3)	Foreign General Cargo
(4)	Domestic or Coastwise Ballast
(5)	Domestic or Coastwise Bulk
(6)	Domestic or Coastwise General Cargo

Block 4 - **Vessel Operating Draft:** (not the design draft)

Deepest draft of the vessel on entrance (in feet and inches)
Deepest draft of the vessel on clearance (in feet and inches)

Block 5 - **Vessel Types:** List one of the codes and descriptions from below.

111	Crude Oil Tanker	350	Passenger
112	Crude/Products Tanker	410	Fish Processing & Catching
140	Tank Barge	421	Drilling Ship
150	Other Tanker	422	Tug/Supply Offshore Support
210	Bulk/Oil Carrier	431	Tug/Tow boat
229	Bulk Carrier	432	Pushboat
310	Container	492	Research/Survey
325	Vehicle Carrier	493	Dredger
330	General Cargo	494	Yacht
333	RO-RO Cargo	499	Other NEI
340	Dry Cargo Barge	600	Lakers Vessels
341	Deck Barge		

Block 9 -- Operator as listed on the Certificate of Financial Responsibility (Oil Pollution): unless other verifiable charter or lease arrangement indicates otherwise.

Block 13 -- If IMO # is available list that and cross out other two titles. If IMO # not available list either or both the official number and/or call sign and cross out the IMO #.

Block 14 -- Additional information

Block 15 -- Additional information

FIG. 4   287

CUSTOMS FORM 1302 (1-14-77)

Form Approved OMB No. 48R0230

DEPARTMENT OF THE TREASURY
UNITED STATES CUSTOMS SERVICE

CARGO DECLARATION
(Oath to be taken on Customs Form 1300)
4.7(a), C.R.

THIS COLUMN FOR U. S. CUSTOMS USE ONLY

Page Nr.

☐ Arrival ☐ Departure

1. Name of ship

2. Port where report is made (not required by United States)

3. Nationality of ship

4. Name of master

5a. Port of loading

5b. Port of discharge

6. Marks and Nrs. (MN)
Container Nrs. (CN)
Seal Nrs. (SN)

7. Number and kind of packages; Description of goods

8. (Answer Col. 8 OR Col. 9)
Gross Weight
(lb. or kg.)

9. Measurement
(per T.S(S)

B/L Nr.

Shipper (SH); Consignee (CO); Notify address (NF)

Final destination (not required by U.S) Date of sailing from port of loading

288

FIG. 5

DEPARTMENT of the TREASURY ● UNITED STATES CUSTOMS SERVICE

CARGO DECLARATION
Outward With Commercial Forms
(Oath to be taken on Customs Form 1300)

Form Approved
OMB No. 1515-0078

Page Nr.

19 CFR 4.62
4.63, 4.75,
4.82, 4.87-
4.89

B/L Nr.	6. Marks and Nrs. (MN) Container Nrs. (CN) Seal Nrs. (SN)	7. Number and kind of packages; Description of goods	(Answer Col. 8 OR Col. 9) 8. Gross Weight (lb. or kg.)	9. Measurement (per TSUS)

1. Name of ship — **2. Port where report is made (not required by United States)**

3. Nationality of ship — **4. Name of master** — **5a. Port of loading** — **5b. Port of discharge**

PAPERWORK REDUCTION ACT NOTICE: We ask for this information to carry out the Customs Service laws of the United States. This form is used by vessel carriers to list all inward cargo on board and for the clearance of all cargo on board with commercial forms. It is mandatory and to your benefit.
This form may be printed by private parties provided it conforms to the official form in size, wording, arrangement, style and size of type, and quality and color of paper. (19 CFR 4.99) For sale by district directors of customs. ☆U.S. GPO: 1987-742-011/41063

Customs Form 1302A (050785)

FIG. 6

289

DEPARTMENT OF THE TREASURY UNITED STATES CUSTOMS SERVICE 19 CFR 4.7, 4.7a, 4.81, 4.85, 4.87	SHIP'S STORES DECLARATION ☐ Arrival ☐ Departure	Form Approved O.M.B. No. 1515-0059 Page No.
1. Name of ship	2. Port of arrival/departure	3. Date of arrival/departure
4. Nationality of ship	5. Port arrived from/Port of destination	
6. Number of persons on board	7. Period of stay	8. Place of storage*

9. Name of article	10. Quantity	11. For Official Use

12. Date and signature by master, authorized agent or officer

This form may be printed by private parties provided the supply printed conforms to the official form in size, wording, arrangement, and quality and color of paper.

* Not required by the United States

PAPERWORK REDUCTION ACT NOTICE: The Paperwork Reduction Act of 1980 says we must tell you why we are collecting this information, how we will use it, and whether you have to give it to us. This information is collected to perform the responsibilities of the U.S. Customs Service. This form is used by the master to declare ship's stores in a format that can be readily audited and checked by U.S. Customs. Your response is mandatory.

Statement Required by 5 CFR 1320.21: The estimated average burden associated with this collection of information is 15 minutes per respondent or recordkeeper depending on individual circumstances. Comments concerning the accuracy of this burden estimate and suggestions for reducing this burden should be directed to U.S. Customs Service, Paperwork Management Branch, Washington DC 20229. DO NOT send completed form(s) to this office.

Customs Form 1303 (040596)

Form Approved
O.M.B. No. 1515-0061

CREW'S EFFECTS DECLARATION

19 CFR 4.7(a), 4.7a(b)

Page No.

1. Name of ship

3. Nationality of ship

4. No.	5. Family name, given name	6. Rank or rating

8. Date and signature by master, authorized agent or officer

This form may be printed by private parties (see 19 CFR 4.99).

Customs Form 1304 (012897)

The United States of America

DEPARTMENT OF THE TREASURY
UNITED STATES CUSTOMS SERVICE

CLEARANCE OF VESSEL TO A FOREIGN PORT

District of ____________________

Port of ____________________

These are to certify all whom it doth concern:

That ____

Master or Commander of the ______________________________________

burden __________________ *Tons, or thereabouts, mounted with* __________

Guns, navigated with ______________ *Men* ______________________________

____________ *built, and bound for* ________________________________

____

____

____

____

with passengers and having on board ______________________________

____

____

MERCHANDISE AND STORES,

hath here entered and cleared his said vessel, according to law.

Given under our hands and seals, at the Customhouse of ________________

____________________ *, this* ____________________ *day of* ________________

one thousand nine hundred ____________________ *,and in the* ________________

year of the Independence of the United States of America.

____
(Customs Officer)

★U.S.GPO:1993-0-343-023/70566

Customs Forms 1378 (122386)

DEPARTMENT OF THE TREASURY
UNITED STATES CUSTOMS SERVICE

Form Approved O.M.B. No. 1515-0013

CUSTOMS USE ONLY
APPROVED
NO.
DATE
SIGNATURE OF CUSTOMS OFFICER

APPLICATION – PERMIT – SPECIAL LICENSE
UNLADING-LADING-OVERTIME SERVICES

4.10, 4.16, 4.30, 4.37, 4.39, 4.91, 6.2, 10.60,
24.16, 123.8, 146.12, 146.14, C.R.; 4.30, 4.39, C.M.

1. PORT

2. NAME OF CARRIER   3. NAME OF OWNER OR OPERATOR   4. NAME OF AGENT

5. ARRIVING FROM   6. DATE OF ARRIVAL   7. LOCATION *(Pier, Terminal, Etc.)*

8. APPLICATION IS MADE FOR A PERMIT FOR THE OPERATIONS INDICATED:

☐ (1) To unlade merchandise (intended to be unladen at this port, as shown by the manifest), baggage, or passengers. To discharge ballast, and To land "in bond" merchandise (Sec. 551, Tariff Act of 1930).

☐ (2) To land supplies, ship's stores, sea stores, or equipment not to be reladen, subject, however, to free or duty-paid entry. (Sec. 446, Tariff Act of 1930).

☐ (3) To lade merchandise or baggage requiring customs supervision.

☐ (4) To land and release for repair, adjustment, or refilling and to relade under customs supervision articles of the carrier's equipment. (Articles to be listed on reverse side hereof showing date and hour of unlading and relading.) The undersigned certifies that the articles listed on the reverse hereof for release under this item are to be landed only for the purpose mentioned in this item and will be reladen on this carrier.

☐ (5) To allow unentered cargo, viz: ....
to remain upon wharf until .... o'clock on the .... day after the expiration of the 5-day period granted by statute for making entry. (NOT GRANTED ON TERM BASIS).

☐ (6) OTHER: ....
....
....
....
....

9. APPLICATION IS MADE FOR A SPECIAL LICENSE FOR OVERTIME SERVICES OF CUSTOMS OFFICERS AND EMPLOYEES FOR:

☐ Entrance, Clearance   ☐ Unlading, Lading, Etc.

☐ OTHER: ....

☐ ON .... AT .... OR ☐ Per Supplemental Oral Request
    (Date)   *(Time)*

10. APPLICATION IS MADE FOR A TERM PERMIT AND SPECIAL LICENSE
From: TO:

11. PRINCIPAL ON BOND	12. SURETY COMPANY CODE	13. AMOUNT OF BOND	14. DATE OF BOND	15. BOND EXPIRES
16. IMPORTER NUMBER *(Party to be Billed - Show Hyphens)*	17. ADDRESS OF AGENT			
	18. SIGNATURE			19. DATE

This PERMIT is not valid until properly lodged with a customs officer at the point of discharge and all operations indicated therein are performed under customs supervision

(Instructions and Paperwork Reduction Act Notice on reverse)   Customs Form 3171 (030882)

FIG. 9—*Continued* 293

RECORD OF ARTICLES RELEASED AND RELADEN UNDER ITEM NO. 8 (4)

UNLADEN AND RELEASED					RELADEN		
Date	Hour	Description of Articles	Released to (Signature)	Inspector	Date	Hour	Inspector

INSTRUCTIONS

Customs Form 3171 shall be filed in duplicate. (When a term permit is requested, additional copies may be required for local purposes). Items shall be completed as follows:

1. Port at which application is filed.

2. Name or number of vessel, vehicle, or aircraft (On term permit show "Not Applicable.")

3. Name of shipping company, airline, etc., which owns or operates the vessel, vehicle or aircraft.

4. Name of party filing application.

5. Name of port or place from which a vessel, vehicle, or aircraft is arriving. (On term permit show "Not Applicable.")

6. Give the date of arrival or expected arrival when request covers a specific vessel, vehicle, or aircraft.

7. Place of lading, unlading, etc.. If request is for overtime services only, state where services are to be performed.

8. Check appropriate items.

9. Indicate purpose for which services are requested and date and time. (If date and time are not known, check "per supplemental oral reques.")

10. When requesting a term permit, show dates or period to be covered.

11. Name of principal on bond. (When a cash deposit is made, write "cash deposit.")

12. Record the name of the surety company and the three-digit surety code.

13. Amount of bond or cash deposit.

14-18. Self-explanatory.

19. Signature of party submitting request.

PAPERWORK REDUCTION ACT NOTICE: The Paperwork Reduction Act of 1980 says we must tell you why we are collecting this information, how we will use it, and whether you have to give it to us. We ask for the information to carry out the Customs Service laws of the United States. This form is used by carriers to request specific Customs services relating to the lading or unlading of merchandise and by Customs to authorize requested activities. It is also used to permit and control various statutes. Another major use of this form is to request Customs services during other than regular hours of service. It is mandatory and to your benefit.

☆U.S. GPO: 1987-742-011/41182

294   FIG. 10

DEPARTMENT OF THE TREASURY
UNITED STATES CUSTOMS SERVICE

CREW MEMBER'S DECLARATION

Form Approved O.M.B. No. 1515-0063

1. CREW MEMBER'S ARTICLE NO.

Customs Form 5129 (110984)   19 CFR 4.7, 4.7a, 4.81, 6.7, 6.9, 148.61-67

Nr —C 1828910

2. CARRIER (Vessel Flag, Name) | 3. DATE OF ARRIVAL | 4. PORT OF ARRIVAL

5. CREW MEMBER'S NAME | 6. RANK | 7. DATE OF BIRTH

8. ADDRESS

9. ANSWER EACH QUESTION:

A. Are you carrying any fruits, plants, meats, other plant or animal products, birds, snails, or other live organisms of any kind?
☐ YES ☐ NO

B. Have you been on a farm or ranch outside the U.S.A. in the last 30 days?
☐ YES ☐ NO

C. Are you carrying over $10,000.00 in monetary instruments, such as coin, currency, traveler's checks, money orders, or negotiable instruments in bearer form? (If yes, you must file a report on CF 4790J
☐ YES ☐ NO

INSTRUCTIONS

List all articles obtained abroad and prices paid, or fair value if not purchased. Include serial number with all articles subject to registration such as cameras, radios, etc.

List articles to remain on board separately from those articles to be landed in the United States.

List separately articles intended for sale, barter, exchange, or carried by you as an accommodation for someone else.

See additional instructions and information on reverse.

I. To be filled in by Crew Member | **II. For Customs Officer's Use**

QUANTITY AND DESCRIPTION OF GOODS	COST, OR VALUE OF GIFTS. ETC.	TARIFF DESCRIPTION	VALUE	RATE	DUTY

I certify that the above statement is a just, true and complete account of all articles of foreign origin for which written declaration and entry are required when landed in the United States (defined on reverse side) and I also certify that this statement is a just, true, and complete declaration of all such articles which I am landing in the United States. | **TOTAL ▶**

10. CUSTOMS OFFICER ACCEPTING ENTRY | 11. SIGNATURE OF CREW MEMBER | 12. DATE

RECEIPT FOR DUTY AND RELEASE SLIP
To be filled in by Crew Member

PORT | CREW MEMBER'S ARTICLE NO.

NAME | CARRIER

REPEAT LIST OF ARTICLES TO BE LANDED (Include serial numbers when appropriate.)

Nr —C 1828910

For Customs Officer's Use

DATE	DUTY
	$

Articles listed at left have been examined and passed.

PIECES OF BAGGAGE RELEASED:

of Customs

The customs officer accepting the declaration and entry shall draw lines through unused spaces on receipt with ink.

NOTICE: Liquidation of amount of duties and taxes, if any, due on this entry is effective on date of payment of this amount (Section 159.10. C.R.) For importer's right to protest or Government's right to redetermine this amount, see section 514 Tariff Act of 1930 as amended.   ☆U.S. GOVERNMENT PRINTING OFFICE: 1989 — 644-760   CF 5129

FIG. 11   295

CHECK APPLICABLE INFORMATION ONLY

DEPARTMENT OF THE TREASURY • U.S. CUSTOMS SERVICE
4.12(a), 6.7(h), 8.28(o)(d), 123.9, 158.1 & C.R.

Form Approved
O.M.B. No. 48-RO372

DISCREPANCY REPORT AND DECLARATION

CARRIER & I.R.S. NUMBER

IMPORTING VESSEL, VEHICLE OR AIRCRAFT

ADDRESS

ARR. DATE | MANIFEST NO.

DISTRICT & PORT CODE | FACILITY NO.

RECD ON IN BOND MANIFEST NO. | DATE ISSUED | FROM PORT OF

DATE | CUSTOMS ISSUING OFFICER

NOTICE

DISCREPANCIES MUST BE PROPERLY ACCOUNTED FOR OR CARRIER MAY BE ASSESSED PENALTIES, DUTIES, TAXES OR LIQUIDATED DAMAGES.

SEC. 1 - DISCREPANCY IDENTIFICATION (1) Report only shortage or overage. (2) Report full-case shortage and within-case shortage on different numbered lines.

Line No.	CUSTOMS, IMPORTER/BROKER, OR CARRIER 1			2	3 CUSTOMS DISCREP-ANCY CODE	CUSTOMS USE ONLY					IMPORTER/BROKER 8		CARRIER 9
	a. NUMBER OF PIECES AND DESCRIPTION			ENTRY, I.D. OR G.O. NO. OR "NONE"		4 LIQUIDATED DAMAGES IF APPLICABLE	5 PENALTIES IF APPLICABLE	6 CONCEALED SHORTAGE ACTION	7 VALUE	8 RATE a. DUTY b. TAX	NET REFUND a. DUTY b. TAX		EXPLANATION CODE (SEE REVERSE)
	B/L NO. & CASE NO.	b. T.S.U.S. NO. (NOT REQUIRED FOR CARRIER)						INITIALS CUSTOMS OFF.					
1	a.									a.	a.	a.	
	b.									b.	b.	b.	
2	a.									a.	a.	a.	
	b.									b.	b.	b.	
3	a.									a.	a.	a.	
	b.									b.	b.	b.	
4	a.									a.	a.	a.	
	b.									b.	b.	b.	
5	a.									a.	a.	a.	
	b.									b.	b.	b.	

TOTAL:

SEC. II - DECLARATION

(NAME OF IMPORTER/BROKER)

☐ Merchandise reported on Lines _____ above was not received. Any such merchandise later received will be entered properly. (If importer checks this declaration the carrier must execute section III or V.)

☐ Shortage of merchandise on Lines _____ was concealed. To the best of my knowledge the merchandise was landed in that condition at the original port of landing. The merchandise and packing have been set aside, and request is hereby made for customs examination at importer's premises at expense of importer. (It is not necessary to obtain carrier's signature in section III for concealed shortage.)

_____
SIGNATURE OF IMPORTER OR HIS AGENT   DATE

SEC. III - DECLARATION OF IMPORTING CARRIER OR HIS AGENT.

Carrier certifies explanation code shown in column 9 regarding discrepancies is correct.

Unless explanation code indicates otherwise, carrier agrees to non-delivery and/or removal without customs release.

Manifest is amended and post entry requested if necessary.

I Certify that required evidence to support above code will be retained in my files for one year.

_____
SIGNATURE OF IMPORTING CARRIER OR HIS AGENT   DATE

SEC. IV - POST ENTRY

RECEIPT NO. _____

_____
SIGNATURE OF CUSTOMS OFFICER   DATE

SEC. V - DECLARATION OF BONDED CARRIER OR HIS AGENT

Merchandise reported above was not delivered to importer, or was improperly delivered for the reason shown in column 9 above.

_____
SIGNATURE OF BONDED CARRIER OR HIS AGENT   DATE

Customs Form 5931 (9-26-78)

ORIGINAL-CUSTOMS CONTROL COPY

296

FIG. 12

APHIS/FWS USE ONLY | CUSTOMS USE ONLY

WELCOME
TO THE
UNITED STATES

DEPARTMENT OF THE TREASURY
UNITED STATES CUSTOMS SERVICE

FORM APPROVED
OMB NO. 1515-0041

CUSTOMS DECLARATION

19 CFR 122.27, 148.12, 148.13, 148.110, 148.111

Each arriving traveler or responsible family member must provide the following information (only **ONE** written declaration per family is required):

1. Family Name

2. First (Given) Name

3. Middle Initial(s) 4. Birth Date *(day/mo/yr)*

5. Airline/Flight No. or Vessel Name or Vehicle License No.

6. Number of Family Members Traveling With You

7. (a) Country of Citizenship

7. (b) Country of Residence

8. (a) U.S. Address *(Street Number/Hotel/Mailing Address in U.S.)*

8. (b) U.S. Address *(City)*

8. (c) U.S Address *(State)*

9. Countries visited on this trip prior to U.S. arrival

a. | b.

c. | d.

10. The purpose of my (our) trip is or was:
(Check one or both boxes, if applicable) — Business — Personal

11. I am (We are) bringing fruits, plants, meats, food, soil, birds, snails, other live animals, wildlife products, farm products; or, have been on a farm or ranch outside the U.S.: — Yes — No

12. I am (We are) carrying currency or monetary instruments over $10,000 U.S., or foreign equivalent: — Yes — No

13. I have (We have) commercial merchandise, U.S. or foreign: *(Check one box only)* — Yes — No

14. The total value of all goods, including commercial merchandise, I/we purchased or acquired abroad and am/are bringing to the U.S. is: **$**_____ *(U.S. Dollars)*

(See the instructions on the back of this form under "MERCHANDISE" and use the space provided there to list all the items you must declare. If you have nothing to declare, write "- 0 -" in the space provided above.)

SIGN BELOW AFTER YOU READ NOTICE ON REVERSE
I have read the notice on the reverse and have made a truthful declaration.

X

Signature — Date *(day/month/year)*

U.S. Customs use only -- Do not write below this line -- U.S. Customs use only

INSPECTOR'S BADGE NUMBER | STAMP AREA

TIME COMPLETED

Customs Form 6059B (012799)

FIG. 12—*Continued* 297

NOTICE

**ALL PERSONS ARE SUBJECT TO FURTHER QUESTIONING AND THEIR PERSONS, BE-
LONGINGS, AND CONVEYANCE ARE SUBJECT TO SEARCH. (19 CFR 162.3 - 162.8)**

The unlawful importation of controlled substances (narcotics, chemicals, prescription medicines if not accompanied by a prescription, etc.) regardless of amount is a violation of U.S. law.

AGRICULTURAL AND WILDLIFE PRODUCTS

To prevent the entry of dangerous agricultural pests and prohibited wildlife, the following are restricted: Fruits, vegetables, plants, plant products, soil, meats, meat products, birds, snails, and other live animals or animal products, wildlife and wildlife products. Failure to declare all such items to a Customs/Agricultural/Wildlife officer can result in penalties and the items may be subject to seizure.

CURRENCY AND MONETARY INSTRUMENTS

The transportation of currency or monetary instruments, REGARDLESS OF AMOUNT, IS LEGAL; however, if you take out of or bring into the United States more than $10,000 (U.S. or foreign equivalent, or a combination of the two) in coin, currency, traveler's checks or bearer instruments such as money orders, personal or cashier's checks, stocks or bonds, you are required BY LAW to FILE a report on Form 4790 with the U.S. Customs Service. If you have someone else carry the currency or instruments for you, you must also file the report. FAILURE TO FILE THE REQUIRED REPORT OR FAILURE TO REPORT THE TOTAL AMOUNT YOU ARE CARRYING MAY LEAD TO THE SEIZURE OF ALL THE CURRENCY OR INSTRUMENTS, AND MAY SUBJECT YOU TO CIVIL PENALTIES AND/OR CRIMINAL PROSECUTION.

MERCHANDISE

VISITORS (NON-RESIDENTS) must declare in item 14 the total value of all articles intended for others and all items intended to be sold or left in the U.S. This includes all gifts and commercial items or samples. (EXCEPTION: Your own personal effects, such as clothing, personal jewelry and camera equipment, luggage, etc., need not be declared.)

U.S. RESIDENTS must declare in Item 14 the total value of ALL articles, including commercial goods and samples, they acquired abroad (whether new or used; dutiable or not; and whether obtained by purchase, received as a gift, or otherwise), including those articles purchased in DUTY FREE STORES IN THE U.S. OR ABROAD, which are in their possession at the time of arrival. Articles which you acquired on this trip mailed from abroad, (other than articles acquired in insular possessions and various Caribbean Basin countries) are dutiable upon their arrival in the U.S.

THE AMOUNT OF DUTY TO BE PAID will be determined by a Customs officer. U.S. residents are normally entitled to a duty free exemption of $400 on those items accompanying them; non-residents are normally entitled to an exemption of $100. Duty is normally a flat rate of 10% on the first $1000 above the exemption. If the value of goods declared in Item 14 EXCEEDS $1400 PER PERSON, then list ALL articles below and show price paid in U.S. dollars or, for gifts, fair retail value. Please describe all articles by their common names and material. For example: MAN'S WOOL KNIT SWEATER; DIAMOND AND GOLD RING; etc. Also, please have all your receipts ready to present to the Customs officer, if requested. This will help to facilitate the inspection process.

COMMERCIAL MERCHANDISE can be defined as articles for sale, for soliciting orders, or other goods not considered personal effects of the traveler.

IF YOU HAVE ANY QUESTIONS ABOUT WHAT MUST BE REPORTED OR DECLARED, ASK A CUSTOMS OFFICER

DESCRIPTION OF ARTICLES (List may be continued on another Form 6059B)	VALUE	CUSTOMS USE
TOTAL ▷		

Paperwork Reduction Act Notice: The information collected on this form is needed to carry out the Customs, Agriculture, and Currency laws of the United States. We need it to insure that travelers are complying with these laws and to allow us to figure and collect the right amount of duty and taxes. Your response is mandatory. The estimated average burden associated with this collection of information is 3 minutes per respondent or recordkeeper depending on individual circumstances. Comments concerning the accuracy of this burden estimate and suggestions for reducing this burden should be directed to U.S. Customs Service, Information Services Group, Washington, D.C. 20229. DO NOT send completed form(s) to this office.

Customs Form 6059B (012799)(Back)

C. G. 705 A
(Rev. 1-80)

DEPARTMENT OF TRANSPORTATION
UNITED STATES COAST GUARD
SHIPPING ARTICLES

(R. S. 4612, as amended—U. S. C., title 46, sec. 713)

Notice is hereby given that section 4519 of the U. S. Revised Statutes (U. S. C., title 46, sec. 577) makes it obligatory on the part of the master of a merchant vessel of the United States, at the commencement of every voyage or engagement, to cause a legible copy of the agreement (forecastle card), omitting signatures, to be placed or posted up in such part of the vessel as to be accessible to the crew, under penalty not exceeding ONE HUNDRED DOLLARS.

ARTICLES OF AGREEMENT BETWEEN MASTER AND SEAMEN IN THE MERCHANT SERVICE OF THE UNITED STATES
Required by act of Congress, title LIII, Revised Statutes of the United States (U. S. C., title 46, ch. 18)

NAME OF SHIP	OFFICIAL NO.	PORT OF REGISTRY	DATE OF REGISTER	REGISTERED TONNAGE		VOYAGE NO.
				Gross	Net	

OPERATING COMPANY ON THIS VOYAGE			CLASS OF SHIP
Name	Address (State number of house, street, and town)	NUMBER OF SEAMEN AND APPRENTICES FOR WHICH ACCOMMODATION IS CERTIFIED	

IT IS AGREED between the Master and seamen, or mariners, of the _____ PORT OF _____

_____, 19 _____

of which _____

is at present Master, or whoever shall go for Master, now bound from the Port of [1] _____

and such other ports and places in any part of the world as the Master may direct, and back to a final port of discharge in the United States, for a term of time not exceeding _____, to _____ calendar months. [2]

And the said crew agree to conduct themselves in an orderly, faithful, honest, and sober manner, and to be at all times diligent in their respective duties, and to be obedient to the lawful commands of the said Master, or of any person who shall lawfully succeed him, and of their superior officers, in everything relating to the vessel, and the stores and cargo thereof, whether on board, in boats, or on shore; and in consideration of which service to be duly performed the said Master hereby agrees to pay to the said crew, as wages, the sums against their names respectively expressed, and to supply them with provisions according to the annexed scale. And it is hereby agreed that any embezzlement or willful or negligent destruction of any part of the vessel's cargo or stores shall be made good to the owner out of the wages of the person guilty of the same. And if any person enters himself as qualified for a duty which he proves himself incompetent to perform, his wages shall be reduced in proportion to his incompetency. And it is also agreed that if any member of the crew considers himself to be aggrieved by any breach of agreement or otherwise, he shall represent the same to the Master or officer in charge of the ship in a quiet and orderly manner, who shall thereupon take such steps as the case may require.

GOING ON SHORE IN FOREIGN PORTS IS PROHIBITED EXCEPT BY PERMISSION OF THE MASTER

NO DANGEROUS WEAPONS [3] OR GROG ALLOWED, AND NONE TO BE BROUGHT ON BOARD BY THE CREW

SCALE OF PROVISIONS to be allowed and served out to the Crew during the voyage in addition to the daily issue of lime and lemon juice and sugar, or other antiscorbutic in any case required by law

		Sun. day	Mon. day	Tues. day	Wednes. day	Thurs. day	Fri. day	Satur. day				Sun. day	Mon. day	Tues. day	Wednes. day	Thurs. day	Fri. day	Satur. day
Water	quarts	5	5	5	5	5	5	5	Coffee (green berry)	ounce	3/4	3/4	3/4	3/4	3/4	3/4	3/4
Biscuit	pound	1/2	1/2	1/2	1/2	1/2	1/2	1/2	Tea	ounce	1/8	1/8	1/8	1/8	1/8	1/8	1/8
Beef, salt	pounds		1-1/4		1-1/4		1-1/4	1-1/4	Sugar	ounces	3	3	3	3	3	3	3
Pork, salt	pound	1/2		1/2		1/2			Molasses	pint	3-1/2	3-1/2	3-1/2	3-1/2	3-1/2	3-1/2	3-1/2
Flour	pound	1/2		1/2		1/2		1/2	Dried fruit	ounces							
Corned meat	pound		1		1		1		Vinegar	pint	1/4		1/4		1/4		1/4
Fresh bread	pounds	1-1/2	1-1/2	1-1/2	1-1/2	1-1/2	1-1/2	1-1/2	Pickles	pint	1/2						1/2
Fish, dry, preserved, or fresh	pound	1-1/2							Corn meal	ounces	4	4	4	4	4	4	4
Potatoes or yams	pound	1/2		1/2		1/2		1/2	Onions	ounces	4	4	4	4	4	4	4
Canned tomatoes	pound		1/2	1/2		1/2	1/2		Lard	ounce	2	2	2	2	2	2	2
Peas	pint	1/3					1/2	1/3	Butter	ounce	1	1	1	1	1	1	1
Beans	pint	1/3	1/3	1/3		1/3	1/3	1/2	Mustard, pepper, and salt sufficient for seasoning.								
Rice	pint		1/3		1/3			1/3										

FIG. 13—Continued 299

SUBSTITUTES

One pound of flour daily may be substituted for the daily ration of biscuit or fresh bread: two ounces of desicated vegetables for one pound of potatoes, or yams, six ounces of hominy, oatmeal, or cracked wheat, or two ounces of tapioca, for six ounces of rice; six ounces of canned vegetables for one-half pound of canned tomatoes; one-eighth of an ounce of tea for three-fourths of an ounce of coffee; three-fourths of an ounce of coffee for one-eighth of an ounce of tea; six ounces of dried fruit; one-half ounce of lime juice for the daily ration of vinegar: four ounces of oatmeal or cracked wheat for one-half pint of corn meal; two ounces of pickled onions for four ounces of fresh onions.

When the vessel is in port and it is possible to obtain the same, one and one-half pounds of fresh meat shall be substituted for the daily rations of salt and canned meat; one-half pound of green cabbage for one ration of canned tomatoes; one-half pound of fresh fruit for one ration of dried fruit. Fresh fruit and vegetables shall be served while in port if obtainable. The seamen shall have the option of accepting the fare the Master may provide, but the right at any time to demand the foregoing scale of provisions.

The foregoing scale of provisions shall be inserted in every article of agreement, and shall not be reduced by any contract, except as above, and a copy of the same shall be posted in a conspicuous place in the galley and in the forecastle of each vessel.

It is also agreed that [4] ___

IN WITNESS WHEREOF the said parties have subscribed their names hereto on the days against their respective signatures mentioned.

on the ___ day of ___, 19___

_____, Master, of _____

_____
(Give address)

CITIZENSHIP REQUIREMENTS (crew-exclusive of licensed officers)

	Subsidized Passenger Vessels	Subsidized Cargo Vessels	Nonsubsidized Vessels
	90 percent shall be citizens of United States, either native-born or naturalized; Legally admitted aliens may comprise other 10 percent but may be employed in Steward's Department only.	On and after Sept. 27, 1936, 100 percent citizens of United States, either native-born or naturalized.	On and after Dec. 25, 1936, 75 percent citizens of United States, either native-born or naturalized.
Native-born citizens	Number	Number	Number
Naturalized citizens			
First papers			
Admissible aliens			
Percentage (American citizens)			

I HEREBY CERTIFY that the above statement as to the citizenship of the crew signed on these articles is true and correct

_____
Master or Consular Officer

Continued on next page

ATTENTION OF MASTERS ESPECIALLY INVITED TO THE FOLLOWING REQUIREMENTS OF LAW

Authority of Master

(R. S. 4596 — 46 U. S. C. 566) Whenever the master of any vessel shall engage his crew, or any part of the same, in any collection district where no Coast Guard Official to perform the duties of shipping commissioner shall have been appointed, he may perform for himself the duties of such commissioner.

NOTE: Authority for the master to discharge seamen is contained in R. S. 4551 — 46 U. S. C. 643. In the following statutes, "master" may be substituted for "shipping commissioner" except in those statutes dealing with the shipment/discharge of seamen in foreign ports.

Agreement To Ship in Foreign Trade

(R. S. 4511 — 46 U. S. C. 564) The master of every vessel bound from a port in the United States to any foreign port other than vessels engaged in trade between the United States and the British North American possessions, or the West India Islands, or the Republic of Mexico, or the ports of Central America, and water ports on the Atlantic to a port on the Pacific, or vice versa, shall, before he proceeds on such voyage, make an agreement, in writing, or in print, with every seaman whom he carries to sea as one of the crew, in the manner hereinafter mentioned:

(R. S. 4519 — 46 U. S. C. 577) The master shall, at the commencement of every voyage or engagement, cause a legible copy of the agreement in writing to be placed or posted up in such part of the vessel as to be accessible to the crew, and on default shall be liable to a penalty of not more than $100.

Penalty for Shipment Without Agreement

(R. S. 4514 — 46 U. S. C. 567) If any person shall be carried to sea, as one of the crew on board of any vessel making a voyage to a foreign port (other than vessels mentioned in section 4511) without entering into an agreement with him, as provided in section 4520 of the Revised Statutes, the master, and at the place and times in such cases required, the vessel shall be held liable for each such offense to a penalty of not more than $200. But the vessel shall not be held liable for any person carried to sea, who shall have secretly stowed away himself without the knowledge of the master, mate, or of any of the officers of the vessel, or who shall have falsely personated himself to the master, mate, or officers of the vessel, for the purpose of being carried to sea.

Shipment in Foreign Ports Before Consuls

(R. S. 4517 — 46 U. S. C. 570) Every master of a merchant vessel who engages any seaman at a place out of the United States, in which there is a consular officer, shall, before carrying such seaman to sea, procure the list of the officer and shall engage seamen in his presence; and the rules governing the engagement of seamen before a shipping commissioner in the United States as to proof in such cases of engagement and upon every such engagement, the consular officer shall endorse upon the agreement his sanction thereof, and an attestation to the effect that the same has been signed in his presence and otherwise duly made.

(R. S. 4518 — 46 U. S. C. 571) Every master who engages any seaman in any place in which there is a consular officer otherwise than as required by the preceding section shall incur a penalty of not more than $100, for which penalty the vessel shall be held liable.

Watches — Hours of Labor — Legal Holidays

(R. S. 4551 — Sec. 2 — 46 U. S. C. Supp. IV 673) In all merchant vessels of the United States of more than one hundred tons gross, excepting those navigating rivers, harbors, lakes (other than Great Lakes), bays, sounds, bayous, and canals, exclusively, the licensed officers and sailors, coal passers, firemen, oilers, and water tenders shall, while at sea, be divided into at least three watches, and shall be kept on duty successively for the performance of ordinary work incident to the sailing and management of the vessel. No licensed officer or seaman in the deck or engine department of any tug documented under the laws of the United States (except boats or vessels used exclusively for fishing purposes) navigating the Great Lakes, harbors of the Great Lakes, and connecting and tributary waters between Gary, Ind., Duluth, Minn., Niagara Falls, N. Y., and Ogdensburg, N. Y., shall be required or permitted to work more than eight hours in one day or except in case of extraordinary emergency affecting the safety of the vessel and/or life or property. These watches shall not be shipped to work alternately in the fireroom and on deck, nor shall those shipped for deck duty be required to work in the fireroom, or vice versa; nor shall any licensed officer, or seaman in the deck or engine department be required to work more than eight hours in one day; but these provisions shall not limit either the authority of the master or other officer or the obedience of the seamen when in the judgment of the master or other officer the whole or any part of the crew are needed for maneuvering, shifting berth, mooring, or unmooring, the vessel or the performance of work necessary for the safety of the vessel, her passengers, crew, and cargo, or for the saving of life aboard other vessels in jeopardy, or when in port or at sea, from requiring the whole or any part of the crew to participate in the performance of fire, lifeboat, or other drills. While such vessel is in a safe harbor no seaman shall be required to do any unnecessary work on Sundays or the following-named days: New Year's Day, the Fourth of July, Labor Day, Thanksgiving Day, and Christmas Day; but this shall not prevent the despatch of a vessel on regular schedule or when ready to proceed on her voyage. And at all times while such vessel is in a safe harbor, eight hours, inclusive of the anchor watch, shall constitute a day's work. Whenever the master of any vessel shall fail to comply with this section and the regulation issued thereunder, the owner shall be liable to a penalty not to exceed $500, and the seamen shall be entitled to discharge from such vessel and to receive the wages earned. But this section shall not apply to vessels engaged in salvage operations: Provided, That in all tugs and barges subject to this section when engaged on a voyage of less than six hundred miles, the licensed officers and members of crews other than coal passers, firemen, oilers, and water tenders may, while at sea, be divided into not less than two watches, but

nothing in this proviso shall be construed as repealing any part of section 222 of this title. This section shall take effect six months after June 25, 1936. (As amended June 25, 1936, c. 816, 2, 49 Stat. 1933; June 23, 1938, c. 597, 52 Stat. 944.)

Wages

(R. S. 4552 — 46 U. S. C. 644) The following rules shall be observed with respect to the settlement of wages.

First. Upon the completion, before a shipping commissioner, of any discharge and settlement, the master or owner and each seaman respectively, in the presence of the shipping commissioner, shall sign a mutual release of all claims for wages in respect of the past voyage or engagement, and the shipping commissioner shall also sign and attest it, and shall retain it in a book to be kept for that purpose, provided both the master and seaman assent to such settlement, or the settlement has been adjusted by the shipping commissioner.

(R. S. 4524 — 46 U. S. C. 591) A seaman's right to wages and provisions shall be taken to commence either at the time at which he commences work, or at the time specified in the agreement for the commencement of work or presence on board, whichever first happens.

(R. S. 4530 — 46 U. S. C. 597) Every seaman on a vessel of the United States shall be entitled to receive on demand from the master of the vessel to which he belongs one-half part of the balance of his wages earned and remaining unpaid at the time when such demand is made at every port where such vessel, after the voyage has been commenced, shall load or deliver cargo before the voyage is ended, and all stipulations in the contract to the contrary notwithstanding, unless the same shall be void; Provided, Such a demand shall not be made before the expiration of, nor oftener than once in five days nor more than once in the same harbor on the same entry. Any failure on the part of the master to comply with this demand shall release the seaman from his contract and he shall be entitled to full payment of wages earned. And when the voyage is ended every such seaman shall be entitled to the remainder of the wages which shall then be due him, as provided in section 4529 of the Revised Statutes: Provided further, That notwithstanding any release signed by any seaman under section 4552 of the Revised Statutes any court having jurisdiction may upon good cause shown set aside such release and take such action as justice shall require.

Discharge of Seamen

(R. S. 4551 — 46 U. S. C. 641) All seamen discharged in the United States from merchant vessels engaged in voyages from a port in the United States to a port on the Pacific, or vice versa, shall be discharged and receive their wages in the presence of a duly authorized shipping commissioner under this Title (R. S. 4501 — 4612), except in cases where some competent court otherwise directs; and any master or owner of any such vessel who discharges any such seaman belonging thereto or pays his wages within the United States in any other manner, shall be liable to a penalty of not more than $50.

(R. S. 4518 — 46 U. S. C. Supp. IV 643 (d)(1)) Upon the discharge of any seaman and the payment of his wages, the shipping commissioner shall enter in the continuous discharge book of such seaman, if he have such a book, the name and official number of the vessel, the nature of the voyage (foreign, intercoastal, or coastwise), the class to which the vessel belongs (steam, motor, sail, or barge), the date and place of the shipment and of the discharge of such seaman, the rating (capacity in which employed) then held by such seaman, and the signature of the person making such entries and nothing more.

(R. S. 4551 — Subsec. (k) — 46 U. S. C. Supp. IV 643 (k)) Where vessels are required to sign on and discharge the crew before a shipping commissioner and no shipping commissioner is appointed or is available the functions and duties required by subsections (d) and (e) of this section to be performed by such shipping commissioner may be performed by a collector or deputy collector of customs; and where vessels are not required to sign on and discharge the crew before a shipping commissioner the duties and functions required by subsections (d) and (e) of this section to be performed by the shipping commissioner shall be performed by the master of such vessel. Any master who shall fail to perform such duties or functions shall be fined in the sum of $50 for each offense.

Discharge in Foreign Ports

(R. S. 4580 — 46 U. S. C. 682) Upon the application of the master of any vessel to a consular officer to discharge a seaman, or upon the application of any seaman for his own discharge, if it appears to such officer that said seaman has completed his shipping agreement or is entitled to his discharge under any act of Congress or according to the general principles or usages of maritime law as recognized in the United States, such officer shall discharge said seaman, and require from the master of said vessel, before such discharge shall be made, payment of the wages the master may be due the said seaman; but no payment of extra wages shall be required by any consular officer upon such discharge of any seaman except as provided in this act.

FIG. 13—*Continued* 301

SHIPPING ARTICLES OF _____ PAGE NO. _____

PARTICULARS OF ENGAGEMENT

C. G. 705 A
(Rev. 1-80)

State of _____, Port of _____

On this _____ day of _____ , who, each for himself, acknowledged to me that he had read or had heard read the same; that he was by me made acquainted with the conditions thereof, and understood the same; and that, while sober, and not in a state of intoxication, he signed it freely and voluntarily, for the uses and purposes therein mentioned.

_____
Master or Consular Officer

Continued on next page

C. G. 705 A
(Rev. 1-80)

SHIPPING ARTICLES OF _____ PAGE No. _____

PARTICULARS OF DISCHARGE

RELEASE

Line No.	PLACE, DATE, AND CAUSE OF LEAVING SHIP OR OF DEATH			TIME OF SERVICE		WAGES EARNED	DEDUCTIONS	BALANCE OF WAGES PAID ON DISCHARGE	DATE WAGES PAID AND RELEASE SIGNED	RELEASE	ATTESTATION OF MASTER OR CONSUL	Line No.
	Place	Date	Cause	M	D	Regular Wage				We, the undersigned seamen, do hereby, each one for himself by our signatures herewith given in consideration of settlements made, release the Master and owners from all claims for wages in respect of this voyage or engagement, and I, the Master, do also release each of the undersigned seamen from all claims in consideration of this release signed by them. _____ Master		
1												1
2												2
3												3
4												4
47												47
48												48
49												49
50												50
51												51
52												52
53												53
54												54
55												55
56												56
57												57
58												58
59												59
60												60

I hereby certify that the entries in the Discharge Books of seamen included in these articles agree with the applicable entries herein, or Certificates of Discharge have been issued in accordance therewith.

_____
Master or Consular Officer

FIG. 14   303

OMB Approved No. 2115-0578

CG-948 (Rev. 4-97)

PERMIT TO PROCEED TO ANOTHER PORT FOR REPAIRS

FILE NO. $\frac{T}{V}$

DEPARTMENT OF TRANSPORTATION
UNITED STATES COAST GUARD

PORT _____

DATE _ ____ _____ _____

DISTRICT OF _____

The $\begin{array}{l} S.S. \\ M.V. \end{array}$ of   , in the State of

O.N.   , whereof

is Master, has been examined and inspected this date and I find that the said vessel is

requiring repairs, to wit:

The said Master requesting that the said vessel be permitted to proceed to the

of   for the purpose of making the said repairs, I

do hereby, after due consideration, regarding it as safe to do so, permit her to proceed to

said port, touching at intermediate ports in her course, as if she had, in every particular,

complied with the requirements of law.*

_____
Officer in Charge, Marine Inspection

_____

NOTE: Inspector must state upon the face of this permit "the condition upon which it is granted, and whether the vessel is to be allowed to carry freight or passengers, the quantity and number."

* Provided, however, that no vessel whose certificate has expired will be permitted to carry passengers while en route to another port for repairs. In issuing this permit, inspector shall notify the master, if proceeding into another district, that application must be made for inspection and certificate in the district where the repairs are made.

_____

An agency may not conduct or sponsor, and a person is not required to respond to, a collection of information unless it displays a valid OMB control number.

The Coast Guard estimates that the average burden for this report is 5 mins. You may submit any comments concerning the accuracy of this burden estimate or any suggestion reducing the burden to: Commandant (G-MOC), U.S. Coast Guard, Washington, DC 20593-0001 or Office of Management and Budget, Paperwork Reduction Project (2115-0578), Washington, DC 20503,.

DEPARTMENT OF TRANSPORTATION U. S. COAST GUARD CG-2692 (Rev. 6-87)	**REPORT OF MARINE ACCIDENT, INJURY OR DEATH**	TEST ELECTRONIC VERSION UNIT CASE NUMBER

SECTION I. GENERAL INFORMATION

1. Name of Vessel or Facility	2. Official No.	3. Nationality	4. Call Sign	5. USCG Certificate of Inspection issued at:

6. Type (Towing, Freight, Fish, Drill, etc.)	7. Length	8. Gross Tons	9. Year Built	10. Propulsion (Steam, diesel, gas, turbine ...)

11. Hull Material (Steel, Wood...)	12. Draft (ft. - in.) FWD. AFT.	13. If Vessel Classed, By Whom: (ABS, LLOYDS, DNV, BV, etc.)	14. Date (Of occurrence)	15. Time (Local)

16. Location (See instruction No. I0A)	17. Estimated Loss or Damage TO:
18. Name, Address & Telephone No. of Operating Co.	VESSEL $ _____ CARGO $ _____ OTHER $ _____

19. Name of Master or Person in Charge	USCG License ☐ YES ☐ NO	20. Name of Pilot	USCG License ☐ YES ☐ NO	State License ☐ YES ☐ NO
19a. Street Address (City, State, Zip Code)	19b. Telephone Number ( )	20a. Street Address (City, State, Zip Code)	20b. Telephone Number ( )	

21. Casualty Elements (Check as many as needed and explain in Block 44.)

NO. OF PERSONS ON BOARD _____
☐ DEATH- HOW MANY? _____
☐ MISSING- HOW MANY? _____
☐ INJURED- HOW MANY? _____
☐ HAZARDOUS MATERIAL RELEASED OR INVOLVED
(Identify Substance and amount in Block 44.)
☐ OIL SPILL-ESTIMATE AMOUNT:
_____
☐ CARGO CONTAINER LOST/DAMAGED
☐ COLLISON (Identify other vessel or object in Block 44.)
☐ GROUNDING ☐ WAKE DAMAGE

☐ FLOODING; SWAMPING WITHOUT SINKING
☐ CAPSIZING (with or without sinking)
☐ FOUNDERING OR SINKING
☐ HEAVY WEATHER DAMAGE
☐ FIRE
☐ EXPLOSION
☐ COMMERCIAL DIVING CASUALTY
☐ ICE DAMAGE
☐ DAMAGE TO AIDS TO NAVIGATION
☐ STEERING FAILURE
☐ MACHINERY OR EQUIPMENT FAILURE
☐ ELECTRICAL FAILURE
☐ STRUCTURAL FAILURE

☐ FIREFIGHTING OR EMERGENCY EQUIPMENT FAILED OR INADEQUATE (Describe in Block 44.)
☐ LIFESAVING EQUIPMENT FAILED OR INADEQUATE (Describe in Block 44.)
☐ BLOW OUT (Petroleum exploration/production)
☐ ALCOHOL INVOLVEMENT (Describe in Block 44.)
☐ DRUG INVOLVEMENT (Describe in Block 44.)
☐ OTHER (Specify)
_____

22. Conditions

A. Sea or River Conditions (wave height, river stage, etc.)	B. WEATHER ☐ CLEAR ☐ RAIN ☐ SNOW ☐ FOG ☐ OTHER (Specify)	C. TIME ☐ DAYLIGHT ☐ TWILIGHT ☐ NIGHT	D. VISIBILITY ☐ GOOD ☐ FAIR ☐ POOR	E. DISTANCE (miles) _____ (of visibility) F. AIR TEMPERATURE _____ (F) G. WIND SPEED & DIRECTION _____ H. CURRENT SPEED & DIRECTION _____

23. Navigation Information ☐ MOORED, DOCKED OR FIXED ☐ ANCHORED ☐ UNDERWAY OR DRIFTING	SPEED _____ AND COURSE _____	24. Last Port _____ Where Bound	24a. Time and Date of Departure

25. FOR TOWING ONLY	25a. NUMBER OF VESSELS TOWED	Empty	Loaded	Total	25b. TOTAL H.P. OF TOWING UNITS	25c. MAXIMUM SIZE OF TOW WITH TOW-BOAT(S)	Length	Width	25d.(Describe in Block 44.) ☐ PUSHING AHEAD ☐ TOWING ASTERN ☐ TOWING ALONGSIDE ☐ MORE THAN ONE TOW-BOAT ON TOW

SECTION II. BARGE INFORMATION

26. Name	26a. Official Number	26b. Type	26c. Length	26d. Gross Tons	26e. USCG Certficate of Inspection Issued at:

26f. Year Built	26g. ☐ SINGLE SKIN ☐ DOUBLE SKIN	26h. Draft FWD AFT	26i. Operating Company

26j. Damage Amount	BARGE $ _____ CARGO $ _____ OTHER $ _____	26k. Describe Damage to Barge

FIG. 15—*Continued* **305**

REVERSE OF CG-2692 (REV. 6-87)	SECTION III. PERSONNEL ACCIDENT INFORMATION		
27. Person Involved ☐ MALE or ☐ FEMALE ☐ DEAD ☐ INJURED ☐ MISSING	**27a. Name** *(Last, First, Middle Name)*		**27c. Status** ☐ CREW ☐ PASSENGER ☐ OTHER *(Specify)*
	27b. Address *(City, State, Zip Code)*		

28. Birth Date	29. Telephone No. ( )	30. Job Position	31. *(Check here if off duty)* ☐

32. Employer -*(If different from Block 18., fill in Name, Address, Telephone No.)*

33. Person's Time	YEAR(S)	MONTH(S)	34. Industry of Employer *(Towing, Fishing. Shipping,*
A. IN THIS INDUSTRY -			*Crew Supply, Drilling, etc.)*
B. WITH THIS COMPANY-			
C. IN PRESENT JOB OR POSITION-			35. Was the Injured Person Incapacitated 72 Hours or
D. ON PRESENT VESSEL/FACILITY -			More? ☐ YES ☐ NO
E. HOURS ON DUTY WHEN ACCIDENT OCCURRED -			36. Date of Death

37. Activity of Person at Time of Accident

38. Specific Location of Accident on Vessel/Facility

39. Type of Accident *(Fall, Caught between, etc.)*	40. Resulting Injury *(Cut, Bruise, Fracture, Burn, etc.)*
41. Part of Body Injured	42. Equipment Involved in Accident

43. Specific Object, Part of the Equipment in Block 42., or Substance *(Chemical, Solvent, etc.)* that directly produced the Injury.

SECTION IV. DESCRIPTION OF CASUALTY

44. Describe how accident occured, damage, information on alcohol/drug involvement and recommendations for corrective safety measures. *(See instructions and attach additional sheets if necessary).*

45. Witness *(Name, Address, Telephone No.)*

46. Witness *(Name Address, Telephone No.)*

SECTION V. PERSON MAKING THIS REPORT		47c. Title
47. Name (PRINT) *(Last, First, Middle)*	47b. Address *(City, State, Zip Code)*	
		47d. Telephone No. ( )
47a. Signature		47e. Date

FOR COAST GUARD USE ONLY		REPORTING OFFICE:		
APPARENT CAUSE				
CASUALTY CODE A B C	INVESTIGATOR *(Name)*	DATE	APPROVED BY *(Name)*	DATE

Continued on next page

INSTRUCTIONS

FOR COMPLETION OF FORM CG-2692

REPORT OF MARINE ACCIDENT, INJURY OR DEATH

AND FORM CG-2692A, BARGE ADDENDUM

WHEN TO USE THIS FORM

1. This form satisfies the requirements for written reports of accidents found in the Code of Federal Regulations for vessels, Outer Continental Shelf (OCS) facilities, mobile offshore drilling units (MODUs) and diving. The kinds of accidents that must be reported are described in the following instructions.

VESSELS

2. A vessel accident must be reported if it occurs upon the navigable waters of the U.S. its territories or possessions; or whenever an accident involves a U.S. vessel; wherever the accident may occur. (Public vessels and recreational vessels are excepted from these reporting requirements.) The accident must also involve one of the following (ref. 46 CFR 4.05-1):

A. All accidental groundings and any intentional grounding which also meets any of the other reporting criteria or creates a hazard to navigation, the environment, or the safety of the vessel;

B. Loss of main propulsion or primary steering, or an associated component or control system, the loss of which causes a reduction of the maneuvering capabilities of the vessel. Loss means that systems, component parts, subsystems, or control systems do not perform the specified or required function;

C. An occurrence materially and adversely affecting the vessel's seaworthiness or fitness for service or route including but not limited to fire, flooding, failure or damage to fixed fire extinguishing systems, lifesaving equipment or bilge pumping systems;

D. Loss of life;

E. An Injury that requires professional medical treatment (beyond first aid) and, if a crewmember on a commerical vessel, that renders the individual unfit to perform routine duties.

F. An occurrence not meeting any of the above criteria but resulting in damage to property in excess of $25,000. Damage cost includes the cost of labor and material to restore the property to the condition which existed prior to the casualty, but it does not include the cost of salvage, cleaning, gas freeing, drydocking or demurrage.

MOBILE OFFSHORE DRILLING UNITS

3. MODUs are vessels and are required to report an accident that results in any of the events listed by Instruction 2-A through 2-F for vessels. (Ref. 46 CFR 4.05-1, 46 CRF 109.411)

OCS FACILITIES

4. All OCS facilities (except mobile offshore drilling units) engaged in mineral exploration, development or production activities on the Outer Continental Shelf of the U. S. are required by 33 CFR 146.30 to report accidents resulting in:

A. Death;

B. Injury to 5 or more persons in a single incident;

C. Injury causing any person to be incapacitated for more than 72 hours.

D. Damage affecting the usefulness of primary lifesaving or firefighting equipment;

E. Damage to the facility in excess of $25,000 resulting from a collision by a vessel;

F. Damage to a floating OCS facility in excess of $25,000.

5. Foreign vessels engaged in mineral exploration, development or production on the U. S. Outer Continental Shelf, other than vessels already required to report by Instructions 2 and 3 above, are required by 33 CFR 146.303 to report casualties that result in any of the following:

A. Death;

B. Injury to 5 or more persons in a single incident;

C. Injury causing any person to be incapacitated for more than 72 hours.

DIVING

6. Diving casualties include injury or death that occurs while using underwater breathing apparatus while diving from a vessel or OCS facility.

A. COMMERCIAL DIVING. A dive is considered commercial if it is for commercial purposes from a vessel required to have a Coast Guard certificate of inspection, from an OCS facility or in its related safety zone or in a related activity, at a deepwater port or in its safety zone. Casualties that occur during commercial dives are covered by 46 CFR 197.486 if they result in:

1. Loss of life;
2. Injury causing incapacitation over 72 hours;
3. Injury requiring hospitalization over 24 hours.

FIG. 15—*Continued* 307

In addition to the information requested on this form, also provide the name of the diving supervisor and, if applicable, a detailed report on gas embolism or decompression sickness as required by 46 CFR 197.410(a)(9).

Exempt from the commercial category are dives for:

1. Marine science research by educational institutions;
2. Research in diving equipment and technology;
3. Search and Rescue controlled by a government agency.

B. ALL OTHER DIVING. Diving accidents not covered by Instruction (6-A) but involving vessels subject to Instruction (2), VESSELS, must be reported if they result in death or injury causing incapacitation over 72 hours. (Ref. 46 CFR 4.03-I(c)).

HAZARDOUS MATERIALS

7. When an accident involves hazardous materials, public and environmental health and safety require immediate action. As soon as any person in charge of a vessel or facility has knowledge of a release or discharge of oil or a hazardous substance, that person is required to immediately notify the U.S. Department of Transportation's National Response Center (telephone toll-free 800-424-8802 - in the Washington, D.C., area call 202-426-2675). Anyone else knowing of a pollution incident is encouraged to use the toll-free telephone number to report it. If etiologic (disease causing) agents are involved, call the U.S. Public Health Service's Center for Disease Control in Atlanta, Ga. (telephone 404-633-5313). (Ref. 42 USC 9603; 33 CFR 153; 49 CFR 171.15)

COMPLETION OF THIS FORM

8. This form should be filled out as completely and accurately as possible. Please type or print clearly. Fill in all blanks that apply to the kind of accident that has occurred. If a question is not applicable, the abbreviation "NA" should be entered in that space. If an answer is unknown and cannot be obtained, the abbreviation "UNK" should be entered in that space. If "NONE" is the correct response, then enter it in that space.

9. When this form has been completed, deliver or mail it as soon as possible to the Coast Guard Marine Safety or Marine Inspection Office nearest to the location of the casualty or, if at sea, nearest to the port of first arrival.

10. Amplifying information for completing the form:

A. Block 16 - " LOCATION" - Latitude and longitude to the nearest tenth of a minute should always be entered except in those rivers and waterways where a mile marker system is commonly used. In these cases, the mile number to the nearest tenth of a mile should be entered. If the latitude and longitude, or mile number, are unknown, reference to a known landmark or object (buoy, light, etc.) with distance and bearing to the object is permissible. Always identify the body of water or waterway referred to.

B. Tug or towboat with tow - Tugs or towboats with tows under their control should complete all applicable portions of the CG-2692. SECTION II should be completed if a barge causes or sustains damage or meets any other reporting criteria. If additional barges require reporting, the "Barge Addendum," CG-2692A, may be used to provide the information for the additional barges.

C. Moored/Anchored Barge - If a barge suffers a casualty while moored or anchored, or breaks away from its moorage, and causes or sustains reportable damages or meets any other reporting criteria, enter the location of its moorage in Block (1) of the CG-2692 and complete the form except for Blocks (2) through (13). The details will be entered in SECTION II for one barge and on the "Barge Addendum" CG-2962A, for additional barges.

D. SECTION III - Personnel Accident Information - SECTION III must be completed for a death or injury. In addition, applicable portions of SECTIONS I, II and IV must be completed. If more than one death or injury occurs in a single incident, complete one CG-2692 for one of the persons injured or killed. and attach additional CG-2692's, pilling out Blocks (1) and (2) and SECTION III for each additional person.

E. BLOCK 44 - Describe the sequence of events which led up to this casualty. Include your opinion of the primary cause and any contributing causes of the casualty. Briefly describe damage to your vessel, its cargo. and other vessels/property. Include any recommendations you may have for preventing similar casualties. *ALCOHOL AND DRUG INFORMATION.* Provide the following information with regard to each person determined to be directly involved in the casualty: name, position aboard the vessel, whether or not the person was under the influence of alcohol or drugs at the time of the casualty, and the method used to make this determination. If toxicological testing is conducted the results should be included; if results are not available in a timely manner, provide the results of the toxicological test as soon as practical and indicate that this is the case in block 44 of the casualty form.

NOTICE: The information collected on this form is routinely available for public inspection. It is needed by the Coast Guard to carry out its responsibility to investigate marine casualties, to identify hazardous conditions or situations and to conduct statistical analysis. The information is used to determine whether new or revised safety initiatives are necessary for the protection of life or property in the marine environment.

Continued on next page

DEPARTMENT OF TRANSPORTATION U.S. COAST GUARD CG-2692A (Rev. 6-82)	BARGE ADDENDUM	REPORTS CONTROL SYMBOL GMMI-2115-0003 ELECTRONIC VERSION

NOTE: This form may be used to report data for barges causing or sustaining damage in the accident described on form CG-2692. This form may only be used in addition to form CG-2692, never alone.

NAME OF VESSEL (Use Same Name as Block 1. of CG-2692).   DATE OF ACCIDENT

FOR BARGE CAUSING OR SUSTAINING DAMAGES

26. Name	26a. Official Number	26b. Type	26c. Length	26d. Gross Tons	26e. USCG Certificate of Inspection Issued at:

26f. Year Built	26g. ☐ SINGLE SKIN ☐ DOUBLE SKIN	26h. Draft FWD AFT	26i. Operating Company

26j. Damage Amount

DAMAGE TO BARGE _____

CARGO _____

26k. Describe Damage to Barge

FOR BARGE CAUSING OR SUSTAINING DAMAGES

26. Name	26a. Official Number	26b. Type	26c. Length	26d. Gross Tons	26e. USCG Certificate of Inspection Issued at:

26f. Year Built	26g. ☐ SINGLE SKIN ☐ DOUBLE SKIN	26h. Draft FWD AFT	26i. Operating Company

26j. Damage Amount

DAMAGE TO BARGE _____

CARGO _____

26k. Describe Damage to Barge

FOR BARGE CAUSING OR SUSTAINING DAMAGES

26. Name	26a. Official Number	26b. Type	26c. Length	26d. Gross Tons	26e. USCG Certificate of Inspection Issued at:

26f. Year Built	26g. ☐ SINGLE SKIN ☐ DOUBLE SKIN	26h. Draft FWD AFT	26i. Operating Company

26j. Damage Amount

DAMAGE TO BARGE _____

CARGO _____

26k. Describe Damage to Barge

FOR BARGE CAUSING OR SUSTAINING DAMAGES

26. Name	26a. Official Number	26b. Type	26c. Length	26d. Gross Tons	26e. USCG Certificate of Inspection Issued at:

26f. Year Built	26g. ☐ SINGLE SKIN ☐ DOUBLE SKIN	26h. Draft FWD AFT	26i. Operating Company

26j. Damage Amount

DAMAGE TO BARGE _____

CARGO _____

26k. Describe Damage to Barge

FOR BARGE CAUSING OR SUSTAINING DAMAGES

26. Name	26a. Official Number	26b. Type	26c. Length	26d. Gross Tons	26e. USCG Certificate of Inspection Issued at:

26f. Year Built	26g. ☐ SINGLE SKIN ☐ DOUBLE SKIN	26h. Draft FWD AFT	26i. Operating Company

26j. Damage Amount

DAMAGE TO BARGE _____

CARGO _____

26k. Describe Damage to Barge

SIGNATURE (of person making this report)

PREVIOUS EDITION MAY BE USED

FIG. 15—*Continued* 309

FOR BARGE CAUSING OR SUSTAINING DAMAGES

26. Name	26a. Official Number	26b. Type	26c. Length	26d. Gross Tons	26e. USCG Certificate of Inspection Issued at:

26f. Year Built	26g. ☐ SINGLE SKIN ☐ DOUBLE SKIN	26h. Draft FWD AFT	26i. Operating Company	

26j. Damage Amount	26k. Describe Damage to Barge
DAMAGE TO BARGE _____ CARGO _____	

FOR BARGE CAUSING OR SUSTAINING DAMAGES

26. Name	26a. Official Number	26b. Type	26c. Length	26d. Gross Tons	26e. USCG Certificate of Inspection Issued at:

26f. Year Built	26g. ☐ SINGLE SKIN ☐ DOUBLE SKIN	26h. Draft FWD AFT	26i. Operating Company	

26j. Damage Amount	26k. Describe Damage to Barge
DAMAGE TO BARGE _____ CARGO _____	

FOR BARGE CAUSING OR SUSTAINING DAMAGES

26. Name	26a. Official Number	26b. Type	26c. Length	26d. Gross Tons	26e. USCG Certificate of Inspection Issued at:

26f. Year Built	26g. ☐ SINGLE SKIN ☐ DOUBLE SKIN	26h. Draft FWD AFT	26i. Operating Company	

26j. Damage Amount	26k. Describe Damage to Barge
DAMAGE TO BARGE _____ CARGO _____	

FOR BARGE CAUSING OR SUSTAINING DAMAGES

26. Name	26a. Official Number	26b. Type	26c. Length	26d. Gross Tons	26e. USCG Certificate of Inspection Issued at:

26f. Year Built	26g. ☐ SINGLE SKIN ☐ DOUBLE SKIN	26h. Draft FWD AFT	26i. Operating Company	

26j. Damage Amount	26k. Describe Damage to Barge
DAMAGE TO BARGE _____ CARGO _____	

FOR BARGE CAUSING OR SUSTAINING DAMAGES

26. Name	26a. Official Number	26b. Type	26c. Length	26d. Gross Tons	26e. USCG Certificate of Inspection Issued at:

26f. Year Built	26g. ☐ SINGLE SKIN ☐ DOUBLE SKIN	26h. Draft FWD AFT	26i. Operating Company	

26j. Damage Amount	26k. Describe Damage to Barge
DAMAGE TO BARGE _____ CARGO _____	

310 FIG. 16

DEPARTMENT OF TRANSPORTATION U.S. COAST GUARD CG-2692B(1-91)	REPORT OF REQUIRED CHEMICAL DRUG AND ALCOHOL TESTING FOLLOWING A SERIOUS MARINE INCIDENT *(See Instructions on reverse)*	APPROVED OMB NO. 2115-0003 (Expiration 6-93).5 Burden Hrs. ELECTRONIC TEST VERSION USCG CASE NUMBER

SECTION I—VESSEL INFORMATION

1. Name of vessel	2. Official Number	3. Call Sign	4. Nationality

5. Vessel Type *(Freight, Towing, Fishing, MODU, etc.)*	6. Length	7. Gross Tons	8. Year Built

9. Operating Company	10. Master or Person in Charge
Name:	Name:
Address:	Address:
Telephone Number:	Telephone Number:

SECTION II—INCIDENT INFORMATION

11. Type of Serious Marine Incident *(Check Appropriate Box(es)). (See Instructions on Reverse)*

☐ a. Death *(Append to Form CG-2692)*

☐ b. Injury requiring medical treatment *(Append to Form CG-2692)*

☐ c. Property damage in excess of $100,000 *(Append to Form CG-2692)*

☐ d. Loss of inspected vessel *(Append to Form CG-2692)*

☐ e. Loss of uninspected, self-propelled vessel of over 100 gross tons *(Append to Form CG-2692)*

☐ f. Discharge of oil of 10,000 gallons or more into U.S. waters

☐ g. Discharge of a reportable quantity of hazardous substance into U.S. waters

☐ h. Release of a reportable quantity of hazardous substance into U.S. environment

12. Date of Incident	13. Time *(local)* of Incident	14. Location of Incident *(Latitude and Longitude or River and Milepost)*

SECTION III—PERSONNEL / TESTING INFORMATION

15. Personnel Directly Involved in Serious Marine Incident	16. Drug and Alcohol Testing *(See Instructions on reverse)*

15a. Name *(Last, First, Middle Initial)*	15b. Licensing/Certification *(Check Appropriate Box(es))*			16a. Drug Test Urine Specimen Provided?		16b. Alcohol Test Blood Specimen Provided?		16c. Alcohol Test Breath Specimen Provided?		
	USCG License	USCG MMD	NEITHER	YES	NO	YES	NO	YES	NO	Breath Test Results
	☐	☐	☐	☐	☐	☐	☐	☐	☐	
	☐	☐	☐	☐	☐	☐	☐	☐	☐	
	☐	☐	☐	☐	☐	☐	☐	☐	☐	
	☐	☐	☐	☐	☐	☐	☐	☐	☐	
	☐	☐	☐	☐	☐	☐	☐	☐	☐	

17. Laboratory Conducting Chemical Drug Tests	18. Laboratory Conducting Blood Alcohol Test(s) or Individual Conducting Breath Test(s)
Name:	Name:
Address:	Address:
Telephone Number:	Telephone Number:

19. Person Making This Report *(Please Print)*	20. Signature	21. Date
Name:		
Address:		
Telephone Number:	Title:	

22. Remarks *(See Instructions on Reverse)*

SN 7530-01-GF3-2380

FIG. 16—*Continued* **311**

INSTRUCTIONS FOR COMPLETION OF FORM CG-2692B

REPORT OF REQUIRED CHEMICAL DRUG AND ALCOHOL TESTING FOLLOWING A SERIOUS MARINE INCIDENT

NOTE: When this form is being submitted along with a REPORT OF MARINE ACCIDENT, INJURY OR DEATH (Form CG-2692), Blocks 3-10 and Blocks 12-14 on Form CG-2692B need not be completed.

WHEN TO USE THIS FORM

1. This form satisfies the requirements in the Code of Federal Regulations for written reports of chemical drug and alcohol testing of individuals directly involved in serious marine incidents. Public vessels and recreational vessels are excepted from these reporting requirements.

SERIOUS MARINE INCIDENTS

2. The term "serious marine incident" includes the following events involving a vessel in commercial service:

A. Any marine casualty or accident that occurs upon the navigable waters of the U.S., its territories or possessions, or that involves a U.S. vessel anywhere, and that results in any of the following:

1. One or more deaths;

2. Any injury to a crewmember, passenger, or other person which requires professional medical treatment beyond first aid;

3. Damage to property, as defined in 46 CFR 4.05-1(f), in excess of $100,000;

4. Actual or constructive total loss of any vessel subject to inspection under 46 U.S.C. 3301; or

5. Actual or constructive total loss of any self-propelled vessel, not subject to inspection under 46 U.S.C. 3301, of 100 gross tons or more.

B. A discharge of oil of 10,000 gallons or more into the navigable waters of the United States, as defined in 33 U.S.C. 1321, whether or not resulting from a marine casualty.

C. A discharge of a reportable quantity of a hazardous substance into the navigable waters of the United States, whether or not resulting from a marine casualty.

D. A release of a reportable quantity of a hazardous substance into the environment of the United States, whether or not resulting from a marine casualty.

INDIVIDUAL DIRECTLY INVOLVED IN A SERIOUS MARINE INCIDENT

3. Term "individual directly involved in a serious marine incident" is an individual whose order, action or failure to act is determined to be, or cannot be ruled out as, a causative factor in the events leading to or causing a serious marine incident.

COMPLETION OF THIS FORM

4. This form should be filled out as completely and accurately as possible. Please type or print clearly. Fill in all blanks that apply to the kind of incident that has occurred. If a question is not applicable, the abbreviation "NA" should be entered in that space. If an answer is unknown and cannot be obtained, the abbreviation "UNK" should be entered in that space. If "NONE" is the correct response, then enter it in that space.

5. When this form has been completed, deliver or mail it as soon as practicable to the Coast Guard Marine Safety or Marine Inspection Office nearest to the location of the incident or, if at sea, nearest to the port of first arrival.

6. Upon receipt of a report of chemical test results, the marine employer shall submit a copy of the test results for each person listed in block 15(a) of this form to the Coast Guard Officer in Charge, Marine Inspection whom the CG-2692B was submitted. (Ref. 46 CFR 4.06-60(d)).

7. Amplifying information for completing the form:

A. Block 11—"TYPE OF SERIOUS MARINE INCIDENT" Check each appropriate box. If box a, b, c, or e is checked, append this form to the required form CG-2692, "REPORT OF MARINE ACCIDENT, INJURY OR DEATH", and submit both forms as indicated in 5. above.

B. Block 16c—"ALCOHOL TEST BREATH SPECIMEN PROVIDED?" When breath test results are available alcohol concentration shall be expressed numerically in percent by weight (i.e., .04, .10 etc...).

C. Block 22—"REMARKS" Describe the duties of each individual listed in 15a, at the time of incident (i.e., master, pilot, chief engineer...). If an individual refuses to provide the required specimens, or if specimens are not obtained for any reason, describe the circumstances completely.

NOTICE: The information collected on this form is routinely available for public inspection. It is needed by the Coast Guard to carry out its responsibility to investigate marine casualties, to identify hazardous conditions or situations and to conduct statistical analysis. The information is used to determine whether new or revised safety initiatives are necessary for the protection of life or property in the marine environment.

22. REMARKS *(Continued)*

TAB 3 to ENCLOSURE (2) to NVIC NO. 8-95

BALLAST WATER REPORTING FORM

IS THIS AN AMENDED BALLAST REPORTING FORM? YES ☐ NO ☐

1. VESSEL INFORMATION

Vessel Name:

IMO Number:

Owner:

Type:

GT:

Call Sign:

Flag:

2. VOYAGE INFORMATION

Arrival Port:

Arrival Date:

Agent:

Last Port: Country of Last Port:

Next Port: Country of Next Port:

3. BALLAST WATER USAGE AND CAPACITY

Specify Units Below (m^3, MT, LT, ST)

Total Ballast Water on Board:

Volume   Units   No. of Tanks in Ballast

Total Ballast Water Capacity:

Volume   Units   Total No. of Tanks on Ship

4. BALLAST WATER MANAGEMENT

Total No. Ballast Water Tanks to be discharged:

Of tanks to be discharged, how many: Underwent Exchange: Underwent Alternative Management:

Please specify alternative method(s) used, if any:

If no ballast treatment conducted, state reason why not:

Ballast management plan on board? YES ☐ NO ☐   Management plan implemented? YES ☐ NO ☐

IMO ballast water guidelines on board [res. A.868(20)]? YES ☐ NO ☐

5. BALLAST WATER HISTORY: Record all tanks to be deballasted in port state of arrival;   IF NONE, GO TO #6   *(Use additional sheets as needed)*

Tanks/ Holds List multiple sources/tanks separately	BW SOURCES					BW MANAGEMENT PRACTICES						BW DISCHARGES			
	DATE DD/MM/Y Y	PORT or LAT. LONG.	VOLUME (units)	TEMP (units)	DATE DD/MM/Y Y	ENDPOINT LAT. LONG.	VOLUME (units)	% Each	METHOD (ER/FT/ ALT)	SEA HT. (m)	DATE DD/MM/Y Y	PORT or LAT. LONG.	VOLUME (units)	SALINT Y (units)

Ballast Water Tank Codes: Forepeak = FP, Aftpeak = AP, Double Bottom = DB, Wing = WT, Topside = TS, Cargo Hold = CH, Other = O

6. RESPONSIBLE OFFICER'S NAME AND TITLE, PRINTED AND SIGNATURE:

11

FIG. 17—*Continued* 313

TAB 4 to ENCLOSURE (2) to NVIC NO. 8 – 99

Where to send this form

Vessels bound for Great Lakes

United States or Canadian Flag vessel bound for the Great Lakes

Fax the form to the COTP Buffalo **315-764-3283** at least 24 hours before the vessel arrives in Montreal, Quebec.

Any other Flag vessel bound for the Great Lakes

Fax the form to the COTP Buffalo **315-764-3283** at least 24 hours before the vessel arrives in Montreal, Quebec, or;

Complete the ballast water information section of the St. Lawrence Seaway required "Pre-entry Information from Foreign Flagged Vessels Form" and submit it in accordance with the applicable Seaway notice.

Vessels bound for the Hudson River North Of George Washington Bridge

Vessel bound for the Hudson River north of the George Washington Bridge

Fax the form to the COTP New York at **718-354-4249** before the vessel enters the waters of the United States (12 miles from the baseline).

Vessels bound for all other United States Ports

Vessel bound for all ports within the waters of the United States other than the Great Lakes or Hudson River north of the George Washington Bridge

Before the vessel departs from the first port of call in the waters of the United States send the form by one of the three following methods:

- Mail the form to the **U.S. Coast Guard, c/o Smithsonian Environmental Research Center (SERC), P.O. Box 28, Edgewater, MD 21037-0028**;

- Transmit the form electronically to the National Ballast Information Clearinghouse (NBIC) at **www.serc.si.edu\invasions\ballast.htm**); or

- Fax the form to the Commandant, U.S. Coast Guard, c/o the NBIC at **301-261-4319.**

If any information changes, send an amended form before the vessel departs the waters of the United States.

12

Continued on next page

TAB 4 to ENCLOSURE (2) to NVIC NO.8 – 99

Instructions For Ballast Water Reporting Form
(Please write in English and PRINT legibly.)

Is this an Amended Ballast Reporting Form?: Check Yes or No. Amendments should be submitted if there are any differences between actual ballast discharges and discharge information reported in a prior form. Please mark "Yes" if this form amends a previously submitted ballast reporting form.

SECTION 1. VESSEL INFORMATION

Vessel Name: Print the name of the vessel clearly.

IMO Number: Fill in identification number of the vessel used by the International Maritime Organization.

Owner: Write in the name of the registered owner(s) of the vessel. If under charter, enter Operator name.

Type: List specific vessel type. Use the following abbreviations: bulk (**bc**), roro (**rr**), container (**cs**), tanker (**ts**),passenger (**pa**), oil/bulk ore (**ob**), general cargo (**gc**), reefer (**rf**). Write out any additional vessel types.

GT: What is the Gross Tonnage of the vessel?

Call Sign: Write in the official call sign.

Flag: Fill in the full name of the country under whose authority the ship is operating. No abbreviations please.

SECTION 2. VOYAGE INFORMATION

Arrival Port: Write in the name of your first port of call after entering the U.S. EEZ or St. Lawrence Seaway. No abbreviations.

Arrival Date: Fill in the arrival date to the above port. Please use European date format (DDMMYY).

Agent: List agent used for current port.

Last Port: Fill in the last port at which the vessel called immediately before entering the U.S. EEZ. No abbreviations please.

Country of Last Port: Fill in the last country at which the vessel called immediately before entering the U.S. EEZ. No abbreviations please.

Next Port: Fill in the port at which the vessel will call immediately after departing the current port ("Current Port"="Arrival Port" above). No abbreviations please.

Country of Next Port: Fill in the country of "Next Port" at which the vessel will call immediately after current port. No abbreviations please.

SECTION 3. BALLAST WATER

Total Ballast Water on Board:

Volume: What was the total volume of ballast water on board upon arrival into the waters of U.S. EEZ? Do not count potable water.

Units: Please include volume units (m^3, MT, LT, ST).

FIG. 17—*Continued* **315**

TAB 4 to ENCLOSURE (2) to NVIC NO. 8 – 99

Number of Tanks in Ballast: Count the number of ballast tanks and holds with ballast as vessel enters waters inside the United States EEZ.

Total Ballast Water Capacity:

Volume: What is the maximum volume of ballast water used when no cargo is on board?

Units: Please include volume units (m³, MT, LT, ST).

Total Number of Tanks on Ship: Count all tanks and holds that can carry ballast water (do not include tanks that carry potable water).

SECTION 4. BALLAST WATER MANAGEMENT

Total No. of tanks to be discharged: Count only tanks and holds with ballast to be discharged into waters inside the United States EEZ or into an approved reception facility. Count all tanks and holds separately (e.g., port and starboard tanks should be counted separately).

Of tanks to be discharged, how many Underwent Exchange: Count all tanks that are to be discharged into waters of the United States or into an approved reception facility.

Of tanks to be discharged, how many Underwent Alternative Management: Count all tanks that are to be discharged into waters of the United States or an approved reception facility.

Please specify alternative method(s) used, if any: Specifically, describe methods used for ballast management.

If no ballast treatment conducted, state reason why not: This applies to all tanks and holds being discharged into waters of the United States or into an approved reception facility.

Ballast Management Plan on board?: Is there a written document on board, specific to your vessel, describing the procedure for ballast management? This should include safety and exchange procedures (usually provided by vessel's owner or operator). Check Yes or No.

Management Plan implemented?: Do you follow the above management plan? Check Yes or No.

IMO Ballast Water Guidelines on board?: Is there a copy of the International Maritime Organization (IMO) Ballast Water Guidelines on board this vessel (i.e. "Guidelines for the Control and Management of Ship's Ballast Water to Minimize the Transfer Aquatic Organisms and Pathogens", [Res. A.868(20)])? Check Yes or No.

SECTION 5. BALLAST WATER HISTORY

(Record all tanks to be deballasted in port state of arrival: If none, go to #6)

Tanks/Holds: Please list all tanks and holds that you have discharged or plan to discharge into waters of the United States or into an approved reception facility (write out, or use codes listed below table). Follow each tank across the page listing all source(s), exchange events, and/or discharge events separately. List each tank on a separate line. Port and starboard tanks with identical ballast water histories may be included on same line. Please use an additional page if necessary, being careful to include ship name, date, and IMO number at the top of each. For tanks with multiple sources: list 3 largest sources from last 30 days on separate lines. If more than 3 sources, include a 4th line for the respective tank(s) that indicated "Multiple" in port column and list the remaining tank volume not included in the 3 largest sources (i.e., total tank volume minus volume of the 3 largest sources). See example #1 on sample ballast reporting form.
-BW SOURCES

Date: Record date of ballast water uptake. Use European format (DDMMYY).

Port or latitude/longitude: Record location of ballast water uptake, no abbreviations for ports.

14

Continued on next page

TAB 4 to ENCLOSURE (2) to NVIC NO.8 – 99

Volume: Record total volume of ballast water uptake, <u>with volume units.</u>

Temp: Record water temperature at time of ballast water uptake, in degrees Celsius <u>(include units).</u>

-BW MANAGEMENT PRACTICES-

Date: Date of ballast water management practice. If exchanges occurred over multiple days, list the day when exchanges were completed. Use European format (DDMMYY).

Endpoint or latitude/longitude: Report location of ballast water management practice. If an exchange occurred over an extended distance, list the end point latitude and longitude.

Volume: Report total volume of ballast water moved (i.e., gravitated and pumped into tanks, discharged to reception facility) during management practice , <u>with units.</u>

% Exch.: (Note: for effective flow through exchange, this value should be at least 300%).

$$\% \ Exchange = \frac{\textit{Total Volume of refill or flowthrough water}}{\text{Original Volume of water}} \quad x \ 100\%$$

Method: Indicate management method using code (ER = empty/refill, FT = flow through, ALT = alternative method).

Sea Ht . (m): Estimate the sea height in meters at the time of the ballast water exchange if this method was used. (Note: this is the combined height of the wind-seas and swell, and does <u>not</u> refer to water depth).

-BW DISCHARGES-

Date: Date of ballast water discharge. Use European format (DDMMYY).

Port or latitude/longitude: Report location of ballast water discharge, <u>no abbreviations for ports.</u>

Volume: Report volume of ballast water discharged, <u>with units.</u>

Salinity: Document salinity of ballast water at the time of discharge, <u>with units</u> (i.e., specific gravity (sg) or parts per thousand (ppt)).

SECTION 6. TITLE AND SIGNATURE

Responsible officer's name and title (printed) and signature: Print name and title, include signature.

FIG. 18   317

TAB 6 to ENCLOSURE (2) to NVIC NO. 8 – 99

National Ballast Survey: USCG Questionnaire

Coast Guard Boarding Officer: _____
                                                    Name

━━━━━━━━━━ BOARDING/VESSEL INFORMATION ━━━━━━━━━━

Is this a: random boarding? ☐ Or, Is this boarding in addition to the random boarding schedule? ☐
Was this random boarding conducted in conjunction with another scheduled activity for this vessel? ☐

Today's Date	
COTP (Captain Of The Port) Zone	
This Arrival Port	
Vessel Name	
IMO Number or Official Number	
Vessel Owner or Operator	

Vessel Type: Tanker ☐   Bulk Carrier ☐   Container ☐   General Cargo ☐   Other ☐

━━━━━━━━━━ BALLAST WATER INFORMATION ━━━━━━━━━━

What was your last port of call? [_____]

Are you discharging ballast water in this or other U.S. port(s)?   Yes ☐   No ☐

What volume of ballast water is being discharged in this or other U.S. port(s)? [_____]

What are the units of the volume being discharged?   (Circle One): m^3 **MT** **LT** **ST**

How many ballast water tanks are on this vessel? [_____]

How many of these tanks are in ballast? [_____]

How many of these tanks will be partially or fully discharged in this or other U.S. ports? [_____]

How many of the tanks to be discharged underwent ballast exchange? [_____]

What percentage of the discharged water was exchanged? [_____]

List ballast tanks that underwent exchange and which will be discharged: _____
_____

What is the salinity (ppt) of an exchanged tank? [_____]

If salinity was not measured, name alternative water characteristic measured: _____

What was the value and unit of the alternative water characteristic? [_____]   [_____]
                                                                    Value   Unit

━━━━━━━━━━ INTERNET CAPABILITIES ━━━━━━━━━━

Can you access the World Wide Web on this vessel?   ☐ Yes   ☐ No
Can you send and receive e-mail on this vessel?   ☐ Yes   ☐ No

318   FIG. 19

AIRCRAFT/VESSEL REPORT

Form Approved
OMB No. 43–RO497

☐ ARRIVAL

Last Foreign Port _____

☐ DEPARTURE

First Foreign Port _____

Airline/Vessel (Name and Nationality)	Flight Number	Port of Arr/Dep	Date of Arr/Dep

TYPE OF TRANSPORT—CHECK ONE

1. ☐ U.S. military—including charters to military
2. ☐ Commercial—scheduled
3. ☐ Commercial—chartered
4. ☐ Foreign military

Total Passengers

Do Not Write in These Blocks—For INS Use Only

Passengers Inspected	Passengers Deferred	Deferred Port

Attach CF 7507, ICAO Declaration, or I–418, or List Crew Below.

CREW: Name   Status

FOREIGN PORT AND COUNTRY	PASSENGERS		
	USC	ALIEN	TOTAL
TOTAL			

FORM I–92 *(See instructions on reverse of form)*
(Rev. 6–1–73)N

United States Department of Justice
Immigration and Naturalization Service

FIG. 20   319

U.S. Department of Justice   OMB 1115-0077
Immigration and Naturalization Service

Admission Number   *Welcome to the United States*

1⎵0⎵79339 07

└─┴─┴─┴─┴─┴─┴─┴─┴─┴─┘

I-94 Arrival/Departure Record - Instructions

This form must be completed by all persons except U.S. Citizens, returning resident aliens, aliens with immigrant visas, and Canadian Citizens visiting or in transit.

Type or print legibly with pen in ALL CAPITAL LETTERS. Use English. Do not write on the back of this form.

This form is in two parts. Please complete both the Arrival Record (Items 1 through 13) and the Departure Record (Items 14 through 17).

When all items are completed, present this form to the U.S. Immigration and Naturalization Service Inspector.

Item 7 If you are entering the United States by land, enter **LAND** in this space. If you are entering the United States by ship, enter **SEA** in this space.

Form I-94 (04-15-86)Y

Admission Number

1⎵0⎵79339 07

└─┴─┴─┴─┴─┴─┴─┴─┴─┴─┘

Immigration and
Naturalization Service

I-94
Arrival Record

1.Family Name	
2.First (Given) Name	3.Birth Date (Day/Mo/Yr)
4.Country of Citizenship	5.Sex (Male or Female)
6.Passport Number	7.Airline and Flight Number
8.Country Where You Live	9.City Where You Boarded
10.City Where Visa Was Issued	11.Date Issued (Day/Mo/Yr)
12.Address While in the United States (Number and Street)	
13.City and State	

Departure Number

1⎵0⎵79339 07

└─┴─┴─┴─┴─┴─┴─┴─┴─┴─┘

Immigration and
Naturalization Service

I-94
Departure Record

14.Family Name	
15.First (Given) Name	16.Birth Date (Day/Mo/Yr)
17.Country of Citizenship	

See Other Side   **STAPLE HERE**

Continued on next page

This Side For Government Use Only

Primary Inspection

Applicant's
Name _____
Date
Referred _____ Time _____ Insp. # _____

Reason Referred

☐ 212A   [ ] [ ]   ☐ PP   ☐ Visa   ☐ Parole   ☐ SLB   ☐ TWOV

☐ Other _____

_____

_____

Secondary Inspection

End Secondary
Time _____ Insp. # _____

Disposition _____

18. Occupation	19. Waivers
20. INS File A -	21. INS FCO
22. Petition Number	23. Program Number
24. ☐ Bond	25. ☐ Prospective Student

26. Itinerary/Comments

_____

_____

_____

_____

_____

27. TWOV Ticket Number

L__|__|__|__J   L__|__|__|__|__|__|__|__|__|__J

Warning -A nonimmigrant who accepts unauthorized employment is subject to deportation.
Important - Retain this permit in your possession; *you must surrender it when you leave the U.S.* Failure to do so may delay your entry into the U.S. in the future.
You are authorized to stay in the U.S. only until the date written on this form. To remain past this date, without permission from immigration authorities, is a violation of the law.
Surrender this permit when you leave the U.S.:
   - By sea or air, to the transportation line;
   - Across the Canadian border, to a Canadian Official;
   - Across the Mexican border, to a U.S. Official.
Students planning to reenter the U.S. within 30 days to return to the same school, see "Arrival-Departure" on page 2 of Form I-20 **prior to surrendering this permit.**

Record of Changes

_____

_____

_____

Port: **Departure Record**

Date:

Carrier:

Flight #/Ship Name:

CZ-2150

FIG. 21 321

Family name | Given name | Initial | Soundex

Home address and name of relative or friend residing there

Address in the U.S. | Date and place of birth

Hair	Eyes	Height	Weight	Sex ☐ M ☐ F	

'A' No.

Action by Immigration Officer | Passport (No. and Nationality)

Arrived by

U.S. Immigration Officer

Form I-95A B (Rev. 10-1-84) Y

CREWMAN'S LANDING PERMIT

OMB No. 1115-0040

TO REORDER CALL: (800) 438-0162

APPERSON BUSINESS FORMS, INC.

WHSE. #0425

ANY HANDWRITTEN ENTRIES MUST BE IN BLOCK CAPITAL LETTERS

OMB No. 1115-0073

U.S. Department of Justice
Immigration and Naturalization Service

**Application to Pay Off or
Discharge Alien Crewman**

(To be filed in triplicate. See Instructions on reverse)

I.

Carrier:	Arrival Manifest Filed at *(Port):*	Date of Arrival:

I hereby request authorization to **PAY OFF/DISCHARGE** the alien crewmen listed below.

II.

Name in Full		Nationality and Passport Number	Action by INS
Family Name	Given Name and Middle Initial		

(If additional space is required, attached list in triplicate)

III. Reason for request:

IV. Arrangements for departure from the U.S. of the listed crewmen are (date and port of departure, air carrier and flight number or vessel).

Mailing Address of Carrier:	
	Signature
	Title

FOR GOVERNMENT USE ONLY

Application: ☐ Granted ☐ Denied	Copy: ☐ Mailed ☐ Delivered	Date:
Office:	Date:	Signature:
Signature and Title:		Title:

Form I-408 (Rev. 05/17/00)Y

FIG. 22—*Continued* 323

NOTICE

SECTION 256 OF THE IMMIGRATION AND NATIONALITY ACT (8 USC 1286)

It shall be unlawful for any person, including the owner, agent, consignee, charterer, master or commanding officer vessel or aircraft, to pay off or discharge an alien crewman, except an alien lawfully admitted for permanent residence, employed on board a vessel or aircraft arriving in the United States without first having obtained the consent of the Attorney General. If it shall appear to the satisfaction of the Attorney General that any alien crewman has been paid off or discharged in the United States in violation of the provisions of this section, such owner, agent, consignee, charterer, master, commanding officer or other person, shall pay to the Commissioner the sum of $3,000 for each such violation. No vessel or aircraft shall be granted clearance pending the determination of the question of the liability to the payment of such sums or while such sums remain unpaid, except that clearance may be granted prior to the determination of such question of the liability to the payment of such sums or while such sums remain unpaid, except that clearance may be granted prior to the determination of such question upon the deposit of an amount sufficient to cover such sums, or of a bond approved by the Commissioner with sufficient surety to secure the payment thereof. Such fine may, in the discretion of the Attorney General, be mitigated to not less than $1,500 for each violation, upon such terms as he shall think proper.

INSTRUCTIONS

1. **Filing:** The application must be completed in triplicate and delivered or mailed to the nearest office of the Immigration and Naturalization Service.

2. **Execution:** The signature and title of either the owner, agent, consignee, charterer, master or commanding officer of the vessel or aircraft seeking authorization to pay off or discharge crewmen must be included on the application.

3. **General:** Inadequate or incomplete data required in items III, Reason for request, and IV, Arrangements for departure, may result in denial of the application.

4. **Disposition:** The original and one copy of the granted application will be returned to the applicant. The copy must be submitted with the departure manifest. One copy of the application will be retained by the Immigration and Naturalization Service with the arrival manifest.

REPORTING BURDEN

PUBLIC REPORTING BURDEN. Reporting burden for this collection of information is estimated to average 15 minutes per response. If you have comments regarding the accurancy of this estimate, or suggestions for making this form simpler, you can write to the U.S. Department of Justice, Immigration and Naturalization Service, HQPDI, 425 I Street N.W., Room 4034, Washington, DC 20536; OMB No. 1115-0073. **DO NOT MAIL YOUR COMPLETED APPLICATION TO THIS ADDRESS.**

324   FIG. 23

APPERSON BUSINESS FORMS, INC.

2267LC   TO REORDER CALL: (800) 438-0162

Form Approved
OMB No. 1115-00

TREASURY DEPARTMENT
UNITED STATES CUSTOMS SERVICE

UNITED STATES DEPARTMENT OF JUSTICE
Immigration and Naturalization Service

PASSENGER LIST

CREW LIST
(Cross out one)

(Oath to be taken on Customs Form 1300)

Sheet No.

Class (First, Cabin, Tourist, or Other)

CARRIER (Nationality, name, and official number of carrier)

Date of arrival/departure (Cross out one) | Port of arrival/departure (Cross out one)

Last foreign port before arrival in United States (Place and Country) | (Date departed)

If departing, show first port at and date on which carrier arrived in United States on this trip. | If departing, show first foreign port after departure from United States.

(1) NAME IN FULL (List Alphabetically)		(2) Date of Birth Nationality and passport number	(3) CREW		(4) CREW (Departing U.S. Flag vessels only) USCG Z or C.D.B. number and name and address of next of kin	(5) This column for use Government officials only (except when carrying certain passengers. See Instructions)
Family name	Given name and middle initial		Position	Where shipped or engaged		

Total Number
I-418 (Rev. 10-1-85) Y
WHSE. NO. 0861 (02-91)

Agent

FIG. 23—*Continued* 325

INSTRUCTIONS
ALL NAMES AND OTHER DATA INSCRIBED ON THIS FORM MUST BE IN THE ENGLISH LANGUAGE

PASSENGERS

Incoming.—Complete columns (1) and (2), and (5) when required below. Deliver one complete alphabetical list, regardless of nationality, to United States Public Health Service, United States Immigration Service, and two such lists to United States Customs Bureau on arrival at first port in the United States. If insufficient space in column (2), information may extend into column (3).

In column (5) show opposite a passenger's name the compartment or space occupied if that passenger is not allotted space for his or her exclusive use in the proportion of at least 36 clear superficial feet (steerage); the sex and the married or single status of each passenger in such case; and the age of each passenger of 8 years or under. In addition, the age of each deceased passenger and the cause of death shall be shown, regardless of class.

Departing.—Complete columns (1) and (2). Deliver one complete list to the United States Immigration Service at the last port of departure—to which is attached the Arrival/Departure Card (Form I-94) given to each nonimmigrant alien when he last arrived in the United States; otherwise, prepare and attach a new Form I-94.

CREW

Incoming.—Complete columns (1), (2) and (3). Deliver one complete alphabetical list to United States Public Health Service, United States Immigration Service, and two such lists to the United States Customs Bureau on arrival at the first port in the United States.

Where a crewman is a returning resident alien, show his registration receipt card number in column (2) in lieu of passport number.

Departing.—Submit a single copy of this form to the Immigration office at the port from which the vessel is to depart directly to a foreign port or place, executed in accordance with the following instructions.

Complete all items in the heading of the form and place the following endorsement on the first line of the form: "Arrival Crewlist, Form I-418, filed at *(Show U.S. port of arrival)*." A Form I-418 which does not bear this endorsement will not be accepted.

Notificaton of Changes in Crew.—(1) Under a heading "Added Crewmen," list the names of nonresident alien crewmen who were not members of the crew and manifested on Form I-418 as such when the vessel last arrived in the United States, and attach for each added crewman his Form I-95 or Form I-94 given to him when he last arrived in the United States; otherwise, prepare and attach a new Form I-95. (2) Under a heading "Separated Crewmen," list the names of all alien crewmen who arrived in the United States on the occasion of the vessel's last arrival in the United States but who for any reason are not departing with the vessel, and for each such separated crewman, show his nationality, passport number, specific port and date of separation, and the reasons for failure to depart. (3) If there are no added and/or separated alien crewmen upon departure, endorse the form "No changes in nonresident alien crew upon departure."

The list required under (1) and (2) may be incorporated in single Form I-418, if space permits.

United States Flag Vessels Only.—Complete column (1), (2), (3) and (4). Deliver two complete crew lists to United States Customs Bureau at the last port of departure. The customs officer will certify one copy of this crew list in the space provided below and that copy shall be presented to the United States Customs Bureau at the first port of arrival in the United States and on the return voyage. Show birthplace in column (2) in lieu of passport number.

CREW LIST VISA APPLICATION

Submit form in duplicate to a United States consular officer. For each alien crewman not in possession of a valid individual visa or Immigration and Naturalization Service Form I-151, note columns (4) and (5) of the duplicate copy as follows: column (4) insert his date, city and country of birth, column (5) insert place of issuance and the authority issuing passport held by such crewman. Same information is required at port of entry when applying for waiver of visa.

Execute the following oath before a Customs Officer as to all arriving passengers on all vessels. The oath is to be executed before a Customs Officer as to all departing crew on United States Flag Vessels, and before an Immigration Officer or other officer authorized to administer oaths as to all departing passengers on all vessels.

I certify that Customs baggage declaration requirements have been made known to incoming passengers; that any required Customs baggage declarations have been or will simultaneously herewith be filed as required by law and regulation with the proper Customs officer; and that the responsibilities devolving upon this vessel in connection therewith, if any, have been or will be discharged as required by law or regulation before the proper Customs officer. I further certify that there are no steerage passengers on board this vessel (46 U.S.C. 151-163).

_____
Signature of Master

Show in box below number of United States citizens and alien passengers embarked or to be debarked separately at each foreign port involved. If passenger list consists of more than one page, summarize on last page only. Separate summary should be prepared for each class when manifested separately.

CERTIFICATION OF COPY OF CREW LIST
OF UNITED STATES FLAG VESSEL

I certify that this is a true copy of the original crew list of the above-named American vessel, which original crew list is on file in this office.

Given under my hand and seal of office at the customhouse at

_____ on _____

_____ Customs Officer

Foreign Port of {	Embarkation (Cross out one) Debarkation	Number or passengers	
		U.S.C.	Aliens
Total			

Form **1078** (Rev. November 1996) Department of the Treasury Internal Revenue Service	**Certificate of Alien Claiming Residence in the United States** (This certificate has no effect on citizenship.)	OMB No. 1545-1482

Your name and address	Your social security number
	Date of employment in the U.S.

Under penalties of perjury, I declare that I am a citizen or subject of (country) ------------------------------ ; that I was admitted to the United States on or about (date) ------------------------------ , under a visa or permit (visa number and class) ------------------------------ ; that I have established residence in the United States; and I understand that my income derived from all sources, including sources outside the United States, will be subject to tax under the Internal Revenue laws applicable to residents of the United States until I abandon my residence in the United States.

Date ------------------------------ , 19 ....   --
                                                         Your signature

Privacy Act and Paperwork Reduction Act Notice.—Our legal right to ask for the information on this form is Internal Revenue Code sections 871, 1441, 6001, 6011, and 6109 and their regulations. You are required to give us the information if you are claiming residence in the United States for income tax purposes. We need it to determine if you are a resident alien of the United States and exempt from the withholding of

income tax that applies to nonresident aliens. If you do not provide the information, your income may be subject to income tax withholding. If you provide false information, you may be subject to criminal prosecution. We may give this information to the Department of Justice as provided by law. We may also give it to cities, states, and the District of Columbia to carry out their tax laws.

Cat. No. 17195I

You are not required to provide the information requested on a form that is subject to the Paperwork Reduction Act unless the form displays a valid OMB control number. Books or records relating to a form or its instructions must be retained as long as their contents may become material in the administration of any Internal Revenue law. Generally, tax returns and return information are confidential, as required by Internal Revenue Code section 6103.

The time needed to complete and file this form will vary depending on individual circumstances. The estimated average time is: **Recordkeeping,** 20 min.; **Learning about the law or the form,** 7 min.; **Preparing the form,** 14 min.; and **Copying, assembling and filing the form with the withholding agent,** 14 min.

If you have comments concerning the accuracy of this time estimate or suggestions for making this form simpler, we would be happy to hear from you. You can write to the Tax Forms Committee, Western Area Distribution Center, Rancho Cordova, CA 95743-0001. **DO NOT** send the form to this address. Instead, see **Where To File** on this page.

Instructions

Purpose of Form.—Form 1078 is used by an alien to claim residence in the United States for income tax purposes.

Resident Aliens.—Aliens admitted to the United States with permanent immigration visas are resident aliens. Aliens with other types of visas that limit their stay in the United States, or their activities in this country, may

be resident aliens or nonresident aliens, depending on the nature and length of their stay. Resident status may also be modified under an income tax treaty. For details, see **Pub. 519,** U.S. Tax Guide for Aliens. Also, see Internal Revenue Code section 7701(b) and its regulations.

Social Security Number.—Enter the number from your social security card. If you do not have a social security number, you can apply for one by completing **Form SS-5.** You can get Form SS-5 from a Social Security Administration office.

Where To File.—A resident alien should file this form with the withholding agent. A **withholding agent** is responsible for withholding tax from your income.

The withholding agent should keep the form and is not required to send a copy to the Internal Revenue Service.

Withholding agents may need to adjust social security and Medicare tax withholding because of the effective date of the change in alien status. For details, see **Pub. 515,** Withholding of Tax on Nonresident Aliens and Foreign Corporations.

Which Form To File.—If you are a resident alien, you must report income on Form 1040, Form 1040A, Form 1040EZ, or TeleFile in the same manner as U.S. citizens.

Nonresident aliens must report income on Form 1040NR or Form 1040NR-EZ.

FIG. 25 327

4398 (MRTD)
Rev. 2-2000

AUTORIDAD DEL CANAL DE PANAMA
SHIP'S INFORMATION AND QUARANTINE DECLARATION

SIN	Radio Letters	Arrived	DD/MM/YY	Hour of Arrival	Day Boarded	Hour Boarded	Hour Cleared	Delay Code
		BALBOA/CRISTOBAL						

Ship's Name (M.V.)	Class (Passenger, Cargo, Tanker, other)	Port of Registry	Nationality

DATA FROM INTERNATIONAL TONNAGE CERTIFICATE (ITC) 69

				Overall length	Extreme beam	FUEL ON BOARD	DAILY CONSUMPTION OF FUEL
Gross	Net	ITC length	ITC beam			Tons or bbls. of oil	Tons or bbls. / Speed (Knots)

MEAN AUTHORIZED TROPICAL DRAFT		Fwd.	PRESENT DRAFT	Aft.	DISPLACEMENT (at present draft)
Salt Water	Fresh Water	S.W.			

Transit to the account of	CODE	FW	SUMMER DEADWEIGHT

Owners	Operators	Charterers

From: (Original Loading Port)	Last Port and date of departure	To: (Final port of discharge of cargo now aboard)	First port of call after leaving Canal waters

Via: (All ports in order and dates visited within past 90 days including original loading port and wayports to final port of discharge)   Agents

EXPIRATION DATE	SAFETY EQUIP CERT
	MARPOL CERT (I.O.P.P.)
	CERT. OF FITNESS (LPG, CHEM, TKR)
	INT. SAFETY MANAGEMENT (ISM)

SHIP CLASSIFICATION SOCIETY

VESSEL DOCKING AT: ☐ MIT/XTOBAL/E.G. ☐ Balboa ☐ Cargo Operation ☐ Bunkers _____ Tons

CARGO (TONS) FOR DISCHARGE AT:		CARGO (TONS) FOR LOADING AT:		Cargo on board (tons)	Type of cargo	Deckload (Type and Tonnage)
Balboa	MIT/XTOBAL/E.G.	Balboa	MIT/XTOBAL/E.G.			

DANGEROUS CARGO DATA

TECHNICAL NAME	FLASH POINT	TRADE NAME	UN NUMBER	IMO CLASS	QUANTITY	LOCATION	CONTAINMENT

TANKERS IN BALLAST	LAST CARGO CARRIED:				GAS FREE?		HOW?	
Certified for passengers (number)	PASSENGERS ON BOARD (Total)	Transit	DISEMBARKING Balboa / Cristobal	SHIP's PERSONNELL ON BOARD	Officers	Crew	Stowaways	H.O.B.'s

HEALTH QUESTIONS: (If more than 4 weeks have elapsed since the voyage began, it will suffice to give particulars for the last 4 weeks.) | YES | NO

1. Has there been on board during the voyage any case or suspected case of plague, cholera, yellow fever, typhus or relapsing fever? (Give particulars in the schedule)
2. Has plague occurred or been suspected among the rats or mice on board during the voyage, or has there been an abnormal mortality among them?
3. Has any person died on board during the voyage otherwise than as a result of accident? (Give particulars in schedule)
4. Is there on board or has there been during the voyage any case of disease which you suspect to be of an infectious nature? (Give particulars in schedule)
5. Is there any sick person on board now? (Give particulars in schedule)
6. Are you aware of any other condition on board which may lead to infection or the spread of disease?

NOTE: -In the absence of a surgeon, the master should regard the following symptoms as grounds for suspecting the existence of disease of an infectious nature. Fever accompanied by prostration or persisting for several days or attended with glandular swelling or any acute skin rash or eruption with or without fever, severe diarrhea with symptoms of collapse, jaundice accompanied by fever

SCHEDULE TO THE DECLARATION
Particulars of every case of illness of death occurring on board, and dead bodies on board
*Recovered, still ill, died   **On board; landed at (name of port); buried at sea

Name	Class/Rating	Age	Sex	Nationality	Port of embarkation	Date of embarkation	Nature of illness	Date of its onset	Results of illness*	Disposal of Case**

DERATING RECORD	Date of last exemption from derrating	Where	Origin of meat in ship's stores

NUMBER, KIND AND ORIGIN OF ANIMALS ON BOARD	NUMBER AND KIND FOR LOCAL DISCHARGE

I HEREBY CERTIFY THAT the foregoing statements and answers to all questions are true to the best of my knowledge and belief, that the list of all live animals now on board my vessel is complete; and that I acknowledge receipt of instructions regarding quarantine requirements. Sea stores, Meat and garbage, the landing of passengers and/or members of the crew, & discharge of cargo

Signature of Ship's surgeon	Signature of Ship's Master
Name typed or printed	Name typed or printed

FOR BOARDING OFFICER USE ONLY

☐ NSQI ☐ SQI ☐ Veterinary inspection required ☐ Hatches will remain closed, and cargo discharge operation delayed until authorized by Sanitation Inspector.

PRATIQUE GRANTED: ☐ R/P ☐ Free ☐ Provisional ☐ Detained for quarantine: Reason: Remarks:

Reason for provisional pratique: ☐ Restricted meat ☐ Animals held on board ☐ Invalid derat ☐ Illness or death on board

Released signed for: Over Draft ☐ Under Draft ☐ Excessive Drag ☐ Down by the head ☐ Docking ☐ Other:

☐ Advised re garbage ☐ Discharge RA/RH cargo   Subscribed and sworn to in my presence; vessel cleared

☐ Sanitation Inspection ☐ M.O.I.C. notified

☐ MTC notified by radio ☐ Hold for quarantine | Boarding Official | BO code | V Insp | HL Insp

ADMEASURERS   **ATTENTION:** Before signing this form be sure the set includes a total of four pages

Continued on next page

AUTORIDAD DEL CANAL DE PANAMA
WARNING TO SHIPMASTERS

You are hereby warned that WHILE YOUR VESSEL IS IN WATER OF THE PANAMA CANAL, regulations prohibit the introduction and, except as specifically authorized by the Republic of Panama, the unloading FOR ANY PURPOUSE of cattle, sheep, other ruminants, or swine, or of fresh, chilled, or frozen meats on board your vessel which originated or were loaded aboard in a country where foot-and-mouth disease or rinderpest exists. The introduction or unloading of undrawn poultry carcasses from any such countries is restricted.

You are also informed that under regulations that garbage (see Item IV) containing scraps, parts, or other waste of these meats: (1) Shall not be thrown overboard in the waters of the Panama Canal Authority; (2) Must be kept in leakproof covered receptacles inside the guard rail while on board your vessel; (3) May be unloaded only in tight receptacles for incineration or other proper disposal under official supervision of the Departamento de Salud.

NAVIGATION REGULATIONS OF THE PANAMA CANAL AUTHORITY

Item I. Prohibits the introduction into the Republic of Panama of cattle, sheep, other ruminants, or swine, which originated in a country in which foot-and-mouth disease or rinderpest exists and further prohibits any vessel having such live animals on board from transiting the Canal until such animals have been examined by the proper veterinarian authority.

Item II. Prohibits, generally, introduction into the Republic of Panama of any fresh, chilled, or frozen beef, veal, mutton, lamb, or pork from any country in which foot-and-mouth disease or rinderpest exists.

Item III. Prohibits the unloading of cattle, sheep, other ruminants, swine, or generally, of fresh, chilled, or frozen beef, veal, mutton, lamb, or pork from any country in which foot-and-mouth disease or rinderpest exists as specifically authorized by the Republic of Panama.

Item IV. Provides that no garbage derived from fresh, chilled, or frozen meat which has originated in any country in which foot-and-mouth disease or rinderpest exists shall be unloaded from any vessel in the Republic of Panama, including Panama Canal waters, except in tight receptacles for destruction under the direction of the Departamento de Salud.

Item V. During the entire time this vessel is moored to any pier or wharf, all connecting lines should be properly fitted with Rat guards placed 3 to 5 feet from side of vessel.

Item VI. Papers required by boarding party. On arrival, there shall be ready for immediate delivery to the boarding party for inspection or delivery, as the case may be, such papers, and numbers of copies of each, concerning tonnage of vessel, cargo, persons on board, health conditions, pratique, and such other matters upon which information is necessary, as may be prescribed by the Administrator. The required manifests, lists, and statements shall be sworn to by the master or agent of the vessel. Failure to have the prescribed papers upon arrival will subject the vessel to delay, but not to fine.

ALL PAPERS REQUIRED BY BOARDING PARTY AS HEREIN LISTED SHOULD BE READY FOR IMMEDIATE INSPECTION

	All Vessels arriving	Additional forms for Transiting vessels
(a) Ship's information and Quarantine Declaration (Panama Canal Form) (set of four)	1	0
(b) cargo Declaration (Panama Canal Form)	1	0
(c) Crew List (Panama Canal Form)	1	0
(d) Passenger list: passengers transiting / landing (Panama Canal Form)	1 [2]	0
(e) Dangerous cargo manifest and / or lading plan	1 [4]	1
(f) Declaration of all arms and munitions of war aboard, other than explosives declared separately	1 [5]	0
(g) Ship's plans (general arrangement, capacity, midship section, etc.)	0	1 [13]
(h) Panama Canal UMS Net Tonnage Certificate	0	1 [1]
(i) Ship's documents for inspection. See (Maritime Regulations for the Operations of the Panama Canal)	1	0

1 For examination and possible retention.
2 Not required unless such persons or cargo are carried
3 For taking up and subsequent return through agent or otherwise
4 Not required unless vessel is carrying packaged, dangerous goods
5 Not required on vessels of war or auxiliary vessels, as those terms are defined in the treaty concerning the permanent neutrality and operation of the Panama Canal (Sept 7, 1977)

INSTRUCTIONS FOR DANGEROUS CARGOES SECTION

TYPE	TECHNICAL NAME	TRADE NAME	UN NUMBER	IMO CLASS	QUANTITY	LOCATION	CONTAINMENT
DANGEROUS CARGOES IN BULK	Give the correct technical name of each dangerous cargo. DO NOT USE ABBREVIATIONS	Give the common or trade name of each dangerous cargo, if known	Give the United Nations ID number of each dangerous cargo	Give the International Maritime Organization's classification and division number of each dangerous cargo	Give the total amount (in tons) of each dangerous cargo	Give the location of each dangerous cargo according to the area, as shown in the diagram below	State how each dangerous cargo is contained. (Cargo tank or hold)
EXPLOSIVES	Same as above	Same as above	Same as above	Same as above	Same as above	Same as above	(Container, etc)
RADIOACTIVE SUBSTANCES	Same as above	Same as above	Not applicable	Same as above	Same as above	Same as above	(Container, cask, etc.)
PACKAGED DANGEROUS GOODS (other than explosives or radioactive substance)	Not required	Not required	Not required	Same as above, except, group all dangerous cargoes within the same IMO class and division and show as one	Give the total amount (in tons) of all the dangerous cargoes within the same IMO class and division	Same as above	(Container, portable tank, drum, vehicle, boxed, etc.)

LOCATION	BELOW DECK					ABOVE DECK				
	5	4	3	2	1	6 5	4	3	2	1
A						A X				X
B						B Y				Y
C						C Z				Z

Note: Vessels carrying flammable liquids in bulk, state name of liquid and flashpoint, or if vessel is in ballast condition and not gas free, state the name of the flammable liquid last carried and the flashpoint. No other information is required. (A liquid is considered flammable when the flashpoint is 61°C or 141°F or less)

The information requested on the shipping and navigation forms will be used by the Panama Canal Authority for economic analysis of traffic, for development of traffic forecasts. And for budget and planning formulations. Further, the information will be used for identification, billing, safety, sanitation, evaluation and statistical purposes. Customs, quarantine, and immigration information is for use by Panama Government agencies. Some of the information is used by vessel agents to assist in expediting vessel transits through the Canal. The information requested on the shipping and navigation forms is required in order to transit the Panama Canal or to book a transit in advance (Maritime Regulations for the Operations of the Panama Canal).

The declarations are the basis of important statistics which are published for the benefit of shipper's or ship's operators generally, but no information is disclosed concerning shipments by individual ships or lines.

FIG. 26 329

4363 (MRTD)
Rev. 1-2000

AUTORIDAD DEL CANAL DE PANAMA
CARGO DECLARATION
OF VESSEL PASSING THROUGH THE CANAL

Instructions.- A declaration of cargo through the Panama Canal is required-from each vessel making transit. The declarations are the basis of important statistics which are published for the benefit of shippers and ship's operators generally, but no information is disclosed concerning shipments by individual ships or lines.

Accurate information is desired concerning cargo, but is not expected that small and unimportant items of cargo will be listed separately. Fractional parts of tons need not be shown. Cargo listed under the classification of general cargo should not exceed 500 metric tons, if possible.

Please state cargo in metric tons, if possible, but if another unit of measurement is used, state clearly what it is. The numbers in parenthesis following the names of commodities are code indexed for use in making tabulations and should be ignored.

Origin and destinations may be indicated by either country or port. However, if port is not stated, shipments to or from the Atlantic Coast of the United States should be shown as Great Lakes, North Atlantic, South Atlantic, or Gulf. Great Lakes includes all U.S. Great Lakes ports. Canadian Great Lakes includes all ports West of Montreal.

If cargo has been laden at more than one country, the tons from each country must be shown separately. For each of these separate countries the corresponding quantities and countries of discharge for cargo must be shown.

Computer generated cargo declarations that comply with these requirements may be submitted by attaching them to this form with the heading and Master's certification completed.

Note: Not having this form ready and completed on arrival may delay your transit.

NAME OF VESSEL:				ACP SIN:	
TOTAL METRIC TONS OF CARGO:			PASSENGERS:	DATE OF ARRIVAL:	

CONTAINER UNITS

	ON DECK								BELOW DECK							
	LOADED		EMPTIES		REEFER		TOTAL		LOADED		EMPTIES		REEFER		TOTAL	
	Unit	Tons	Unit	Tons	Unit	Tons	Unit	Tons	Unit	Tons	Unit	Tons	Unit	Tons	Unit	Tons
20 FEET																
40 FEET																
TOTAL																

CHECK ONLY IF

☐ Scheduled common carrier
☐ Voyage charter
☐ Time charter
☐ Other (specify) _____
☐ Round the world

DESCRIPTION OF CARGO	TOTAL TONNAGE BY COMMODITY	COUNTRY OR PORT OF ORIGIN (SHOW TONS LOADED IN EACH)		COUNTRY OR PORT OF DESTINATION (SHOW TONS TO BE DISCHARGED IN EACH)	
Asbestos (4)					
Asphalt (6)					
Beans, edible (8)					
Bricks & tile (4)					
Canned foods: (specify) Fish (16)					
Fruit (18)					
Milk (22)					
Vegetables (26)					
Other (specify)					
Cement (32)					
Chemicals: (specify) Amonium compounds (34)					
Borax (sodium borate) (36)					
Carbon black (38)					
Caustic soda (sodium hydroxide) (40)					
Other (specify)					
Chemicals, petroleum: (specify) Benzen Toluene (54)					
Other (specify)					
Clay, fire & china (58)					
Coal (60)					
Cocoa & cocoa beans (processed & unprocessed)62 (92)					
Coffee (processed & unprocessed) (64)					
Coke (coal type) (66)					
Coldstorage cargo: (specify) Bananas (68)					
Dairy products (70)					

Continued on next page

DESCRIPTION OF CARGO	TOTAL	COUNTRY OR PORT OF ORIGIN (TONS)					COUNTRY OR PORT OF DESTINATION (TONS)			
Fish (72)										
Fruit(excluding bananas)(74)										
Meat (76)										
Other (80)										
Copra & coconuts (84)										
Cotton, raw (86)										
Fertilizers (specify)										
Fibers, natural (specify)										
Fishmeal (96)										
Flour, wheat (98)										
Glass & glassware (102)										
Grains:(specify) Barley (104)										
Corn (106)										
Oats (108)										
Rice (110)										
Sorghum (112)										
Soybeans (296)										
Wheat (114)										
Other (specify)										
Groceries (118)										
Infusorial earth (124)										
Iron & steel mfg.: (specify) Angles, shapes & sec's. (126)										
Nails, tacks, spikes, bolts, screws, etc. (128)										
Plates, sheets & coils (130)										
Tubes, pipes & fittings (132)										
Wire, bars & rods (134)										
Other (specify)										
Liquors (142)										
Lumber: (specify) Boards & planks (144)										
Plywood, veneers, composition board (148)										
Other (specify)										
Machinery: (specify) Agricultural machinery & implements (152)										
Autos & trucks (unboxed) (154)										
Autos & trucks (boxed), accesories & parts (155)										
Construction machinery & equipment (156)										
Electrical machinery & apparatus (158)										
Motorcycles, bicycles & parts (160)										
Others (specify)										
Metals: (specify) Aluminium (166)										
Copper (170)										
Iron (172)										
Lead (174)										
Scrap (176)										
Tin & tinplate (178)										
Zinc (180)										
Other (specify)										
Molasses (190)										
Nitrate of soda (44)										
Oil, fish (194)										
Oil, vegetable (specify) Oil seeds (excluding soybeans)(196)										
Ores: (specify) Alumina & bauxite (206)										
Chrome (210)										
Copper (212)										
Iron (214)										
Lead (216)										

FIG. 26—*Continued* 331

DESCRIPTION OF CARGO	TOTAL	COUNTRY OR PORT OF ORIGIN (TONS)				COUNTRY OR PORT OF DESTINATION (TONS)			
Manganese (218)									
Tin (220)									
Zinc (224)									
Other (specify)									
Paper & paper products (232)									
Peas, dried (234)									
Petroleum & products: (specify) Crude petroleum (238)									
Diesel oil (240)									
Gasoline (242)									
Jet fuel (244)									
Kerosene (246)									
Liquified gas (247)									
Lubricating oils (248)									
Residual fuel oils (250)									
Petroleum coke (252)									
Other (specify)									
Phosphates (258)									
Porcelainware (260)									
Potash (262)									
Pulpwood (264)									
Resin (270)									
Rubber (specify raw, manufactured, scrap)									
Salt (282)									
Seeds (excluding oil seeds) (286)									
Skins & hides (288)									
Sugar, raw (300)									
Sulfur (302)									
Tallow (304)									
Textiles (308)									
Tobacco & tobacco manufactures (310)									
Wax, paraffin (314)									
Wines (316)									
Wool, raw (320)									
Other cargo (specify below)									

Continued on next page

ONLY FOR CONTAINERIZED CARGO

LOADED AT (COUNTRY OR PORT OF ORIGIN)

DISCHARGE AT (COUNTRY OR PORT OF DESTINATION)

TYPE

GENERAL CARGO

TOTAL:

HAZARDOUS CARGO

TOTAL:

REEFER CARGO

TOTAL:

EMPTIES

TOTAL:

GRAND TOTAL

RECEIVED BY:

CERTIFIED CORRECT TO THE BEST OF MY KNOWLEDGE AND BELIEF:

SIGNATURE OF MASTER

PANAMA CANAL BOARDING OFFICIAL

Public reporting for this collection of information is estimated to vary from 5 minutes to 4 hours per response. The above includes the time for reviewing instructions, searching existing data sources, gathering and maintaining the data needed, and completing and reviewing the collection of information. Send comments regarding the burden estimate or any other aspect of this collection of information, including suggestions for reducing this burden to the Manager of Management and Budget.

The information requested on the shipping and navigation forms will be used by the Autoridad del Canal de Panama for economic analysis of traffic, for development of traffic forecast, and for budget and planning formulations. Further, the information will be used for identification, billing, safety, sanitation, evaluation and statistical purposes. Customs, quarantine and immigration information is for use by both the Autoridad and the Government of the Republic of Panama. Some of the information is used by vessels agents to assist in expediting vessel transits through the Canal. As required, the information provided may be made available to other Panamanian Government agencies. The information requested on the shipping and navigation forms is required in order to transit the Panama Canal or to book a transit in advance (Maritime Regulations for the Operations of the Panama Canal).

FIG. 27

333

1509 (MRTD)
Rev. 2-2000

AUTORIDAD DEL CANAL DE PANAMA
CREW LIST FOR INCOMING VESSELS

Persons composing the crew of the (M.V.) _____ Flag _____

    Last port _____ Next Port _____

      ❏ Balboa   ❏ Cristobal   Panama _____, 20 ____

	Last Name	First name	Middle Initial	Capacity or Duty	Birthplace Country	Birthday (Day/Mo/Yr)	Nationality	Identification or Z. No.
1								
2								
3								
4								
5								
6								
7								
8								
9								
10								
11								
12								
13								
14								
15								
16								
17								
18								
19								
20								
21								
22								
23								
24								
25								
26								
27								
28								
29								
30								
31								
32								
33								
34								
35								
36								
37								
38								
39								
40								
41								
42								
43								

The undersigned solemnly swears that the within list contains the names of all the crew of said vessel, including stowaways and workaways, so far as I can ascertain.

Subscribed and sworn to this _____ day of

_____, 20 _____

_____
Boarding Official

_____
Master

(See reverse side)

Continued on next page

BOARDING OFFICIAL WILL FILL IN BELOW THIS LINE

Hour boarded vessel _____

Master, M/V) _____ ; You are hereby informed that the following-named person or persons now on board the vessel under tour command is/are (a) to be detained on board while your vessel is within the waters of Panama Canal or (b) be delivered by you to the Immigration Officer at Balboa/Cristobal, Panama.

NAME OF PERSON	REASON FOR EXCLUSION	DISPOSITION

Above instructions received:

_____
Master

Inspected : Crew _____

_____
Boarding Official

Public reporting for this collection of information is estimated to vary from ¼ hour to 7 hours per response for passenger vessels. The above includes the time for reviewing instructions, searching existing data sources, gathering and maintaining the data needed, and completing and reviewing the collection of information. Send comments regarding the burden estimate or any other aspect of this collection of information, including suggestions for reducing this burden to the Manager, Records Management Branch, Panama Canal Authority, 7801 NW 37 Street, Miami FL 33166 - 6559.

The information requested on the shipping and navigation forms will be used by the Panama Canal Authority for economic analysis of traffic, for development of traffic forecasts, and for budget and planning formulations. Further, the information will be used for identification, billing, safety, sanitation, evaluation and statistical purposes. Customs, quarantine, and immigration information is for use by Panama Government agencies. Some of the information is used by vessel agents to assist in expediting vessel transits through the Canal. As required, the information provided may be made available to other Panamanian Government agencies. The information requested on the shipping and navigation forms is required in order to transit the Panama Canal or to book a transit in advance (Maritime Regulations for the Operations of the Panama Canal)

FIG. 28 335

20
Rev. 3-2000

AUTORIDAD DEL CANAL DE PANAMÁ
PASSENGER LIST   Sheet No. ———

☐ Landing

☐ Transit

Vessel's Name: ————————————————

Last Port: ———————— Next port ————————

☐ Balboa ☐ Cristobal   Panama, ——————————,20 ———

	Last Name	First Name	M.I.	Nationality	Landing passengers only		
					Birthplace (Country)	Birthday (Day/Mo./Yr.)	Passport or travel document
1							
2							
3							
4							
5							
6							
7							
8							
9							
10							
11							
12							
13							
14							
15							
16							
17							
18							
19							
20							
21							
22							
23							
24							
25							
26							
27							
28							
29							
30							
31							
32							
33							
34							
35							
36							
37							
38							
39							
40							

The undersigned certifies that this list contains the names of all landing/transit, passengers of said vessel.

——————————————
Master

Continued on next page

BOARDING OFFICIAL WILL FILL IN BELOW THIS LINE

Hour boarded vessel _____

Master, SS _____ :You are hereby informed that the following-named person or persons now on board the vessel under your command is/are (a) to be detained on board while your vessel is within the waters of Panama Canal or (b) be delivered by you to the Immigration Officer at Balboa/Cristobal, Panama.

NAME OF PERSON	REASON FOR EXCLUSION	DISPOSITION

Above instructions received:

_____
Master

_____
Boarding Official

Inspected: Crew _____

Public reporting for this collection of information is estimated to vary from ½ hour to 7 hours per response for passenger vessels. The above includes the time for reviewing instructions, searching existing data sources, gathering and maintaining the data needed, and completing and reviewing the collection of information. Send comments regarding the burden estimate or any other aspect of this collection of information, including suggestions for reducing this burden to the Manager, Records Management Branch, Panama Canal Authority, 7801 NW 37 Street, Miami FL 33166 - 6559.

The information requested on the shipping and navigation forms will be used by the Panama Canal Authority for economic analysis of traffic, for development of traffic forecasts, and for budget and planning formulations. Further, the information will be used for identification, billing, safety, sanitation, evaluation and statistical purposes. Customs, quarantine, and immigration information is for use by Panamanian Government agencies. Some of the information is used by vessel agents to assist in expediting vessel transits through the Canal. As required, the information provided may be made available to other Panamanian Government agencies. The information requested on the shipping and navigation forms is required in order to-transit the Panama Canal or to book a transit in advance (Maritime Regulations for the Operations of the Panama Canal).

FIG. 29   337

United States Department of State

MARINE NOTE OF PROTEST

(22 United States Code 1173)

Port of _____

On this _____ day of _____ , 19 _____ , before me, _____

_____ , American _____ for

_____ and the dependencies thereof, personally appeared

_____ , Master of the vessel, called the_____

_____ of the burden of _____ tons or thereabout, and declared that on

the _____ day of _____ last past he/she sailed in and with the ship from the

port of _____ , laden with_____ , and arrived in the ship,

at _____ on _____ , and having
                                                                          (Insert the date and hour)

experienced _____
                        (State facts which constitute the protest)

_____

hereby enters this Note of Protest accordingly, to serve and avail him/her hereafter, if found necessary.

_____

_____ of the United States
of America.

Attested:

_____
                    Master

        [SEAL]
                                        _____   _____
                                              (Date)   *(Place)*

I HEREBY CERTIFY that the within document is a true copy of a Marine Note of Protest, the original of which
is deposited as a part of the permanent archives of the American Consulate

at _____

_____
                        (Signature of Officer)

_____ of the United States
        (Title)   of America.

FORM
4-84   FS-281d

Continued on next page

MARINE EXTENDED PROTEST

(22 United States Code 1173)

Port of _____

By this public instrument of declaration and protest be it known and made manifest to all whom these presents shall come or
may concern, that on the _____ day of _____ , 19 _____ , before _____ ,
American _____ for _____ , and dependencies
thereof, personally came and appeared _____ , Master of the vessel
called the _____ ,Official No. _____
of the burden of _____ tons or thereabout, then lying in this port of _____
_____laden with _____ cargo, who
duly noted and entered with the said _____
his/her protest, for the uses and purposes hereafter mentioned; and now, on this day, the_____ day of _____ ,
19 ____ before me, _____ , American _____
at_____ , comes the said _____ and requires me to extend this protest;
and together with the said Master also come _____ and
_____all crew
members of said ship, all of whom, being by me duly sworn, do voluntarily asseverate as follows: That these appears, on the_____
_____ day of _____ , sailed in and with the said _____ from the
port of _____ laden with _____and bound to the
port of _____ : That the said ship was then properly staffed and equipped in every respect
seaworthy; that* _____

And these said appearers, upon their oaths aforesaid, do further declare and say: That during the said voyage they, together with the
others of the said ship's company, used their utmost endeavors to preserve the said_____
and cargo from all manner of loss, damage, or injury. Wherefore the said_____ , Master has protested
in accordance with law and declares that all losses, damages, costs, charges, and expenses as stated herein that have happened to
the said _____ or cargo, or to either , are and ought to be borne
by those to whom the same by right may appertain by way of average or otherwise, the same having occurred as before mentioned,
and not by or through the insufficiency of the said_____ , the ship's tackle or apparel, or fault or neglect of this
appearer, his/her officers, or any of his/her mariners, or fault or neglect in the proper loading, stowage, custody, and care of the cargo.
This done and protested in the port of_____ this _____ day of _____ , 19 ____ .
IN TESTIMONY WHEREOF, these appearers have hereunto subscribed their names, and I, the said_____
_____ , have granted to the said Master this public instrument, under my
hand and the seal of this _____to serve and avail him/her, and all others whom it does or may concern as need and
occasion may require.

_____ ,*Master.*   _____

                                          Signature of Officer

_____ , *First Officer.* _____ of the United

                                                        States of America.

_____

                                          (Position in Crew)

_____

                                          (Position in Crew)

_____

* Here insert narrative of the facts of the voyage as they occurred, with full and minute particulars, with date, latitude, longitude, etc. If
additional

FIG. 30 339

NOTE OF PROTEST
Notary Form

State of_____County of_____City of_____

On this, the_____day of_____19____personally appeared

before me_____a Notary Public for and in the

State of_____at large in the city of_____

County of_____ _____ Master of
                          (Name of Master)

the S.S._____ of the burden of _____Tons
      (Name of vessel)   (Net tons)

or thereabouts, and declared that said vessel sailed on a voyage

from_____ on _____ bound for_____
  (Port of departure)   (Date)   (Name port)

with a cargo of_____Protests_____
                                 (Give state of weather,etc.)

_____

_____

_____

_____

and fearing damages from causes as above stated, the said Master

notes this, his Protest, before me, reserving the right to extend

the same at any time and place convenient.

                                              _____

Subscribed and sworn before me,   Master

this_____day of_____

19_____.

_____

(Notary's signature and seal)

SEVEN SEAS STEAMSHIP CORPORATION

S.S. SEVEN SEAS   STATEMENT OF FACTS   Voy.90

LOSS OF BLADE

		1965	EST	
(1) Lost blade in Lat.39-40N Long.70-00W		15 May	0415 Hrs	0945GMT
(2) Returning to New York		15 May	0510 "	
(3) Arrived Ambrose. Pilot on board		16 May	1310 "	
(4) Made fast, Todds Drydock #10		16 May	1730 "	
(5) Left Drydock		18 May	1300 "	
(6) Discharged Pilot;Departure Ambrose		18 May	1545 "	2045GMT
(7) Arrived Deviation point Lat.39-40 N. Long.70-00 W.		19 May	0450 "	0950GMT

	Date	Time	Dist	Fuel
From Lat. 39-40 N. Long. 70-00 W.	15 May	0415		8355
To: Ambrose Pilot	16 May	1310	192	
Todd Drydock #10	16 May	1730	23	8249
Left drydock	18 May	1300		8225
Departure Ambrose	18 May	1545	23	
Arrived Deviation point Lat.39-40 N. Long.70-00 W.	19 May	0450	192	8050

From Deviation point Lat.39-40 N. Long.70-00 W

To New York (Todds) and return   4days 00 hrs   45 min.

     Total distance   430 miles

     Fuel consumed   305 bbls.

      Chief Engineer   Master

FIG. 32   341

CHANGE LIST

S.S. __Seven Seas_____ Dept. ____Deck____ Voy. No. ___90_____

Total Wages	BILLS						CHANGE					Total
	$100	$50	$20	$10	$5	$1	50¢	25¢	10¢	5¢	1¢	
1,255.60	12	1			1		1		1			1,255.60
1,125.80	11		1		1		1	1		1		1,125.80
1,015.75	10			1	1		1	1				1,015.75
1,010.00	10			1								1,010.00
1,145.58	11		2		1		1			1	3	1,145.58
800.50	8						1					800.50
702.45	7					2		1	2			702.45
715.56	7			1	1		1			1	1	715.56
695.98	6	1	2		1		1	1	2		3	695.98
685.90	6	1	1	1	1		1	1	1	1		685.90
555.20	5	1			1				2			555.20
595.43	5	1	2		1			1	1	1	3	595.43
430.90	4		1	1			1	1	1	1		430.90
455.65	4	1			1		1		1	1		455.65
480.23	4	1	1	1					2		3	480.23
476.31	4	1	1		1	1	1		1	1		476.31
12,146.84	114	8	11	6	11	3	10	8	13	8	14	12,146.84

Hundreds	114 =	$11,400.00
Fifties	8 =	400.00
Twenties	11 =	220.00
Tens	6 =	60.00
Fives	11 =	55.00
Ones	3 =	3.00
Halves	10 =	5.00
Quarters	8 =	2.00
Dimes	13 =	1.30
Nickels	8 =	.40
Cents	14 =	.14
Deck Depart. total		$12,146.84

Other departments are made up in a similar manner or the entire crew can be put on one change list.

SEVEN SEAS STEAMSHIP CORPORATION
CHARTERING DIVISION
TIME SHEET

Name of vessel:_____Port_____

Cargo:_____Quantity_____

Arrival: Day_____Date_____Time_____

Draft before commencing: F_____A_____M_____S.G._____

Notice of Readiness served: Day_____Date_____Time_____

Notice accepted; Day_____Date_____Time_____

Docked or anchored: Day_____Date_____Time_____

Commenced Loading/Discharging: Day_____Date_____Time_____

Completed Loading/Discharging: Day_____Date_____Time_____

Draft on completing Load./Disch.F_____A_____M_____S.G._____

Undocked: Day_____Date_____Time_____

Sailed: Day_____Date_____Time_____

TIME WORKED. LIST SUNDAYS AND HOLIDAYS WHERE THEY OCCUR.

Day:_____Date:_____From:_____To:_____Hours_____Min._____

Day:_____Date:_____From:_____To:_____Hours_____Min._____

Day:_____Date:_____From:_____To:_____Hours_____Min._____

Day:_____Date:_____From:_____To:_____Hours_____Min._____

Day:_____Date:_____From:_____To:_____Hours_____Min._____

Day:_____Date:_____From:_____To:_____Hours_____Min._____

Day:_____Date:_____From:_____To:_____Hours_____Min._____

TIME NOT WORKED ACCOUNT OF WEATHER, HOLIDAYS, GEAR BREAKDOWN,ETC.

Day:_____Date:_____From:_____To:_____Reason_____

Day:_____Date:_____From:_____To:_____Reason_____

Day:_____Date:_____From:_____To:_____Reason_____

	DAYS	HOURS	MIN.

Total Time Used:

Time Allowed:_____Per Charter Party.

Despatch/Demurrage:
Signed without prejudice to any of the terms, conditions and
exceptions of governing charter party.

_____   _____
Charterer's Agent   Master

FIG. 34   343

SEVEN SEAS STEAMSHIP CORPORATION

STEVEDORE DAMAGE REPORT
To
Ship, Cargo, Equipment
Or Gear.

S.S._____VOY. NO._____PORT_____

DATE OF THIS REPORT_____

DATE AND TIME OF DAMAGE_____

EXTENT OF DAMAGE_____

HOW DID DAMAGE OCCUR?_____

WAS SHIP'S GEAR AT FAULT? EXPLAIN_____

WAS DAMAGE SURVEYED?_____DATE_____PORT_____

NAMES OF THOSE ATTENDING SURVEY_____

WAS DAMAGE TO

VESSEL REPAIRED?_____TEMPORARILY_____PERMANENTLY_____

DATE OF REPAIRS_____PORT_____

WAS FULL COST OF REPAIRS PAID BY STEVEDORES?_____

_____   _____
   CHIEF OFFICER   MASTER

RECEIVED COPY OF THE ABOVE REPORT: DATE_____TIME_____

            I/WE ADMIT
                  DENY   LIABILITY_____
                                         STEVEDORE

                         ADDRESS_____

THIS REPORT TO BE MADE UP WHEN DAMAGE IS CAUSED BY STEVEDORE, BARGEE,
LIGHTERMEN, REPAIRMEN, ETC.

Six copies of this report are to be made up and distributed as

follows: One copy to stevedore or other causing damage.
         Three copies to home office, attention Insurance Dept.
         One copy to Agent.
         One copy for vessel's file.

FIG. 35

VESSEL DATA

S.S._____CALL LETTERS_____OFFICIAL NUMBER_____

HOME PORT _____	PANAMA CANAL TONNAGE:
NET TONNAGE _____	NET _____
GROSS TONNAGE _____	GROSS _____
DISPLACEMENT: SUMMER _____TONS	SUEZ CANAL TONNAGE:
" WINTER _____TONS	NET _____
" TROPICAL _____TONS	GROSS _____
DEADWEIGHT: SUMMER _____TONS	HORSEPOWER _____
" WINTER _____TONS	SPEED, NORMAL _____
" TROPICAL _____TONS	PROPELLER DIAM. _____
DRAFT: SUMMER _____	" PITCH _____
DRAFT: WINTER _____	LENGTH O.A. _____
DRAFT: TROPICAL _____	LENGTH REG. _____
F.W. ALLOWANCE _____	LENGTH B.P. _____
FREEBOARD: SUMMER _____	BREADTH, MLD _____
FREEBOARD: WINTER _____	DEPTH " _____
FREEBOARD: TROPICAL _____	WHERE BUILT _____
CAPACITY: BALE _____CU.FT.	DATE BUILT _____
CAPACITY: GRAIN _____CU.FT.	LENGTH OF ANCHOR CHAIN
F.W. CAPACITY _____TONS	PORT _____ STBD._____ SIZE _____
CONSUMPTION PER DAY _____TONS	WEIGHT OF ANCHORS
FUEL CAPACITY: _____BBLS	PORT _____ STBD._____
CONSUMPTION:	SPARE ANCHOR _____
PER DAY, STEAMING, LOADED _____BBLS	STREAM _____ KEDGE _____
PER DAY, STEAMING, LIGHT _____BBLS	BBLS PER MILE, LOADED
IN PORT, WORKING _____BBLS	BBLS PER MILE, LIGHT
IN PORT, IDLE _____BBLS	

FIG. 36   345

LOF 2000

LLOYD'S STANDARD FORM OF
SALVAGE AGREEMENT

(APPROVED AND PUBLISHED BY THE COUNCIL OF LLOYD'S)

NO CURE - NO PAY

1. Name of the salvage Contractors: (referred to in this agreement as "the Contractors")	2. Property to be salved. The vessel: her cargo freight bunkers stores and any other property thereon but excluding the personal effects or baggage of passengers master or crew (referred to in this agreement as "the property")
3. Agreed place of safety:	4. Agreed currency of any arbitral award and security (if other than United States dollars)
5. Date of this agreement:	6. Place of agreement:
7. Is the Scopic Clause incorporated into this agreement? State alternative : Yes/No	
8. Person signing for and on behalf of the Contractors Signature:	9. Captain or other person signing for and on behalf of the property Signature:

A. **Contractors' basic obligation:** The Contractors identified in Box 1 hereby agree to use their best endeavours to salve the property specified in Box 2 and to take the property to the place stated in Box 3 or to such other place as may hereafter be agreed. If no place is inserted in Box 3 and in the absence of any subsequent agreement as to the place where the property is to be taken the Contractors shall take the property to a place of safety.

B. **Environmental protection:** While performing the salvage services the Contractors shall also use their best endeavours to prevent or minimise damage to the environment.

Continued on next page

C. **Scopic Clause:** Unless the word "No" in Box 7 has been deleted this agreement shall be deemed to have been made on the basis that the Scopic Clause is not incorporated and forms no part of this agreement. If the word "No" is deleted in Box 7 this shall not of itself be construed as a notice invoking the Scopic Clause within the meaning of sub-clause 2 thereof.

D. **Effect of other remedies:** Subject to the provisions of the International Convention on Salvage 1989 as incorporated into English law ("the Convention") relating to special compensation and to the Scopic Clause if incorporated the Contractors' services shall be rendered and accepted as salvage services upon the principle of "no cure - no pay" and any salvage remuneration to which the Contractors become entitled shall not be diminished by reason of the exception to the principle of "no cure - no pay" in the form of special compensation or remuneration payable to the Contractors under a Scopic Clause.

E. **Prior services:** Any salvage services rendered by the Contractors to the property before and up to the date of this agreement shall be deemed to be covered by this agreement.

F. **Duties of property owners:** Each of the owners of the property shall cooperate fully with the Contractors. In particular:

   (i) the Contractors may make reasonable use of the vessel's machinery gear and equipment free of expense provided that the Contractors shall not unnecessarily damage abandon or sacrifice any property on board;

   (ii) the Contractors shall be entitled to all such information as they may reasonably require relating to the vessel or the remainder of the property provided such information is relevant to the performance of the services and is capable of being provided without undue difficulty or delay;

   (iii) the owners of the property shall co-operate fully with the Contractors in obtaining entry to the place of safety stated in Box 3 or agreed or determined in accordance with Clause A.

G. **Rights of termination:** When there is no longer any reasonable prospect of a useful result leading to a salvage reward in accordance with Convention Articles 12 and/or 13 either the owners of the vessel or the Contractors shall be entitled to terminate the services hereunder by giving reasonable prior written notice to the other.

H. **Deemed performance:** The Contractors' services shall be deemed to have been performed when the property is in a safe condition in the place of safety stated in Box 3 or agreed or determined in accordance with Clause A. For the purpose of this provision the property shall be regarded as being in safe condition notwithstanding that the property (or part thereof) is damaged or in need of maintenance if (i) the Contractors are not obliged to remain in attendance to satisfy the requirements of any port or harbour authority, governmental agency or similar authority and (ii) the continuation of skilled salvage services from the Contractors or other salvors is no longer necessary to avoid the property becoming lost or significantly further damaged or delayed.

I. **Arbitration and the LSSA Clauses:** The Contractors' remuneration and/or special compensation shall be determined by arbitration in London in the manner prescribed by Lloyd's Standard Salvage and Arbitration Clauses ("the LSSA Clauses") and Lloyd's Procedural Rules. The provisions of the LSSA Clauses and Lloyd's Procedural Rules are deemed to be incorporated in this agreement and form an integral part hereof. Any other difference arising out of this agreement or the operations hereunder shall be referred to arbitration in the same way.

J. **Governing law:** This agreement and any arbitration hereunder shall be governed by English law.

K. **Scope of authority:** The Master or other person signing this agreement on behalf of the property identified in Box 2 enters into this agreement as agent for the respective owners thereof and binds each (but not the one for the other or himself personally) to the due performance thereof.

L. **Inducements prohibited:** No person signing this agreement or any party on whose behalf it is signed shall at any time or in any manner whatsoever offer provide make give or promise to provide or demand or take any form of inducement for entering into this agreement.

IMPORTANT NOTICES :

1. **Salvage security.** As soon as possible the owners of the vessel should notify the owners of other property on board that this agreement has been made. If the Contractors are successful the owners of such property should note that it will become necessary to provide the Contractors with salvage security promptly in accordance with Clause 4 of the LSSA Clauses referred to in Clause I. The provision of General Average security does not relieve the salved interests of their separate obligation to provide salvage security to the Contractors.

2. **Incorporated provisons.** Copies of the Scopic Clause; the LSSA Clauses and Lloyd's Procedural Rules may be obtained from (i) the Contractors or (ii) the Salvage Arbitration Branch at Lloyd's, One Lime Street, London EC3M 7HA.

Tel.No. + 44(0)20 7327 5408

Fax No. +44(0)20 7327 6827

E-mail: lloyds-salvage@lloyds.com.

www.lloyds.com

LLOYD'S

15.1.08
3.12.24
13.10.26
12.4.50
10.6.53
20.12.67
23.2.72
21.5.80
5.9.90
1.1.95
1.9.2000

FIG. 37　　　　347

LOF 1995

LLOYD'S

STANDARD FORM OF

SALVAGE AGREEMENT

(APPROVED AND PUBLISHED BY THE COUNCIL OF LLOYD'S)

NO CURE - NO PAY

On board the_____

Dated_____

NOTES

1. *Insert name of person signing on behalf of Owners of property to be salved. The Master should sign wherever possible.*

2. *The Contractor's name should always be inserted in line 4 and whenever the Agreement is signed by the Master of the Salving vessel or other person on behalf of the Contractor the name of the Master or other person must also be inserted in line 4 before the words "for and on behalf of." The words "for and on behalf of" should be deleted where a Contractor signs personally.*

3. *Insert place if agreed in clause 1(a)(i) and currency if agreed in clause 1(e).*

IT IS HEREBY AGREED between Captain[1]_____ for and on behalf of the Owners of the "_____ _____" her cargo, freight, bunkers, stores, and any other property thereon (hereinafter collectively called "the Owners") and _____ for and on behalf of _____ (hereinafter called "the Contractor"[2]) that:–

1.　(a)　The Contractor shall use his best endeavors:–

　　(i)　to salve the " _____ "and/or her cargo, freight, bunkers, stores, and any other property thereon and take them to[3] ___ _____ or to such other place as may hereafter be agreed either place to be deemed a place of safety or if no such place is named or agreed to a place of safety and

　　(ii)　while performing the salvage services to prevent or minimize damage to the environment.

　　(b)　Subject to the statutory provisions relating to special compensation the services shall be rendered and accepted as salvage services upon the principle of "no cure - no pay."

　　(c)　The Contractor's remuneration shall be fixed by Arbitration in London in the manner hereinafter prescribed and any other difference arising out of this Agreement or the operations thereunder shall be referred to Arbitration in the same way.

　　(d)　In the event of the services referred to in this Agreement or any part of such services having been already rendered at the date of this Agreement by the Contractor to the said vessel and/or her cargo freight bunkers stores and any other property thereon the provisions of this Agreement shall apply to such services.

　　(e)　The security to be provided to the Council of Lloyd's (hereinafter called "the Council") the Salved Value(s) the Award and/or any Interim Award(s) and/or any Award on Appeal shall be in[3] _____ currency.

Continued on next page

(f) If clause 1(e) is not completed then the security to be provided and the Salved Value(s) the Award and/or Interim Award(s) and/or Award on Appeal shall be in Pounds Sterling.

(g) This Agreement and Arbitration thereunder shall except as otherwise expressly provided be governed by the law of England, including the English law of salvage.

PROVISIONS AS TO THE SERVICES

2. *Definitions:* In this Agreement any reference to "Convention" is a reference to the International Convention on Salvage 1989 as incorporated in the Merchant Shipping (Salvage and Pollution) Act 1994 (and any amendment thereto). The terms "Contractor" and "services"/"salvage services" in this Agreement shall have the same meanings as the terms "salvor(s)" and "salvage operation(s)" in the Convention.

3. *Owners Cooperation:* The Owners their Servants and Agents shall co-operate fully with the Contractor in and about the salvage including obtaining entry to the place named or the place of safety as defined in clause 1. The Contractor may make reasonable use of the vessel's machinery, gear, equipment, anchors, chains, stores, and other appurtenances during and for the purpose of the salvage services free of expense but shall not unnecessarily damage, abandon, or sacrifice the same or any property the subject of this Agreement.

4. *Vessel Owners Right to Terminate:* When there is no longer any reasonable prospect of a useful result leading to a salvage reward in accordance with Convention Article 13, the owners of the vessel shall be entitled to terminate the services of the Contractor by giving reasonable notice to the Contractor in writing.

PROVISIONS AS TO SECURITY

5. (a) The Contractor shall immediately after the termination of the services or sooner notify the Council and where practicable the Owners, of the amount for which he demands salvage security (inclusive of costs, expenses, and interest) from each of the respective Owners.

(b) Where a claim is made or may be made for special compensation, the owners of the vessel shall, on the demand of the Contractor whenever made, provide security for the Contractor's claim for special compensation, provided always that such demand is made within two years of the date of termination of the services.

(c) The amount of any such security shall be reasonable in the light of the knowledge available to the Contractor at the time when the demand is made. Unless otherwise agreed such security shall be provided (i) to the Council (ii) in a form approved by the Council and (iii) by persons, firms, or corporations either acceptable to the Contractor or resident in the United Kingdom and acceptable to the Council. The Council shall not be responsible for the sufficiency (whether in amount or otherwise) of any security which shall be provided nor the default or insolvency of any person firm or corporation providing the same.

(d) The owners of the vessel their Servants and Agents shall use their best endeavors to ensure that the cargo owners provide their proportion of salvage security before the cargo is released.

6. (a) Until security has been provided as aforesaid the Contractor shall have a maritime lien on the property salved for his remuneration.

FIG. 37—*Continued* **349**

(b) The property salved shall not, without the consent in writing of the Contractor (which shall not be unreasonably withheld), be removed from the place to which it has been taken by the contractor under clause 1(a). Where such consent is given by the Contractor on condition that the Contractor is provided with temporary security pending completion of the voyage the Contractor's maritime lien on the property salved shall remain in force to the extent necessary to enable the Contractor to compel the provision of security in accordance with clause 5(c).

(c) The Contractor shall not arrest or detain the property salved unless:–

(i) security is not provided within 14 days (exclusive of Saturdays or Sundays or other days observed as general holidays at Lloyd's) after the date of the termination of the services or

(ii) he has reason to believe that the removal of the property salved is contemplated contrary to clause 6(b) or

(iii) any attempt is made to remove the property salved contrary to clause 6(b).

(d) The Arbitrator appointed under clause 7 or the Appeal Arbitrator(s) appointed under clause 13(d) shall have power in their absolute discretion to include in the amount awarded to the Contractor the whole or part of any expenses reasonably incurred by the Contractor in:–

(i) ascertaining demanding and obtaining the amount of security reasonably required in accordance with clause 5.

(ii) enforcing and/or protecting by insurance or otherwise or taking reasonable steps to enforce and/or protect his lien.

PROVISIONS AS TO ARBITRATION

7. (a) Whether security has been provided or not, the Council shall appoint an Arbitrator upon receipt of a written request made by letter, telex, facsimile, or in any other permanent form provided that any party requesting such appointment shall if required by the Council undertake to pay the reasonable fees and expenses of the Council and/or any Arbitrator or Appeal Arbitrator(s).

(b) Where an Arbitrator has been appointed and the parties do not proceed to arbitration the Council may recover any fees, costs, and/or expenses which are outstanding.

8. The Contractor's remuneration and/or special compensation shall be fixed by the Arbitrator appointed under clause 7. Such remuneration shall not be diminished by reason of the exception to the principle of "no cure - no pay" in the form of special compensation.

REPRESENTATION

9. Any party to this Agreement who wishes to be heard or to adduce evidence shall nominate a person in the United Kingdom to represent him, failing which the Arbitrator or Appeal Arbitrator(s) may proceed as if such party had renounced his right to be heard or adduce evidence.

CONDUCT OF THE ARBITRATION

10. (a) The Arbitrator shall have power to:-

(i) admit such oral or documentary evidence or information as he may think fit

(ii) conduct the Arbitration in such manner in all respects as he may think fit subject to such procedural rules as the Council may approve

Continued on next page

(iii) order the Contractor in his absolute discretion to pay the whole or part of the expense of providing excessive security or security which has been unreasonably demanded under clause 5(b) and to deduct such sum from the remuneration and/or special compensation

(iv) make Interim Award(s) including payment(s) on account on such terms as may be fair and just

(v) make such orders as to costs fees and expenses including those of the Council charged under clauses 10(b) and 14(b) as may be fair and just.

(b) The Arbitrator and the Council may charge reasonable fees and expenses for their services whether the Arbitration proceeds to a hearing or not and all such fees and expenses shall be treated as part of the costs of the Arbitration.

(c) Any Award shall (subject to Appeal as provided in this Agreement) be final and binding on all the parties concerned whether they were represented at the Arbitration or not.

INTEREST & RATES OF EXCHANGE

11. *Interest:* Interest at rates per annum to be fixed by the Arbitrator shall (subject to Appeal as provided in this Agreement) be payable on any sum awarded taking into account sums already paid:-

(i) from the date of termination of the services unless the Arbitrator shall in his absolute discretion otherwise decide until the date of publication by the Council of the Award and/or Interim Award(s) and

(ii) from the expiration of 21 days (exclusive of Saturdays and Sundays or other days observed as general holidays at Lloyd's) after the date of publication by the Council of the Award and/or Interim Award(s) until the date payment is received by the Contractor or the Council, both dates inclusive.

For the purpose of sub-clause (ii) the expression "sum awarded" shall include the fees and expenses referred to in clause 10(b).

12. *Currency Correction:* In considering what sums of money have been expended by the Contractor in rendering the services and/or in fixing the amount of the Award and/or Interim Award(s) and/or Award on Appeal the Arbitrator or Appeal Arbitrator(s) shall to such an extent and, in so far as it may be fair and just in all the circumstances, give effect to the consequences of any change or changes in the relevant rates of exchange which may have occurred between the date of termination of the services and the date on which the Award and/or Interim Award(s) and/or Award on Appeal is made.

PROVISIONS AS TO APPEAL

13. (a) Notice of Appeal if any shall be given to the Council within 14 days (exclusive of Saturdays and Sundays or other days observed as general holidays at Lloyd's) after the date of the publication by the Council of the Award and/or Interim Award(s).

(b) Notice of Cross-Appeal if any shall be given to the Council within 14 days (exclusive of Saturdays and Sundays or other days observed as general holidays at Lloyd's) after notification by the Council to the parties of any Notice of Appeal. Such notification if sent by post shall be deemed received on the working day following the day of posting.

(c) Notice of Appeal or Cross-Appeal shall be given to the Council by letter, telex, facsimile, or in any other permanent form.

FIG. 37—*Continued* 351

(d) Upon receipt of Notice of Appeal the Council shall refer the Appeal to the hearing and determination of the Appeal Arbitrator(s) selected by it.

(e) If any Notice of Appeal or Cross-Appeal is withdrawn the Appeal hearing shall nevertheless proceed in respect of such Notice of Appeal or Cross-Appeal as may remain.

(f) Any Award on Appeal shall be final and binding on all the parties to that Appeal Arbitration whether they were represented either at the Arbitration or at the Appeal Arbitration or not.

CONDUCT OF THE APPEAL

14. (a) The Appeal Arbitrator(s) in addition to the powers of the Arbitrator under clauses 10(a) and 11 shall have power to:-

(i) admit the evidence which was before the Arbitrator together with the Arbitrator's notes and reasons for his Award and/or Interim Award(s) and any transcript of evidence and such additional evidence as he or they may think fit.

(ii) confirm, increase, or reduce the sum awarded by the Arbitrator and to make such order as to the payment of interest on such sum as he or they may think fit.

(iii) confirm, revoke, or vary any order and/or Declaratory Award made by the Arbitrator.

(iv) award interest on any fees and expenses charged under paragraph (b) of this clause from the expiration of 21 days (exclusive of Saturdays and Sundays or other days observed as general holidays at Lloyd's) after the date of publication by the Council of the Award on Appeal and/or Interim Award(s) on Appeal until the date payment is received by the Council, both dates inclusive.

(b) The Appeal Arbitrator(s) and the Council may charge reasonable fees and expenses for their services in connection with the Appeal Arbitration whether it proceeds to a hearing or not and all such fees and expenses shall be treated as part of the costs of the Appeal Arbitration.

PROVISIONS AS TO PAYMENT

15. (a) In case of Arbitration, if no Notice of Appeal be received by the Council in accordance with clause 13(a) the Council shall call upon the party or parties concerned to pay the amount awarded and in the event of non-payment, shall subject to the Contractor first providing to the Council a satisfactory Undertaking to pay all the costs thereof realize or enforce the security and pay therefrom to the Contractor (whose receipt shall be a good discharge to it) the amount awarded to him together with interest if any. The Contractor shall reimburse the parties concerned to such extent as the Award is less than any sums paid on account or in respect of Interim Award(s).

(b) If Notice of Appeal be received by the Council in accordance with clause 13, it shall, as soon as the Award on Appeal has been published by it, call upon the party or parties concerned to pay the amount awarded and in the event of non-payment shall subject to the Contractor first providing to the Council a satisfactory Undertaking to pay all the costs thereof realize or enforce the security and pay therefrom to the Contractor (whose receipt shall be a good discharge to it) the amount awarded to him together with interest if any. The Contractor shall reimburse the parties concerned to such extent as the Award on Appeal is less than any sums paid on account or in respect of the Award or Interim Award(s).

Continued on next page

(c) If any sum shall become payable to the Contractor as remuneration for his services and/or interest and/or costs as the result of an agreement made between the Contractor and the Owners or any of them the Council in the event of non-payment shall subject to the Contractor first providing to the Council a satisfactory Undertaking to pay all the costs thereof realize or enforce the security and pay therefrom to the Contractor (whose receipt shall be a good discharge to it) the said sum.

(d) If the Award and/or Interim Award(s) and/or Award on Appeal provides or provide that the costs of the Arbitration and/or of the Appeal Arbitration or any part of such costs shall be borne by the Contractor, such costs may be deducted from the amount awarded or agreed before payment is made to the Contractor unless satisfactory security is provided by the Contractor for the payment of such costs.

(e) Without prejudice to the provisions of clause 5(c) the liability of the Council shall be limited in any event to the amount of security provided to it.

GENERAL PROVISIONS

16. *Scope of Authority:* The Master or other person signing this Agreement on behalf of the property to be salved enters into this Agreement as agent for the vessel, her cargo, freight, bunkers, stores, and any other property thereon, and the respective Owners thereof and binds each (but not the one for the other or himself personally) to the due performance thereof.

17. *Notices:* Any Award notice authority order or other document signed by the Chairman of Lloyd's or any person authorized by the Council for the purpose shall be deemed to have been duly made or given by the Council and shall have the same force and effect in all respects as if it had been signed by every member of the Council.

18. *Sub-Contractor(s):* The Contractor may claim salvage and enforce any Award or agreement made between the Contractor and the Owners against security provided under clause 5 or otherwise, if any, on behalf of any Sub-Contractors, his or their Servants, or Agents including Masters and members of the crews of vessels employed by him or by any Sub-Contractors in the services provided that he first provides a reasonably satisfactory indemnity to the Owners against all claims by or liabilities to the said persons.

19. *Inducements prohibited:* No person signing this Agreement or any party on whose behalf it is signed shall at any time or in any manner whatsoever offer, provide, make, give, or promise to provide, demand, or take any form of inducement for entering into this Agreement.

For and on behalf of the Contractor	**For and on behalf of the Owners of property to be salved.**
(To be signed by the Contractor personally or by the Master of the salving vessel or other person whose name is inserted in line 4 of this Agreement.)	(To be signed by the Master or other person whose name is inserted in line 1 of this Agreement.)

INTERNATIONAL CONVENTION ON SALVAGE 1989
The following provisions of the Convention are set out for information only.

FIG. 37—*Continued* 353

Article I

Definitions

(a) *Salvage operation* means any act or activity undertaken to assist a vessel or any other property in danger in navigable waters or in any other waters whatsoever

(b) *Vessel* means any ship or craft, or any structure capable of navigation

(c) *Property* means any property not permanently and intentionally attached to the shoreline and includes freight at risk

(d) *Damage to the environment* means substantial physical damage to human health or to marine life or resources in coastal or inland waters or areas adjacent thereto, caused by pollution, contamination, fire, explosion or similar major incidents

(e) *Payment* means any reward, remuneration or compensation due under this Convention

Article 6

Salvage Contracts

1. This Convention shall apply to any salvage operations save to the extent that a contract otherwise provides expressly or by implication.

2. The master shall have the authority to conclude contracts for salvage operations on behalf of the owner of the vessel. The master or owner of the vessel shall have the authority to conclude such contracts on behalf of the owner of the property on board the vessel.

Article 8

Duties of the Salvor and of the Owner and Master

1. The salvor shall owe a duty to the owner of the vessel or other property in danger:

(a) to carry out the salvage operations with due care;

(b) in performing the duty specified in subparagraph (a), to exercise due care to prevent or minimize damage to the environment;

(c) whenever circumstances reasonably require, to seek assistance from other salvors; and

(d) to accept the intervention of other salvors when reasonably requested to do so by the owner or master of the vessel or other property in danger; provided however that the amount of his reward shall not be prejudiced should it be found that such a request was unreasonable.

2. The owner and master of the vessel or the owner of other property in danger shall owe a duty to the salvor:

(a) to co-operate fully with him during the course of the salvage operations;

(b) in so doing, to exercise due care to prevent or minimize damage to the environment; and

(c) when the vessel or other property has been brought to a place of safety, to accept redelivery when reasonably requested by the salvor to do so.

Article 13

Criteria for Fixing the Reward

1. The reward shall be fixed with a view to encouraging salvage operations, taking into account the following criteria without regard to the order in which they are presented below:

Continued on next page

(a) the salved value of the vessel and other property;

(b) the skill and efforts of the salvors in preventing or minimizing damage to the environment;

(c) the measure of success obtained by the salvor;

(d) the nature and degree of the danger;

(e) the skill and efforts of the salvors in salving the vessel, other property and life;

(f) the time used and expenses and losses incurred by the salvors;

(g) the risk of liability and other risks run by the salvors or their equipment;

(h) the promptness of the services rendered;

(i) the availability and use of vessels or other equipment intended for salvage operations;

(j) the state of readiness and efficiency of the salvor's equipment and the value thereof

2. Payment of a reward fixed according to paragraph 1 shall be made by all of the vessel and other property interests in proportion to their respective salved values

3. The rewards, exclusive of any interest and recoverable legal costs that may be payable thereon, shall not exceed the salved value of the vessel and other property

Article 14

Special Compensation

1. If the salvor has carried out salvage operations in respect of a vessel which by itself or its cargo threatened damage to the environment and has failed to earn a reward under Article 13 at least equivalent to the special compensation assessable in accordance with this Article, he shall be entitled to special compensation from the owner of that vessel equivalent to his expenses as herein defined

2. If, in the circumstances set out in paragraph 1, the salvor by his salvage operations has prevented or minimized damage to the environment, the special compensation payable by the owner to the salvor under paragraph 1 may be increased up to a maximum of 30% of the expenses incurred by the salvor. However, the Tribunal, if it deems it fair and just to do so and bearing in mind the relevant criteria set out in Article 13, paragraph 1, may increase such special compensation further, but in no event shall the total increase be more than 100% of the expenses incurred by the salvor

3. Salvor's expenses for the purpose of paragraphs 1 and 2 means the out-of-pocket expenses reasonably incurred by the salvor in the salvage operation and a fair rate for equipment and personnel actually and reasonably used in the salvage operation, taking into consideration the criteria set out in Article 13, paragraph 1(h), (i) and (j)

4. The total special compensation under this Article shall be paid only if and to the extent that such compensation is greater than any reward recoverable by the salvor under Article 13

5. If the salvor has been negligent and has thereby failed to prevent or minimize damage to the environment, he may be deprived of the whole or part of any compensation due under this Article

6. Nothing in this Article shall affect any right of recourse on the part of the owner of the vessel

FIG. 38   355

SCOPIC 2000
SPECIAL COMPENSATION PROTECTION AND INDEMNITY CLUB (SCOPIC) CLAUSE

1. General
This SCOPIC clause is supplementary to any Lloyd's Form Salvage Agreement "No Cure - No Pay" ("Main Agreement") which incorporates the provisions of Article 14 of the International Convention on Salvage 1989 ("Article 14"). The definitions in the Main Agreement are incorporated into this SCOPIC clause. If the SCOPIC clause is inconsistent with any provisions of the Main Agreement or inconsistent with the law applicable hereto, the SCOPIC clause, once invoked under sub-clause 2 hereof, shall override such other provisions to the extent necessary to give business efficacy to the agreement. Subject to the provisions of Clause 4 hereof, the method of assessing Special Compensation under Convention Article 14(1) to 14(4) inclusive shall be submitted by the method of assessment set out hereinafter. If this SCOPIC clause has been incorporated into the Main Agreement the Contractor may make no claim pursuant to Article 14 except in the circumstances described in sub-clause 4 hereof. For the purposes of liens and time limits the services hereunder will be treated in the same manner as salvage.

2. Invoking the SCOPIC Clause
The Contractor shall have the option to invoke by written notice to the owners of the vessel, the SCOPIC clause set out hereafter at any time of his choosing regardless of the circumstances and, in particular, regardless of whether or not there is a "threat of damage to the environment". The assessment of SCOPIC remuneration shall commence from the time the written notice is given to the owners of the vessel and services rendered before the said written notice shall not be remunerated under this SCOPIC clause at all but in accordance with Convention Article 13 as incorporated into the Main Agreement ("Article 13").

3. Security for SCOPIC Remuneration

(i) The owners of the vessel shall provide to the Contractor within 2 working days (excluding Saturdays and Sundays and holidays usually observed at Lloyd's) after receiving written notice from the contractor invoking the SCOPIC clause, a bank guarantee or P&I Club letter (hereinafter called "The Initial Security") in a form reasonably satisfactory to the Contractor providing security for his claim for SCOPIC remuneration in the sum of US$3 million, inclusive of interest and costs.

(ii) If, at any time after the provision of the Initial Security the owners of the vessel reasonably assess the SCOPIC remuneration plus interest and costs due hereunder to be less than the security in place, the owners of the vessel shall be entitled to require the Contractor to reduce the security to a reasonable sum and the Contractor shall be obliged to do so once a reasonable sum has been agreed.

(iii) If at any time after the provision of the Initial Security the Contractor reasonably assesses the SCOPIC remuneration plus interest and costs due hereunder to be

Continued on next page

greater than the security in place, the Contractor shall be entitled to require the owners of the vessel to increase the security to a reasonable sum and the owners of the vessel shall be obliged to do so once a reasonable sum has been agreed.

(iv) In the absence of agreement, any dispute concerning the proposed Guarantor, the form of the security or the amount of any reduction or increase in the security in place shall be resolved by the Arbitrator.

4.   Withdrawal

If the owners of the vessel do not provide the Initial Security within the said 2 working days, the Contractor, at his option, and on giving notice to the owners of the vessel, shall be entitled to withdraw from all the provisions of the SCOPIC clause and revert to his rights under the Main Agreement including Article 14 which shall apply as if the SCOPIC clause had not existed. PROVIDED THAT this right of withdrawal may only be exercised if, at the time of giving the said notice of withdrawal the owners of the vessel have still not provided the Initial Security or any alternative security which the owners of the vessel and the Contractor may agree will be sufficient.

5.   Tariff Rates

(i)   SCOPIC remuneration shall mean the total of the tariff rates of personnel; tugs and other craft; portable salvage equipment; out of pocket expenses; and bonus due.

(ii)   SCOPIC remuneration in respect of all personnel; tugs and other craft; and portable salvage equipment shall be assessed on a time and materials basis in accordance with the Tariff set out in Appendix "A". This tariff will apply until reviewed and amended by the SCR Committee in accordance with Appendix B(l)(b). The tariff rates which will be used to calculate SCOPIC remuneration are those in force at the time the salvage services take place.

(iii)   "Out of pocket" expenses shall mean all those monies reasonably paid by or for and on behalf of the Contractor to any third party and in particular includes the hire of men, tugs, other craft and equipment used and other expenses reasonably necessary for the operation. They will be agreed at cost, PROVIDED THAT:

(a)   If the expenses relate to the hire of men, tugs, other craft and equipment from another ISU member or their affiliate(s), the amount due will be calculated on the tariff rates set out in Appendix "A" regardless of the actual cost.

(b)   If men, tugs, other craft and equipment are hired from any party who is not an ISU member and the hire rate is greater than the tariff rates referred to in Appendix "A" the actual cost will be allowed in full, subject to the Shipowner's Casualty Representative ("SCR") being satisfied that in the particular circumstances of the case, it was reasonable for the Contractor to hire such items at that cost. If an SCR is not appointed or if there is a dispute, then the Arbitrator shall decide whether the expense was reasonable in all in the circumstances.

(iv)   In addition to the rates set out above and any out of pocket expenses, the Contractor shall be entitled to a standard bonus of 25% of those rates except that if the out of pocket expenses described in sub-paragraph 5(iii)(b) exceed the applicable tariff rates in Appendix "A" the Contractor shall be entitled to a bonus such that he shall receive in total

(a)   The actual cost of such men, tugs, other craft and equipment plus 10% of the tariff rate, or

FIG. 38—*Continued* 357

(b) The tariff rate for such men, tugs, other craft and equipment plus 25% of the tariff rate whichever is the greater.

6. Article 13 Award

(i) The salvage services under the Main Agreement shall continue to be assessed in accordance with Article 13, even if the Contractor has invoked the SCOPIC clause. SCOPIC remuneration as assessed under sub-clause 5 above will be payable only by the owners of the vessel and only to the extent that it exceeds the total Article 13 Award (or, if none, any potential Article 13 Award) payable by all salved interests (including cargo, bunkers, lubricating oil and stores) after currency adjustment but before interest and costs even if the Article 13 Award or any part of it is not recovered.

(ii) In the event of the Article 13 Award or settlement being in a currency other than United States dollars it shall, for the purposes of the SCOPIC clause, be exchanged at the rate of exchange prevailing at the termination of the services under the Main Agreement.

(iii) The salvage award under Article 13 shall not be diminished by reason of the exception to the principle of "No Cure - No Pay" in the form of SCOPIC remuneration.

7. Discount
If the SCOPIC clause is invoked under sub-clause 2 hereof and the Article 13 Award or settlement (after currency adjustment but before interest and costs) under the Main Agreement is greater than the assessed SCOPIC remuneration then, notwithstanding the actual date on which the SCOPIC remuneration provisions were invoked, the said Article 13 Award or settlement shall be discounted by 25% of the difference between the said Article 13 Award or settlement and the amount of SCOPIC remuneration that would have been assessed had the SCOPIC remuneration provisions been invoked on the first day of the services.

8. Payment of SCOPIC Remuneration

(i) The date for payment of any SCOPIC remuneration which may be due hereunder will vary according to the circumstances.

(a) If there is no potential salvage award within the meaning of Article 13 as incorporated into the Main Agreement then, subject to Appendix B(5)(c)(iv), the undisputed amount of SCOPIC remuneration due hereunder will be paid by the owners of the vessel within 1 month of the presentation of the claim. Interest on sums due will accrue from the date of termination of the services until the date of payment at US prime rate plus 1%.

(b) If there is a claim for an Article 13 salvage award as well as a claim for SCOPIC remuneration, subject to Appendix B(5)(c)(iv), 75% of the amount by which the assessed SCOPIC remuneration exceeds the total Article 13 security demanded from ship and cargo will be paid by the owners of the vessel within 1 month and any undisputed balance paid when the Article 13 salvage award has been assessed and falls due. Interest will accrue from the date of termination of the services until the date of payment at the US prime rate plus 1%.

(ii) The Contractor hereby agrees to give an indemnity in a form acceptable to the owners of the vessel in respect of any overpayment in the event that the SCOPIC remuneration due ultimately proves to be less than the sum paid on account.

Continued on next page

9.   Termination

(i)   The Contractor shall be entitled to terminate the services under this SCOPIC clause and the Main Agreement by written notice to owners of the vessel with a copy to the SCR (if any) and any Special Representative appointed if the total cost of his services to date and the services that will be needed to fulfill his obligations hereunder to the property (calculated by means of the tariff rate but before the bonus conferred by sub-clause 5(iii) hereof will exceed the sum of:-

(a)   The value of the property capable of being salved; and

(b)   All sums to which he will be entitled as SCOPIC remuneration

(ii)   The owners of the vessel may at any time terminate the obligation to pay SCOPIC remuneration after the SCOPIC clause has been invoked under sub-clause 2 hereof provided that the Contractor shall be entitled to at least 5 clear days' notice of such termination. In the event of such termination the assessment of SCOPIC remuneration shall take into account all monies due under the tariff rates set out in Appendix A hereof including time for demobilisation to the extent that such time did reasonably exceed the 5 days' notice of termination.

(iii) The termination provisions contained in sub-clause 9(i) and 9(ii) above shall only apply if the Contractor is not restrained from demobilising his equipment by Government, Local or Port Authorities or any other officially recognised body having jurisdiction over the area where the services are being rendered.

10.   Duties of Contractor
The duties and liabilities of the Contractor shall remain the same as under the Main Agreement, namely to use his best endeavours to salve the vessel and property thereon and in so doing to prevent or minimise damage to the environment.

11.   Shipowner's Casualty Representative ("SCR")
Once this SCOPIC clause has been invoked in accordance with sub-clause 2 hereof the owners of the vessel may at their sole option appoint an SCR to attend the salvage operation in accordance with the terms and conditions set out in Appendix B.

12.   Special Representatives
At any time after the SCOPIC clause has been invoked the Hull and Machinery underwriter (or, if more than one, the lead underwriter) and one owner or underwriter of all or part of any cargo on board the vessel may each appoint one special representative (hereinafter called respectively the "Special Hull Representative" and the "Special Cargo Representative" and collectively called the "Special Representatives") at the sole expense of the appointor to attend the casualty to observe and report upon the salvage operation on the terms and conditions set out in Appendix C hereof. Such Special Representatives shall be technical men and not practising lawyers.

13.   Pollution Prevention
The assessment of SCOPIC remuneration shall include the prevention of pollution as well as the removal of pollution in the immediate vicinity of the vessel insofar as this is necessary for the proper execution of the salvage but not otherwise.

14.   General Average
SCOPIC remuneration shall not be a General Average expense to the extent that it exceeds the Article 13 Award; any liability to pay such SCOPIC remuneration shall be that of the Shipowner alone and no claim whether direct, indirect, by way of indemnity or re-

FIG. 38—*Continued* 359

course or otherwise relating to SCOPIC remuneration in excess of the Article 13 Award shall be made in General Average or under the vessel's Hull and Machinery Policy by the owners of the vessel.

15. Any dispute arising out of this SCOPIC clause or the operations thereunder shall be referred to Arbitration as provided for under the Main Agreement.

APPENDIX A (SCOPIC)

1. PERSONNEL

(a) The daily tariff rate, or pro rata for part thereof for personnel reasonably engaged on the contract, including any necessary time in proceeding to and returning from the casualty, shall be as follows:

Office administration, including communications	US$1,000
Salvage Master	US$1,500
Naval Architect or Salvage Officer/Engineer	US$1,250
Assistant Salvage Officer/Engineer	US$1,000
Diving Supervisor	US$1,000
Diver	US$ 750
Salvage Foreman	US$ 750
Riggers, Fitters, Equipment Operators	US$ 600
Specialist Advisors–Fire Fighters, Chemicals, Pollution Control	US$1,000

(b) The crews of tugs, and other craft, normally aboard that tug or craft for the purpose of its customary work are included in the tariff rate for that tug or craft but when because of the nature and/or location of the services to be rendered, it is a legal requirement for an additional crewmember or members to be aboard the tug or craft, the cost of such additional crew will be paid.

(c) The rates for any person not set out above shall be agreed with the SCR or, failing agreement, be determined by the Arbitrator.

(d) For the avoidance of doubt, personnel are "reasonably engaged on the contract" within the meaning of Appendix A sub-clause l(a) hereof if, in addition to working, they are eating, sleeping or otherwise resting on site or travelling to or from the site; personnel who fall ill or are injured while reasonably engaged on the contract shall be charged for at the appropriate daily tariff rate until they are demobilised but only if it was reasonable to mobilise them in the first place.

(e) SCOPIC remuneration shall cease to accrue in respect of personnel who die on site from the date of death.

2. TUGS AND OTHER CRAFT

(a) (i) Tugs, which shall include salvage tugs, harbour tugs, anchor handling tugs, coastal/ocean towing tugs, off-shore support craft, and any other work boat in excess of 500 b.h.p., shall be charged at the following rates, exclusive of fuel or lubricating oil, for each day, or pro rata for part thereof, that they are reasonably engaged in the services, including proceeding towards the casualty from the tugs' location when SCOPIC is invoked or when the tugs are mobilised (whichever is the later) and from the tugs' position when their

Continued on next page

involvement in the services terminates to a reasonable location having due
regard to their employment immediately prior to their involvement in the
services and standing by on the basis of their certificated b.h.p.:

For each b.h.p. up to 5,000 b.h.p.	US$2.00
For each b.h.p. between 5,001 & 10,000 b.h.p.	US$1.50
For each b.h.p. between 10,001 & 20,000 b.h.p.	US$1.00
For each b.h.p. over 20,000 b.h.p.	US$0.50

(ii) Any tug which has aboard certified fire fighting equipment shall, in addition
to the above rates, be paid:

US$500 per day, or pro rata for part thereof, if equipped with Fi Fi 0.5

US$1,000 per day, or pro rata for part thereof, if equipped with Fi Fi 1.0

for that period in which the tug is engaged in fire fighting necessitating the
use of the certified fire fighting equipment.

(iii) Any tug which is certified as "Ice Class" shall, in addition to the above, be
paid US$1,000 per day, or pro rata for part thereof, when forcing or breaking
ice during the course of services including proceeding to and returning from
the casualty.

(iv) For the purposes of paragraph 2(a)(i) hereof tugs shall be remunerated for
any reasonable delay or deviation for the purposes of taking on board essential salvage equipment, provisions or personnel which the Contractor reasonably anticipates he shall require in rendering the services which would not
normally be found on vessels of the tugs size and type.

(b) Any launch or work boat of less than 500 b.h.p. shall, exclusive of fuel and lubricating oil, be charged at a rate of US$3.00 for each b.h.p.

(c) Any other craft, not falling within the above definitions, shall be charged out
at a market rate for that craft, exclusive of fuel and lubricating oil, such rate to be agreed
with the SCR or, failing agreement, determined by the Arbitrator.

(d) All fuel and lubricating oil consumed during the services shall be paid at cost
of replacement and shall be treated as an out of pocket expense.

(e) For the avoidance of doubt, the above rates shall not include any portable salvage equipment normally aboard the tug or craft and such equipment shall be treated in
the same manner as portable salvage equipment and the Contractors shall be remunerated in respect thereof in accordance with Appendix A paragraphs 3 and 4 (i) and (ii)
hereof.

(f) SCOPIC remuneration shall cease to accrue in respect of tugs and other
craft which become a commercial total loss from the date they stop being engaged in the
services plus a reasonable period for demobilisation (if appropriate) PROVIDED that such
SCOPIC remuneration in respect of demobilisation shall only be payable if the commercial
total loss arises whilst engaged in the services and through no fault of the Contractors,
their servants, agents or sub-contractors.

3.   PORTABLE SALVAGE EQUIPMENT

(a) The daily tariff, or pro rata for part thereof, for all portable salvage equipment reasonably engaged during the services, including any time necessary for mobilisa-
tion and demobilisation, shall be as follows:

FIG. 38—*Continued* **361**

Generators	Rate—US$.
Up to 50 kW	60
51 to 100 kW	125
101 to 300 kW	200
Over 301 kW	350
Portable Inert Gas Systems	
1,000m^3/hour	1,200
1,500m^3/hour	1,400
Compressors	
High Pressure	100
185 Cfm	150
600 Cfm	250
1200 Cfm	400
Air Manifold	10
Blower; 1,500m^3/min.	850
Pumping Equipment	
Air	
2"	75
Diesel	
2"	50
4"	90
6"	120
Electrical Submersible	
2"	50
4"	150
6"	500
Hydraulic	
6"	600
8"	1,000
Hoses	
Air Hose	
¾"per 30 metres or 100 feet	20
2"per 30 metres or 100 feet	40
Layflat	
2" per 6 metres or 20 feet	10
4" per 6 metres or 20 feet	15
6" per 6 metres or 20 feet	20
Rigid	
2" per 6 metres or 20 feet	15
4" per 6 metres or 20 feet	20
6" per 6 metres or 20 feet	25
8" per 6 metres or 20 feet	30
Fenders	
Yokohama	
1.00m. × 2.00m.	75
2.50m. × 5.50m.	150
3.50m. × 6.50m.	250
Low Pressure Inflatable	
3 metres	70
6 metres	70
9 metres	150
12 metres	250
16 metres	250
Shackles	
Up to 50 tonnes	10
51 to 100 tonnes	20
101 to 200 tonnes	30
Over 200 tonnes	50
Distribution Boards	
Up to 50 kW	60
51 to 100 kW	125
101 to 300 kW	200
Over 301 kW	350

Welding & Cutting Equipment	Rate—US$.
Bolt Gun	300
Gas Detector	100
Hot Tap Machine, including supporting equipment	1,000
Oxy-acetylene Surface Cutting Gear	25
Underwater Cutting Gear	50
UnderwaterWelding Kit	50
250 Amp Welder	150
400 Amp Welder	200
Pollution Control Equipment	
Oil Boom, 24", per 10 metres	30
Oil Boom, 36", per 10 metres	100
Oil Boom, 48", per 10 metres	195
Lighting Systems	
Lighting String, per 50 feet	25
Light Tower	50
Underwater Lighting System, 1,000 watts	75
Winches	
Up to 20 tons, including 50 metres of wire	200
Storage Equipment	
10' Container	25
20' Container	40
Miscellaneous Equipment	
Air Bags, less than 5 tons lift	40
5 to 15 tons lift	200
Air Lift 4"	100
6"	200
8"	300
Air Tugger, up to 3 tons	75
Ballast/Fuel Oil Storage Bins, 50,000 litres	100
Chain Saw	20
Damage Stability Computer and Software	250
Echo Sounder, portable	25
Extension Ladder	20
Hydraulic Jack, up to 100 tons	75
Hydraulic Powerpack	75
Pressure washer, water	250
steam	450
Rigging Package, heavy	400
Light	200
Rock, Drill	50
Splitter	400
Steel Saw	20
Tirfors, up to 5 tonnes	10
Thermal Imaging Camera	250
Tool Package, per set	175
Ventilation Package	20
VHF Radio	10
Z Boat, including outboard up to 14 feet	200
over 14 feet	350
Protective Clothing	
Breathing Gear.	50
Hazardous Environment Suit	100
Diving Equipment	
Decompresson Chamber,	
2 man, including compressor	500
4 man, including compressor	700
Hot Water Diving Assembly	250
Underwater Magnets	20
Underwater Drill	20
Shallow Water Dive Spread	225

Continued on next page

(b) Any portable salvage equipment engaged but not set out above shall be charged at a rate to be agreed with the SCR or, failing agreement, determined by the Arbitrator.

(c) The total charge (before bonus) for each item of portable salvage equipment, owned by the contractor, shall not exceed the manufacturer's recommended retail price on the last day of the services multiplied by 1.5.

(d) Compensation for any portable salvage equipment lost or destroyed during the services shall be paid provided that the total of such compensation and the daily tariff rate (before bonus) in respect of that item do not exceed the actual cost of replacing the item at the Contractors' base with the most similar equivalent new item multiplied by 1.5.

(e) All consumables such as welding rods, boiler suits, small ropes etc. shall be charged at cost and shall be treated as an out of pocket expense.

(f) The Contractor shall be entitled to remuneration at a stand-by rate of 50% of the full tariff rate plus bonus for any portable salvage equipment reasonably mobilised but not used during the salvage operation provided

> (i) It has been mobilised with the prior agreement of the owner of the vessel or its mobilisation was reasonable in the circumstances of the casualty, or
>
> (ii) It comprises portable salvage equipment normally aboard the tug or craft that would have been reasonably mobilised had it not already been aboard the tug or craft.

(g) SCOPIC remuneration shall cease to accrue in respect of portable salvage equipment which becomes a commercial total loss from the date it ceases to be useable plus a reasonable period for demobilisation (if appropriate) PROVIDED that such SCOPIC remuneration in respect of demobilisation shall only be payable if the commercial total loss arises while it is engaged in the services and through no fault of the Contractors, their servants, agents or sub-contractors.

4. DOWNTIME
If a tug or piece of portable salvage equipment breaks down or is damaged without fault on the part of the Contractor, his servants, agents or sub-contractors and as a direct result of performing the services it should be paid for during the repair while on site at the stand-by rate of 50% of the tariff rate plus uplift pursuant to sub-clause 5(iv) of the SCOPIC clause.

If a tug or piece of portable salvage equipment breaks down or otherwise becomes inoperable without fault on the part of the Contractor, his servants, agents or sub-contractors and as a direct result of performing the services and cannot be repaired on site then:

(a) If it is not used thereafter but remains on site then no SCOPIC remuneration is payable in respect of that tug or piece of portable salvage equipment from the time of the breakdown.

(b) If it is removed from site, repaired and reasonably returned to the site for use SCOPIC remuneration at the standby rate of 50% of the tariff rate plus bonus pursuant to sub-clause 5(iv) of the SCOPIC clause shall be payable from the breakdown to the date it is returned to the site.

(c) If it is removed from the site and not returned SCOPIC remuneration ceases from the breakdown but is, in addition, payable for the period that it takes to return it di-

FIG. 38—*Continued* 363

rectly to base at the stand-by rate of 50% of the tariff rate plus bonus pursuant to sub-clause 5(iv) of the SCOPIC clause.

APPENDIX B (SCOPIC)

1. (a) The SCR shall be selected from a panel (the "SCR Panel") appointed by a Committee (the "SCR Committee") comprising of representatives appointed by the following:

- 3 representatives from the International Group of P and I Clubs
- 3 representatives from the ISU
- 3 representatives from the IUMI
- 3 representatives from the International Chamber of Shipping

(b) The SCR Committee shall be responsible for an annual review of the tariff rates as set out in Appendix A.

(c) The SCR Committee shall meet once a year in London to review, confirm, re-confirm or remove SCR Panel members.

(d) Any individual may be proposed for membership of the SCR Panel by any member of the SCR Committee and shall be accepted for inclusion on the SCR Panel unless at least four votes are cast against his inclusion.

(e) The SCR Committee shall also set and approve the rates of remuneration for the SCRs for the next year.

(f) Members of the SCR Committee shall serve without compensation.

(g) The SCR Committee's meetings and business shall be organised and administered by the Salvage Arbitration Branch of the Corporation of Lloyd's (hereinafter called "Lloyds") who will keep the current list of SCR Panel members and make it available to any person with a bona fide interest.

(h) The SCR Committee shall be entitled to decide its own administrative rules as to procedural matters (such as quorums, the identity and power of the Chairman etc.)

2. The primary duty of the SCR shall be the same as the Contractor, namely to use his best endeavours to assist in the salvage of the vessel and the property thereon and in so doing to prevent and minimise damage to the environment.

3. The Salvage Master shall at all times remain in overall charge of the operation, make all final decisions as to what he thinks is best and remain responsible for the operation.

4. The SCR shall be entitled to be kept informed by or on behalf of the Salvage Master or (if none) the principal contractors' representative on site (hereinafter called "the Salvage Master"). The Salvage Master shall consult with the SCR during the operation if circumstances allow and the SCR, once on site, shall been entitled to offer the Salvage Master advice.

5. (a) Once the SCOPIC clause is invoked the Salvage Master shall send daily reports (hereinafter called the "Daily Salvage Reports") setting out:

- the salvage plan (followed by any changes thereto as they arise)
- the condition of the casualty and the surrounding area (followed by any changes thereto as they arise)

Continued on next page

- the progress of the operation
- the personnel, equipment, tugs and other craft used in the operation that day.

(b) Pending the arrival of the SCR on site the Daily Salvage Reports shall be sent to Lloyd's and the owners of the vessel. Once the SCR has been appointed and is on site the Daily Salvage Reports shall be delivered to him.

(c) The SCR shall upon receipt of each Daily Salvage Report:

    (i) Transmit a copy of the Daily Salvage Report by the quickest method reasonably available to Lloyd's, the owners of the vessel, their liability insurers and (if any) to the Special Hull Representative and Special Cargo Representative (appointed under clause 12 of the SCOPIC clause and Appendix C) if they are on site; and if a Special Hull Representative is not on site the SCR shall likewise send copies of the Daily Salvage Reports direct to the leading Hull Underwriter or his agent (if known to the SCR) and if a Special Cargo Representative is not on site the SCR shall likewise send copies of the Daily Salvage Reports to such cargo underwriters or their agent or agents as are known to the SCR (hereinafter in this Appendix B such Hull and Cargo property underwriters shall be called "Known Property Underwriters").

    (ii) If circumstances reasonably permit consult with the Salvage Master and endorse his Daily Salvage Report stating whether or not he is satisfied and

    (iii) If not satisfied with the Daily Salvage Report, prepare a dissenting report setting out any objection or contrary view and deliver it to the Salvage Master and transmit it to Lloyd's, the owners of the vessel, their liability insurers and to any Special Representatives (appointed under clause 12 of the SCOPIC clause and Appendix C) or, if one or both Special Representatives has not been appointed, to the appropriate Known Property Underwriter.

    (iv) If the SCR gives a dissenting report to the Salvage Master in accordance with Appendix B(5)(c)(iii) to the SCOPIC clause, any initial payment due for SCOPIC remuneration shall be at the tariff rate applicable to what is in the SCR's view the appropriate equipment or procedure until any dispute is resolved by agreement or arbitration.

(d) Upon receipt of the Daily Salvage Reports and any dissenting reports of the SCR, Lloyd's shall distribute upon request the said reports to any parties to this contract and any of their property insurers of whom they are notified (hereinafter called "the Interested Persons") and to the vessel's liability insurers.

(e) As soon as reasonably possible after the Salvage services terminate the SCR shall issue a report (hereinafter call the "SCR's Final Salvage Report") setting out:

- the facts and circumstances of the casualty and the salvage operation insofar as they are known to him.
- the tugs, personnel and equipment employed by the Contractor in performing the operation.
- A calculation of the SCOPIC remuneration to which the contractor may be entitled by virtue of this SCOPIC clause.

The SCR's Final Salvage Report shall be sent to the owners of the vessel and their liability insurers and to Lloyd's who shall forthwith distribute it to the Interested Persons.

6. (a) The SCR may be replaced by the owner of the vessel if either:

FIG. 38—*Continued* 365

(i)   the SCR makes a written request for a replacement to the owner of the vessel (however the SCR should expect to remain on site throughout the services and should only expect to be substituted in exceptional circumstances); or

(ii) the SCR is physically or mentally unable or unfit to perform his duties; or

(iii) all salved interests or their representatives agree to the SCR being replaced.

(b) Any person who is appointed to replace the SCR may only be chosen from the SCR Panel.

(c) The SCR shall remain on site throughout the services while he remains in that appointment and until the arrival of any substitute so far as practicable and shall hand over his file and all other correspondence, computer data and papers concerning the salvage services to any substitute SCR and fully brief him before leaving the site.

(d) The SCR acting in that role when the services terminate shall be responsible for preparing the Final Salvage Report and shall be entitled to full co-operation from any previous SCRs or substitute SCRs in performing his functions hereunder.

7.   The owners of the vessel shall be primarily responsible for paying the fees and expenses of the SCR. The Arbitrator shall have jurisdiction to apportion the fees and expenses of the SCR and include them in his award under the Main Agreement and, in doing so, shall have regard to the principles set out in any market agreement in force from time to time.

APPENDIX C (SCOPIC)
The Special Representatives

1.   The Salvage Master, the owners of the vessel and the SCR shall co-operate with the Special Representatives and shall permit them to have full access to the vessel to observe the salvage operation and to inspect such of the ship's documents as are relevant to the salvage operation.

2.   The Special Representative shall have the right to be informed of all material facts concerning the salvage operation as the circumstances reasonably allow.

3.   If an SCR has been appointed the SCR shall keep the Special Representatives (if any and if circumstances permit) fully informed and shall consult with the said Special Representatives. The Special Representatives shall also be entitled to receive a copy of the Daily Salvage Reports direct from the Salvage Master or, if appointed, from the SCR.

4.   The appointment of any Special Representatives shall not affect any right that the respondent ship and cargo interests may have (whether or not they have appointed a Special Representative) to send other experts or surveyors to the vessel to survey ship or cargo and inspect the ship's documentation or for any other lawful purpose.

5.   If an SCR or Special Representative is appointed the Contractor shall be entitled to limit access to any surveyor or representative (other than the said SCR and Special Representative or Representatives) if he reasonably feels their presence will substantially impede or endanger the salvage operation.

TABLE 161.18(A).—THE IMO STANDARD SHIP REPORTING SYSTEM

A	ALPHA	Ship	Name, call sign or ship station identity, and flag.
B	BRAVO	Dates and time of event	A 6 digit group giving day of month (first two digits), hours and minutes (last four digits). If other than UTC state time zone used.
C	CHARLIE	Position	A 4 digit group giving latitude in degrees and minutes suffixed with N (north) or S (south) and a 5 digit group giving longitude in degrees and minutes suffixed with E (east) or W (west); or.
D	DELTA	Position	True bearing (first 3 digits) and distance (state distance) in nautical miles from a clearly identified landmark (state landmark).
E	ECHO	True course	A 3 digit group.
F	FOXTROT	Speed in knots and tenths of knots.	A 3 digit group.
G	GOLF	Port of departure	Name of last port of call.
H	HOTEL	Date, time and point of entry system.	Entry time expressed as in (B) and into the entry position expressed as in (C) or (D).
I	INDIA	Destination and expected time of arrival.	Name of port and date time group expressed as in (B).
J	JULIET	Pilot	State whether a deep sea or local pilot is on board.
K	KILO	Date, time and point of exit from system.	Exit time expressed as in (B) and exit position expressed as in (C) or (D).
L	LIMA	Route information	Intended track.
M	MIKE	Radio	State in full names of communications stations/ frequencies guarded.
N	NOVEMBER	Time of next report	Date time group expressed as in (B).
O	OSCAR	Maximum present static draught in meters.	4 digit group giving meters and centimeters.
P	PAPA	Cargo on board	Cargo and brief details of any dangerous cargoes as well as harmful substances and gases that could endanger persons or the environment.
Q	QUEBEC	Defects, damage, deficiencies or limitations.	Brief detail of defects, damage, deficiencies or other limitations.
R	ROMEO	Description of pollution or dangerous goods lost.	Brief details of type of pollution (oil, chemicals, etc) or dangerous goods lost overboard; position expressed as in (C) or (D).
S	SIERRA	Weather conditions	Brief details of weather and sea conditions prevailing.
T	TANGO	Ship's representative and/or owner.	Details of name and particulars of ship's representative and/or owner for provision of information.
U	UNIFORM	Ship size and type	Details of length, breadth, tonnage, and type, etc., as required.
V	VICTOR	Medical personnel	Doctor, physician's assistant, nurse, no medic.
W	WHISKEY	Total number of persons on board.	State number.
X	XRAY	Miscellaneous	Any other information as appropriate. [i.e., a detailed description of a planned operation, which may include: its duration; effective area; any restrictions to navigation; notification procedures for approaching vessels; in addition, for a towing operation: configuration, length of the tow, available horsepower, etc.; for a dredge or floating plant: configuration of pipeline, mooring configuration, number of assist vessels, etc.].

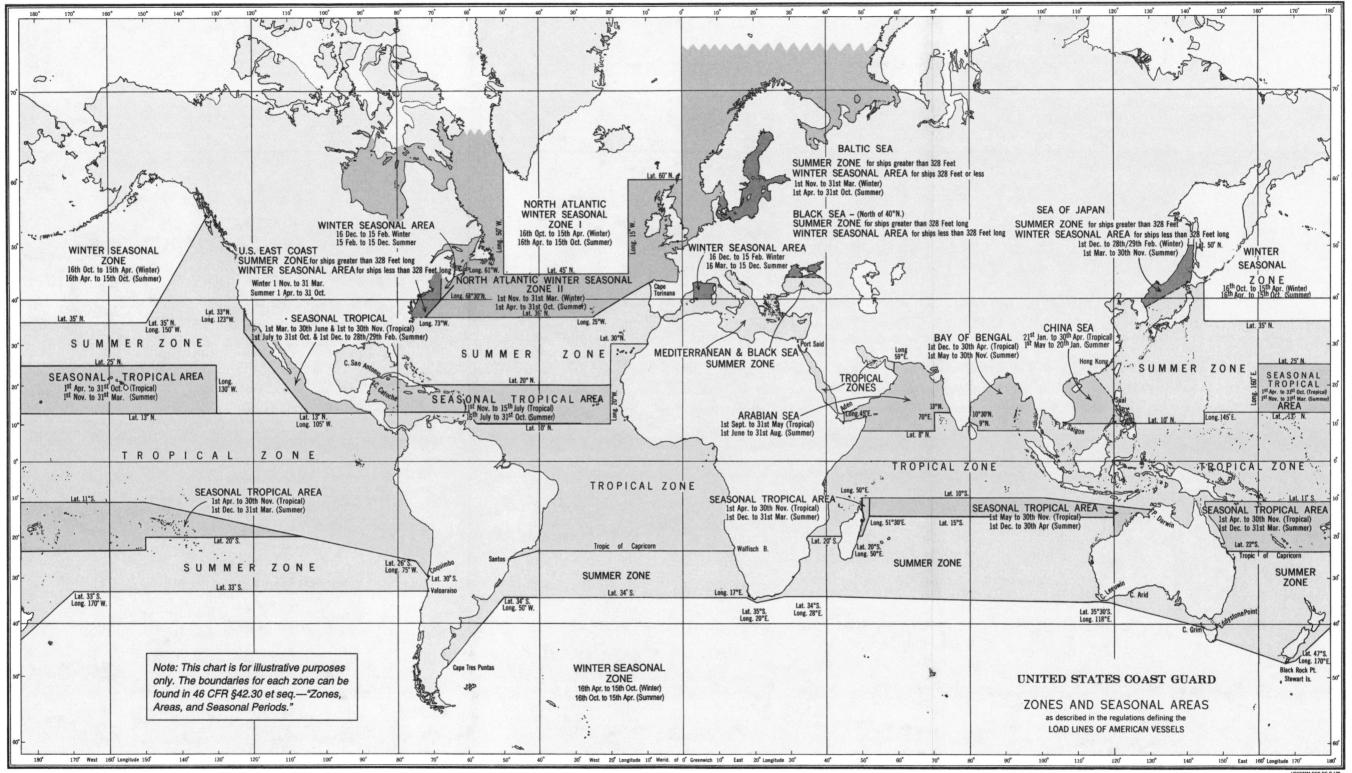

BALTIC SEA

SUMMER ZONE for ships greater than 328 Feet
WINTER SEASONAL AREA for ships 328 Feet or less
1st Nov. to 31st Mar. (Winter)
1st Apr. to 31st Oct. (Summer)

BLACK SEA – (North of 40°N.)
SUMMER ZONE for ships greater than 328 Feet long
WINTER SEASONAL AREA for ships less than 328 Feet long

SEA OF JAPAN
SUMMER ZONE for ships greater than 328 Feet
WINTER SEASONAL AREA for ships less than 328 Feet long
1st Dec. to 28th/29th Feb. (Winter)
1st Mar. to 30th Nov. (Summer)

NORTH ATLANTIC
WINTER SEASONAL
ZONE I
16th Oct. to 15th Apr. (Winter)
16th Apr. to 15th Oct. (Summer)

WINTER SEASONAL AREA
16 Dec. to 15 Feb. Winter
15 Feb. to 15 Dec. Summer

WINTER SEASONAL AREA
16 Dec. to 15 Feb. Winter
16 Mar. to 15 Dec. Summer

WINTER SEASONAL
ZONE
16th Oct. to 15th Apr. (Winter)
16th Apr. to 15th Oct. (Summer)

U.S. EAST COAST
SUMMER ZONE for ships greater than 328 Feet long
WINTER SEASONAL AREA for ships less than 328 Feet long
Winter 1 Nov. to 31 Mar.
Summer 1 Apr. to 31 Oct.

WINTER SEASONAL
ZONE
16th Oct. to 15th Apr. (Winter)
16th Apr. to 15th Oct. (Summer)

NORTH ATLANTIC WINTER SEASONAL
ZONE II
1st Nov. to 31st Mar. (Winter)
1st Apr. to 31st Oct. (Summer)

SEASONAL TROPICAL
1st Mar. to 30th June & 1st to 30th Nov. (Tropical)
1st July to 31st Oct. & 1st Dec. to 28th/29th Feb. (Summer)

WINTER
SEASONAL
ZONE
16th Oct. to 15th Apr. (Winter)
16th Apr. to 15th Oct. (Summer)

SUMMER ZONE

SUMMER ZONE

SUMMER ZONE

MEDITERRANEAN & BLACK SEA
SUMMER ZONE

BAY OF BENGAL
1st Dec. to 30th Apr. (Tropical)
1st May to 30th Nov. (Summer)

CHINA SEA
21st Jan. to 30th Apr. (Tropical)
1st May to 20th Jan. (Summer)

SUMMER ZONE

SEASONAL TROPICAL AREA
1st Apr. to 31st Oct. (Tropical)
1st Nov. to 31st Mar. (Summer)

SEASONAL TROPICAL AREA
1st Nov. to 15th July (Tropical)
16th July to 31st Oct. (Summer)

TROPICAL
ZONES

ARABIAN SEA
1st Sept. to 31st May (Tropical)
1st June to 31st Aug. (Summer)

SEASONAL
TROPICAL
AREA
1st Apr. to 31st Oct. (Tropical)
1st Nov. to 31st Mar. (Summer)

TROPICAL ZONE

TROPICAL ZONE

TROPICAL ZONE

TROPICAL ZONE

SEASONAL TROPICAL AREA
1st Apr. to 30th Nov. (Tropical)
1st Dec. to 31st Mar. (Summer)

SEASONAL TROPICAL AREA
1st Apr. to 30th Nov. (Tropical)
1st Dec. to 31st Mar. (Summer)

SEASONAL TROPICAL AREA
1st May to 30th Nov. (Tropical)
1st Dec. to 30th Apr. (Summer)

SEASONAL TROPICAL AREA
1st Apr. to 30th Nov. (Tropical)
1st Dec. to 31st Mar. (Summer)

SUMMER ZONE

SUMMER ZONE

SUMMER ZONE

SUMMER ZONE

SUMMER ZONE

Note: This chart is for illustrative purposes
only. The boundaries for each zone can be
found in 46 CFR §42.30 et seq.—"Zones,
Areas, and Seasonal Periods."

WINTER SEASONAL
ZONE
16th Apr. to 15th Oct. (Winter)
16th Oct. to 15th Apr. (Summer)

UNITED STATES COAST GUARD

ZONES AND SEASONAL AREAS
as described in the regulations defining the
LOAD LINES OF AMERICAN VESSELS

USCOMM-CGS-DC-R-176

Conversion Factors

Mathematical solutions are only as precise as the least precise of the entered values. For example, when one multiplies 12.34 by 38.21135, the least precise term is 12.34 since it only goes to the hundredth place. Thus the answer generated by calculator (471.528059) gives a false level of precision and should be rounded to the hundredth place (471.53) to correctly reflect the level of precision of the executed function. For this reason, the listed conversion factors have been rounded to more accurately reflect shipboard operational constraints on mathematical precision.

Additionally, if a conversion factor is an exact ratio, no decimal places will be indicated, as in 12 inches to 1 foot (and not 12.00 inches).

To convert from:	*To:*	*Multiply by:*
Barrels, oil (US)	Cubic feet	5.61
	Cubic meters	0.16
	Gallons (imperial)	35
	Gallons (US)	42
	Hectoliters	1.59
	Liters	158.98
	Long tons	0.15 (or divide by 6.6)
	Metric tons	0.15 (or divide by 6.49)
	Pounds	339.40
	Short tons	0.17 (or divide by 5.89)
Board feet (bm)	Cubic feet	0.08
	Cubic inches	144
	Cubic meters	0.002
Bushels (imperial)	Bags (imperial)	0.33
	Bushels (US)	1.03
	Cubic feet	1.28

To convert from:	To:	Multiply by:
Bushels (imperial)	Cubic inches	2,219.36
	Cubic meters	0.04
	Dekaliters	3.64
	Gallons (imperial)	8
	Liters	36.38
	Quarts (imperial)	0.13
Bushels (US)	Bushels (imperial)	0.97
	Cubic feet	1.24
	Cubic inches	2,150.42
	Cubic meters	0.04
	Dekaliters	3.52
	Liters	35.24
	Quarts, dry	32
Cables (British)	Cables (US)	0.83
	Feet	600
	Kilometers	182.88
	Miles, nautical	0.099
	Yards	200
Cables (US)	Cables (British)	1.20
	Feet	720
	Kilometers	0.22
	Meters	219.46
	Miles, nautical	0.12
	Yards	240
Centimeters	Decimeters	0.1
	Feet	0.03
	Inches	0.39
	Meters	0.01
	Millimeters	10
	Yards	0.01
Cubic centimeters	Board feet (bm)	0.0004
	Cubic inches	0.06
	Ounces, liquid (US)	0.03
Cubic feet	Barrels, oil (US, 42 gal)	0.18
	Board feet	12
	Bushels (US)	0.80
	Bushels (imperial)	0.78
	Cubic centimeters	28,316.85
	Cubic decimeters	28.32

To convert from:	To:	Multiply by:
Cubic feet	Cubic inches	1,728.00
	Cubic meters	0.03
	Cubic yards	0.04
	Gallons (imperial)	6.23
	Gallons (US)	7.48
	Hectoliters	0.28
	Liters	28.32
Cubic inches	Board feet (bm)	0.007
	Bushels (US)	0.0005
	Cubic centimeters	16.39
	Cubic feet	0.000579
	Gallons (imperial)	0.0036
	Gallons (US)	0.0043
	Gills	0.14
	Liters	0.02
	Ounces, liquid (US)	0.55
	Pints, liquid (US)	0.03
	Quarts, liquid (US)	0.02
Cubic meters	Barrels, liquid (31.5 gal)	8.39
	Barrels, oil (42 gal)	6.29
	Board feet (bm)	423.77
	Bushels (imperial)	27.49
	Bushels (US)	28.38
	Cubic decimeters	1,000.0
	Cubic feet	35.31
	Cubic inches	61,023.74
	Cubic yards	1.31
	Gallons (imperial)	219.97
	Gallons (US)	264.17
	Liters	999.97 (1,000)
Cubic yards	Cubic feet	27
	Cubic inches	46,656.00
	Cubic meters	0.76
	Liters	764.55
Decimeters	Centimeters	10
	Feet	0.33
	Inches	3.94
	Meters	0.1
	Yards	0.11

To convert from:	To:	Multiply by:
Feet	Centimeters	30.48
	Decimeters	3.05
	Inches	12
	Kilometers	0.0003
	Meters	0.305
	Miles, nautical	0.00017
	Miles, statute	0.00019
	Yards	0.33
Gallons (imperial)	Barrels, oil (US)	0.03
	Cubic centimeters	4,546.09
	Cubic feet	0.16
	Cubic inches	277.42
	Gallons (US)	1.20
	Liters	4.55
	Ounces (imperial)	160
	Ounces, liquid (US)	153.72
	Quarts (imperial)	4
	Quarts, liquid (US)	4.80
Gallons (US)	Barrels, oil (US)	0.02
	Cubic centimeters	3,785.43
	Cubic feet	0.13
	Cubic inches	231
	Cubic meters	0.004
	Gallons (imperial)	0.8328
	Gills	26.6
	Liters	3.785
	Ounces, liquid (US)	128
	Pints, liquid (US)	8
	Quarts, liquid (US)	4
Hectoliters	Bushels (imperial)	2.75
	Bushels (US)	2.84
	Cubic feet	3.53
	Cubic inches	6,102.34
	Cubic meters	0.1
	Cubic yards	0.13
	Dekaliters	10
	Gallons (imperial)	21.99
	Gallons, dry (US)	22.70
	Gallons, liquid (US)	26.42

To convert from:	To:	Multiply by:
Hectoliters	Liters	100
Hogsheads	Cubic feet	8.42
	Cubic inches	14,553
	Cubic meters	0.34
	Gallons (US)	63
	Liters	238.48
Hundredweights, long (US)	Kilograms	50.80
	Pounds	112
	Tons, long	0.05
	Tons, metric	0.051
	Tons, short	0.056
Hundredweights, short (US)	Kilograms	45.36
	Pounds	100
	Tons, long	0.0446
	Tons, metric	0.0454
	Tons, short	0.05
Inches	Centimeters	2.54
	Decimeters	0.254
	Feet	0.08
	Meters	0.0254
	Millimeters	25.40
	Yards	.028
Kilograms	Grams	1,000
	Ounces (avdp)	35.27
	Pounds	2.20
	Tons, long	0.00098
	Tons, metric	0.001
	Tons, short	0.0011
Kilometers	Feet	3,280.83
	Meters	1,000
	Miles, nautical	0.54
	Miles, statute	0.62
	Yards	1,093.61
Kips	Short tons	0.50
	Pounds	1,000
Liters	Barrels, oil (US)	0.006
	Bushels (imperial)	0.027
	Bushels (US)	0.028
	Cubic centimeters	1,000.028

To convert from:	To:	Multiply by:
Liters	Cubic feet	0.04
	Cubic inches	61.03
	Gallons (imperial)	0.22
	Gallons (US)	0.26
	Ounces, liquid (US)	33.81
	Pints, liquid (US)	2.11
	Quarts, dry (US)	0.91
	Quarts, liquid (imperial)	0.88
	Quarts, liquid (US)	1.06
Meters	Centimeters	100
	Decimeters	10
	Fathoms	0.55
	Feet	3.28
	Inches	39.37
	Kilometers	0.001
	Miles, nautical	0.00054
	Miles, statute	0.00062
	Yards	1.09
Miles, nautical	Cables (British)	10
	Cables (US)	8.44
	Feet	6,076.12
	Kilometers	1.85
	Meters	1,852
	Miles, Statute	1.15
	Yards	2,025.37
Miles, statute	Feet	5,280
	Kilometers	1.61
	Meters	1,609.35
	Miles, nautical	0.87
	Yards	1,760
Millimeters	Centimeters	0.1
	Feet	0.003
	Inches	0.04
	Meters	0.001
Pounds (avdp)	Grams	453.59
	Kilograms	0.45
	Ounces (avdp)	16
Square feet	Square centimeters	929.03
	Square inches	144

To convert from:	*To:*	*Multiply by:*
Square feet	Square meters	0.09
	Square yards	0.11
Square inches	Square centimeters	6.45
	Square decimeters	0.06
	Square feet	0.007
	Square meters	0.0006
	Square millimeters	645.16
Square meters	Square centimeters	10,000
	Square feet	10.76
	Square inches	1,549.997
	Square yards	1.196
Square yards	Square centimeters	8,361.27
	Square feet	9
	Square inches	1,296
	Square meters	0.84
Tons, long	Hundredweights, long (US)	20
	Hundredweights, short (US)	22.4
	Kilograms	1,016.05
	Pounds	2,240
	Tons, metric	1.02
	Tons, short	1.12
Tons, metric	Hundredweights, long (US)	19.68
	Hundredweights, short (US)	22.05
	Kilograms	1,000
	Pounds	2,204.62
	Tons, long	0.98
	Tons, short	1.10
Tons, short	Hundredweights, long (US)	17.86
	Hundredweights, short (US)	20
	Kilograms	907.18
	Kips	2
	Pounds	2,000
	Tons, long	0.89
	Tons, metric	0.91
Yards	Centimeters	91.44
	Decimeters	9.144
	Feet	3

To convert from:	*To:*	*Multiply by:*
Yards	Inches	36
	Kilometers	0.0009
	Meters	0.91
	Miles, nautical	0.00049
	Miles, statute	0.00057

Agencies and Contacts

IMPORTANT PHONE NUMBERS

USCG National Response Center
800-424-8802

Chemtrec (chemical data information)
800-424-9300

U.S. Customs Smuggling Report
Hotline
800-BE-ALERT
(800-232-5378)

Violence at Sea (Office of Naval
Intelligence)
301-669-3261

Hostile Ship Actions (MARAD)
202-366-5735

Center for Disease Control
404-687-6571

AT&T Cable Areas
800-235-CHARTS for free charts
showing cable areas. Have vessel's
name and documentation number
ready.

INTERNATIONAL AGENCIES

As shown, phone numbers include the prefix for international calls (011), the country code (for example, 44 for United Kingdom), and the city code (for example, 207 for London) to be used when making calls from the United States to other countries.

Baltic and International Maritime
    Council (BIMCO)
Bagsvaerdvej 161
2880 Bagsvaerd
Copenhagen, Denmark
Tel: 011-45-44-36-68-00
Fax: 011-45-44-36-68-68

INMARSAT
40 Melton Street
London, United Kingdom
NW1 2EQ
Tel: 011-44-207-728-1100
Fax: 011-44-207-728-1746

International Association of Dry Cargo
Ship Owners (INTERCARGO)
2nd Floor, 4 London Wall Buildings
Blomfield Street
London, United Kingdom
EC2M 5NT
Tel: 011-44-207-638-3989
Fax: 011-44-207-638-3943

International Association of
Independent Tanker Owners
(INTERTANKO)
Bogstadveien 27B
P.O. Box 5804 Majorstua
N-0308 Oslo, Norway
Tel: 011-47-22-12-26-40
Fax: 011-47-22-12-26-41

International Association of
Lighthouse Authorities (IALA)
20 Ter Rue Schnapper
78100 St. Germain
En Laye, France
Tel: 011-33-01-3451-7001
Fax: 011-33-01-3451-8205

International Chamber of Shipping
(ICS) and
International Shipping Federation
(ISF)
12 Carthusian Street
London, United Kingdom
EC1M 6EZ
Tel: 011-44-207-417-8844
Fax: 011-44-207-417-8877

International Labor Organization
(ILO)
4 Route des Morillons
CH-1211 Geneva 22
Switzerland
Tel: 011-41-22-799-6111
Fax: 011-41-22-798-8685

International Maritime Bureau
Maritime House
1 Linton Road
Barking, Essex, United Kingdom
1G11 8HG
Tel: 011-44-208-591-3000
Fax: 011-44-208-594-2833
Telex: 8956492 IMBLDN G

International Maritime Organization
(IMO)
4 Albert Embankment
London, United Kingdom
SE1 7SR
Tel: 011-44-207-735-7611
Fax: 011-44-207-587-3210
Telex: 23588 IMOLDN G

International Organization for
Standardization (ISO)
1 Rue de Varembe
Case Postale 56, CH-1211
Geneva 20, Switzerland
Tel: 011-41-22-749-0111
Fax: 011-41-22-733-3430

International Telecommunications
Institute (ITU)
Place des Nations
CH-Geneva 20, Switzerland
Tel: 011-41-22-730-5111
Fax: 011-41-22-733-7256

The Nautical Institute
202 Lambeth Road
London, United Kingdom
SE1 7LQ
Tel: 011-44-207-928-1351
Fax: 011-44-207-401-2817

Oil Companies International Marine
Forum (OCIMF)
27 Queen Anne's Gate
London, United Kingdom
SW1H 9BU
Tel: 011-44-207-654-1200
Fax: 011-44-207-654-1205

Panama Canal Authority
ACP-MR
P.O. Box 5413
Miami, FL 33102-5413
Tel: 011-507-272-3202/3165
Fax: 011-507-272-3892
Telex: 3023 PCCMTCC PG

United Nations High Commissioner
for Refugees (UNHCR)
Case Postale 2500
CH-1211 Geneva 2 Depot, Switzerland
Tel: 011-41-22-739-8111
Fax: 011-41-22-739-7369
or
1775 K Street NW, Suite 300
Washington, DC 20006

UNITED STATES GOVERNMENT AGENCIES

Federal agencies are best located on the Internet.

Centers for Disease Control
1600 Clifton Road
Atlanta, GA 30333
Tel: 404-639-3311

Environmental Protection Agency
1200 Pennsylvania Ave., NW
Washington, DC 20460
Tel: 202-260-2090

Federal Communications Commission
445 12th Street, SW
Washington, DC 20554
Tel: 202-418-0190
Tel: 888-CALL-FCC

National Imagery and Mapping
Agency
NIMA (CODH/J-52)
3200 South 2nd Street
St. Louis, MO 63118-3399
Tel: 800-455-0899
Tel: 314-263-4802
Fax: 314-260-5024

National Oceanographic and Atmo-
spheric Administration (NOAA)
Includes the following agencies:
National Environmental Satellite
Data and Information Service
National Marine Fisheries (NMF)
National Ocean Service (NOS)
National Weather Service (NWS)
14th Street and Constitution Ave.,
NW
Room 6013
Washington, DC 20230
Tel: 202-482-6090
Fax: 202-482-3154
888-212-7283 or www.sarsat.noaa.gov
(for registering EPIRBs)

National Ocean Service (NOS)
SSMC 4, 13th Floor
1305 E/W Highway
Silver Spring, MD 20910
Tel: 301-713-3070
To order nautical charts:
National Ocean Service, NOAA
Distribution Branch (N/CG33)
6501 Lafayette Avenue
Riverdale, MD 20737
Tel: 301-436-6829

National Technical Information
Service (for copies of
international treaties, etc.)
5285 Port Royal Road
Springfield, VA 22161
Tel: 703-605-6000

U.S. Coast Guard—National Maritime
Center
4200 Wilson Blvd.
Arlington, VA 22203-1804
Tel: 202-493-1010
Fax: 202-493-1060

U.S. Customs Service
1300 Pennsylvania Avenue NW
Washington DC 20229
Tel: 202-927-1000
Carrier Initiative Program
Manager, Anti-Smuggling Division
Office of Field Operations
U.S. Customs Service
1300 Pennsylvania Ave., NW
Washington D.C. 20229
Tel: 800 BE ALERT (800-232-5378) to
report smuggling

U.S. Department of Agriculture
1400 Independence Ave., SW
Washington, DC 20250
Tel: 202-720-2791
Fax: 202-720-2166

U.S. Department of State
2201 C St., NW
Washington, DC 20520
Tel: 202-647-4000

U.S. Department of Transportation
400 7th Street, SW
Washington, DC 20590
Tel: 202-366-4000

U.S. Federal Maritime Commission
800 North Capitol Street, NW
Room 900
Washington, DC 20573
Tel: 202-523-5783/5860
Fax: 202-523-5785/3725

U.S. Fish and Wildlife Service
1849 C Street, NW
Washington, DC 20240
Tel: 202-208-4717

U.S. Maritime Administration
(MARAD)
U.S. Department of Transportation
400 7th Street SW
Washington, DC 20590
Tel: 800-99-MARAD

U.S. Public Health
Hubert H. Humphrey Building
200 Independence Avenue SW
Washington, DC 20201
Tel: 202-690-7694
Fax: 202-690-6960

UNITED STATES COMMERCIAL AGENCIES

American Institute of Merchant
Shipping
1000 16th Street NW, Suite 511
Washington, DC 20036-5705
Tel: 202-775-4399
Fax: 202-659-3795

National Cargo Bureau
90 West Street, Suite 2000
New York, NY 10006-1039
Tel: 212-571-5000
Fax: 212-571-5005

Ship Operations Cooperative Program
(SOCP)
Tel: 202-366-1928 (contact at MARAD)
This group has no formal address.
This program, founded in 1993, is a forum for industry and federal and
state agencies to work together to
solve common problems. It boasts
members as diverse as the Coast
Guard, NOAA, maritime acade-
mies, shipowners, ship operators,
and classification societies. It provides a common voice for the maritime industry when making
recommendations to local, state,

and federal regulatory bodies. It is producing a database for STCW reference and has produced several training videos. The program also provides a platform for testing and reporting on new products and technology.

Society of Naval Architects and
  Marine Engineers (SNAME)
601 Pazonia Ave.
Jersey City, NJ 07306
Tel: 800-798-2188
Fax: 201-798-4975

CLASSIFICATION SOCIETIES

American Bureau of Shipping
ABS Plaza
16855 Northchase Dr.
Houston, TX 77060
Tel: 281-877-6000
Fax: 281-877-6001
Telex: 232099 ABNY UR

Bureau Veritas–London
2nd Floor, Tower Bridge Ct.
224-226 Tower Bridge Rd.
London, United Kingdom
SE1 2TX
Tel: 011-44-207-550-8900
Fax: 011-44-207-403-1590

Det Norske Veritas—U.S. Group
16340 Park Ten Place, Suite 100
Houston, TX 77084
Tel: 281-721-6600
Fax: 281-721-9600

Germanischer Lloyd
Department Fleet Service
Vorsetzen 32
D-20459 Hamburg, Germany

International Association of
  Classification Societies (IACS)
5 Old Queen Street
London, United Kingdom
SW1H 9JA
Tel: 011-44-207-976-0660
Fax: 011-44-207-976-0440

Korean Register of Shipping
Yusung P.O. Box 29
Taejon, Republic of Korea
Tel: 011-82-42-869-9114
Fax: 011-82-42-862-6011

Lloyd's Register
71 Fenchurch St.
London, United Kingdom
EC3M 4BS
Tel: 011-44-207-709-9166
Fax: 011-44-207-488-4796
Telex: 888379 LR LON G

Polish Register of Shipping
Al. Gen. J. Hallera 126
80-416 Gdansk, Poland
or Polski Rejest Statkow
P.O. Box 445
80-958 Gdansk, Poland
Tel: 011-46-58-346-17-00
Fax: 011-48-58-346-03-92
Telex: 0512952 prs pl

Registro Italiano Navale
P.A. via Corsica 19 16128
Genova, Italy
Tel: 011-39-01-057-2381
Fax: 011-39-01-056-1499

MARINE EXCHANGES

Chamber of Shipping of British
Columbia
100-1111 W. Hastings Street
Vancouver, British Columbia
V6E 2J3
Tel: 604-681-2351
Fax: 604-681-4364

Marine Exchange of Los Angeles/Long
Beach Harbor
3601 S. Gaffey St, #803
San Pedro, CA 90731
or:
P.O. Box 1949
San Pedro, CA 90733-1949
Tel: 310-832-6411
Fax: 310-833-7051

Marine Exchange of Puget Sound
2701 1st Avenue, Suite 110
Seattle, WA 98121-1123
Tel: 206-443-3830
Fax: 206-443-3839

Marine Exchange of the San Francisco
Bay Region
Fort Mason Center, Building B, Room
325
San Francisco, CA 94123-1380
Tel: 415-441-6600
Fax: 415-441-1025
Telex: 6502052782
Answerback:
6502052782MCI_UW

Marine Exchange of the West Gulf,
Inc.
1520 Texas Avenue, Suite 304
Houston, TX 77002-3682
Tel: 713-222-0123
Fax: 713-222-2194

Maritime Association of Greater
Boston
Charleston Navy Yard
33 Third Avenue
Boston, MA 02129-4518
Tel: 617-242-3303
Fax: 617-242-4546

Maritime Association of New York and
New Jersey
17 Battery Place, Suite 913
New York, NY 10004
Tel: 212-425-5704
Fax: 212-635-9498

Maritime Exchange for the Delaware
River and Bay
240-242 Cherry Street
Philadelphia, PA 19106-1906
Tel: 215-925-2615
Fax: 215-925-3422
24-hour ship reporting: 215-925-1524

Merchants Exchange of Portland
200 SW Market Street, Suite 190
Portland, OR 97201
Tel: 503-228-4361
Fax: 503-295-3660

New Orleans Board of Trade
316 Board of Trade Place
New Orleans, LA 70130
Tel: 504-525-3271

Port of San Diego Unified Port District
P.O. Box 120488
3165 Pacific Hwy.
San Diego, CA 92101-1128
Tel: 800-854-2757
Tel: 619-686-6236
Fax: 619-686-6215

Foreign Medical Evacuation and Travelers' Insurance Companies

UNITED STATES–BASED COMPANIES

Acadian Ambulance and Air Service
Inc.
Lafayette, LA
800-259-1111 / 318-267-1111
504-267-1111

Advanced Air Ambulance
Miami, FL
800-633-3590 / 305-599-7700

Air Ambulance America—AAA
Austin, TX
800-222-3564 / 512-479-8000

Air Ambulance Network
Sarasota, FL
800-327-1966 / 813-934-3999

Air Ambulance Professionals
Ft. Lauderdale, FL
800-752-4195 / 954-491-0555

AIRescue International
Van Nuys, CA
800-922-4911 / 818-994-0911

AirEvac
Phoenix, AZ
800-421-6111

Air Medic – Air Ambulance of America
Washington, PA
800-321-4444 / 412-228-8000

Air Response
Orlando, FL
877-366-6266 / 518-993-4153
407-384-6100

Air Star International
Thermal, CA
877-570-0911 / 800-991-2869

American Care Inc.
San Diego, CA
800-941-2582 / 619-486-8844

Care Flight – Air Critical Care
International
Clearwater, FL
800-282-6878 / 813-530-7972

Critical Air Medicine
San Diego, CA
800-247-8326 / 619-571-0482

Critical Care Medflight
Lawrenceville, GA
800-426-6557 / 770-513-9148

Global Care/Medpass
Alpharetta, GA
800-860-1111

Inflight Medical Services
International, Inc.
Naples, FL
800-432-4177 / 941-594-0800

Intensive Air Ambulance
Morganville, NJ
800-543-3759 / 908-946-1200

International SOS Assistance
Philadelphia, PA
800-523-8930 / 215-244-1500
(Also provides travel insurance
services.)

Life Jet
Baltimore, MD
877-LIFEJET / 877-543-3538

Medical Escort International, Inc.
Allentown, PA
800-255-7182 / 610-791-3111

Medex Assisstance Corp.
Timonium, MD
800-537-2029 / 410-453-6300 (call
collect)

Medjet International, Inc.
Birmingham, AL
800-356-2161 / 205-592-4460

Mercy Medical Airlift, Inc.
Manassas, VA
800-296-1217 / 703-361-1191
(Service area: Caribbean and part of
Canada only. If necessary, will
meet commercial flights with incoming patients at JFK, Miami,
and other airports.)

National Air Ambulance
Ft. Lauderdale, FL
800-327-3710 / 305-525-5538

Smartravel
4600 King St.
Suite 6J
Alexandria, VA
800-730-3170 / 703-379-8645
(Provides a range of travel medical
services.)

Travelcare International, Inc.
Eagle River, WI
800-524-7633 / 715-479-8881

Travelers Emergency Network
Durham, NC
800-275-4836 / 800-ASK-4-TEN

FOREIGN-BASED COMPANIES

*As shown, phone numbers include the
prefix for international calls (011), the
country code (for example, 44 for United
Kingdom), and the city code (for example, 207 for London) to be used when
making calls from the United States to
other countries.*

AEA International
331 North Bridge Rd.
#17-00 Odeon Towers
Singapore
188720
U.S. Phone: 800-468-5232
(Service worldwide, also provides
travel insurance services.)

Austrian Air Ambulance
Vienna, Austria
Tel: 011-43-1-40-1-44
Fax: 011-43-1-40-1-55

Euro-Flite, Ltd.
Helsinki International Airport
Vantaa, Finland
011-358-0-870-25-44

Europassistance
Johannesburg, South Africa
011-27-11-315-3999

Jet Flite
Vantaa, Finland
011-358-0-822-766 / 011-358-0-6996
(after hours)

Medical Rescue International
P.O. Box 91622
Auckland Park, South Africa 2006
011-27-11-403-7080

Medic'air
Paris, France
011-33-1-41-72-14-14

Tyrol Air Ambulance
Innsbruck, Austria
011-43-512-22-4-22

TRAVEL INSURANCE COMPANIES

Access America, Inc.
Richmond, VA
800-284-8300

AIG Assist
American International Group, Inc.
New York, NY
800-382-6986

ASA, Inc.
International Health Insurance
Phoenix, AZ
888-ASA-8288

Axa Assistance
Bethesda, MD
301-214-8200

Gateway
Seabury & Smith
Washington, DC
800-282-4495 / 202-457-7707

Health Care Global
(also known as Medhelp or Wallach &
   Co. or Healthcare Abroad)
Middleburg, VA
800-237-6615 / 540-687-3166
   540-281-9500

International Medical Group (IAG)
Indianapolis, IN
800-628-4664 / 317-655-4500

Medex International
Timonium, MD
800-732-5309

Petersen International Insurance
   Brokers
Valencia, CA
800-345-8816

Travelex
Omaha, NE
800-228-9792

Travel Guard
Stevens Point, WI
800-826-1300

Travel Insurance Services
InterMedical Division
Walnut Creek, CA
800-937-1387 / 925-932-1387

Travel Insured International
E. Hartford, CT
800-243-3174

Unicard Travel Association
Overland Park, KS
800-501-0352

Universal Service and Assistance
Alexandria, VA
800-770-9111 / 703-370-7800

Worldwide Assistance
Washington, DC
800-821-2828 / 202-331-1609

EXECUTIVE MEDICAL SERVICES

Healthquest Travel, Inc.
888-899-3633

World Clinic
Burlington, MA
800-636-9186

Acronyms

AB	Able-bodied seaman
ABS	American Bureau of Shipping
ACS	Automated commercial system (of U.S. Customs Service)
AMVER	Automated mutual assistance vessel rescue system
APPS	Act to Prevent Pollution from Ships
ARPA	Advanced radar plotting aid
BAC	Blood alcohol content
BIMCO	Baltic and International Maritime Council
B/L or BL	Bill of lading
BV	Bureau Veritas
CDC	Center For Disease Control
CERCLA	Comprehensive Environmental Response, Compensation and Liability Act
CFR	*Code of Federal Regulations* (U.S.A.)
COFR	Certificate of financial responsibility
COGSA	Carriage of Goods by Sea Act
COI	Certificate of inspection
COTP	U.S. Coast Guard captain of the port
CWA	Clean Water Act
DEA	Drug Enforcement Agency
ECDIS	Electronic chart and data information system
ECS	Electronic chart system
EEZ	Exclusive economic zone (extends 200 miles offshore)
EMS	Emergency medical service
EPA	Environmental Protection Agency
EPIRB	Emergency position indicating radio beacon
ETA	Estimated time of arrival
FBI	Federal Bureau of Investigation
FCC	Federal Communications Commission
FMC	Federal Maritime Commission
FPA	United States Coast Guard's foreign port assessment program

FWPCA	Federal Water Pollution Control Act
GMDSS	Global maritime distress and safety system
HAZMAT	Hazardous materials
IHSA	Intervention on the High Seas Act
ILO	International Labor Organization
IMO	International Maritime Organization
INS	United States Immigration and Naturalization Agency
INTERCARGO	International Association of Dry Cargo Ship Owners
INTERTANKO	International Association of Independent Tanker Owners
IOPP	International oil pollution prevention certificate
ISGOTT	*The International Guide to Oil Tankers and Terminals*
ISM	International Management Code for the Safe Operation of Ships and for Pollution Prevention; International Safety Management Code
ISO	International Organization for Standardization
ITU	International Telecommunications Union
LOF	Lloyd's Open Form, a type of salvage agreement
MARAD	U.S. Maritime Administration
MARPOL	International Convention for the Prevention of Pollution from Ships, 1973, as modified by the Protocol of 1978 (MARPOL 73/78)
MC	Mutual consent (used as a log entry when discharging mariners)
MMD	Merchant mariner's document
MSDS	Material safety data sheet
NANCPA	Non-indigenous Aquatic Nuisance Prevention and Control Act of 1990
NAVINFONET	Navigation information network
NBIC	National ballast water information clearinghouse
NCB	National Cargo Bureau
NFFD	Not fit for duty
NIMA	National Imagery and Mapping Agency
NISA	National Invasive Species Act of 1996
NLS	Noxious liquid substance
NOAA	National Oceanographic and Atmospheric Administration
NOS	National Ocean Service
NPDES	National pollutant discharge elimination system
NVIC	*Navigation and Vessel Inspection Circular* (issued by USCG)
OCIMF	Oil Companies International Marine Forum
OCMI	Officer-in-charge, marine inspection (U.S. Coast Guard)
OPA or OPA '90	Oil Pollution Act of 1990 (USA)
OSHA	Occupational Safety and Health Administration
P & I	Protection and indemnity
PWSA	Ports and Waterways Safety Act
QI	Qualified individual
RCC	Rescue coordination center
SAR	Search and rescue

SARSAT	Search and rescue satellite
SIGTTO	Society of International Gas Tanker and Terminal Operators
SMCP	Standard marine communication phrases (IMO phrases)
SMS	Safety management system
SOCP	Ship operations cooperative program
SOLAS	International Convention for the Safety of Life at Sea 1974
SOPEP	Shipboard oil pollution emergency plan
STCW	Standards of Training, Certification and Watchkeeping
TOVALOP	Tanker owners voluntary agreement concerning liability for oil pollution
UNHCR	United Nations High Commission on Refugees
USC	*United States Code*
USCG	United States Coast Guard
USCS	United States Customs Service
USDA	United States Department of Agriculture
USPHS	United States Public Health Service
VDR	Voyage data recorder
VHF	Very high frequency radio
VMRS	Vessel movement reporting system
VRP	Vessel response plan
VTS	Vessel traffic service or system

Notes

Chapter 1. The Master

1. 46 USC §2304.
2. 46 USC §3315.
3. Load line information can be found in 46 USC §5101 *et seq.*
4. 46 USC §5114.
5. 46 USC §5116.
6. 46 USC §10104.
7. Federal alcohol regulations can be found in 46 USC §2115, §2302, §6101, §7702, §8101, and in 46 CFR §16 and 33 CFR §95. Information on the National Driver Register is found in 49 USC §30301 *et seq.*
8. Federal regulations on hours of work and rest can be found in 46 USC §8104. Additional regulations may be promulgated by states and may apply only to certain classes of vessels. For example, OPA '90 has strict work and rest hour rules pertaining to deck officers aboard tankers.
9. 46 USC §2114.

Chapter 2. United States Laws

1. In March 2000, the captain of the Norwegian tanker *Freja Jutlandic* was arrested in Baltimore for failing to notify the U.S. Coast Guard of an oily bilge-water leak from his vessel and for making false statements in the Oil Record Book, which was in violation of the Port and Waterways Safety Act. The master was charged criminally for "making false statements" because no mention of the leak, an oil discharge required to be noted in the Oil Record Book, was recorded. A crewmember had surreptitiously notified the Coast Guard of the vessel's condition. The master had telexed his head office asking for advice in effecting repairs to the hull and was told specifically not to notify the Coast Guard. The Coast Guard, local police, and U.S. Attorney's office conducted the investigation jointly.
2. 46 USC §7101, §7109, and §7302, and as amended by OPA '90.

3. FWPCA/CWA information can be found in 33 USC §1251 *et seq.*

4. In 1999 three employees of Holland America Lines were sentenced to two years probation and a $10,000 fine for violations of the Clean Water Act when their ship, the *Rotterdam*, pumped oily bilge water into the waters of the Inland Passage off Alaska. One of the men, Mr. Hogendoorn, was the director of technical operations. This was the first time a shore-based employee in the cruise industry had ever been sentenced for a criminal violation of this act. Mr. Hogendoorn knew the oily-water separator of the vessel was having problems but did not order repairs to the equipment. This omission was considered criminally negligent. The other two men were second engineers who bypassed the oily-water separator when pumping bilges. The chief engineer was also charged but has failed to appear in the United States. The Dutch operator of the vessel, HAL Beheer BV, was charged with felony violation of the Act to Prevent Pollution From Ships and was sentenced to pay a $1 million fine as well as $1 million in restitution.

5. OPA '90 is codified, in part, in 33 USC §2701 *et seq.*

6. Pollution regulations found in 46 CFR §7101 and §7302 prohibit the Coast Guard from issuing a license, MMD, or certificate of registry unless the National Driver Register information for that applicant is reviewed. The Coast Guard cannot use information that is older than three years unless that information pertains to a driver's license suspension still in effect. The National Driver Register Act of 1982 is codified in 49 USC §30301 *et seq.*

7. 33 CFR §2732 discusses federal escort regulations for Alaska. States publish their own regulations.

8. Guidance for drug and alcohol testing can be found in 46 CFR §2115, §2301 *et seq.*, §7702, and §8101.

9. Criminal and civil fines and penalties can be found in 33 USC §1319.

10. 33 USC §2704 has information on limiting liability and cleanup funds.

11. The Intervention on the High Seas Act is found in 33 CFR §1471 *et seq.*

12. The Act to Prevent Pollution from Ships is found in 33 USC §1901 *et seq.*

13. The Refuse Act is codified in 33 USC §407.

14. The following is a reprint of a press release issued by EPA Headquarters on October 16, 1998.

"A former assistant engineer on Holland America's cruise ship SS *Rotterdam* was awarded $500,000 on Oct. 8, by the U.S. District Court for the District of Alaska in Anchorage for providing information concerning the illegal pumping of untreated bilge water into the ocean in violation of the Act to Prevent Pollution from Ships. During the summer of 1994, the engineer refused an order to pump untreated bilge water into the sea while the ship was sailing through Alaska's Inside Passage which is an ecologically sensitive area. When other crew members complied with the order, he reported the illegal dumping to the U.S. Coast Guard. In the same case, the ship's owner, Holland America Cruise Line, which is a subsidiary of the Dutch company HAL Beheer BV, was ordered to pay a $1 million fine, half of which was awarded to the engineer. As part of the settlement, Holland America will also provide $1 million to the National Park Foundation to benefit marine ecosystems. In addition to the $2 million payment, Holland America must establish a company environmental compliance plan, add pollution reduction equipment on each of its vessels, and serve five years probation. The case was investigated by EPA's Criminal Investigation Division, the U.S. Coast Guard and the FBI."

15. NANPCA can be found in 33 CFR §151.2000 *et seq.* and 16 USC §4701 *et seq.*

16. 33 CFR §151.2040. Vessels completing the forms should submit them as follows:

A. All vessels bound for the Great Lakes are to fax the form to COTP Buffalo at 315-764-3283 at least twenty-four hours before the vessel arrives in Montreal, Quebec.

B. Vessels bound for the Hudson River north of George Washington Bridge are to fax the form to COTP New York at 718-354-4249 before the vessel enters the waters of the United States (twelve miles from the baseline).

C. For vessels bound for all other United States ports, before the vessel departs from the first port of call in the waters of the United States, the form should be sent by one of the three following methods:

1. Mail the form to the following address:
U.S. Coast Guard
c/o Smithsonian Environmental Research Center (SERC)
P.O. Box 28
Edgewater, MD 21037-0028

2. Transmit the form electronically to the National Ballast Information Clearinghouse (NBIC) at http://invasions.si.edu/ballast.htm, or

3. Fax the form to the Commandant, U.S. Coast Guard, c/o the NBIC at 301-261-4319.

17. The Uniform National Discharge Standards for Vessels of the Armed Forces is codified in 33 USC §1322 *et seq.* These regulations govern every sort of vessel discharge, including cooling water, rain or washdown runoff, stack emissions, etc. Although these rigorous requirements are not imposed on commercial vessels, there is a high probability they soon will be.

18. Alternative ballast water management plans can be submitted to the Coast Guard for approval at the following address:
Commandant (G-MSO-4)
U.S. Coast Guard Headquarters
2100 Second Street, SW
Washington, D.C. 20593-0001
202-267-0500

19. CERCLA is codified in 42 USC §9601 *et seq.*

20. The Shore Protection Act is codified in 33 USC §2601 *et seq.* and regulations are in 33 CFR §151.1000 *et seq.*

21. The federal alcohol statutes of 46 USC §2302 are implemented by the regulations in 33 CFR §95.

22. Ports and Waterways Safety Act can be found in 33 USC §1221 *et seq.* and 33 CFR §161.1.

23. Information on the Northern Right Whales Protection Act is found in 33 CFR §169.100 *et seq.*

24. The U.S. Cable Act is codified in 47 USC §21 *et seq.*

25. Benzene regulations are found in 46 CFR §197.501.

26. The Clean Air Act is codified in 42 USC §7401 *et seq.* More information can be found at the EPA's Web site.

Chapter 3. International Codes and Conventions

1. The International Convention for the Prevention of Pollution from Ships, 1973, as modified by the Protocol of 1978 (MARPOL 73/78) and the Protocol on Environmental Protection to the Antarctic Treaty as it Pertains to Pollution from Ships (Annexes I, II, and V) are codified in 33 CFR §151 *et seq.* The full text of MARPOL is available from the National Technical Information Service, reference "ADA 168-505."

2. These ISM requirements can be found in 33 CFR §96.100 *et seq.;* NVICs 2-94 and 4-98 provide the Coast Guard's enforcement policy.

3. STCW provisions can be found in 46 CFR §10, §12, and §15.

4. GMDSS regulations can be found in 47 CFR §80.1065 *et seq.*

5. ILO recommendations can be reviewed at the ILO website http://us.ilo.org/. More information can be found in the USCG *Maritime Security Manual,* volume 2, chapter 24. This manual can be viewed and downloaded from www.uscg.mil/hq/g-m/nmc/pubs/msm.

Chapter 4. Vessel Accidents and Incidents

1. Coast Guard regulations regarding casualty reporting can be found in 46 CFR §4.01 *et seq.* Also see appendix B of this book, "Figures: Sample Forms," for reporting forms.

2. See 29 CFR §1904 for OSHA reporting requirements.

3. Drug and alcohol testing requirements and information are found in 46 CFR §16.101 *et seq.* and 33 CFR §95.

4. Information on SOPEPs can be found in 33 CFR §151.26.

5. 46 USC §11506.

6. 46 USC §11501.

7. 46 USC §11505.

8. 46 USC §11501.

9. Ibid.

10. Ibid.

11. Ibid.

12. Ibid.

13. Ibid.

Chapter 5. Vessel Security

1. BIMCO has a text on vessel security: *The Ship Master's Security Manual* was published in July 1998 and is available to its members. BIMCO also offers courses on vessel security. In 1999, the International Chamber of Shipping published the third edition of *Pirates and Armed Robbers—A Master's Guide.* The U.S. Coast Guard has published information in the *Marine Safety Manual,* which is available to view or download at www.uscg.mil/hq/g-m/nmc/pubs/msm. IMO has

published two circulars, numbers 443 and 623, relating to this issue; they are available at www.imo.org. Another interesting Web site is www.maritimesecurity.com.

2. IMO publication MSC/Circ. 443, "Measures to Prevent Unlawful Acts Against Passengers and Crews Aboard Ships," September 26, 1986. This document was the basis for most of the U.S. legislation that followed.

3. The Coast Guard's National Security Branch has several roles including counter-terrorism, foreign port assessment, antipiracy, and military environmental response operations. It also works jointly with the Office of Naval Intelligence in preparing reports on the worldwide threat to shipping. The Foreign Port Assessment Program (FPA) evaluates the vulnerability to terrorist attack of foreign ports frequented by U.S. cruise ship passengers. Since 1993, over sixty cruise ship ports have been assessed throughout the world. It is requested that masters add the Office of Naval Intelligence to the list of addressees when reporting hostile actions against vessels. The contact point is:

ONI Violence at Sea (VAS) Desk
4251 Suitland Rd.
Washington, DC 20395-5720
Tel: 301-669-3261
Fax: 301-669-3247
E-mail: cdragonette@nmic.navy.mil

Reports may also be routed through the U.S. Department of Transportation response center hotline at 800-424-0201 or the Maritime Administration Office of Ship Operations, MAR-613, at 202-366-5735 (opcenter@marad.gov).

4. These passenger safety requirements can be found in 33 CFR §120 and §128. Further information can be found in NVIC 3-96 and the USCG *Marine Safety Manual* COMDTINST M16000.12, which can be accessed at www.uscg.mil/hq/g-m/nmc/pubs/msm.

5. The requirement for a safety management system is found in 46 USC §3203.

6. Information can be found in the USCG *Marine Safety Manual,* volume 7, chapter 6; in the USCG *Physical Security Manual* COMDTINST M5530.1; and in 33 CFR §6.14.

7. Reports on piracy, armed robbery, and stowaway incidents can be found at the IMO Web site at www.imo.org. IMO has also published a circular (number 623) offering guidance to shipmasters; this is available to view or download at the IMO Web site. Some of the areas known for relatively frequent hostile boarding incidents are Bangladesh, Belize, Brazil, Colombia, Congo, Ecuador, Guatemala, Gulf of Aden, Honduras/Nicaragua border, Indonesia, Ivory Coast, Malacca Straits, Mexico (Gulf area), Nigeria, Phillip Channel, Singapore Straits, Socotra Island, Solomon Islands, Somalia, Spratly Islands (and surrounding areas), and Sri Lanka. Information is also available from the State Department and the Coast Guard.

8. Federal law states that any person who stows away on board a vessel in a U.S. port, or any person who stows away on board a vessel in a foreign port and is found on board in a U.S. port, is subject to a fine of $1,000 or imprisonment for up to one year, or both.

9. 8 USC §1101 *et seq.*

10. 8 USC §1231.

11. Ibid.

12. The United Nations High Commission for Refugees (UNHCR), in an effort to encourage the rescue of refugees at sea, has published guidelines, which if followed, will minimize delay and may allow for compensation to vessels that rescue refugees on the high seas. The guidelines are published in a booklet entitled *Guidelines for the Embarkation of Refugees*.

13. 8 USC §1101 defines refugee.

14. 8 USC §1158.

Chapter 6. Communications

1. 46 USC §2306.

2. These phrases can be found in NVIC 7-98.

3. GMDSS regulations are found in 47 CFR §80 *et seq*.

4. More information on GMDSS can be found at www.navcen.uscg.mil/marcomms/gmdss.

Chapter 7. Shipping Articles

1. Information on shipping articles can be found in 46 USC §10302 and 46 CFR §14 *et seq*.

2. 46 USC §10502.

3. 46 USC §10303(a).

4. 46 USC §10509.

5. 46 USC §10315.

6. 46 USC §8103.

7. The owner, charterer, master, managing operator, or agent may act as shipping commissioner if a shipping commissioner is not available. 46 USC §10102.

8. 46 CFR §14.

9. NVICs may be accessed online at www.uscg.mil/hq/g-m/nvic/

10. STCW language proficiency requirements dictate that the crew be proficient in English.

11. 46 CFR §10.205 requires that an applicant for an original license must have fingerprints taken during the application process in order to check if a criminal record exists for the candidate. A more thorough treatment of criminal and driving offenses is found in 46 CFR §10 and §12. Additionally, a driving history review is made for each applicant seeking a merchant mariner's document. The National Driver Register Act prohibits the Coast Guard from reviewing files older than three years, unless the information concerns license revocation or suspension that is still in effect. The National Highway Traffic Safety Administration (NHTSA) of the Department of Transportation (DOT) maintains the NDR. 49 USC §30301 *et seq*.

12. Marine employer testing and vessel operating requirements can be found in 49 CFR §16 and 33 CFR §95. In March 1997, the Eleventh Coast Guard District published a pamphlet for marine employers to help them better understand and meet the chemical testing requirements of the industry. Copies can be obtained from the Drug and Alcohol Program Inspector.

13. The International Vaccination Certificate is issued by the Public Health Department, part of the U.S. Department of Health, Education, and Welfare, and is approved by the World Health Organization.

14. This may be handled by Human Resources or the unions before hiring. This is a blood test required by the USCG benzene program for persons working on tankers. Benzene regulations are found in 46 CFR §197.501 *et seq.*

15. Respirator fit cards are issued by a certified doctor using special equipment. Valid for one year, the card states the brand and size of the respirator that fits the individual.

16. 46 USC §10318 (foreign and intercoastal articles) and §10504 (coastwise articles).

17. If a seaman is discharged involuntarily, and it appears that the discharge was not due to neglect of duty, incompetency, or injury, the master shall provide the seaman with employment on a vessel agreed to by the seaman or shall provide the seaman with one month's additional wages. 46 USC §10318.

Chapter 8. Logbooks

1. The Official Logbook is Coast Guard form CG-706B and can be obtained from any Marine Safety Office. Statutes pertaining to the Official Logbook can be found in 46 USC §11301.

2. Required entries, as excerpted from the *U.S. Code,* can also be found on pages 18 and 19 of the Official Logbook.

3. Information on the handling of a deceased seaman's effects starts at 46 USC §10701.

4. 33 CFR §164.25.

5. 46 USC §10509.

6. Princess Cruise Lines and P & O Ferries, to name just two operators, equip their vessels with voyage data recorders (VDRs).

7. Information can be found in IMO Resolution A.861(20).

8. Oil Record Book requirements can be found starting in 33 CFR §151.25.

9. NISA and NANPCA ballast water regulations can be found in 33 CFR §151.1500 *et seq.* Record keeping requirements are found in 33 CFR §151.2045. For more discussion of mandatory and voluntary ballast practices, see chapter 2, U.S. Federal Laws. Details of this regulation are found in NVIC 8-99.

10. Ballast water reporting forms should be kept aboard. See Appendix B of this book, "Figures: Sample Forms." The form can also be found in the Appendix to 33 CFR §151, Subpart D. Submittal of the IMO Ballast Water Reporting Form will also fulfill U.S. requirements, but for data entry purposes, the U.S. form is preferred.

11. Ballast reports must be submitted as follows:
- Foreign-flagged vessel bound for Great Lakes:
  Telefax to COTP, Buffalo, at 315-764-3283
- Vessels bound for Hudson River:
  Telefax to COTP, New York, at 718-354-4249 before vessel enters U.S. waters, twelve miles from the baseline
- All other vessels:
  Telefax to Commandant, U.S. Coast Guard, at 301-261-4319, or transmit

the report electronically to the National Ballast Water Clearinghouse at www.serc.si.edu\invasions\ballast.htm, or mail it to U.S. Coast Guard c/o Smithsonian, P.O. Box 28, Edgewater, MD 21037-0028.
For additional information, contact:
Commandant (G-MSO-4)
U.S. Coast Guard
2100 2nd Street, SW
Washington, DC
20593-0001
202-267-0500
12. 33 CFR §151.51 et seq.
13. Requirements for GMDSS logs can be found in 47 CFR §80.175.

Chapter 9. Documents and Certificates

1. Information on documentation can be found in 46 USC §12105.
2. General information on inspection and certificates of inspection can be found in 46 USC §3101 and 46 CFR §31.01 et seq., §71.01 et seq., §91.01 et seq., §176.01 et seq., and §189.01-1 et seq.
3. 46 USC §3314.
4. Information on load lines can be found starting at 46 USC §5101.
5. See 46 CFR §91 et seq., for regulations pertaining to inspections. If the records required by the regulations are in the form of cargo gear certificates and registers issued by the American Bureau of Shipping or other classification society recognized by the Coast Guard, the marine inspectors will accept such records as prima facie evidence of compliance with the regulations.
6. Information on COFRs can be found in 33 CFR §138 et seq.
7. Information on IOPPs and MARPOL is found in 33 CFR §151.01 et seq.
8. SOPEP information can be found in 33 CFR §151.26.
9. Requirements for vessel response plans are found starting in 33 CFR §155.1010.
10. See chapter 2, "United States Laws," as well as chapter 8, "Logbooks," for ballast water regulation information.
11. Derat certificate is form CDC 75-5. To schedule an appointment, call the Miami, Florida, office at 954-356-6650. Center for Disease Control can be reached at 404-687-6571.
12. HAZMAT regulations can be found in 49 CFR §171 et seq.

Chapter 10. Crew Lists

1. Immigration regulations are found in 8 CFR.
2. This change is reflected in customs regulations 19 CFR §4.9(b) and §4.68.

Chapter 11. Customs

1. Customs statutes can be found in 19 USC, regulations in 19 CFR. The customs Web site at www.customs.ustreas.gov is an excellent resource.

2. To mention a few of the major locations, customs attachés are found in Bangkok, Bonn, Dublin, Hong Kong, London, Mexico City, Ottawa, Paris, Rome, Tokyo, Seoul, Panama City, Vienna, and the Hague.

3. The 1993 Customs Modernization Act (Pub. L. 103-182, 107 Stat. 2507) was codified by revisions to 19 USC.

4. Questions regarding operational aspects can be directed to the Office of Field Operations at 202-927-3654

5. The act repealed 19 USC §1435 and amended 19 USC §1434.

6. Public health regulations regarding foreign quarantine are found in 42 CFR §71.

7. 19 CFR §4.2.

8. 19 USC §1433 and §1436, and 19 CFR §4.3.

9. Arrival reporting regulations are found in 19 CFR §4.2.

10. Preliminary entry requirements can be found in 19 CFR §4.8.

11. Formal entry requirements can be found in 19 CFR §4.9. Formal entry for vessels is governed by the Tariff Act of 1930 found in 19 USC §1434 et seq.

12. Inward foreign manifests are covered in 19 CFR §4.7.

13. 19 USC §1431, §1584.

14. 19 USC §1202.

15. Foreign-made items that have already been declared and cleared by customs, or items taken aboard for use during the voyage, can be listed on CF-4455 before departure as proof that the item was not purchased overseas. Also available is form CF-4457 if a crewmember wants to mail an item that was boarded in the United States back to the United States from abroad.

16. 19 USC §1453, §1497.

17. Complete crew list regulations can be found in 8 CFR §231.

18. 19 USC §1466.

19. Tonnage tax and fees can be found starting in the most recent edition of 19 CFR §24 and §420, and in 46 USC §§2110-12.

20. See 15 CFR §30.24 for regulations of the Department of Commerce.

21. 19 USC §1453. Information regarding aiding unlawful importation can also be found in 19 USC 1595.

22. Controlled substance information is found in 19 USC §1584 and §1594.

23. For a referral to the proper local office, contact:
U.S. Customs Carrier Initiative Program
Manager, Anti-Smuggling Division
Office of Field Operations
U.S. Customs Service
1300 Pennsylvania Ave., NW
Washington D.C. 20229
Web site: www.customs.gov

Chapter 13. Accounting

1. 46 USC §10314.

2. Information on allotments is found in 46 USC §10315.

3. Slop chest requirements can be found in 46 USC §11103.

Chapter 16. Panama Canal

1. The Panama Canal Authority (Autoridad del Canal de Panama, ACP) can be reached at

Panama Canal Authority
ACP-MR
P.O. Box 5413
Miami, FL 33102-5413
Tel: 011-507-272-3202 / 3165
Fax: 011-507-272-3892
Telex: 3023 PCCMTCC PG
Web site: www.pancanal.com

2. Detailed information can be found in the Panama Canal Authority's Notice to Shipping Number N-01-2000, which was published January 1, 2000. It is available on-line at www.pancanal.com/eng/maritime/notices/note-01-2000/

Chapter 17. Suez Canal

1. An excellent Web site is www.muslimtents.com/abdelazeem.
2. Contact "SUQ" 24 hours:
On approach—Radio telex ID No. 4820 (Tx 4250/Rx 6310/4205) Mode F1B
In transit—Radio Telex ID No. 4820 (Tx 1612/Rx 2147 [Ch. 211])
INMARSAT telex 581-1622570
INMARSAT voice 871-1622570
INMARSAT fax 871-1622574
International land telex number 63528
International fax number 002-064-393517

Index

About the Author

Tuuli Messer is a graduate of the U.S. Merchant Marine Academy at Kings Point, New York, having earned a bachelor of science degree in marine transportation. She also holds a law degree from the University of San Francisco. She has an unlimited master's license, with sea service aboard tankers, car carriers, RO-ROs, surveillance vessels, semi-submersibles, containerships, and breakbulk ships.

Captain Messer teaches in the Marine Transportation Department and is the Chair of the Academic Senate at the California Maritime Academy, a campus of Califonia State University. She has served as both navigator and watch officer aboard the training ship *Golden Bear* and also as a deck training officer, overseeing deck department instructors during cruises. As a consultant, she provides expert witness testimony on issues involving maritime law. She is also a pollution and safety advisor for a large shipping company.

Captain Messer, a lieutenant commander in the Naval Reserve, is a member of the United States Naval Institute, the National Association of Maritime Educators, and the Admiralty Law Society.

US $50.00

9 780870 335310   5 5 0 0 0

ISBN: 978-0-87033-531-0